A HISTORY OF MODERN LIBRARIANSHIP

Constructing the Heritage of Western Cultures

Pamela Spence Richards,
Wayne A. Wiegand,
and Marija Dalbello, Editors

LIBRARIES
UNLIMITED™
An Imprint of ABC-CLIO, LLC
Santa Barbara, California • Denver, Colorado

Library of Congress Cataloging-in-Publication Data

A history of modern librarianship : constructing the heritage of western cultures / Pamela Spence Richards, Wayne A. Wiegand, and Marija Dalbello, editors.
      pages cm
  ISBN 978-1-61069-099-7 (paperback) — ISBN 978-1-4408-3473-8 (ebook)
  1. Library science—History.   2. Libraries and society—History.   I. Richards, Pamela Spence, 1941– editor.   II. Wiegand, Wayne A., 1946– editor.   III. Dalbello, Marija, editor.
  Z665.H576   2015
  020.9—dc23   2015002077

ISBN: 978-1-61069-099-7
EISBN: 978-1-4408-3473-8

19 18 17 16 15   1 2 3 4 5

This book is also available on the World Wide Web as an eBook.
Visit www.abc-clio.com for details.

Libraries Unlimited
An Imprint of ABC-CLIO, LLC

ABC-CLIO, LLC
130 Cremona Drive, P.O. Box 1911
Santa Barbara, California 93116-1911

This book is printed on acid-free paper ∞

Manufactured in the United States of America

A HISTORY OF
MODERN LIBRARIANSHIP

In Memory of Pamela Spence Richards, 1941–1999

Contents

Preface

A History of Modern Librarianship: Constructing the Heritage of Western Cultures has been a long time coming. In 1992 Pamela Spence Richards (at the time at Rutgers University) and Wayne Wiegand (at the time on the University of Wisconsin–Madison faculty) sat down in Pam's New York apartment to craft a project to consist of essays by library history scholars that would cover seven regions of modern world library history. Wayne agreed to write the essay on the United States and Canada. Pam volunteered to become the sole editor of the essays. In the year following she commissioned authors for the essays, during which time Wayne drafted his essay as a model others could follow. In 1994, however, Pam contracted brain cancer. Although she vowed to carry on with the project during her recuperation (Wayne had finished the first draft of his essay in 1996), her condition worsened, and she died in 1999. Her husband Wim Smits (a historian at Columbia University) told Wayne he would take the project on as a memorial to her, but unfortunately Wim died soon after Pam. For the next few years the project languished.

In 2007 Wayne decided to resurrect Pam's project. To help him he asked Marija Dalbello to become co-editor; Marija had been very active in international librarianship and—like Pam—was on the Rutgers faculty. Together, we agreed to keep Pam's name as first editor and to donate all royalties the book generated to a scholarship established in Pam's honor at Rutgers.

When we contacted authors Pam had originally commissioned in the 1990s, however, we discovered one had passed away and those still living thought the project had died with Pam. When informed the project was once again active, most said they could no longer meet the requirements outlined in project guidelines Pam had written. For Wayne and Marija, it was back to the drawing board if we wanted to save even part of the project. Because Peter Hoare—(originally commissioned by Pam in the 1990s to write the essay on Europe) and Tony Olden (who joined the project in 2004 to do the essay on Africa) graciously agreed to complete their work, we decided to reconceptualize the project to focus primarily on librarianship's Western traditions through the end of the twentieth century in Europe (Peter), the United States and Canada (Wayne), those parts of Africa colonized in the nineteenth century by Western powers (Tony), and Australia and New Zealand, and add to it an essay on the early twenty-first-century innovations and the intellectual techniques and information technologies leading to this development. When Ross Harvey graciously accepted our invitation to do the essay on Australia and New Zealand and Marija offered to write the concluding essay on digital convergence, we had the makings of the book you now have in your hand.

The editors want to thank Peter and Tony for honoring a commitment to the project they made years earlier and working through several revisions, and to Ross for coming to our aid at such a late date. On behalf of all the authors, we also want to thank the librarians and libraries across the Western world that enabled and facilitated all of these essays (many actually "made" the library history we discuss), and the institutions employing all of us for making careers in librarianship (whether in teaching or practice) so fun and rewarding. We hope some of those characteristics are evident in our individual essays. Finally, we want to thank Barbara Ittner, our Libraries Unlimited editor, who showed exceptional patience as coeditors and essay authors laboriously worked through numerous (and sometimes painful) revisions, and once the manuscript arrived provided invaluable comments that substantially tightened the book's scope. Naturally, we dedicate this book to Pam's memory. We hope it stands as testimony to her dedication to an international library history that informs contemporary practice and carries out her vision for *A History of Modern Librarianship: Constructing the Heritage of Western Cultures.*

Introduction

The historical study of libraries as collections of books and the buildings that house them and the study of books themselves—including their preservation and destruction—are a common focus of library histories. In our collection, we take a different approach as we present cross-national dimensions of librarianship in the context of modernity. The five essays in this volume are aimed at a general informed reader and specialists in library and information studies. The essays in this book present a history of Western librarianship primarily since the eighteenth century. They contextualize modern developments of the library institution, professionalization of librarianship, the library systems, and technological innovations that shaped the practice and the philosophy of librarianship. Each essay is organized around critical points related to the practice and theory of modern librarianship, following an organization common with conventional histories of this type, which include Michael Harris's classic, *History of Libraries in the Western World*, published in 1993. Harris's history is an authoritative work, acknowledged as definitive in its coverage of the history of writing, libraries, and librarianship, especially in the ancient world. Our book extends his work by deepening the history of the entire twentieth century and the shaping of modern librarianship, including coverage of the English-speaking colonial world (in its Africa and Australia–New Zealand chapters), the post–Cold War Western world since the 1990s, and a history of librarianship's digital convergences of the twentieth and the twenty-first centuries. Our intended audience is interdisciplinary and international, including students and educators in information science and library programs across the Western world, but also historians of print and practicing professionals in all types of libraries who are interested in the history of one of the world's most important cultural institutions.

HISTORICAL TRANSITIONS

Librarianship has a history several millennia long, but our focus here is on the period between the eighteenth and early twenty-first centuries. We reference historical antecedents and consequent developments of the entire modern era (strictly believed to cover the sixteenth century through World War II) for contextual purposes.

During the time span of this volume, and mirroring broader historical processes, the profession underwent three general transitions. First, with the advent of urbanized industrial mass society in the mid-nineteenth century, librarians in the Anglo-American world ceased seeing themselves as "keepers of the book," a role their eighteenth-century predecessors had prioritized in order to preserve cultural artifacts for an elite clientele. In keeping with the needs of the new science- and technology-based society and its political and economic ideologies, they became instead members of a practical and pragmatic profession committed to serving the public at large, and to disseminating the new as well as preserving the old. Seeing as their task the development of new techniques to enhance access to useful knowledge, they did their work in the service of public enlightenment in the quest for scientific, impartial truth. A belief that this quest was value-free, that is, free of particular cultural characteristics, was very much part of the intellectual climate of the time.

In the second of our historical transitions, as Anglo-American hegemony grew, this new professional self-image and set of techniques spread to continental Europe and to Russia, and, with the growth of colonialism and imperialism, to much of the rest of the world.

Finally, in the postcolonial era, that globalizing process accelerated. High-tech tools like the Internet and expanding digital collections changed the library to such an extent that little connection appeared to remain between the eighteenth-century pre-electronic profession and its twenty-first-century successor. Besides technological changes, the organization and dissemination of knowledge more and more frequently took place in institutions other than libraries; and, accordingly, graduates of library schools got jobs in other, less traditional environments. Yet contemporary libraries and their offshoots in the information business continued to encounter many of the same problems as their predecessors. We dub these problems—bound up not only with the broader contradictions of globalizing and modernizing processes but also with the elusive ideal of value neutrality implicit in the ethos of the Anglo-American and generally Western library—the "core tensions" of modern international librarianship. Exploring these core tensions frames the narrative for all the essays in this volume.

CORE TENSIONS OF MODERN INTERNATIONAL LIBRARIANSHIP

It has often been claimed that Anglo-American librarianship, with its apparent commitment to unbiased collection building, to equal user access, and to scientific systems of indexing, is free of the ideological bias that marks other traditions. Scientific and therefore objective (and good), the librarianship based on that tradition is not—some argue—culture bound. Such has been the principal justification for its export. But is value neutrality in fact always good? And even if it is good in principle, is it possible to achieve?

While it is true that the ethos of value-free dissemination of knowledge to any user may be a powerful force for good, a belief in the technical benefits of modern librarianship can be dangerous unless coupled with vigilance to preserve universal access. It is one of the ironies of the twentieth century that many of the techniques developed by modern librarianship to enhance access to information—like standardized indexing—were also useful to the hegemony of totalitarian regimes such as those of Nazi Germany and the Soviet Union that had little interest in the free flow of information. And, despite the shift away from the "keeper of the book" role, is not the librarian's function as well to help preserve and maintain a culture? (This is a point to which we shall return.) Focusing merely on the technique itself—especially when it is simply assumed to be good—can lead to neglect of the context in which it is used. But, even when most people would agree that neutrality is a force for good, it is, unfortunately, both in theory and in practice, elusive. On the most basic material level, one need only ask whether libraries can remain unaffected by the aims and values of those that found and fund them, be they national governments, the military, religious institutions, private businesses, foundations, or international organizations like UNESCO—organizations and institutions whose role, where relevant, is explored by this book's contributors.

More specifically, even the core principles of the defenders of value neutrality are plagued by ambiguities, contradictions, and constraints: Is not equal access, for example, no matter how noble, conditioned by other civic factors—from leisure time to transportation to literacy, to say nothing of broader, and often unquestioned, worldviews? In the American South, to take but one glaring case in point, racist ideology outweighed the profession's hallowed equal access principle. No less did it shape scientific indexing. Indeed, even the more cursory reading of Michel Foucault, for example, or any other theorist of discourse, shatters the illusion of objectivity in classification and indexing. For without constant comparison with other worldviews, it is easy to see why people tend to take as universal givens the concepts and categories of their culture. But the problem extends beyond indexing and classification. Take one of the core principles of the Anglo-American school—that of "unbiased" collection building. In 1879 Melvil Dewey came up with a motto for the American Library Association that proudly asserted: "The best reading for the largest number at the least cost," naively assuming that like number and cost "the best reading" was an easily defined category, free from cultural limitations that might create dogmas and reify categories.

The relationship between libraries and their cultural context, however, is in no way without politics, religion, or morality: in their work, librarians exercise judgments that are not always apparent. Once librarians have selected "the best" materials and indexed them "scientifically," they have, whether consciously or not, worked to define and reinforce the concepts and categories of their culture. Indeed, for all their pretenses of value neutrality, librarians—even librarians who style themselves in the Anglo-American mode—are agents of cultural reproduction perpetuating prevailing ideologies of surveillance and control of information inherent in the "scientific" ideal of objectivity. Put differently, they might even be said to be forging what the Italian Marxist philosopher Antonio Gramsci called "cultural hegemony"—a means of building a consensus society that tends to preserve the social and political status quo. Librarians are gatekeepers of privileged forms of scientific authority under the guise of neutrality.

In short, though guided by the ideal of transcending culture, librarians in the Anglo-American tradition nonetheless both shape and are shaped by it. Caught between ideal and reality, they navigate a civic maze that all too often places obstacles before their goal. And, once their de facto relationship to broader civic culture is acknowledged, they steer between two other roles that too often conflict in a rapidly changing global society—preserving a cultural heritage and organizing and disseminating new information and knowledge.

The tensions inherent in the Anglo-American tradition were only highlighted by the second and third of the transitions in librarianship—the spread of Anglo-American cultural hegemony to continental Europe and the so-called Third World. For, if Gramscian hegemony applies to libraries in Europe and America, it is even more applicable in the West's colonial empires. The British, the Germans, and the French (who had adopted new models of librarianship), for example, used the export of cultural institutions like libraries, archives, museums, and schools to ensure the replication of their own views and values—the views and values of those in power—rather than those of indigenous populations. Just how this process operated is a central theme of this book's chapters. Privileged Western forms of knowledge were reinforced across cultures and languages through processes of globalization and modernization.

Of equal importance for our book is the fact that when elements of Anglo-American culture—like the modern library establishment with its technical apparatus and bureaucracy—became, as sociologist Anthony Giddens calls it, "disembedded" from their original sites and "re-embedded" in cultures for which they were not designed, the dynamic interaction created tensions. Especially in the decolonized world the foreign intrusion of Western practices in their cultures stimulated many colonial peoples to defend their own heritage. Thus, for some librarians, tensions arose between the demands of their role as guardians of their own cultural heritage and as providers of value-free knowledge that is delocalized and universal.[1] It was in a new form the old dilemma inherent in the function of the librarian but much exacerbated by the political demands of that situation. Our contributors examine the problems of adaptation in the regions they study and take into consideration the peculiar cultural, socioeconomic, and political makeup and mind-sets.

Clearly, the modern development of librarianship has not solved the clash between its two roles: provider to all of culturally constrained knowledge on the one hand, provider of tools to keep alive (or sometimes forge) a cultural or national identity on the other. After all, the business of providing the ways of expression in these new electronic forms is, just like the pre-electronic library, not a passive technical activity, but is deeply rooted in its social and cultural environment. The logic of modernization and its technical abilities—if severed from the idea of accompanying "progress" with its replacement of traditional and local by modern and "better" forms of knowledge— can be transformative in validating multiple bases of authority built on humanistic values of difference and particularism, and continuities of the present and the past. The library, whether public or catering to specialized interests, is a social institution, and as such it everywhere reflects the influence of the civic life of the communities and individuals it serves. Libraries of the traditional eighteenth-century preservation model as well as the twenty-first-century user-oriented variety have never been passive depositories of records of knowledge. They are creative social and cultural institutions that play an important role in the process of cultural reproduction, the process by which a culture preserves and defends, as well as transforms, its own heritage. The contributors to this book hope to make both practicing and aspiring librarians aware of the cultural determinants of their own profession's history and the opportunities as well as the problems they create.

NOTE

1. Anthony Giddens, *The Consequences of Modernity* (Cambridge, UK: Polity, 1990), 108–9.

Wayne A. Wiegand
F. William Summers Professor of Library and Information Studies Emeritus
Florida State University

Marija Dalbello
Associate Professor
School of Communication and Information
Rutgers, The State University of New Jersey

I

Europe

Peter Hoare

INTRODUCTION

This chapter traces the history of modern European librarianship, principally since 1800. Libraries in Europe date back more than two thousand years, and although important libraries and significant developments in their care and management are well documented through the Middle Ages and succeeding centuries, modern librarianship emerged in its present meaning only in the late eighteenth century. For the purposes of this chapter Europe is defined as extending westward from the Urals and Caucasus mountains and south to the Mediterranean, so including the western part of Russia and the largely Slavic-speaking nations of central Europe, down to the Balkans and Greece and westward to Spain and Portugal. The islands of Great Britain and Ireland have historically stood somewhat outside "Europe" but are increasingly seen as part of the continent in cultural as well as political terms. Most countries have a well-established industrial base (as of this writing under threat from international competition), though traditional agriculture tends to be stronger in the continent's southern parts; good transport and information technology (IT) links generally offer effective communication between all areas.

Many of today's national borders are recent: some are still unsettled, while others have moved back and forth in the last two centuries. After the Congress of Vienna (1815), which followed the Napoleonic wars and French occupation of much of western Europe, new states emerged and others disappeared into larger nations. Similar changes came to central and eastern Europe, some due to the breakup of major blocs such as the Ottoman (Turkish) and Austro-Hungarian empires after 1918, others following invasion, occupation, and treaties. Italy and Germany became single countries only after unification in the 1860s–1870s, and both have gained and lost territory since then. The Soviet Union dominated most of Eastern Europe for decades after World War II, and some cities that for centuries had been major centers of German publishing and library activity (Breslau, Danzig, and Königsberg) were lost to Germany after 1945 and developed new roles within Poland and Russia (as Wrocław, Gdańsk, and Kaliningrad), with most of their German culture now a matter of history. Germany itself was divided for forty-five years after 1945, with the German Democratic Republic under close Soviet control from 1949 to 1990, with radical effects on its librarianship, as essays in Peter Vodosek and Konrad Marwinski's 1999 book describe. Such developments have, however, not always had such revolutionary effects and may have left older traditions of librarianship unchanged.

Wars affected much of Europe in the past 150 years, with destruction of libraries (and the consequent challenges) a major element from the professional point of view. From the Prussian bombardment of the Strasbourg city library in 1870 to the destruction of the university library in Louvain in both 1915 and 1940, from the multiple losses across Europe during World War II—in Germany, Italy, France, England, and across Eastern Europe—to the deliberate targeting of the National Library in Sarajevo in 1992, the effect of war has been dramatic. But librarianship somehow continued to develop through this turmoil, taking opportunities for reconstruction and redirection of the profession—not least in building up an awareness of the need to organize information for both military and civil purposes, leading to continuing advances in documentation.

The political dimension is crucial to understanding librarianship, as has been noted in the German Democratic Republic. National politics often dictate the way libraries operate or develop: libraries may be founded or administered for political ends rather than through pressure from librarians. This affects the history of librarianship, since the profession has to operate within the structure of the library world and its political context. Libraries were in many instances the carriers of "modern" ideas: the battles against censorship and for free access (which can be traced separately in many countries and were often led by librarians combating conservative cultures) show how libraries often stood for cultural, social, and political progress. The part libraries played in widening access to education is also indisputable. However, the growth of professionalism often depends more on the character and initiative of individual librarians than on political considerations. Across a continent such as Europe, the diversity of libraries and contexts makes a single view of librarianship impossible.

Though a relatively small continent, Europe does not form a single cultural or linguistic bloc. It contains many separate nations, some witnessing many changes to their borders, political hegemony, and cultural identity over the past two hundred years. It encompasses many different languages, some largely "national" such as Hungarian or Greek, others like German shared between different countries. By the end of the twentieth century, public education was generally well advanced and literacy levels high throughout the continent. A thriving publishing industry is common within most linguistic blocs, even small ones (though discouraged at some periods for political reasons), and historically this had an important interaction with libraries. In most countries the expansion of publishing through the nineteenth century, with technological advances facilitating mass markets for printed material (so widening the readership base), paralleled the spread of libraries to all classes. A symbiosis between publishing and libraries developed, with libraries responding to new formats, ranging from three-decker novels to scientific periodicals. This relationship is threatened in the twenty-first century by electronic publishing and digitization—though librarians address the challenge by stressing the primacy of information content rather than format.

The cultural and social background of the history of European librarianship since the late eighteenth century is therefore complex: a mosaic of patterns and trends differing between and within countries. Language problems, a serious barrier to developing a common European conception or practice of librarianship, have been more marked in the modern than earlier centuries: until the Reformation in the sixteenth century there was considerable religious and cultural cohesion (particularly in western Europe), and Latin dominated the contents of libraries. In the seventeenth and much of the eighteenth centuries this cohesion began to break down, but widespread use of Latin and French maintained some linguistic agreement—and there was relatively little library provision except at a serious or scholarly level. The international dominance of the English language is a recent development: in many countries German was in the eighteenth and nineteenth centuries the most common alternative to the vernacular, as French was elsewhere. In fact, loyalty to indigenous languages has been an important factor in the history of libraries. In some countries vernacular publication was unknown or suppressed until the nineteenth century, but it soon came to contribute powerfully to nationalism and linguistic diversity. Similarly, a library world open to a wide readership has been, for most European countries, a development of the past two centuries or even more recent.

But language and culture are not identical, and cultural differences within a language bloc are not uncommon, such as a distinct Scottish identity within Great Britain, or Protestant-Catholic divides in the Netherlands or Ireland. Much of Europe's history has been Christian, though there have long been divisions, not only between Catholicism and Protestantism (the latter with its own variations) but also with the Orthodox churches prominent in the east and southeast of the continent. Judaism has had a significant effect on culture, especially nineteenth-century Jewish immigration from eastern Europe and emigration from Nazi Germany in the 1930s, notably to Great Britain as well as to the United States. Several countries witnessed the arrival of more immigrant groups from farther afield, such as Turkish workers in Germany since 1961; some welcomed ethnic minorities from former colonies (as Arab, African, and West Indian arrivals in France and Britain from the 1950s onward). By the later twentieth century these increasingly represented Muslim, Hindu, and other Asian and Middle Eastern cultures, all presenting cultural and linguistic challenges to host countries and their libraries.

The spread of English as a lingua franca alongside the vernacular—a late-twentieth-century phenomenon accelerated by the Internet—has not led to cultural and linguistic conformity. Since the mid-nineteenth century librarians in the British Isles have felt more comfortable with the English-speaking world than with their European neighbors, and collaboration with North America has been close in a number of professional areas like cataloging rules. Many British libraries used the Anglo-American *Joint Code* of 1908 for more than half a century, and the various editions of the *Anglo-American Cataloguing Rules* or *AACR* have been recognized worldwide since 1967. Total European coordination was not, however, easily achieved in practice. Other traditions like the influential "Prussian Instructions" dominated libraries in Germany and Central Europe in the earlier twentieth century, and Soviet rules for cataloging, dating from the 1930s and partly reflecting different types of publishing formats, also influenced parts of Europe in the mid- to late twentieth century.

Historiography

"In setting out to study library systems and library developments in Europe," Leif Kajberg and Marian Koren write (2009), "a striking difficulty is that of coming to grips with the comparative, cross-country and inter-cultural perspective. A fairly large body of professional and academic literature exists on the systems, state of the art, role and history, etc. of libraries in *individual* European countries, but there is a remarkable dearth of comparative research approaches and studies. [. . .] In brief, comparative, contrasting and over-arching research studies that look at European libraries and librarianship from the broader perspective of a region or continent are difficult to identify."[1] Even in an area once seen as monolithic, such as the former "Iron Curtain" countries of Central and Eastern Europe in the period from 1945 to 1990, the most recent patterns of development reveal many local differences, as seen in the many single-country studies in a double issue of *Library Trends*, "Libraries in a Post-Communist World" (2014–2015).

Some examples of wider treatment of Europe's library world can, however, be quoted, as background to the discussion that follows. In 1848 Edward Edwards published "A Statistical View of the Principal Public Libraries in Europe and the United States," later used as part of the evidence submitted to the Select Committee on Public Libraries of 1849; the libraries described did not represent public libraries of the modern kind and most were "research libraries" in the continental sense. Edwards undertook another survey in the 1860s, covering Britain, France, Germany, and the United States in some detail, which took in a much wider range of libraries than the title *Free Town Libraries* (1869) suggests. A little earlier V. I. Sobol'shchikov traveled around western Europe to assess library buildings and management on behalf of the Russian imperial library; his *Obzor bol'shikh bibliotek Evropy v nachalie 1859 goda* (1860; "Survey of the great libraries of Europe in early 1859"), is full of interest for his view of librarianship in those countries he visited.

In 1936–1937 senior British librarians visited libraries in most European countries (but not Spain, Portugal, or Italy), as well as Britain and North America, on behalf of the Library Association. Their report, *A Survey of Libraries* (1938), edited by L. R. McColvin, gives a valuable critical account of European librarianship in the countries visited in the years before World War II. J. H. P. Pafford's *Library Co-operation in Europe* (1935) and Arundell Esdaile's two-volume *The World's Great Libraries* (1934–1937) provide much historical information on European librarianship from the same period. The modern world of information, however, has European roots back to the seventeenth century, as Peter Hoare showed in a 1998 article, "The Development of a European Information Society."

General histories of libraries and librarianship do not always show a specifically European context. Examples are Elmer D. Johnson's *History of Libraries in the Western World* (1965; 4th ed. by Michael H. Harris, 1995), or B. F. Volodin's *Vsemirnaia istoriia bibliotek* ("World history of libraries," 2002). Frédéric Barbier's *Histoire des bibliothèques, d'Alexandrie aux bibliothèques virtuelles* (2013) concentrates on Europe but is more concerned with the earlier period (and is less interested in librarianship). Wiegand and Davis's *Encyclopedia of Library History* (1994) is very useful on specific countries and libraries, with some articles on broad topics, but again cannot always give a European perspective. David Stam's *International Dictionary of Library Histories* (2 vols., 2001) is mostly devoted to studies of individual libraries, but its introductory surveys do provide comparisons between libraries of different types in Europe and more widely.

European librarians' views of their profession tend to focus on the national level, and much historical writing reflects this preference. Multiauthored histories cover some single countries or areas, such as the *Cambridge History of Libraries in Britain and Ireland* (3 vols., 2006), and the *Histoire des bibliothèques françaises* (4 vols., 1988–1992). Some monographs provide a single-country overview, such as Christine Senser's *Die Bibliotheken der Schweiz* (1991) for Swiss libraries. For Germany Ladislaus Buzás's *Deutsche Bibliotheksgeschichte* (3 vols., 1975–1978) was compressed into a one-volume English translation by William D. Boyd, *German Library History, 800–1945* (1986), while Wolfgang Schmitz's *Deutsche Bibliotheksgeschichte* (1984) gives a more succinct account. For the postwar period and the reconstruction of libraries and librarianship in Germany after 1945, the papers in Vodosek and Leonhard's collection *Die Entwicklung des Bibliothekswesens in Deutschland 1945–1965* (1993) give a good picture. For the Netherlands, Paul Schneiders's *Nederlandse bibliotheekgeschiedenis* (1999) is comprehensive and has a good English summary. For Italy, Enzo Bottasso's *Storia della biblioteca in Italia* (1984) is complemented by Paolo Traniello's *Storia delle biblioteche in Italia dall'Unità a oggi* (2002) for the modern period from the 1860s onward to the end of the twentieth century, while a 1990 issue of *Libraries & Culture* covers many aspects of "Libraries and Librarianship in Italy." It is not always possible, however, in material with a specific national coverage, to see a country's librarianship in its full European context. Furthermore, countries such as Portugal and Greece have a rich library heritage but have contributed relatively little to the growth of librarianship or its history. Some area studies are helpful—for example, special issues of *Libraries & Culture* like "The History of Reading and Libraries in the Nordic Countries" (1993), which expands K. C. Harrison's 1969 book on Scandinavia and in turn is complemented by Martin Dyrbye's 2009 book on the Nordic and Baltic countries.

The impact of "Anglo-Saxon" and particularly U.S. professional ideas on European countries other than Britain is an important part of library history, especially since 1945. Paolo Traniello's *La biblioteca pubblica: storia di un istituto nell'Europa contemporanea* (1997), while particularly concerned with public libraries, has a section devoted to the achievements of "the Anglo-Saxon model" throughout Europe. Even at the first International Conference on Bibliography (Brussels, 1895), the brainchild of Belgian librarians Paul Otlet and Henri La Fontaine, many contributors were English or American. That conference led to the establishment of the Institut international de la bibliographie, embodying Otlet's ambitious aim of universal bibliographical control, and in due course to worldwide enterprises such as the Universal Decimal Classification (UDC) and the Fédération internationale de documentation (FID), all showing strong English-language input to genuine Europe-based international initiatives.

But it is difficult to perceive a single European model of librarianship, and certainly not one incorporating the United Kingdom into a European pattern—this despite important contributions from the International Federation of Library Associations (IFLA) and other international organizations. There have been several moves toward collaboration, either Europe-wide or in particular areas. Scandinavia is a prime example, with initiatives such as NORDINFO to coordinate work in research and special libraries across five countries. Other collaborative projects include LIBER, the Ligue des bibliothèques européennes de recherche or Association of European Research Libraries, founded in 1972, and the Conference of European National Libraries, which produced the European Library, a website accessing collections of all its members and linked to a larger digital *Europeana* project. Links between professional associations, as well as between libraries, helped develop librarianship across the continent, though this was slower in Eastern Europe where independent professional associations were not favored under communism. Since 1992 EBLIDA, the European Bureau of Library, Information and Documentation Associations, has united professional bodies to address areas such as copyright and intellectual property. Initiatives linked to the European Union have addressed some problems of interstate and intercultural collaboration through projects such as CACAO, which in 2007–2009 offered "an innovative approach for understanding and navigating texts in different languages . . . enabling users to better exploit European electronic content." The success of such initiatives proved the value of international collaboration despite the difficulties.

It is tempting to think that librarians across Europe have always worked in a "progressive" manner for the greater good. In fact, over the centuries, values in librarianship changed due to different political situations and cultural contexts. Pronouncements made in good faith by earlier librarians do not always reflect later professional viewpoints. James Duff Brown's *Manual of Library Economy* (1903), for example, complains of "the craze for critical 'evaluation' or 'appraisal'" in catalogs.[2] Within the widely accepted socialist philosophy of 1920s Russia, control over library users' reading was not simply tolerated by librarians—it became an unchallengeable orthodoxy, seen as a vital part in the battle against illiteracy. Similar control in Nazi Germany grew out of earlier desires to encourage "good" reading. Acceptance of censorship by librarians within communities with strong religious identities (e.g., Catholic Poland or Ireland, or community pressure in some Protestant communities) must be understood in its historical context. Debates over the provision of fiction and "light reading" in public-funded libraries—sometimes reflecting political views about the place of the lower classes— persist in the twenty-first century as librarians continue to react to their political and cultural world. No doubt change will continue and orthodoxies of the early twenty-first century will be superseded in years to come.

THE BACKGROUND TO MODERN EUROPEAN LIBRARIANSHIP

Libraries had developed across Europe in many different forms through the Middle Ages (e.g., royal, monastery), then under the influence of the Renaissance and Reformation (and Counter-Reformation), and notably by the Enlightenment of the eighteenth century. By the end of that century Europe had two main areas of librarianship, different in many ways but not mutually exclusive, and the eighteenth-century scene forms a background for the development of modern librarianship.

First came *scholarly collections*, often of great extent and long standing, where book selection was subject to private or institutional priorities over the centuries. Some were called "public" libraries, some were controlled by cities or city-states. Some admitted members of the public selectively; a few had features recognizable in modern public libraries. The curators' approaches were not always conservative but tended toward preservation of inherited riches rather than exploitation of them. Progressive thinking is evident in a few great royal or ducal libraries, such as the French Royal Library in Paris, or Wolfenbüttel in Germany, where librarians not only planned the library's growth but experimented with new arrangements and management. Monastic and other ecclesiastical libraries across Europe, many with rich collections that later passed into public hands, served their religious communities and did not usually look further afield. In some other cases, too, positive developments were less marked. Despite the riches of its foundation collections, even the British Museum library was slow to assume the role of a national library after opening in 1753.

Second, there were more *popular libraries* of various kinds and sizes, sometimes operated by societies such as the "Common Use" libraries of the Netherlands and northern Germany; sometimes by learned societies that served a select membership by forming scholarly collections, as across Britain from the mid-eighteenth century; sometimes on a commercial basis, where a "circulating library" lent books on a subscription basis and aimed principally at a popular market. Such circulating libraries spread rapidly across Europe from the mid-eighteenth century and the movement gained momentum with the rise of the popular novel, improving literacy rates—though their popularity led some cultural authorities to condemn them as peddlers of trash. (Some, however, had a wider-based stock to serve specialized needs, and some were restricted by class, gender, or religion.) Both these types of popular libraries can be seen as predecessors of the modern public library, though normally they had no element of state funding.

Scholarly and popular libraries fed the gradual development of a professional view of librarianship that became more focused and explicit across Europe through the nineteenth century. Both types of library provided reading material for formal and more popular education. Popular libraries were one of the main vehicles for disseminating Enlightenment philosophy and in turn opened up a mass culture across Europe. The development of the modern library world—and indeed of many elements in modern culture—can be traced to the French Revolution of 1789, which aimed to give power to the people and abolish the *ancien régime* of aristocracy and church power, giving rise to the concept of public ownership (in the intellectual sphere as in other areas). The development of a public sphere in France led the way in many areas of librarianship, for example, the transfer of the French Royal Library into state hands as the Bibliothèque nationale expanded its existing public role into something wider and more explicit. (Similar changes occurred after the Russian Revolution of 1917 in the transformation of the Imperial Public Library in St. Petersburg into a library with wider public access, now the National Library of Russia, as Zaitsev's book indicates.)

Similarly, the sequestration or nationalization of monastic and ecclesiastical libraries, and of large private collections, was not restricted to France (England had led the way in the sixteenth century with the dissolution of the monasteries). Such secularization took place in Austria in the earlier eighteenth century and was followed in Bavaria in the early nineteenth century when the Bavarian State Library overtook the Hofbibliothek in Vienna to become the largest library in German-speaking countries. In Austria sequestrated books went largely to existing state or university libraries, as also happened in Czechoslovakia under Communist rule after World War II, when such libraries were deposited in the national library. In revolutionary France, however, the sequestrated collections were used to form municipal libraries as a centrally planned distribution of the nation's patrimony to the regions. This French initiative created the first local "public" libraries to receive national recognition, though they were primarily concerned with conservation of historic collections and it was many years before they became fully accessible to the public. The ideas behind their foundation, however, are significant as an early formulation of a national library system.

France also first established the concept of public employment in the late eighteenth century. The regulation of French librarians as civil servants—with the advantages and disadvantages that entailed—was one of the earliest manifestations of the recognition of a library profession on a national scale. The creation of an administrative class or *Beamtentum* in Prussia and in the German Empire after 1870 had a similar effect, and the constitutional situation of many librarians in France and Germany, in public-funded libraries of all kinds, has led to a degree of central control of appointments, job definitions, and professional education. Napoleon's abolition of the Holy Roman Empire led, after 1815, to a more secular pattern of government (if not more liberal or efficient) in German-speaking countries. This transformed many old ducal and monastic collections into state libraries, somewhat along the French pattern (but mostly not under municipal or national control). At the same time, in the Napoleonic wars the French transferred many collections (of books and art objects) to France, where some remained even after 1815—though others were sold and became important acquisitions for the British Museum and other European libraries in Europe and later in the United States.

The broad idea of "liberty" (not always the same as democracy) spreading through other countries, notably those falling under French hegemony during the revolutionary and Napoleonic wars, had its roots in the Enlightenment philosophy of the eighteenth century; it also led to the growth of "Enlightened" librarians and the beginnings of a modern view of librarianship. For example, the French occupation of the Netherlands led to the establishment of a national library there in 1798. Furthermore, the political ideas developed in France after 1789 inspired later revolutions spreading across Europe in the 1830s and especially around 1848, which in their turn opened up political and cultural thinking and had significant effects on the history of librarianship.

LIBRARIES AND LIBRARIANSHIP OF DIFFERENT TYPES

This section covers three broad groups: national libraries, academic and research libraries and special libraries, and public libraries. (For purposes of historical analysis this is admittedly too simplified a categorization.) Within each group the particular type is discussed in general terms, followed by studies of individual countries, in the same order in each group (beginning with the British Isles, then running roughly from east to west and from north to south). The nature of libraries is not always determined by librarians but reflects government directives or social requirements. The different ways in which libraries develop under these influences has a direct effect on the philosophy and practice of librarianship, and in turn influences professional organizations, which have often come to articulate the philosophy of librarianship.

One feature of many continental European countries (less true in Britain and Ireland) is the dominance of large "research" libraries—national, regional, academic, and even some "public" libraries—which, while supported from public funds of some kind, have been largely a separate species from public libraries for the wider community. In some countries these larger libraries led the way in developing professional thinking—especially in the absence of an effective network of more popular libraries. In some cases (particularly Germany) the division between the two types of libraries created separate professional structures with parallel training and career paths for "research" and "public" librarians that constrained professional librarians seeking to transfer between them, which then led to divergent concepts of librarianship. In Denmark the two wings were well integrated for many years, until internal tensions caused a split in the 1970s (though later legislation drew them closer again).

Public libraries of the popular type were a later development in many countries, following the spread of more liberal ideas of democracy and education. The growth of libraries was not, however, always in step with the growth of political democracy. In nineteenth-century France successive constitutional changes were not matched by a parallel development of public libraries, while in contrast in Tsarist Russia the autocratic government still permitted many public libraries to exist (and the repressive Communist regime that followed strongly advocated public libraries throughout the country, as Simsova's and Raymond's books show). Public libraries also faced open opposition: in nineteenth-century Britain ratepayers (local voters) were inclined to oppose their taxes being spent on books for others to read.

The academy library, a particular type of research library found in most European countries, reflected a developing commitment to science. Academy libraries sometimes housed a country's major heritage and research collections—for example, the Royal Irish Academy in Dublin, or the academies in Tallinn (Estonia) and Riga (Latvia). The academies in Estonia and Latvia (no longer in existence, though their libraries survive) were based on academies founded under the Russian Empire and predated national and university libraries in their cities. Similarly, Hungary and some other countries have strong academy libraries (for different subject areas), and in Russia they form a significant part of the nation's library wealth. In Britain the nearest equivalent of the "academy library" is the learned society, from the Royal Society, founded in 1660, to the libraries of the numerous Royal Colleges in the medical field. These, like a few large research libraries created by private enterprise, such as the Wellcome Historical Medical Library in London or the John Rylands Library (a Manchester rare book collection later absorbed into the university library), and the legal libraries of the Inns of Court in London, became part of a spectrum of library heritage, though they do not fit neatly into the structure of "academic" libraries. Some have had a "national" status recognized, as when the National Library of Scotland absorbed the library of the Royal Society of Edinburgh in the 1980s as the basis of a proposed Scottish Science Library.

The boundaries between the twin disciplines of "librarianship" and "documentation" can best be understood in libraries such as these, devoted to the provision of specialized current information as well as to conservation of their heritage. In the twentieth century the concept of "documentation" led to specialist training for a role recognized as separate from "librarianship." British documentalists founded Aslib (originally the Association of Special Libraries and Information Bureaux) in 1926 to represent the interests of commercial and other information-oriented library members not adequately covered by the Library Association; its *Handbook of Special Librarianship and Information Work*, originally compiled by Wilfred Ashworth (1955 and later editions) set out principles for work in this area. (An Institute of Information Scientists established in Britain in 1958 offered a separate training and qualification structure, which lasted until the institute merged with the Library Association in 2002 to form the Chartered Institute of Library & Information Professionals, or CILIP.) Many other countries repeated these patterns with separate professional associations, career paths, educational provisions, and qualification systems. A comparative study of the "documentation profession" would provide many parallels with the history of librarianship, though it is probably less constrained by national characteristics.

A wider development, similar to the growth of "documentation" in the early twentieth century, gained strength in the twenty-first century. The "information revolution" led to posts outside the traditional library field in areas such as Web management, knowledge or data management, and information analysis. While such posts are often available to nonlibrarians, librarians found it easy to adapt their professional skills to the new demands. In many parts of the world, this has led to recognition of a wider "information profession," a development that has a clear logic but risks losing some elements important in traditional librarianship, notably the concern with the book as a physical object.

I. NATIONAL LIBRARIES

For national libraries the question of definition is significant, as K. W. Humphreys showed in his 1987 Panizzi lectures. In many modern developing countries, the national library is the natural center of the public library network and is itself essentially a "public" library. This is less common in Europe, though wider roles are being taken in the twenty-first century. "National library" functions have often been grafted on to libraries founded without these responsibilities, notably university libraries or other large research libraries. In most cases one of the principal "national" functions is the preservation and recording of the archive of the nation's literary heritage (often, but not always, held as a permanent, nonlending stock). This function in turn presupposes strong collections of early printing and manuscripts, legal deposit, and a national bibliography—but this is not always the case, since in some countries the strongest collections of early printing are found elsewhere and bibliographic functions are handled independently. The degree of networking based on a national library can also vary widely.

Ian R. Willison's 1989 article "The National Library in Historical Perspective" sketches the development of the principle in both Europe and North America, giving an excellent overview of the major libraries and the librarians who created them. He stresses the significance of the "national archive" (of printed material as well as manuscripts—in the twenty-first century expanded to a much wider range of media)—and the concept of a "universal library" as keynotes for the particular role of the national library, something adopted in countries establishing such a library as part of the furniture of a new state. International Federation of Library Associations (IFLA) extended the principle by espousing the concept of "universal bibliographic control," which depends on national libraries to maintain current and retrospective national bibliographies.

Because many types of libraries assumed a "national" role, the typology is not always clear. Historically, libraries played a role in national development or the establishment of a "national" identity within a larger state. A small-scale example of this is the place of libraries and museums in nineteenth-century Transylvania, a multiethnic province now in Romania but associated with the Habsburg crown until 1918: it contained three national groups (Romanian, Hungarian, and German), each feeling a need to establish an identity through "national" libraries-in-museums—a concept deriving from the British Museum library in London. Some countries possess several libraries called "national," sometimes for distinct areas (as with the Biblioteca de Catalunya in Spain), sometimes for historically based differences (as the separate national libraries across Italy), sometimes for special purposes (like the All-Russia State Library of Foreign Literature in Moscow described by Skorodenko, which offers public access to its rich collections but is also the national center for the librarianship of worldwide literature).

A common feature of a national library is legal deposit—that is, the right to receive all the nation's publications, now expanding to include electronic material. The twenty-first-century extension of legislation to electronic and other nonbook publications has been uneven across the continent, though its introduction has to a large extent been driven by librarians stressing the long-term value of the national archive, rather than by politicians or publishers. National libraries are often not the only recipients of legal deposit; major university libraries sometimes have similar privileges. Sometimes regional research libraries receive only those publications relevant to their region. When nations changed their borders, combining or separating, a national library was sometimes placed in a difficult position regarding legal deposit material. Ex-Soviet nations in the 1990s, for example, stopped receiving material formerly deposited under pan-Soviet legislation. On the other hand, the creation of the Irish Free State (now the Republic of Ireland) in 1922 did not change legal deposit arrangements for the United Kingdom, and the new state adopted the same pattern; as a result, UK and Irish publishers are required to deposit their works in a foreign country.

Britain

In 1753 the newly founded British Museum library was not initially given an official "national" status; this remained true even after the gift of King George III's library in 1828, until its charismatic director Antonio Panizzi (Italian by birth) developed the principle in the 1840s. Panizzi worked with (and fought against) the book trade to maximize the library stock through purchase and legal deposit; he created practical and influential cataloging rules and laid the foundations for a comprehensive printed catalog. He established the concept of a national library in a museum context, inspirational to librarians in other countries—the national library as a scholarly resource of material of all kinds, a combination of written material and *realia* or objects. This "universality" existed in London until the departure of the library departments from the British Museum when the British Library's new building opened in 1997.

Panizzi also erected a pioneering building, with fireproof cast-iron stacks and an iconic domed reading room, which made the library recognizable worldwide. The Russian librarian V. I. Sobol'shchikov visited in 1859, two years after it opened, and reported that he was dumbstruck with admiration; he also approved of the library administration, though remaining critical of some aspects. Later Russian radical visitors were also enthusiastic about what the library offered, as Robert Henderson's article shows—but in terms of its stock, which Karl Marx, Lenin, and others used for political ends; yet this too illustrates an important part of its librarianship philosophy—making available the widest possible range of material. Panizzi's reign effectively gave national libraries their classic form. The obvious European competitor was the French Bibliothèque nationale; Panizzi explicitly aimed to "outdo Paris," and because of the turmoils of French politics and the lack of a strong guiding hand there, he succeeded.

The British Museum began a new printed catalog in 1881; it was completed in 1905 under the supervision of Richard Garnett and others (but only after political debate about its nature and its cost, even reaching Parliament). It remained a major reference tool in libraries throughout the country, indeed worldwide, for much of the twentieth century, providing not only a prototype national bibliography but also a rich bibliographical source across a range of subjects. It generated supplements, partial new editions, and eventually a photolithographic cumulation, introduced by Sir Frank Francis in the 1960s to break the logjam of updating. Only after the creation of the British Library in 1973 did electronic cataloging begin—based partly on the *British National Bibliography* (started in 1950 with Francis's support but kept independent of the museum library systems in 1973). By then the British Library was leading the United Kingdom's input on new internationally acceptable cataloging standards, following the IFLA-sponsored 1961 conference, which produced the twelve "Paris Principles." This had resulted in the *Anglo-American Cataloguing Rules*, first published in 1967 in British and American editions and quickly achieving worldwide recognition, with various editions and translations into the twenty-first century. In the same way the British Library was prominent in the development of RDA (Resource Description and Access), the successor to AACR for a multimedia world, and adopted RDA for its own catalogs in 2013.

Panizzi's successors built on his foundations and made the British Museum library a world center of scholarship, particularly in the humanities. Garnett and Francis were prominent, as was A. W. Pollard, bibliographer of early English printing and a founder of the Central Library for Students, later the National Central Library (NCL), an agency for interlibrary lending. But as an institution the British Museum stood aside from many professional developments in the twentieth century, despite pressure from librarians such as Francis. It was thus not surprising, for example, that when the government established the National Lending Library for Science and Technology (NLLST) in 1960 to replace the document-supply role of the old Science Museum Library, it rejected links with the British Museum library and deliberately located the new institution at Boston Spa in Yorkshire, 200 miles north of London (Bernard Houghton has described its radical nature in *Out of the Dinosaurs*).

The NLLST aroused professional hostility for being a library "without a catalog"—not wholly true—and its first director, Donald Urquhart, who had little confidence in the traditional library profession (as shown in his autobiography), revolutionized the provision of scientific literature by supplying books and, crucially, journal articles directly to libraries and even users around the country, greatly reducing the need for interlibrary loan. This ground-breaking development derived from an awareness of the special needs of science and technology, and represented a "scientific" vision of librarianship parallel to the "humanities" tradition exemplified by the British Museum, which had a huge influence on professional thinking. The NLLST drew praise throughout Europe and indeed worldwide, though it was not replicated elsewhere. Remarkably, until the arrival of the Internet, its international service proved more economic for many libraries in Europe and beyond than local provision of similar services. The NLLST crystallized a new understanding of document supply, in contrast to the British Museum, which kept its stock intact and did not participate in interlibrary lending, either directly or through the NCL.

Not until the report of the National Libraries Committee in 1969, under the chairmanship of Sir Fred Dainton, was a "national library" role legally clarified. The visionary Dainton Report represented views of influential members of the library profession, as well as scholars, politicians, and others, and led directly to the founding of the British Library in 1973. As a national library this incorporated not only the library departments of the British Museum, the National Central Library, and the British National Bibliography, but also the former Patent Office Library as a reference library for science and invention, and most significantly the NLLST, so that it was eventually based in both London and Yorkshire.

The British Library quickly assumed a dominant role in professional activities. Direct links with public libraries were not part of its remit, but it developed strong connections with academic and research libraries and facilitated wide-ranging developments in the provision of information. Like many huge institutions it sometimes appeared unwieldy and unresponsive to specific developments in librarianship, but for several years it funded research into librarianship that provided great value to professional development. The new London building, opened in 1997, proved a popular success—though in the twenty-first century it struggles to meet all readers' demands. As in many other national libraries, ambitious digitization programs (largely librarian-driven but acclaimed by the scholarly world) expanded the library's impact by making materials available worldwide. These programs included digitizing early books and manuscripts and comprehensive digitization of newspapers from the seventeenth century onward (allowing the library to close its newspaper library in Colindale, north London, in favor of electronic access in the main building).

National Libraries of Ireland, Scotland, and Wales

Elsewhere in the United Kingdom, the National Libraries of Ireland (NLI), Scotland (NLS), and Wales (NLW) were founded in the late nineteenth and early twentieth centuries, without being given a clear role within the United Kingdom or without any explicit relationship with the British Museum. Nonetheless, the idea of the British Museum, as developed under Panizzi, was clearly in the founders' minds, though each library concentrated on its own country's literature and history and they consequently developed different policies. In Scotland and Wales, national libraries became a focus for professional library activity (in each case affected by national characteristics), compiling national bibliographies and, with more devolved government in recent years, increasing responsibilities as national libraries: for example, the National Library of Scotland absorbed the Scottish Central Library in 1974 and assumed the major role in interlibrary lending and library cooperation in Scotland. The National Library of Ireland played a similar role but with a number of differences (due to political and other reasons).

The NLI, NLS, and NLW did not share equally in one common function of national libraries—legal deposit. The National Library of Scotland, founded in 1925, inherited the UK-wide legal deposit privilege of the Faculty of Advocates Library on which it was based. The National Library of Wales, a new institution of 1907 and from the start bilingual (Welsh and English), had more limited access to publications until 1987, though its collection of Welsh publications was always comprehensive. The National Library of Ireland has a more complicated history. It was founded on the basis of the Royal Dublin Society in 1877, when Ireland was still a full part of the United Kingdom; it never had UK legal deposit and was at first under the shadow of the rich and ancient library of Trinity College Dublin (TCD), traditionally a Protestant bulwark in a largely Catholic country, which held UK legal deposit privilege. Catholic and Protestant communities both supported the new National Library, and its concentration on Irish material—in both English and Irish Gaelic—gave it a distinctive character, especially in the growing movement for Irish independence. It was also one of the first libraries in Britain to adopt the Dewey Decimal Classification (DDC). After the establishment of the Irish Free State, now the Republic of Ireland, in 1922 it continued as the new country's national library, and despite funding problems provided a focus for professional activity and bibliography. In 1927 it received legal deposit rights for Irish publications, though TCD continues to receive UK publications as well, even though after 1922 it was in a foreign country (this was sometimes problematic when deposited books were on the Catholic Index of works banned in the Republic). The two libraries—and indeed many libraries on both sides of the border—evolved a harmonious relationship once religious and political differences diminished. The province of Northern Ireland, which after 1922 remained part of the United Kingdom, had no "national" library and no legal deposit, though other institutions assumed some functions (one of the strongest collections of Northern Ireland publications being in Belfast's Linen Hall Library, a semiprivate subscription library with some state subvention).

Scandinavia

In Scandinavia, Denmark, Sweden, and Norway have "royal" libraries, while Iceland and Finland have national libraries. All have similar responsibilities. The Danish, Norwegian, Swedish, and Icelandic languages are closely linked, but linguistic distinctions are part of national identities. Finnish and Sami (spoken in arctic Norway, Sweden, and Finland) are unrelated languages.

The Danish Royal Library is linked to Copenhagen University, with its former off-shoot, the National Library for Science and Medicine, operating as a faculty library. Daniel Gotthild Moldenhawer (librarian, 1788–1832) remodeled the royal library, informally known as a national library since 1793, on the lines of Göttingen University library in Germany (where he had studied). For example, he created a systematic catalog in 192 volumes, which remained in use for over a century. In 1902 Denmark established another state library in Århus (or Aarhus) to act as a second legal deposit center (with special concern for audiovisual material from the 1980s) and to serve as a public research library with lending facilities. After the creation of a university in Århus in 1928 it came to serve as both a national and a university library, and in the twenty-first century accommodated the national interlibrary loan services. More recently it assumed responsibility for public library services to ethnic minorities and immigrant communities, a special remit rarely found in other countries.

Iceland was a Danish dependency until 1918, but a national library, now Landsbókasafn Islands, was founded in Reykjavik in the early nineteenth century (housed first in the cathedral tower, then in its own building from the 1880s) and had legal deposit from 1887. In a country with a historically strong book culture, the library flourished. In the late nineteenth century the national library's Jón Ólafsson worked in the United States and Canada, and when he returned he introduced the Dewey Decimal Classification, which has dominated Icelandic libraries ever since. The new national library building (by a British architect, and now united with Reykjavik University Library) houses interlending and cooperative cataloging for the whole country.

Norway, too, was a dependency, first of Denmark, then Sweden from 1814 under a union of crowns. In 1905 it attained full independence with its own king. National library functions were for many years carried out in Christiania (now Oslo) by the country's only university library. This had been founded in 1811 with a large donation from the royal library in Copenhagen but was without legal deposit for much of the nineteenth century. It was a "universal" collection, available to the public as well as to the university, and in the twentieth century developed a national bibliography (automated from the 1970s), as well as a union catalog of all Norwegian libraries. Cataloging and classification long followed German patterns, though UDC was introduced in 1982. During the Nazi occupation, librarians in Oslo preserved Jewish books and archives (though lending them was forbidden) and collected illegal publications. In 1989 Norway established a separate national library depository at Mo i Rana (within the Arctic Circle), where ideal storage conditions ensured conservation of both print and electronic media. Over the next ten years the new national library separated from the university library under its first librarian, the charismatic Bendik Rugaas. In 2005 the national library occupied the university library's handsome old building in Oslo, while retaining a presence at Mo i Rana. This gave it a significant base in the capital, and its special collections (inherited from the university) and other functions allowed it to act as a national center for library activity of all kinds.

In Sweden, the Royal Library is the national library, though from the sixteenth century it was technically the property of successive monarchs who added extensively from northern European conquests in the seventeenth century during Sweden's "Great Power" period. In the early nineteenth century the library clarified its national role by initiating a national bibliography, conducting cataloging projects, and developing reader services, and in 1877 it moved to a new building using modern cast-iron techniques inspired by British and French libraries. By the late nineteenth century the Royal Library was competing with Uppsala University's older library as the country's major research library. Strong twentieth-century librarians brought further progress and a clearer mission, including responsibility for the national bibliography from 1956 and retrospective bibliographies (in the twenty-first century accessible online). Under Uno Willers in the 1950s, the Royal Library served as Stockholm University's main research library, an arrangement that lasted until 1976, when the university built a new library. In the twenty-first century the Royal Library functions as the center for library activity throughout Sweden, including national policy planning, and it is a major player in the country's professional identity.

Finland has a complicated history: first a Swedish province, then part of the Russian empire from 1809 to 1917, then independent but with a period under German occupation. A strong Swedish-speaking minority complicated its "national library" responsibilities (Finnish language and literature only became recognized in the nineteenth century). In 1640 Sweden founded the royal academy in Åbo (now better known by its Finnish name, Turku); it also functioned as a university, and its library grew rapidly in the eighteenth century, before the institution transferred to Helsingfors (now Helsinki) in 1829 after a disastrous fire. Russian domination in the nineteenth century awarded the library legal deposit, but other library systems broadly followed the German pattern familiar elsewhere in Scandinavia. After Finland achieved independence in 1917, the university library became accessible to the public and adopted U.S. and British practices, again common elsewhere in Scandinavia; so the university library evolved into the National Library of Finland, though the formal name change did not occur until 2006. In the twenty-first century its "national" activities form a separate section within a single institution, which also serves the university. Like other national libraries, it is responsible for the preservation and continuing development of the country's "historic archive" and leads Finland's digital development. At the same time it acts as a national center for scientific periodicals and the negotiation of licenses for electronic publications (a role not commonly found in other national libraries).

Russia

In Russia the history of "national" libraries covers the Tsarist empire, which collapsed in 1917, and the Soviet Union (USSR—also effectively an empire) up to the 1990s, followed by a still-federal but rather smaller Russian republic. Throughout much of its history Russia has been the controlling center of more than one single nation; in the twenty-first century it has national libraries in Moscow and St. Petersburg, which, as under the Soviet Union, share the "national" function. These two libraries played important roles in the development of librarianship throughout this vast country.

The idea of a national library in Russia dates from 1714 and the foundation of Peter the Great's academy in his new capital of St. Petersburg, modeled on the learned societies springing up across Europe. This continues today as the Russian Academy of Sciences, a major research center with a substantial library (though it suffered a disastrous fire in 1988). In 1936 British visitors judged it one of the finest libraries in Russia and applauded its methods. From the start the Russian Academy library had a national role, including legal deposit, but Empress Catherine II wished to expand services to a wider populace, and she founded a new Imperial Public Library in 1795 (described by Zaitsev, Stuart, and others). From the start this library also assumed a national role with responsibility for "the social enlightenment of Russian subjects" and for collecting material relating to Russia wherever published. Its collections were significantly strengthened by the 1794 transfer from Warsaw of the rich "public" library founded by the Załuski brothers in 1747 (what was left of the library was returned to Poland in the 1920s but suffered great losses in World War II). Director Alexei Olenin initiated a program of modernization; in 1809 he published the country's first manual on library management (in French and Russian), which opened the door to improvements in Russian librarianship. Olenin's success paved the way for Baron Modest Korf (director, 1849–1861), who reinvigorated the library by introducing subject-specialist departments and encouraging professional development. In 1859 his colleague V. I. Sobol'shchikov published (in French) a book on library organization and toured western European libraries to study library architecture and systems, producing a valuable report. Later in the nineteenth century Alexander II's political reforms enabled Afanasy Bychkov (director, 1882–1899) to redefine Russian librarianship by stressing reader service. By the 1917 revolutions, the library had staff with social-democratic leanings who raised questions of how far it should open to the masses. New Bolshevik statutes issued in 1920 did not help the desperate financial situation, and with little money available for book purchases the library developed exchange programs with U.S. and European libraries, including the New York Public Library and the Bibliothèque nationale in Paris. During this period the library also segregated politically "dangerous" literature, inaccessible to all but approved readers (known as the "Spetskhran" or special reserve, and not opened up until the 1990s). This policy became common in other libraries and countries adopting Marxist-Leninist philosophies. During the siege of Leningrad in 1941–1942, the main collections were evacuated and services continued at a much reduced level, but the presence of the library helped the spirit of resistance against the German invaders. Postwar developments followed the general pattern of Soviet librarianship with an isolationist and autocratic management, though still offering a tradition of reader service. The opening in 1992 of a new building outside the city center and a new feeling of openness after the collapse of the Soviet Union allowed the library, under its new title, National Library of Russia, to assume a larger role in the country's professional library development.

Russia's second "national library" is the Russian State Library in Moscow, formerly known as the Lenin Library and one of the world's two or three largest libraries. Its origins lie in the museum and library opened by Count Nikolai Rumiantsev in St. Petersburg in 1831. It moved to Moscow in 1862 as the first library in the city open to the general public. After the 1917 revolution, Moscow became the capital and in 1921 the library was formally named as the national library. The library continued to grow through donations of major collections and international exchange programs, and after the revolution by incorporating sequestrated private, religious, and institutional collections. As the major library in the capital it had great powers to coordinate library practices throughout the USSR by liaising with the nationalized publishing industry to develop cataloging services. After World War II it played a crucial role in the development of library practices across the whole Soviet bloc, covering much of eastern Europe and central Asia. For example, it was responsible for the cataloging rules and the Marxist-Leninist classification scheme adopted by most libraries under Soviet control. As with the St. Petersburg library, progress toward electronic information management became possible only in the last few years of the twentieth century.

The other Soviet socialist republics constituting the USSR also had national libraries; those in Minsk (Belarus) and Kiev (Ukraine) are among the largest and historically most important in what was European Russia. All broadly followed Russian professional development and after independence in the 1990s remained in the same mold. Libraries in the Baltic republics of Estonia, Latvia, and Lithuania showed more independence and developed a more Western outlook as their countries joined the European Union. These countries also had strong academy libraries under the Tsarist regime, small sisters of the St. Petersburg Academy, also with pan-Russian legal deposit privileges through the nineteenth century. Their historic collections form an important complement to the newer national libraries in each country, though they had suffered serious depletion at different times from occupying forces.

Poland

Poland's national library is a twentieth-century creation, reflecting Poland's reemergence in 1918 as an independent nation after more than a century, though it traces its roots back to the library established in Warsaw by the Załuski brothers in 1747 and long exiled in St. Petersburg. Its foundation in 1928 was a conscious part of the founding of a new state, though it had no separate home for many years—the collections, drawn from existing state holdings and private collections, were housed initially in the School of Economics and in the Potocki Palace—and plans for a new building were disrupted by World War II. German occupation led to its renaming as a municipal library, then to the deliberate burning of its special collections in 1944 as part of the German reprisals following the Warsaw Uprising, resulting in the loss of many thousands of volumes. Re-creation of the library after 1945, though subject to Soviet direction, succeeded in gathering rich collections concerning Poland's history and has left it as one of the most important cultural institutions in the country. Automation began in the late 1960s and soon developed Polish versions of machine-readable cataloging (MARC) for use in wide-ranging networking. In modern accommodation it acts as the national bibliographic center and as the main source of advice on preservation and conservation.

Germany

In Germany, the story of national libraries is less straightforward, though the country overall has one of the strongest histories of library development in Europe. The complex political nature of the "German Empire" that came together in 1870 made it difficult to create a national library in a country with a strong tradition of local or regional autonomy. For example, the Federal Republic's 1949 constitution gives the federal states autonomy in cultural matters, including libraries. Many *Staatsbibliotheken*— state libraries, sometimes sharing the role with a university or city library—have strong local or regional positions, some even with quasi-national status, but coordination and collaboration proved difficult over the generations. Bernhard Fabian's 1983 book *Buch, Bibliothek und geisteswissenschaftliche Forschung* analyzed shortcomings in the supply of research materials for the humanities scholar and quickly influenced library policies in the Federal Republic. Under Fabian's direction, the multivolume *Handbuch der historischen Buchbestände in Deutschland* described in detail research library holdings throughout Germany (later expanded to other countries and now available online), facilitating a better understanding of collections at a national level and also giving valuable data on the history of the libraries listed.

The reunified Germany eventually created an official national library in 1999. Die Deutsche Bibliothek is based partly on the Deutsche Bücherei in Leipzig, founded in 1912 by the German book trade association and under Soviet control after 1945, and partly on the parallel Deutsche Bibliothek in Frankfurt am Main, established in 1946 (again by the book trade) to maintain a West German equivalent. In 1999 the two were joined, together with the German Music Archive in Berlin, to make a single national library. It operates on two main sites—neither in the federal capital of Berlin but both close to the main centers of the publishing trade (the Frankfurt and Leipzig book fairs are a major fixture in the book trade calendar worldwide). It fulfills many national library functions, including countrywide legal deposit and the publication of the national bibliography. It does not, however, act as the principal "historic archive" of German literature or early printing (which originated in Germany in the fifteenth century): these functions are performed by other libraries across the country.

Die Deutsche Bibliothek is also not the center of interlending or document supply, which to some extent is covered by regional cooperatives. For science and engineering, however, the Technische Informationsbibliothek (TIB) in Hannover carried out a role reminiscent of the former NLLST in Britain for many years in the later twentieth century. The TIB, now linked with the university library in Hannover, has a remit to collect technical scientific literature (print and electronic) comprehensively and on a worldwide basis and to make it available to libraries or even individual users in the most effective way. In 2014 it has the additional title of German National Library of Science and Technology, another example of how Germany has decentralized its national library functions.

The common form of state libraries or *Staatsbibliotheken* grew from former princely collections or ancient town libraries, and in some cases continued royal libraries of former independent kingdoms such as Bavaria (Munich), Saxony (Dresden), or Württemberg (Stuttgart). From these *Staatsbibliotheken* came many core texts of modern librarianship, including Schrettinger's *Versuch eines vollständigen Lehrbuchs der Bibliotheks-Wissenschaft* (1808–1810) ("Attempt at a complete manual of library science"—one of the first known uses of the term), and Ebert's *Die Bildung des Bibliothekars* (1820; "The education of a librarian"), based on their work at Munich and Dresden respectively. The two men disagreed on the primacy of classified or alphabetical catalogs, a debate that persisted in German academic libraries; and in 1859 Sobol'shchikov observed good professional practices in reader services and cataloging at both Dresden and Munich, but found classification more of a problem. In 1840 Julius Petzholdt, also of Dresden, founded one of the earliest library periodicals, *Anzeiger für Bibliographie und Bibliothekswissenschaft*, and in 1856 he published his *Katechismus der Bibliothekslehre* ("Catechism of librarianship"), which went through several editions and was heavily drawn on by later professional writers in both Germany and Italy.

In Berlin the Deutsche Staatsbibliothek was formerly the Prussian Royal Library, with a history dating back to the seventeenth century. Under King Frederick II, "the Great," the royal library became important as part of the state's educational policy, though regulations of 1790 restricted access to certain classes. These were amended when the library became part of the new university and academy established in Berlin in 1810 under the scholar Wilhelm von Humboldt, a reforming minister for education. Reflecting Humboldt's aims, in 1813 Friedrich Schleiermacher wrote a *Reglement für die Königliche Bibliothek*, setting out a constitution that influenced other libraries in Prussia for many years (as discussed by Gustav Abb). This *Reglement* called for autonomy for the library and for a librarian who was also a scholar—the tradition of the "scholar-librarian" recognized in most countries but with particular strength in Germany.

Rapidly expanding collections needed organization, but not until the 1840s did the library complete a subject catalog with an alphabetical catalog appended after 1865 (alongside an older author catalog from the 1830s, which continued in use until World War II). From this, and particularly from the printed *Preussische Gesamtkatalog* or Prussian union catalog begun in 1895 (but never completed), arose the influential *Preussische Instruktionen für die alphabetischen Katalogisierung*, the classic German cataloging code, soon recognized as a standard for scholarly libraries in much of Europe; however, other rules, such as those published in 1886 by Carl Dziatzko for the Royal and University Library in Breslau (now Wrocław in Poland), had more influence in Britain and the United States. The Prussian Instructions were eventually replaced in the late twentieth century by the *Regeln für die alphabetische Katalogisierung* (RAK), a remarkable initiative by librarians from both halves of a divided Germany and from other German-speaking countries, in general agreement with the *Anglo-American Cataloging Rules.*

The Royal Library in Berlin provided several influential figures in German librarianship at the turn of the twentieth century. Friedrich Althoff, director of the Ministry for Ecclesiastical, Educational, and Medical Affairs (1882–1907), played a strong political role in reducing the Staatsbibliothek's isolation and coordinating Prussian scholarly libraries into an implicit network. Adolf von Harnack, director of the Royal Library (1905–1921), further developed the concept of the scholar-librarian. Harnack doubled the Staatsbibliothek's staff and budget and set it up as the principal library of the Reich, considerably influencing other German research libraries. It was, however, never fully recognized as the "national library," partly because of the political strength of other large libraries such as Munich (now the Bavarian State Library) or Göttingen University, and partly because of the constitutional tradition of cultural devolution, which elevated the practical fragmentation of libraries into a principle of national culture. This failure to secure "national" status led to the establishment of the Deutsche Bücherei in Leipzig, but this did not prevent the Staatsbibliothek from expanding in 1914 from its baroque home, familiarly known as the "Kommode" or chest of drawers, to a massive new building on Berlin's main thoroughfare, Unter den Linden. Although acclaimed as a "temple of scholarship," its impracticalities soon became apparent ("Only an earthquake can help," commented one librarian on first seeing it). Nonetheless, the national significance of the library continued.

Fritz Milkau, Harnack's successor as director (1921–1925), believed the librarian's primary duty was "orderliness," but his achievements went far beyond. He guided the Staatsbibliothek into its new home and through the financial rigors of postwar Germany, and further developed an interlending network for research libraries. But he is best remembered for his three-volume *Handbuch der Bibliothekswissenschaft* (1931–1933), which with later editions under Georg Leyh defined German professional philosophy and practice for the rest of the twentieth century. Typically, this concentrated on research libraries, reflecting Milkau's early experience at the university libraries in Greifswald and Breslau and in the Staatsbibliothek; it stressed the primacy of reader services and an active rather than a passive role for the librarian. Leyh, who had collaborated with Milkau on the first edition, worked briefly at the Staatsbibliothek before World War I but spent his later years at Tübingen University Library; his attempt to return to the Staats-bibliothek in 1934 failed, probably on political grounds. Like other significant figures, Leyh survived the Nazi regime (though, as Werner Arnold notes, without developing progressive ideas on academic freedom), finally retiring in 1947. His second edition of Milkau's *Handbuch* appeared in 1952–1965.

In 1945 Berlin was divided into eastern and western sectors: Unter den Linden fell into the Soviet sector and the Staatsbibliothek soon became inaccessible to western users. In response, West Berlin built a new Staatsbibliothek Preussischer Kulturbesitz in 1978, with a title indicating its role in preserving Prussian cultural heritage. The library build-ing attracted international acclaim, and it joined other great libraries in West Germany in developing a strong network to support scholarship. The eastern library remained largely neglected in war-shattered buildings for more than forty years. Despite reaching some accommodation with the Communist regime its activities suffered compared with its western counterpart. Marxist-Leninist policies in the German Democratic Republic (GDR) allowed it the exceptional status of an *öffentliche wissenschaftliche Bibliothek* or public research library, and effectively—but never explicitly—a national library for the GDR. It took the title Deutsche Staatsbibliothek and received legal deposit, and had responsibility for all GDR research libraries. It suffered severe shortages: in 1980 nearly half its acquisitions came from international exchange programs, computerization was slow to develop, and photocopying, which could have eased some supply problems, was viewed as politically suspect.

With the reunification of Germany in 1990 the two libraries were merged as a single Staatsbibliothek zu Berlin (retaining the reference to Prussian culture in a subtitle) on two sites a mile apart. Differences in professional attitudes and salaries between east and west, as well as heavy costs of restoring the building on Unter den Linden, created stumbling blocks to an easy merger. With the development of a common professional language, however, the Staatsbibliothek began serving a wider scholarly community and included major digitization projects.

Austria and the Former Austro-Hungarian Empire

In 1807 Custos Paul Strattmann declared the imperial Hofbibliothek or court library in Vienna, with its handsome Baroque building, "a library for the cultured classes of the city—the national library of the Austrian Empire." Irina Kubadinow's history explains that it had high status within the wide-ranging Austrian domains (which then extended to parts of Italy and the Dalmatian coast, as well as Bohemia and Hungary). After being evacuated during the revolutions of 1848, it reopened with greater emphasis on public access and longer opening hours. It continued to collect widely, with new catalogs pre-pared in 1871–1891 under Ernst von Birk (replacing a slip-catalog of 1780, claimed as the oldest in the world). Professional activity mirrored German research libraries. When the empire disappeared in 1918, the library's title became Austrian National Library. Austrian research librarians had joined German professional associations before the Nazi takeover in 1938; Nazi policies and a party-appointed director led to the seques-tration of private libraries, many from Jewish families, and to collection policies con-centrating on German and racist material. After World War II Austria was separated from Germany but remained under joint Allied control until 1955. Only after the Soviet occupation ended was it possible to establish a new republic (but Austrian librarians established a professional association as early as 1946). The national library became a symbol of the new nation politically and socially, and expanded coordination activities with other libraries, such as the Austrian Library Co-operative, using automated catalogs and the pan-German RAK code. The library began digitizing early Austrian newspapers in 2003 and led the way with other Web-based initiatives.

In other parts of the former Austro-Hungarian empire national boundaries changed even in the nineteenth century. The present National Library of the Czech Republic in Prague (since 1924 housed in the Clementinum, a former Jesuit college) evolved from the former "public and university library," which itself had grown from the city's academic and religious collections. It received its present title in 1990 but for decades had a national role, and it continues to coordinate library activities across the country. A strong rival for "national" status emerged in the National Museum library, founded in 1818 (Jaroslav Vrchotka describes its early history); its librarians influenced the development of Czech librarianship and culture. The Clementinum library in Prague had a notional responsibility for Slovak culture in the former state of Czechoslovakia, but the Matica Slovenská in Martin, founded in 1863, was already a major focus and became the National Library of Slovakia in 2000 after the two states separated, though it had had quasi-national status since 1941. Cooperation between these libraries and other research libraries in Brno and Bratislava began in the 1980s and was strongly supported by the A. W. Mellon Foundation: since 1992 the library has implemented a common automated library system and has transformed professional activity in both the Czech Republic and Slovakia.

In Hungary, a separate kingdom within the Austro-Hungarian Empire with a distinctive linguistic identity, Count Ferenc Széchényi established in 1802 what was in effect a national library linked to a national museum; it became a focus of national pride. This, together with an academy of sciences and some university libraries, came to share many "national library" functions. In the twenty-first century the National Széchényi Library in Budapest is the center for collecting and disseminating all material published in or relating to Hungary, presenting itself as "the memory of the nation." Research libraries in Serbia, Croatia, Slovenia, Macedonia, Montenegro, and Kosovo, some based on old collections and mostly linked to universities with strong German traditions in their librarianship, became national libraries for their republics after the dissolution of Yugoslavia in 1991. The national library of Bosnia-Herzegovina in Sarajevo, with its particularly strong collections including much Muslim and Arabic material from its Ottoman past, was virtually destroyed in 1992 by Serbian troops intent on eliminating a monument of multiethnicity, built by generations of librarians devoted to this inclusive culture. Librarians from around the world marshaled efforts to reconstruct the "national archive," but with mixed success; too much unique material had disappeared.

Switzerland

Switzerland has a federal structure with few "national" institutions and four national languages (German, French, Italian, and Romansch, all providing alternative titles for the national library). The foundation of the library in Bern in 1894 was part of a move to create a national identity, and although it collects material on all aspects of Swiss life, its constitution specified its role primarily as a center for national bibliography. Open to the public for more than a century (and including a remarkable postal lending service to scattered localities), it has an unusual relationship with the twenty-six cantons, which are responsible for most library services in Switzerland, in that its collections complement cantonal collections rather than forming the country's major resource. Switzerland has no legal deposit, only a voluntary agreement with the book trade. The presence of the League of Nations library in Geneva (later, the United Nations), and the libraries of its related bodies, heavily influenced Swiss librarianship in the twentieth century. Since 1992 the library revivified with electronic cataloging and storage facilities for different media, at the same time expanding its readership base from researchers to a wider public.

Belgium and the Netherlands

National libraries in Belgium and the Netherlands both have royal titles, but different histories. The Royal Library of Belgium in Brussels, named after King Albert I, dates soon after the establishment of the new kingdom in 1830 (it was previously under first French, then Dutch control). It grew from the library of the dukes of Burgundy, dating back to the fifteenth century, which in 1795 merged with the city's municipal library as a general public research library known as the Library of Burgundy. After independence the two libraries separated and the Royal Library was formally established in 1837, with legal deposit for Belgian publications. The bilingual nature of the country caused problems, since the subject catalog used only French for headings from 1857 to 1959; from 1960 new subject catalogs used both French and Dutch (or Flemish), and from 1988 the library used Library of Congress subject headings in English as a compromise (with translations into French and Dutch). The library evolved a role as the country's central research library, not always easy to manage given the degree of autonomy for Dutch- and French-speaking parts of the country: the Royal Library is one of a small number of "national" entities, however, with its official title in French and Dutch.

The Royal Library of the Netherlands in The Hague began in 1798 under the French-inspired Batavian Republic, when the library of the House of Orange was combined with other collections explicitly as a national library, though it suffered changes in title and role under French occupation in its early years. When the Netherlands became an independent kingdom in 1815 the library was given the royal title of Koninklijke Bibliotheek. In the mid-nineteenth century the library suffered from poor government funding and restricted accessions; by the 1880s matters had improved with new catalogs and expanded reading rooms and reference services, as well as an important museum of the book reflecting the historic importance of printing in the Netherlands. Dutch legal deposit has always relied on a voluntary deposit system, but the national bibliography, produced jointly with a commercial company, has achieved high standards. Administrative control of the library—through a board of governors set up in 1987—led to reorganization and the opening of a new building in 1982. This enhanced the institution's role as a national library, although it largely focused on the humanities and social sciences, with other libraries covering the natural sciences.

France

In France the royal library was long considered originator of the concept of a national library. It established a dominant role among European libraries in the eighteenth century, under librarians such as the abbé Jean-Paul Bignon and Pierre Le Noir, by strongly enforcing legal deposit. In 1791 it published the first national cataloging code, which also provided for the pioneering use of catalog cards, as Judith Hopkins records. It was one of the first institutions taken over by the state after the French Revolution, formally achieving the status of Bibliothèque nationale or national library in 1795. In the nineteenth and twentieth centuries it led library developments in France, though administrative paralysis prevented it from playing a leading role in Europe like the British Museum. Sobol'shchikov's report of 1859 notes this paralysis under Jules Taschereau and comments on the institution's general lethargy and the inaccessibility of the catalog. He instead preferred the Bibliothèque Sainte-Geneviève, a heavily used academic library in a fine new building. Taschereau remained in charge of what became the Bibliothèque Impériale under Napoleon III until the Paris Commune of 1871, but the democratic reforms for the library proposed by the Communards failed when the Commune itself collapsed after a few weeks.

Reforms in the later nineteenth century revived the library's fortunes by building on its rich collections and catalogs, with librarians such as Léopold Delisle (who had been dismissed under the Commune). The earlier twentieth century saw more difficult times and an unclear national remit, and although library staff member Eugène Morel became a major player in public librarianship by promoting ideas gleaned from British and North American professional contacts, he did not significantly change the attitude of the Bibliothèque nationale. The library temporarily achieved a new role under Bernard Faÿ, director under the Vichy regime and German occupation after 1940, when it coordinated all library activity in France, a situation Martine Poulain describes very powerfully. At the same time, however, it suffered from the preoccupations of the Nazi regime and Faÿ's own fierce mistrust of dissent, especially socialist and anti-Catholic movements. When banished staff returned after liberation in 1944 the library addressed postwar reconstruction. By the 1970s it acquired wider national library responsibilities and better financial support. Further change and opportunities for new advances in librarianship came in the 1980s and 1990s, when political initiatives under President François Mitterrand led to establishing the Bibliothèque nationale de France in a controversial new building, opened in 1996, with greatly expanded responsibilities. While librarians had little direct influence on the plans, the response led to significant developments in electronic information, an area in which French librarians made distinctive contributions to one of the twenty-first century's most notable phenomena.

Italy

Italy has several libraries with the title "national," reflecting the country's complicated history with political unity only being achieved in the 1860s. Two libraries, in Florence and Rome, are known as Biblioteca Nazionale Centrale and share many national library functions, including a national center for cataloging, laying down standards for more than a thousand libraries across the country. The national library created in Florence in 1861 reflected the city's status as the temporary capital of the new Kingdom of Italy: it was based on the sixteenth-century Magliabechi library, which had passed to the city as a public library with local legal deposit in 1747 (it acquired national legal deposit rights, along with its counterpart in Rome, in 1885). It started issuing records of deposits in 1886, which developed into a full national bibliography in 1958 (a task now shared with Rome). The national library in Rome, established when Rome had become capital in 1870 but incorporating older collections, had a history of poor management during the early twentieth century but in the twenty-first plays the major part in central state library services.

Other "national" libraries exist in Naples (growing out of royal and other collections), Venice (the Marciana, dating back to the fifteenth century), Milan (the Braidense, established for public use in 1770 by the empress Maria Theresa of Austria), Turin (with two—one the former royal library of Savoy), and Bari, but these "national" titles reflect their heritage rather than a special function. The Biblioteca Nazionale di Palermo has had the title Biblioteca Centrale della Regione Siciliana since 1977, retaining its "national" functions and supporting the Sicilian library school. By the turn of the century the national Ministry of Culture funded these functions, together with more than thirty other libraries sharing responsibilities for "national" coverage, though under overall direction from Rome and Florence.

Spain and Portugal

In Spain, the royal library became the national library when revolution abolished the monarchy in 1836, after which it developed a more professional role, though it remained very much a research library little used by the public. Government reorganization in 1900 led to a clearer role within a national network of libraries, including a school of archives, a national bibliography, cataloging and classification, and reader services, under the leadership of Marcelino Menéndez Pelayo. After his death in 1912 the tradition of scholar-librarians continued but a more broadly based profession of librarianship also evolved. The Civil War of 1936–1939 and the subsequent Franco regime brought hard times for the national library: government policies strengthened other libraries and removed some of its own functions. With the return of the monarchy after Franco's death in 1975, the library experienced more freedom, and librarianship developed along European lines. Automated cataloging, in an Iberian MARC format using new rules of 1985, had a strong influence in the Spanish library world more generally.

In Portugal, a Royal Public Library founded in 1797 became the National Library in Lisbon in 1860 and established a strong professional position under Jaime Cortesão in the 1920s; his colleague Raúl Proença did much to coordinate cataloging standards across the country. Antonio de Oliveira Salazar's Fascist government, which controlled the country from 1932 to 1968, did little for libraries, and the university library in Coimbra took on some national library functions. Only in the late twentieth century could the national library improve its services, particularly with the opening of a new building in 1969 and automation of the national union catalog, PORBASE. In 1997 the library came under the Ministry of Culture, with a greater degree of autonomy, and in the twenty-first century seeks to combine its heritage collections with a modern international approach to public services. In 2009 it started a major project to record Portuguese culture through digitization of books, maps, manuscripts, and other material.

2. ACADEMIC AND RESEARCH LIBRARIES

The principal role of academic libraries is serving the teaching and research needs of higher education, though they may also have wider responsibilities. This combination of functions has been an important determinant of the development of European librarianship. "Research libraries" is a term used in English for many academic libraries but also for scholarly libraries not associated with universities or other higher education institutions—though these again have many different forms. Many have a role similar to a national or regional library, some even with legal deposit privileges. Some university libraries—like Göttingen (Germany), Kraków (Poland), Leiden (Netherlands), Uppsala (Sweden), and the Bodleian Library at Oxford in England—have historically been at the center of library development in their countries, as "universal" libraries standing above local needs, with recognized national and international status. Elsewhere, historic universities maintain their country's great libraries: examples are the universities of Coimbra (Portugal), Salamanca (Spain), or Tartu in Estonia (originally a seventeenth-century Swedish foundation, formerly known as Dorpat). In many of these the research function is seen as predominant, as opposed to provision for students.

University libraries, however, may also double as public libraries; for example, in Germany a number of institutions shared the title *Stadt- und Universitätsbibliothek* ("city and university library"). This is not a recent development or restricted to Germany: the ancient Scottish universities, such as Glasgow and Edinburgh, originated as "the town's college," with libraries serving a wider public than students and professoriat into the nineteenth century. For more than a hundred years the university library in Moscow, founded in 1756, was the only "public" library in the city. On the whole, however, a clear distinction exists between the role of librarians in academic and research libraries and those in public libraries, reflected in different practices and philosophies of librarianship.

The pattern of higher education and the provision for libraries within it have varied through history and in different countries, as is seen in the papers in the 1993 collection edited by Lucilla Conigliello and Anna Maria Milizia. In many countries, as in the United Kingdom, academic and university libraries are funded through the parent body. In others—Germany and Italy are examples—funds are provided by the state specifically for the library, separately from any state funding for the university. In many countries, too (Germany, Hungary, and Portugal are examples), sectional libraries developed under the control of faculties or specialist institutes and are not formally related to the main library: these bring problems of coordination, economy of scale, and general library management. Because France had no universities for much of the nineteenth century, old scholarly libraries found new ways of surviving; Catherine Minter looks at this question, in comparison with Germany and England, in her 2013 article on library reform. Some countries favored technical colleges as a source of higher education. Newly established universities in all countries presented challenges to librarians charged with growing their libraries from scratch. Many of the new universities founded in England and Germany in the 1960s received strong professional leadership from their first librarians, free to develop new ideas without the constraints of long-established practices. Many innovations, technical and administrative, owed their origins to initiatives taken by librarians, whether policies of centralization or decentralization, or pioneering new building designs to serve changing readership patterns. In much of Europe the adoption of automation and use of electronic information originated in academic, not national, libraries, and within academic institutions it was often the librarians, not academics, who pushed forward with electronic information in ways that transformed educational practice.

United Kingdom and the Republic of Ireland

University libraries in Great Britain and Ireland vary considerably in their history and influence on modern librarianship. Their relationship with other professional sectors has not always been comfortable, and for many years there was little cross-sector influence. In particular, the early involvement of university librarians in the Library Association (LA), the main professional body founded in 1877, became less marked in the twentieth century, though G. H. Bushnell's book argued for closer links in 1930; W. A. Munford's centenary history of the LA also makes this clear. A separate body was set up in 1950 to look after the interests of this sector at the institutional level. As T. H. Bowyer describes, SCONUL (originally the Standing Conference of National and University Libraries but now the Society of College, National and University Libraries) has become a major player, especially in its ability to liaise with government. The LA (now the Chartered Institute of Library and Information Professionals, or CILIP) continued to serve many members in university and research libraries with a separate section, but it was less influential than SCONUL in setting the agenda for professional development in the sector. The modern academic and research librarian has benefited from a history of professionalism developed by significant individuals over 150 years; changing views can be appreciated by comparing successive classic manuals for university librarians such as those by Bushnell (1930), G. Woledge and B. S. Page (1940), and James Thompson and Reg Carr (1987).

As well as the ancient universities and the large civic universities, higher education (and libraries) reached out through "university colleges" in towns and cities throughout England and Wales (and a similar pattern through the whole of Ireland) in the later nineteenth and early twentieth centuries. These were by no means always solely directed at local needs but helped spread a common view of the profession. They later became full universities and were followed by other institutions founded, especially in the 1960s, in response to social changes and a need for more science and technology in university education. Collections continued to grow strongly until the 1980s. By the early twenty-first century many smaller institutions had acquired university status, though their libraries did not equal their larger forerunners. These developments brought a wider range of students than in earlier centuries, and more structured educational methods ushered in a need for more guidance and direction in the use of library materials (including media other than print).

Professional principles emerged from practice. For example, R. W. Chambers, librarian and professor of English at University College London in the early 1900s, stressed the need for a strong personal involvement between the library and its users, as Wilks shows. This philosophy of librarianship passed to his successors and to university libraries such as Birmingham, Leeds, and Glasgow. Twentieth-century textbooks encouraged the development of these broad priorities, though older traditions were not neglected. The orthodoxies of the later twentieth century are now being revisited in an electronic environment.

In Scotland the four oldest universities, dating back to the fifteenth and sixteenth centuries, all have strong historic collections and complement the National Library of Scotland in preserving the "national archive," but they are otherwise more similar to the large civic universities of England than to Oxford or Cambridge. They were joined by newer institutions of varying backgrounds, some with scientific or technical emphasis, others working from dispersed sites with consequences for the practice of librarianship. The University of the Highlands and Islands, for example, has thirteen campuses and research centers linked with local learning centers, but also has a strong online presence for distance learning.

All the older foundations have traditions of rich donations. Some also benefited from legal deposit (historically accorded to some university libraries, including the four oldest Scottish universities, but currently only to Oxford and Cambridge in England and Trinity College Dublin in Ireland). Through Sir Thomas Bodley, Oxford established the privilege of receiving all English publications since 1610—though this was by agreement with the book trade rather than by state action. As a result, the Bodleian Library (named after its refounder) quickly became Britain's largest and richest collection well before the foundation of a national library. Under various acts of Parliament the university library at Cambridge (until the nineteenth century the only other university in England) also acquired legal deposit, and through donations and active purchasing policies also developed rich collections. In the modern period the libraries of these two institutions, often referred to as "Oxbridge," heavily influenced the British library world, though their scale and modus operandi meant not all their policies or practices were relevant elsewhere. In many ways they compare more to the librarianship philosophies in German-speaking Europe.

The balance between the teaching and research needs of staff and students in Britain developed pragmatically, but mostly without the distraction of the strong departmental libraries (under professorial control) seen in Germany and elsewhere. However, the split between research requirements and ordinary student needs lingered for many years, with main library collections often inaccessible to students, for whom a separate reading room with a selected collection of texts was often provided. In Glasgow in 1899 the library curator (William Purdie Dickson) argued against open access because the sexes might meet in the book stacks and because overgenerous access to the whole of the library's collection could perplex a young student. The U.S. tradition of large separate undergraduate libraries did not find much favor in Britain: this was partly a matter of scale, since collections and funding were usually much smaller than in the United States, but also reflected a desire not to restrict undergraduates' use of the widest possible range of material.

Though professional accomplishments were also important, some large universities such as Manchester, Oxford, and Cambridge fostered the concept of the scholar-librarian. Other universities gave more priority to the professional role of the librarian, although academic ability also had its place, especially in subject-specialist posts. In the last half of the twentieth century, emphasis on the library as an information resource rather than a book repository became more common. In some cases, libraries created subject-specialist departments that combined the advantages of a departmental library (i.e., its smaller scale and specific holdings) with those of the larger library: R. O. MacKenna of Glasgow University wrote on this aspect as well as on library organization more widely. Later still, financial pressures and electronic systems made this pattern less attractive. From the 1980s onward, academic institutions increasingly integrated information technology (IT) and library services, with many universities amalgamating their libraries and computing centers and developing a unified "information systems" model, in which students and staff relied increasingly on electronic information and digital versions of hard-copy book collections. This evolved largely as a result of collaboration between librarians in the United Kingdom and the Republic of Ireland, and in turn led to new ideas of what librarianship meant in an electronic or "virtual" environment—both for reader service and for conservation of historic collections.

For most of these changes librarians—not the state—took the initiative, even though the majority of university funding had come from the state since the early twentieth century. Despite commending the library as "the power-house of the university," the University Grants Committee (UGC) established in 1919 gave little direction on library developments. The UGC's Parry Report of 1967 recommended standards but did nothing to make them obligatory, and by the end of the century underfunding caused serious problems, not least because of the spiraling costs of scientific journals, which unbalanced library budgets already under strain. SCONUL and other bodies mounted repeated campaigns on this international problem, largely in vain. The move to electronic publication changed budgeting practices in the twenty-first century (also creating, through restrictive licensing deals, new challenges to the librarian's wish to offer services beyond the institution's walls). In such ways the development of librarianship was heavily influenced by technology, though this also allowed new insights into professional work.

Scandinavia and the Baltic States

In both Norway and Finland the major university library (Oslo and Helsinki respectively) has some national library provision responsibilities. In Denmark and Sweden the national library and university libraries also formed close links. For example, the university founded in Århus in 1928 shares facilities with the branch of the Danish Royal Library there. The Royal Library absorbed the sixteenth-century University of Copenhagen library in 1989 to provide comprehensive service to a wide range of readers—thus manifesting advantages of active professional cooperation in a small country. In Scandinavia the oldest university is Sweden's Uppsala University, founded in 1477 (though its library did not begin until 1620), benefiting from royal patronage and the deposit of material collected from across Europe during Sweden's period as a great power in the mid-seventeenth century. Pehr Fabian Aurevillius, who served as librarian from 1787 to 1829, drew on ideas from Germany and elsewhere to consolidate the library's collections and produce new catalogs and other facilities. Consolidation continued through the nineteenth century, and under Claes Annerstedt (1883–1904) expansion progressed through exchange agreements with the Bibliothèque Sainte-Geneviève in Paris and with libraries in Russia in 1887 and the United States in 1904, thus extending the library's awareness of professional developments across the world. Modernization of professional activity continued in the early twentieth century (helped by Sweden's neutrality in two world wars), and in the 1950s the library undertook the difficult process of incorporating Uppsala's many departmental libraries. As elsewhere, computerization helped, and Uppsala took the lead in developing a national union catalog.

Other long-standing Swedish universities include Lund, founded in 1668, and Gothenburg (Göteborg), founded in 1890 but on the basis of an older museum library. New universities founded in the twentieth century reflected the expansion of education throughout Scandinavia and brought new ideas into the library world (the 1970 library at Umeå, for example, was the first in Sweden to base its planning on open-access stacks). Denmark similarly developed new universities with updated patterns of library provision, particularly in the multisite institutions such as the University of Southern Denmark (founded in 1998, with six campuses in 2010). As in several Scandinavian universities, because some courses were taught in English it was necessary to provide a wider range of library material, but this also simplified use of library management systems developed in Britain or the United States.

For most of the nineteenth century Finland was a grand duchy within Russia. In the twentieth century the old university in Helsinki, with a library effectively serving as a national library (its early years are described by Arne Jörgensen), was joined by a number of new institutions. Among these was Turku University, promoted by nationalist interests after independence from Russia and opened in 1920. A library followed a year later and developed along the usual lines (though with only a small number of subordinate libraries). By the late twentieth century it had become Finland's second-largest university, with legal deposit for Finnish publications. Åbo Akademi—a Swedish-speaking university also in Turku, founded in 1918 to serve the Swedish minority in Finland (reviving the seventeenth-century Åbo Akademi transferred to Helsinki in 1829)—acquired a fine functionalist building in the 1930s dubbed the "book tower," which aroused much interest in McColvin's 1938 *Survey of Libraries*, where it was described as "very fine" and "of the most modern pattern." However, the library soon outgrew its accommodation and opened new buildings, beginning in the 1950s. Librarians struggled to combine main-library resources with many other university collections and welcomed common computerized systems for all Finnish libraries from the 1970s onward.

Estonia, Latvia, and Lithuania regained independence in 1991 after five years of German occupation and forty years within the Soviet Union, but they had a history of some complexity, with periods under Swedish, Polish, and Russian rule. All have historic libraries of importance, with universities in Vilnius (Lithuania) and Tartu (Estonia) going back to the seventeenth century; their pattern of operations reflected the German university model, though Tartu (earlier Dorpat) had Swedish roots. Academies founded under the Tsarist regime in Tallinn (Estonia; previously known as Reval) and Riga (Latvia) continued their role as major research libraries alongside the national libraries and supplemented newer university libraries in those cities. After 1991, all these libraries developed new systems influenced by the European Union and other Western interests.

Russia

University libraries in the nineteenth-century Russian empire were led by Moscow University Library (which also had an important public role from the time of its foundation by the scientist M. V. Lomonosov in 1756). Much of the library was destroyed by fire when Napoleon occupied the city in 1812, but appeals by the university to "lovers of societal enlightenment" soon produced thousands of donated volumes, including many from the Imperial Academy of Sciences in St. Petersburg. Its librarians followed German practices in publishing a systematic catalog in 1826. The library continued to expand and was housed in fifteen different buildings across central Moscow. After the 1917 revolution the expansion continued, though like all other libraries in the Soviet Union its work was heavily politicized. Although many rare books were temporarily evacuated during German bombardment in World War II (some as far away as Kazakhstan), the library continued to offer services throughout the war. The campus occupied a new site on the edge of the city in the 1950s, when it brought many departmental libraries into the main library. This encouraged the development of professional studies of many kinds, including those relating to cataloging and classification (for many years following the standard "Marxist-Leninist" system and generally under the guidance of the Lenin Library). Automation and the *glasnost* (liberalization) of the 1980s brought more awareness of international developments. Remarkably, in 1990 the Soviet Union introduced a policy of cataloging all new acquisitions by U.S. Machine Readable Cataloging (U.S. MARC) and created a comprehensive electronic catalog.

Other Russian university libraries followed similar patterns of development (and politicization), with standardization of systems across the USSR being a matter of pride, though local differences could sometimes be accommodated—for example, using local languages alongside the predominant Russian. Research libraries, notably the Academy of Sciences of the USSR (with its Siberian outpost in Novosibirsk) and the similar but smaller academies of the various Soviet republics such as Ukraine and Belarus, accumulated large collections and supported the work of university libraries. As in Russia, after 1991 other post-Soviet republics contacts with the West influenced library practice and professional thinking, though politics still played a part and the Soviet tradition did not wholly disappear. A double issue of *Library Trends* (2014–2015) discusses the position across the whole of former Communist Europe.

Poland

In Poland, from a library point of view one of the most significant parts of eastern Europe, the Jagiellonian University library in Kraków dates back to the fourteenth century and is one of Europe's great libraries, comparable in many ways to the Bodleian. It acquired many books over the centuries from donations, and the range of its collections reflects the complex history of Poland with alliances, conquests, partitions, and political change. Although Kraków ceased to be the capital in 1596, it remained the royal seat and so retained some political importance. From 1797, and for the entire nineteenth century, the city was within Austria (while retaining its Polish identity). This gave the library the advantage of legal deposit from the whole Austro-Hungarian Empire, and thus the efforts of successive librarians like Karol Estreicher (director, 1868–1905) created a particularly national collection that grew steadily. By the twentieth century it was effectively, and later in reality, a second national library, and though the Communist regime after 1945 placed tight constraints on its international dealings, the library developed its buildings and collections of Eastern European material. The end of the Cold War released the Jagiellonian from these constraints, and computerization from as early as 1974 revealed to the world the riches of this remarkable library.

After the loss of Kraków to Austria in 1797, a new university was founded in Warsaw in 1815. It remained under Russian control for the rest of the century (though the university was closed from 1831 to 1857 following its members' involvement in the 1830 uprising). It became officially a center for the Russification of Poland after 1870, but student dissent and socialist agitation persisted, and many Polish students boycotted the institution. In 1915 German occupation permitted the restitution of some Polish teaching (the "Russian" university, and its library, was relocated to Rostov-on-Don in Russia—the historic book collections did not return to Poland for many years). After Polish independence in 1918 the university grew quickly, but the German occupation of 1939–1945, followed by appalling destruction, meant an almost total collapse of the university and its library. Some large collections came to the university in the postwar settlement, and for a while the university remained relatively independent of political interference, though restoration of the library was slow. The Communist regime, increasingly stringent in its policies after 1956, handicapped the library's development, as it did other academic and research libraries in Poland, and it was not until the freedom movements of the 1980s that the library made further progress.

The university in Wrocław, a Polish city since 1945, traces its history back to 1815; under its German name of Breslau the library played a strong role in the nineteenth and early twentieth centuries in developing the German model of librarianship. Many books were lost during the Red Army's advance in 1945, and the resources of the city library were turned over to the university by the new Polish authorities. Reconstruction and new buildings allowed new developments, and like other Polish libraries Wrocław received U.S. funding to install computer systems in 1993. Major digitization programs began in 2004, and a formal "Digital Library" opened in 2006. The university library in Poznań (founded as a German university in Posen, but Polish since 1919) developed Polish collections through the twentieth century and followed similar paths in forming a Polish library identity.

Germany, Austria, and Central Europe

In the growth of university libraries in the German-speaking world in the eighteenth century and after, the example of Göttingen was paramount. The strength of its collections, its fine catalog and systematic arrangement, and its healthy relationship with the state as well as its manifestation of Enlightenment philosophy were unmatched. Its librarians and their nascent professional views were admired by librarians and scholars into the nineteenth century. Classification practices, both in shelf-arrangement and subject catalogs, constituted a battleground of professional debate across German-speaking countries. The influence of Göttingen's systematic classification continued in wider discussion of subject catalogs, though many librarians preferred "home-grown" arrangements and wanted to define their own roles as intermediary librarians. Active debate on professional matters continued vigorously, with many writers from state and university libraries contributing to the debate—the distinction between the two types of library being almost irrelevant as university libraries built up "public" functions as well as serving the academic community.

The way in which professional commitment interfaced with political necessity is well shown in the Nazi period (1933–1945), when many university librarians and research library directors continued their work in what were for some very painful circumstances. This period has been very controversial among later German library historians. Librarians working in universities or the redefined research libraries in the German Democratic Republic (GDR) had to work within the constraints of a Communist state (in many cases, be it said, with enthusiasm for socialist principles and library philosophies). The creation of new forms of "unitary" research libraries in the GDR, on a model combining research and public functions, was partly a political matter, but was welcomed by librarians wishing to extend the reader-base for their scholarly collections. Librarians in the GDR then had to face change after reunification in 1990, when the Federal Republic imposed on the eastern states its different pattern of library organization, more inclined to follow prewar models, and with university and research libraries returned to the western pattern.

The postwar period also brought new professional developments to the Federal Republic. Most significant, perhaps, were generous funding from the Deutsche Forschungsgemeinschaft ("German Research Council," a government body), and the new universities in the 1960s that diverged sharply from older library thinking, largely under the influence of British and American library planning. One example is the University of Konstanz, established in 1966, which reversed the traditional pattern of departmental libraries in competition with the university library tradition by introducing longer opening hours and a high degree of open access for all readers, as described by the first librarian, Joachim Stoltzenburg. A campus plan supposedly inspired by "Anglo-Saxon" models had departments clustering round the single central library, to which they had direct access. Konstanz inspired other library designers, but its main developments in the last years of the twentieth century were in pioneering the use of electronic information, a move widely welcomed by German and Austrian librarians whose professional thinking expanded rapidly to embrace IT.

Many older libraries, whether ecclesiastical, royal, or ducal, developed into "state libraries" (*Staatsbibliotheken* or *Landesbibliotheken*) under librarians who continued the traditions of academic and research librarianship. A major example is the Herzog August Bibliothek in Wolfenbüttel. Its early history is complex: the older ducal collections passed to the nearby University of Helmstedt in 1614, but following the university's closure in 1810 under French occupation much of its collections came back to Wolfenbüttel. Under the librarianship of notable scholars like Gottfried Leibniz and Gotthold Lessing, the ducal library flourished in the eighteenth century, then with reduced funding became less significant until it was made over to the then Free State of Brunswick in 1918. A new librarian, Erhart Kästner (in office 1950–1968), began modernizing, but the turning point came with massive support from the Volkswagen Foundation and the state of Lower Saxony. Kästner's successor Paul Raabe made the library a world-class institution, efficient and user-friendly but never losing sight of the huge role such a library could play in the world of scholarship. From what he described as "Bibliosibirsk" or "Library Siberia," for more than twenty years very close to the impenetrable East German border, he created a mecca for scholars in many fields, and also for librarians eager to see what could be achieved with vision. After retiring from Wolfenbüttel in 1992 Raabe became director of the Frankesche Stiftung in Halle, in the former GDR, another rich historic collection from the seventeenth century in need of restoration to public appreciation—which he achieved by the end of the century.

Elsewhere in central Europe similar patterns are evident, with many old libraries surviving and turning to new ways of serving their readers. German influence affected not only Austria but also libraries and universities in other countries within their orbit. In Prague the old religious libraries and the Charles University came together to create a national library, confirming the essential unity of German library thought in research libraries of different kinds. In Hungary, old university libraries developed in much the same way as in Germany and Austria, bringing problems of fragmentation but also serious commitment by librarians to scholarship and professional development. In Budapest, the Széchényi collections from the university library became the nucleus of the national library.

Belgium and the Netherlands

Belgium, a new country in 1830, already had three universities: the medieval foundation in Louvain (otherwise Leuven) and the more recent universities in Ghent and Liège; a new university in Brussels followed in the new state capital. Of these, Louvain and Brussels were bilingual (using both Dutch or Flemish and French), while Ghent used Dutch and Liège used French. New foundations from the 1960s were mostly monoglot, depending on where they were situated in a country increasingly divided along linguistic and cultural boundaries.

The story of the Louvain university library is remarkable. It suffered total destruction in 1914 under German occupation, but rapid international aid after 1918, including a massive reparation exercise from Germany, restored its collections, and U.S. funds helped erect a new building in 1922–1928. The reconstructed (and supposedly fireproof) library then suffered a second destruction in 1940 with the loss of over a million books, though the library somehow continued to provide services throughout the German occupation. Again, international efforts after the war restored the 1920s building and the reconstructed collections. Further drama ensued in 1968, when linguistic and cultural pressures led the university to split in two, with the erection of a new French-speaking institution in 1972 in the newly planned town of Louvain-la-Neuve several miles away. Dividing library collections was clearly traumatic for the library staff, forcing many arbitrary decisions. In 2014 the two universities exist side by side, both claiming part of the divided heritage.

The four older universities developed central libraries with many departmental or faculty libraries (not always well coordinated). In the twenty-first century progress toward centralization was greatly helped by automated systems. Newer universities from the 1960s, like the French university of Louvain, had more centralized structures. Few laws direct library operations (and there is no legal deposit): state funding goes to the institutions, but there are concerns about "private" funds from research grants and other sources that go to research units but do not support central library activities.

The Netherlands also witnessed problems in relation to sponsoring bodies, with a so-called "pillar" system with parallel provision for different religious denominations affecting university libraries for much of the nineteenth and twentieth centuries. But Dutch university libraries have a longer history (Leiden, one of Europe's great international institutions, dates back to 1575), and although full-time librarians only appeared in the nineteenth century, university libraries in Utrecht, Amsterdam, and Groningen were founded in the seventeenth century (in the first two cases the library predates the university). Other universities were founded in the nineteenth and twentieth centuries, some with strong Catholic affiliations, others devoted to science and technology, as with the Delft University of Technology, founded in 1842 and in the twenty-first century a major center of information technology. Libraries founded before 1900 were much influenced by German librarianship, especially as practiced at Göttingen, but innovation also came from strong Dutch professional associations. P. A. Tiele, the influential librarian at Leiden and later at Utrecht, introduced sheaf-catalogs with printed entries in the nineteenth century, and the widespread adoption by university libraries of the automated system PICA (Project for Integrated Catalogue Administration), led by Johan R. de Groot of Leiden and developed in the Dutch Royal Library, is another example of Dutch initiative. Outside the Netherlands PICA was adopted by several union catalogs in Germany and France as well as by the National Library of Australia.

The history of Nijmegen (now Radbout) University sheds light on the problems of modern Dutch librarianship more widely. Founded in 1923, the library was originally seen as a crucial element in Catholicism's battle for the souls of a nation—with a narrow remit, not the easiest basis for modernization. Librarians like A. J. M. Cornelissen (librarian, 1927–1941) took a less strict view of their role and stressed that a university must be "informed about all ideas." German occupation of the Netherlands in 1940 led to more problems for the library (e.g., confiscation of "undesirable" literature), but more serious damage came during the 1944 Allied advance when the library burned down, probably as part of the German scorched-earth policy. Efforts by librarians led to its restoration, with much help from Catholic communities both in the Netherlands and the United States—partly from a campaign in the United States that aroused new tensions because it stressed Catholic loyalties rather than losses to practical library work and scholarship more generally. When the university moved its library to a new modernist building in 1967 the library immediately had to address social change, notably the

1968 student riots that opened up universities to student interests and libraries to staff participation.

Similar developments could be traced in other universities in the twentieth century, particularly attempts to reduce wasteful duplication of effort and expenditure due to a large number of subordinate and uncoordinated libraries. Through amalgamation and rationalization Utrecht reduced the number of libraries from 144 in 1974 to eight in 1991. Leiden too reduced the number of its libraries drastically, despite fears for the central library's strengths. As in many European countries, and partly in reaction to problems of decentralization, Dutch university librarians led the way in automation, notably in the creation of union catalogs using PICA and the use of shared datasets.

France

The disappearance of France's twenty-two universities—and their libraries—in the turmoil after the 1789 revolution left the country with only isolated "faculties" or professional colleges. This situation was not resolved for nearly a century. In consequence, France's universities are largely modern institutions compared to those in many other countries. Paris was an exception: it maintained three rich old libraries at public expense; the Arsénal, the Mazarine, and the Bibliothèque Sainte-Geneviève—as well as the Sorbonne library, formerly of the University of Paris, later the major part of the restored university library system. The Sainte-Geneviève became one of the largest and most popular public research libraries in the capital, with strong staffing levels, rich collections, and an enthusiastic staff, which impressed Sobol'shchikov when he visited it in 1859 in its new building. He also approved the provision of a textbook collection, a practical idea he had seen in Dresden and Munich. In 1930 the Sainte-Geneviève became part of the university library system, while retaining its public role; the Arsénal became part of the national library, while the Mazarine came under the Institut de France.

Not until 1877 did patriotic feeling raise the question of France's lack of a structure for higher education and the inadequate scale of the libraries available to students. Libraries of all the French faculties contained only 400,000 volumes, fewer than Göttingen alone. An 1878 decree introduced a "library allocation" based on the number of students in the faculty (with disastrous effects in 1914 when military conscription drastically reduced student numbers). Subsequent government instructions in the 1880s established a new basis for university libraries, laying down precise instructions for implementation and bringing together all the academic libraries in a town or city under the title "university library." This was not always practical, however: not until 1910 did Paris finally achieve, on paper at least, a single university library. In one or two cities—Clermont-Ferrand most successfully—the university and city libraries merged (the latter being primarily research-based rather than popular public libraries); elsewhere, local difficulties prevented mergers.

Despite these efforts the state failed to provide a structure for library staff. A single librarian was often the only salaried staff member (this was the case as late as 1913 in Caen and Grenoble), and he had to undertake the entire range of duties with the help of "supernumeraries" outside the civil service whose wages had to be squeezed from the book fund. Improvements came slowly. In 1909 six librarians were elected by their peers in national and university libraries to sit (as a minority) on the national library commission, which continued strict controls over library practices. It was soon clear, however, that the commission would not change its conservative habits. By 1914 the system of university libraries was creaking, maintained only by devoted librarians—though now released from minute central state control and under the direction of the individual university. The majority of staff, however, had no professional or even academic education, and appeals to the national commission for professional education were ignored or rejected as inappropriate "trade union activity."

The World War I depressed public activity in all areas of French life, including universities and their libraries. Damage was not widespread: Nancy University library was devastated by a bomb only twelve days before the Armistice, but Lille was occupied by the Germans for four years and little library activity was possible. The postwar settlement returned to France the city and university libraries of Strasbourg, lost to Germany in 1870: the mediocre academic library had been reorganized and transformed under German rule into a major research library—which was hard to fit into the French model of university libraries. It was consequently renamed "national and university" (with public access but insufficient funding). This was unfortunately typical of academic libraries in the interwar years, with state funding inadequate for the work required.

Librarians pushed for new systems, new staffing structures, a national school of librarianship, and more, but the political establishment was unimpressed. Because authorities blocked all their proposals, university librarians made little progress. Even when frustrated academics and scholars used the League of Nations initiatives on intellectual cooperation to develop a proposal for a central collection of scientific periodicals, the effort failed. This demonstrated, however, increased interest in "documentation" based on special libraries (often those of specialized higher-education institutions, the *grandes écoles*), which in subsequent years became characteristic of the French information world, bringing more women into this special branch of the profession, as Sylvie Fayet-Scribe records.

The German occupation of France in 1940 brought many losses, not so much through bombardment (until the Allied advance in 1944 when, for example, the university at Caen was destroyed, including its library) as through German pillage of important collections from research libraries of all kinds. The situation after liberation was hard for librarians, who had to rebuild their professional structure as well as their libraries. Although in 1945 seventeen French "academies" or university-level institutions had control over their libraries, they received no state guidance on what should be done. Postwar recovery was slow—though student numbers rose fivefold by the late twentieth century—since higher education took a lower priority in state spending than secondary education, and not until the 1960s was progress made on developing university libraries. Soon after the end of World War II some collections of periodicals and other material arrived from England—where they had been acquired by the Free French government in exile—and from the United States, where the American Library Association acted as intermediary, and by 1951 French librarians operated a center for international exchange based at the Sorbonne. Lacking dedicated funds, however, libraries benefited little from these contacts with other countries.

In the 1960s economic recovery and political change led France to establish many new universities around the country, partly to relieve pressure on the crowded institutions in Paris, but also bringing higher education to more people. With new institutions came new university libraries. Practices like open access for students (though not to the entire stock), classified collections using international schemes, even multiple libraries within a single university, all sparked a revivification of the profession through study days, training courses, and increased funding. State bodies showed greater appreciation of the value of a broad approach to education and to collaboration with public libraries.

When the student-led riots of 1968 led to greater autonomy for universities, specialist libraries within universities grew rapidly. In 1973 the Association des Bibliothécaires de France (ABF) or Association of French Librarians published a "Black Book" criticizing the situation in university libraries, and meetings of professional and academic staff at the national level sought solutions by analyzing what was being done in other countries. Financial crises after 1975 brought further pessimism, though in the late twentieth century France adopted electronic systems with enthusiasm. All this enabled universities—and their libraries—to deal with greatly increased student numbers and to tackle new methods of delivering education and the other challenges of the late twentieth and early twenty-first centuries. France's deliberate preference for a centralized and state-directed organization was combined with a policy of localization, bringing the advantages of higher education to smaller towns and wider areas.

Italy

In Italy, some universities date from the thirteenth century; Bologna and Naples, for example, are among the oldest in Europe. The history of their libraries, however, is complex. In Naples the library founded in 1224 had to be refounded in the seventeenth and eighteenth centuries, and it was eventually separated from the university to become one of Italy's many national libraries. The reverse happened at Genoa when in 1815 the national library of the short-lived Republic of Liguria (under French occupation) became a university library. By unification in the 1860s, most of Italy's university and research libraries contained substantial collections of early printed books and manuscripts from secularized religious houses, which led librarians to concentrate on preservation. Royal commissions of 1869, 1873, and 1876 on state-owned libraries—covering universities as well as "national" and other significant libraries—imposed detailed regulations, again conservative in nature and concentrating on "heritage" collections rather than reader services. However, an 1885 decree devised under the influence of Ferdinando Martini of the Ministry of Public Instruction and Desiderio Chilovi of the Florence national library set out detailed instructions for the operation of libraries, but this made insufficient provision for funding (though its regulations remained the standard until 1967). As a result, libraries soon found themselves in dire straits. In response to an 1899 ministerial inquiry Modena reported that its staff was reduced to one "usher" and Sassari lacked even dictionaries. Chilovi described Genoa university library, in a 1900 paper, as "characterized by a relative abundance in the dead part but not in the living." He also questioned the practice of funding academic libraries separately from their universities, which made them unaccountable to their users.[3]

Other government initiatives failed for lack of funding of libraries, whose share of the ministry's budget fell 80 percent between 1875 and 1920. After his march on Rome in 1922, Benito Mussolini's Fascist regime promised changes, but its cultural and ideological agenda brought only partial success. A new Directorate approved new buildings and considered reader services, but overall the position of university libraries and "state" research libraries remained difficult. Damage during World War II required major reconstruction projects after 1945, including much cataloging, clearing backlogs many years old, and in some cases moving toward international standards. Librarians promulgated new cataloging rules in 1956 and encouraged union catalogs. In 1975 a decree clarified the role of university libraries—to assist students, provide research material, and promote coordination with faculty and institute libraries. The last point tried to address the nagging problem of departmental libraries funded by the university, as opposed to central university libraries, which were funded by the state. Some universities even lacked a central library, which made a professional approach to coordination all the more difficult.

An 1989 law gave more autonomy to the forty-eight state universities, but improvement came slowly. By the twenty-first century, however, information technology, European Union funding, and improvement in library education led many university libraries to offer student-oriented services, open stacks, and more coordination with the institution's departmental libraries. Large state libraries without "national" status had less clarity, though many benefited from the union catalogs of the Servizio Bibliografico Nazionale (SBN; "National Bibliographical Service").

Spain and Portugal

Spain and Portugal's oldest universities had major libraries—in Salamanca in Spain (from the twelfth century) and in Coimbra in Portugal, where the university (founded 1290) and its library were moved from Lisbon in 1537. Both are among the world's great libraries, but they need to accommodate modern needs. A common feature of most universities in both countries are strong faculty or departmental libraries, which manifest, in Javier Lasso de la Vega's words, "nineteenth-century individualism, which particularly characterizes the Spanish academician."[4] Librarians' attempts to adopt the Universal Decimal Classification as the system for all Spanish libraries faced resistance from conservative academics; they were in any case hindered by lack of the funding necessary to reclassify large libraries. Universities in both Spain and Portugal expanded over the years, with new foundations and greater concern for science and technology. Unfortunately, however, this also led to continued fragmentation of library collections as specialist institutes developed.

Professional librarians were not evident in academic libraries in either country until well on in the twentieth century—innovations came from state intervention and academics appointed to run libraries—but the development of automated systems and the opportunities they offered for international collaboration (together with participation in EU initiatives) led to considerable advances from the 1990s onward. The Autonomous University of Barcelona, for example, published an ambitious and optimistic plan for 2011–2014 with the slogan "The library, your digital ally."

3. PUBLIC LIBRARIES

Public libraries are a major and universal phenomenon in the library world, but their nature in different countries and at different times is linked to educational and social factors, and different formulations of the concept are inevitable. An important step came when UNESCO issued a *Public Libraries Manifesto* in 1972 (revised in 1994). IFLA adopted the manifesto and published additional recommendations that set out criteria for judging public libraries: they should be free of charge, with free access and lending to all, free from censorship and commercial pressure, and developed within a national library network. Taking a historical view, these criteria are not always relevant, even within a single country or culture, and they must be regarded as aspirations rather than reality. They certainly cannot be universally applied across even the past hundred years of European librarianship, and librarians in the past have not always felt all criteria were appropriate.

Public libraries came into existence in many different ways. In their origins they often drew on other types of libraries with longer histories, sometimes growing out of workers' libraries, endowed institutions, or even commercially based libraries. In some countries, for example in the Soviet Union and its satellites, and in the coal-mining districts of South Wales, parallel trade union or workers' libraries grew up in the earlier twentieth century, mirroring or rivaling public library provisions. Many private libraries or independent foundations opened for public use (notably in the Catholic countries of Italy and Poland, though not necessarily religious in nature), often retaining their historic constitutional position as private establishments while functioning as public libraries.

Terminology, similarly, is confusing. It cannot be assumed that the term "public library" means or has meant the same thing to the inhabitants of Oxford, Oslo, Osnabrück, Orvieto, or Olomouc at different times. In earlier centuries a "public" library could be the major library in a city, such as the Bodleian in Oxford or the Imperial Public Library in St. Petersburg, both major research libraries with limited public access. Indeed, the term "public library" is not always the most appropriate or most widely used. The French introduced the term *médiathèque* in recent years in preference to *bibliothèque publique* (which was seen as a foreign import) to stress the availability of a variety of media. Other examples include the historic German distinction between *Bibliothek* (often a scholarly library) and *Bücherei* or *Bücherhalle* for more popular libraries (though under Anglo-American influence the term *öffentliche Bibliothek* or "public library" has become more widely accepted since 1945). In the 1920s, Soviet policies in Russia introduced the term *massovaia biblioteka*, or "library for the masses." In contrast, in some Slav-speaking central European countries and also in rural Scandinavia, the emphasis was on reading, with terms like "reading room" used as a common term for a popular library. In Britain the term "free library" was common through the nineteenth century and still has political echoes. What was sometimes thought of as the "Anglo-Saxon model," with local control and wide accessibility, does not accurately reflect the situation in Britain (it is closer to the U.S. pattern), but its assumed principles have been popular for many years, particularly in Scandinavia, and it played an important part in the reconstruction of services in West Germany after 1945. In other countries such as France and Italy the tradition is different, as the following sections demonstrate. McColvin's 1938 *Survey of Libraries* is particularly strong on the public libraries of Europe before World War II, and Marian Koren's 2008 book gives an international perspective on developments through the whole twentieth century.

The United Kingdom of Great Britain and Northern Ireland

The United Kingdom of Great Britain and Northern Ireland, to give its full name, has a distinctive, comprehensive, yet inconsistent pattern of public libraries under some degree of local control. It has been affected by changes in local government and, since 1998, by devolution of many powers to Wales, Scotland, and Northern Ireland. This history began with the 1849 report of the governmental Select Committee on Public Libraries, part of a movement toward public provision of various services, and encouraged city and town councils to establish libraries as a means of improving education and social stability. Under the inspiration of the politician William Ewart and the librarian Edward Edwards, the Select Committee studied libraries in Europe as well as Britain. The resulting Public Libraries Act of 1850, with further acts covering Scotland and Ireland, was one of the first pieces of European legislation to envisage public funding of libraries.

But the 1850 act, like other early legislation on libraries, was "permissive," allowing towns to spend voluntarily on libraries a very limited proportion of income from rates (local taxes) but with no legal requirement for them to do so. Many towns were slow to take up the opportunity, often with vocal opposition to "books on the rates" (i.e., public funding of libraries). Various reports on the condition of libraries led to developments such as county libraries from the 1920s, but these too were essentially permissive. Only with the Public Libraries and Museums Act of 1964 were local authorities in England and Wales required to operate public libraries, with government responsibility limited to ensuring an adequate level (Scotland and Northern Ireland were left out).

Library historians disagree on the intentions of the Public Libraries Act's original political supporters, who may not have intended the wide-ranging service that actually developed. This uncertainty about the purpose of public libraries—which even at the time of writing is politically controversial—influenced developments in the United Kingdom and also the way in which librarianship evolved. Some originators saw libraries as a "general good," others as part of a movement for the "improvement" of the working classes, which took great strength from the 1870 Education Act and its effect on illiteracy. Another late-nineteenth-century government initiative encouraged technical education, with public libraries expected to stock patents and other technical literature.

Larger towns and cities began to establish libraries soon after the 1850 act passed, and they slowly spread across the country (including Wales and Scotland, but more slowly in Ireland). The industrial cities of central and northern England led the way, but London was slow to adopt the act, partly because of its fragmented local government. Libraries were often seen as prestige developments, with local philanthropists erecting buildings or providing books—not least Andrew Carnegie, Scottish by birth but North American in his philanthropy, and the Cornishman John Passmore Edwards. Both men influenced not only the numbers of libraries in Britain and Ireland around the turn of the century but also people's expectations of the libraries' collections and services. Professional advocacy of public libraries—again with examples drawn from other countries—surfaced in publications by Edward Edwards and Thomas Greenwood, whose *Free Public Libraries* (1886) went through several editions. In his own books and in publishing other contributors in his *British Library Year Book* (1900), Greenwood was a force in circulating modern ideas of librarianship, particularly in the public library field. The foundation of the Library Association in 1877—a year after the American Library Association and drawing inspiration from it—gave librarians a focus, and while it was by no means solely concerned with public libraries, that soon became its main concern. By the twentieth century the association was the main forum for public librarians and through training and qualification programs provided support to the development of professional practice and theory, as Munford's history shows.

Public libraries of the last half of the nineteenth century were often starved of resources and professional services were slow to develop, though this improved as legislation enabled more funding from local government. Librarians devoted much ingenuity to forms of controlling access to books in still closed-access libraries. Familiar patterns of reference and lending services, with open access and special facilities for children, began at the dawn of the twentieth century. These developments depended almost entirely on the initiative of individual librarians and their ability to persuade their paymasters and local councils to support their work, rather than any state directive. Such efforts inspired the characteristics of classic British public librarianship.

Besides Edwards and Greenwood, major names in the early period of this development were James Duff Brown, L. Stanley Jast, and Ernest A. Savage. Brown pioneered open access at Clerkenwell, London, in 1897. He created his own subject classification as an alternative to the DDC and also wrote the influential *Manual of Library Economy* (1903), which went through many editions. Jast was librarian at Croydon and later Manchester, and in a 1900 article noted the change from the old concept of the library as "a mere distributing agent for books" to something much more active. He also lamented "no practical recognition among English (as opposed to American—the Continent doesn't count) librarians of the absolute necessity for close classification."[5] Jast's lack of respect for continental European librarianship is ironic in view of his Polish origins, but open-access libraries of the sort he advocated did not yet exist in Europe. Savage, who had worked under Jast at Croydon, introduced services to industry and commerce in the Coventry public library, then from 1922 built up a major public library service in Edinburgh, with emphasis on subject departments.

By the beginning of World War I librarians in many British towns offered services of high quality, with a readership not confined to the working classes, and with a range of special services to children, industry, and education. Competition—at least in the provision of leisure reading—came from middle-class subscription libraries and large commercial circulating libraries like Mudie's, some surviving from the nineteenth century but some in newer forms like Boot's Book-Lover's Library (operated through a chain of chemists' shops beginning in 1898 and popular with the middle classes). But these contributed little to the development of professional standards and are almost wholly neglected in professional discourse of the time—with the notable exception of the London Library, the nation's largest subscription library (its history informally recorded by John Wells), with rich loan collections and led by notable librarians such as Robert Harrison and Charles Hagberg Wright. In Scotland another kind of competition existed. Industrialist and philanthropist James Coats provided rural areas with many small libraries, as documented by John C. Crawford, and in Glasgow privately funded reference libraries such as the Mitchell Library and Baillie's Institution supplemented public library provision (though both later joined the city libraries).

Lack of legislation for small towns and rural areas led to a new Public Libraries Act in 1919, which for the first time allowed English and Welsh county councils to act as library authorities (Scottish counties had had the right since 1918). The consequent spread of well-organized libraries to rural districts—in many cases with their own buildings, elsewhere with mobile libraries or small deposit collections in villages run by volunteers under County Library authority—was a significant step forward and was led by prominent librarians who developed professional standards for a new area of librarianship. With the growth of regional interlending bureaus and a Central Library for Students (founded 1916, from 1930 the National Central Library) as a clearinghouse, librarians claimed that—in theory—any book was available to any reader at any time, a strong statement reflecting the confidence of the library profession that had created this service in the face of political negligence and opposition to the expenditure involved.

Provision of similar services in Ireland—since 1922 divided, with the Free State independent and Northern Ireland still within the United Kingdom—was less successful, largely due to meager public finances, though major cities such as Dublin, Cork, and Belfast established adequate levels of service. Many libraries were built by Andrew Carnegie, though without continuing funding and often without professional staff (described in Brendan Grimes's book). The Carnegie UK Trust set up county libraries in the 1920s in both the north and south of the island, but these attracted political and religious opposition, which led to the demise of the scheme (one dramatic example, in County Mayo, is documented in Pat Walsh's book). Nonetheless, there was, for a few years in the 1920s and 1930s, a positive view of book provision across the whole of Ireland. Later, the two parts of the island went their own way, but the Library Association of Ireland, founded in 1928 as a single professional association, proved effective in maintaining professional standards.

The 1924 Mitchell Report, *The Public Library System of Great Britain and Ireland 1921–1923* (commissioned by the Carnegie UK Trust) and the 1927 Kenyon Report, *Public Libraries in England and Wales* (for the Board of Education) both called for a more expansive national service, but government response was disappointing. Fifteen years later Lionel McColvin produced *The Public Library System in Great Britain* (1942), an ambitious plan for a rational structure in postwar Britain, welcomed by the profession. Despite McColvin's authority as a prominent professional, his plans were not implemented directly, but his report paved the way for new legislation. The 1959 Roberts Report, *The Structure of the Public Library Service in England and Wales* (commissioned by the Ministry of Education), led to the 1964 Public Libraries Act, which for the first time required all local authorities in England and Wales to provide public libraries. Government oversight, however, proved unsatisfactory and formal standards were not imposed (though the newly devolved government in Wales issued standards for public libraries in 2002). London's local government was restructured in 1965, creating larger boroughs, which could support better library services (the first computerized catalogs and issue systems began in London in the early 1960s). Changes in administration in the larger English conurbations in 1972 also created new public library structures, not always for the better since some efficient existing systems were absorbed into larger units.

In Scotland and Northern Ireland legislation led to different solutions. In 1972 Scotland's public libraries became the responsibility of smaller units—breaking up county libraries—until 1995, when larger unitary councils took over, while the devolved Scottish Parliament set up bodies to monitor performance nationally. Northern Ireland established new Boards for Education and Libraries, a logical link that proved its worth, but in 2009 they were replaced by a unitary library service for the whole province under the devolved Northern Ireland executive.

In all these changes, since the mid-twentieth century professional librarians have become steadily less able to influence policy making. In England the culture secretary was placed in charge of implementing standards, without much professional input to support decision making. Such direct government involvement referred only to public libraries—and to the British Library and the national libraries in Wales and Scotland—not to libraries of other kinds, though they might come under governmental authority in other ways, for example, in the education or health sectors.

Nonetheless a variety of initiatives over the past half-century came from the profession's leaders rather than government intervention. A. W. McClellan's influential concept of "service in depth" developed first in the London borough of Tottenham in the 1960s, with the professional librarian becoming more involved with the reader through subject specialization and better exploitation of the stock. Outreach took on new dimensions with the idea of "community librarianship" driven by a socially and politically aware profession addressing the needs of the disadvantaged and taking library provision out into urban and rural communities. This movement, while drawing to some extent on the U.S. experience in the 1960s, gained strength in the 1980s in the face of threats to the welfare state and social dissent—although it never fully became part of mainstream professional thinking and later suffered with the widespread cuts to library funding. The same could be said of services to ethnic and other minority groups, which, while better developed in terms of stock provision and professional interpretation of need, remained a professional specialty rather than common ground. From the 1990s onward, electronic information brought new challenges: while public libraries were early users of automated systems, exploiting the Internet and other sources of online information was another matter. Public libraries at first lagged behind academic and special libraries in this respect. The announcement by Tony Blair's government of a "People's Network" in the mid-1990s to give access to the Internet through state-funded public terminals in libraries gave librarians opportunities to attract library users and exploit electronic resources in new ways, and computer use has become a major feature of public library use.

Scandinavia and the Baltic States

The Scandinavian or Nordic countries show various patterns of public library development, though common currency and wide cooperation helped achieve a high reputation and good exposure in the historical literature. Through much of the nineteenth century, "public" library provision had seen uncoordinated growth of reading societies, church-supported libraries in rural schools, and sometimes endowed libraries in larger towns and cities, which helped create a foundation of literacy and familiarity with books. A tradition of adult education capitalized on the provision of library services (the Library Association's 1938 *Survey of Libraries* noted that adult education was more widespread in Scandinavia than Britain). Early state support for small libraries helped to establish the idea of libraries as a "public good," but the transition into a modern public library framework took time and varied from one country to another. The *Survey* saw Denmark as a benchmark to which Sweden and Norway aspired, and noted the presence of excellent modern library architecture. This favorable picture continued through the rest of the century, recognizing libraries working within and supporting strong welfare states.

Denmark's early legislative program, dating from 1882, established a State Libraries Agency, which supported existing local provision, often through associations, and developed the concept of a "people's university" with librarians as the authoritative experts and interpreters. A major figure in this development was Anders Schack Steenberg (1854–1929), who had become familiar with British and American library practices. Laura Skouvig has studied changing official attitudes through the twentieth century. A Public Libraries Act in 1920 gave towns and cities the power to run libraries, as in Britain, but with central state support that lasted until 1983. Librarians were seen as technocrats with a sense of discipline, a commitment to progress, and a desire to serve the interests of society as a whole rather than the individual reader that made this a distinctive pattern. After 1945 Danish public librarians established cordial relations with their British counterparts, both countries sharing a developing welfare state and a need for reconstruction after wartime deprivations. As other supply methods opened later in the century and Denmark passed a new act in 1964 that strengthened municipal responsibilities, the librarian's role became more consciously democratic and user-driven. A public library "golden age" in the 1970s preceded financial cuts in the 1990s, and the growth of the computer-based information society in the twentieth century raised questions about the librarian's role.

In Iceland, a dependency of Denmark until 1918, the small population had a strong tradition of reading books. Public libraries first grew from provision by local associations, rather than by the state. The first formal public library opened in Reykjavik in 1923 out of a reading society founded in 1901. Its first librarian, Sigurgeir Friðriksson, studied at the new library school in Copenhagen and so introduced a Danish version of the Dewey Decimal Classification (DDC) (also used in the National Library in Reykjavik), which became common throughout Iceland. He had also toured Swedish libraries and visited the New York Public Library and other libraries in the United States and Canada.

Norway, after relying on a wide range of subscription and community libraries (some offering free access) throughout the nineteenth century, became heavily influenced by U.S. librarianship, a connection that continued for many years. The United States was, for many Norwegians, the preferred place to seek professional education (no library school existed in Norway until 1940, and that did not function fully until after 1945), and U.S. influence remained strong throughout the country. In Christiania (now Oslo) the Deichmanske Bibliotek, an endowed public library, experienced a dramatic rise in use under Haakon Nyhuus, director from 1898, who opened the library up and extended services to children and working-class areas as well as the city center. In 1900 Nyhuus introduced open access after a visit to England (where it was still a new concept). The way had been prepared by Hans Tambs Lyche, a Unitarian minister who had worked in the United States and wrote about North American libraries as early as 1894; he appreciated their view of the library within society and the concept of reading with a purpose. Lyche proposed the reorganization of the Deichmanske Bibliotek to provide fuller facilities for the whole population, to encourage self-education and self-development. In the port of Bergen, director Arne Kildal introduced outreach to isolated communities such as lighthouses and military camps, again based on American ideas. After Nyhuus became head of the State Library Office, his work there further expanded familiarity with U.S. practices in all sectors of library work.

The development of Sweden's public libraries followed the Danish pattern, with state funding going first to existing popular libraries in 1905, then in 1912 being extended to municipalities. Valfrid Palmgren was a powerful advocate for public libraries and children's services and in many ways was the founder of Sweden's successful library system. She produced a report in 1911, inspired by her experience in the United States, recommending modern state-funded libraries not for the "lower classes" but for the whole population. A 1912 law built on this and set up a central institution to coordinate and control standards for public libraries. North American concepts of public libraries also inspired Swedish librarians more widely. As in Norway and Denmark about the same time, a professional association established in 1915 began to promote the role of librarians as educators, with lectures and workers' classes organized through independent study-circles with their own book collections. A 1930 decree gave libraries higher constitutional status and allowed public libraries to expand, for example by taking over study-circle collections. As the century progressed, especially after 1945, a growing emphasis on the role of libraries in democracy (as in other Scandinavian countries) was evident in reports from state commissions in 1974 and 1984, then by a definitive library law of 1997 that guaranteed access to libraries for all, including minorities of various kinds. This has been seen as facilitating democratic interaction in a way particular to libraries, not least because they cover the entire country. Modern Swedish library architecture, like that of its neighbors, manifests inspiring design that has made the Scandinavian public library physically attractive to readers and to staff, a principle that forms part of the professional ethos.

Although it had been an independent republic since 1917, Finland was not included under "Scandinavia" in the 1938 Library Association *Survey of Libraries* but was in the section dealing with Russia and Eastern Europe. The *Survey* described Finnish public libraries as a mixture of "dull and antiquated" and ultra-modern, the latter especially in terms of architecture. Partly because of subordination to Russia until 1917, the prehistory of public libraries is less clear, though small voluntary libraries were widespread; the collection edited by Ilkka Mäkinen (2001) takes the story through the whole twentieth century. North American–inspired professionalism in Finnish public libraries emerged after 1945, although the first library legislation came in 1928. Not until the 1960s did a "golden age" of Finnish public librarianship begin, with an act of 1961 that permitted, among other things, expenditure on mobile libraries with professional support (an essential service to a widely scattered population) and strong investment in reader services, especially to children and young people (to the disadvantage of school libraries). High loan figures resulted. By the beginning of the twenty-first century Finland was known for its high educational and social standards, and libraries were recognized as major contributors, with public libraries an obligatory part of a municipality's duties. Finland had come to see itself as closely allied with Sweden, Denmark, and Norway, despite linguistic differences, though there were also links with Estonia and other Baltic states.

After gaining independence from the Soviet Union in 1991, Estonia, Latvia, and Lithuania established professional links with Finland and other Nordic countries. For forty years they had been an integral part of the Soviet Union (and earlier part of the Russian Empire, before independence in the 1920s and 1930s), and they retained large Russian-speaking minorities, making public library provision more costly, as in other multilingual countries. In Lithuania public library history is even more complicated, since much of its territory, including its present capital, Vilnius or Vilna, was part of Poland between the World Wars and suffered particularly heavy depredations in World War II, not least to its very rich Jewish libraries, as Sem Sutter describes. As elsewhere in the Soviet Union, public libraries in the Baltic states were widespread (several thousand in the 1970s) and well organized, but operated within the Communist political framework. The new constitutions for these republics, after 1991, included commitment to modernization of library services.

Russia

Russia itself has had great influence on east European libraries of all types for many years through its control of substantial areas of the continent, first under the Tsarist empire up to 1917, then through the USSR and the Soviet "empire," which lasted from 1945 to 1991. (The latest period, since the end of the USSR and the breakup of its empire, is documented in a double issue of *Library Trends* [2014–2015], "Libraries in a Post-Communist World.")

The nineteenth century witnessed major changes in Russian social and political life, though Tsarist controls remained tight even under more enlightened rulers. The growth of popular education, while not alleviating widespread illiteracy in a scattered and largely rural population, provided a ready audience for small local libraries (founded privately or by the local authority or *zemstvo* or—often illegally—by radical groups who paved the way for communism in the twentieth century), as well as for circulating and subscription libraries and more "official" libraries in larger towns.

Not until the 1890s was the role of libraries in combating Russia's economic and political problems addressed publicly, as Mary Stuart's article on "The Ennobling Illusion" indicates. State provision increased and donors like the publisher F. F. Pavlenkov funded more than 2,000 small popular libraries (against some government opposition). These libraries, however, were mostly small and conservative, with book stocks regulated by the Ministry of Education from 1888. Library activists consequently looked less to these than to models outside Russia, especially in Britain and increasingly the United States. Influential radical figures like Herzen, Marx, Engels, Kropotkin, Lenin, and others had used British libraries, and from these and other contacts like the New York Public Library a new sense of internationalism developed.

The radical political movement in Russia appreciated the public library's utilitarian qualities, particularly its ability to promote social progress. Librarians in the public sphere in the late nineteenth century, mostly members of the liberal urban intelligentsia, reinforced this view with their own professional interests. Most notable of those with Western connections was Liubov Borisovna Khavkina, from Kharkov (now Kharkiv in Ukraine), which had founded a major public library in 1886. Khavkina studied in Berlin in 1898–1901, and based on her experiences there worked for wider library provision, even before the end of the century. In 1914, after publishing a book about it, she visited the New York Public Library, and also visited libraries in Washington DC, Pittsburgh, and Chicago. The 1917 Bolshevik revolution was for Khavkina an optimistic time, offering hope for realizing her ambitions for librarianship and popular education—though claims that the Bolshevik regime developed librarianship on a blank canvas are much exaggerated. She established an Institute of Library Science linked to what became the Lenin Library in Moscow and continued to press for Western models in Russian libraries.

By the time Khavkina next visited the United States in 1926, the Russian political scene had changed significantly. Lenin's interest in public libraries as a medium for change had been taken up strongly by his wife, Nadezhda Krupskaia. After 1917 she played a large part in the People's Commissariat of Enlightenment under Anatoly Lunacharsky and quickly developed programs for education and librarianship within the new Marxist-Leninist policies she helped develop, as evidenced in Simsova's 1968 collection of contemporary documents. Libraries grew enormously across the whole country as they became a fundamental part of the state's work in education and in the battle against illiteracy, but at the same time they were subject to totalitarian policies that later closed the Soviet Union to much outside influence. In 1923 Krupskaia, acting on behalf of Lenin (by then nearing the end of his life), issued a circular banning certain authors and works from Soviet libraries, described in Bertram Wolfe's essay. This became the model for more purging of undesirable literature (including works by earlier Communist writers) under Stalin and the pattern of strongly "orthodox" collections, which spread from Russia to other parts of Europe that came under Soviet control.

The next seventy years in Russian librarianship were characterized by inward-look-ing policies and hardening attitudes, and by a reluctance to be involved with the Western professional world (despite the views of the British librarians who visited the Soviet Union in 1936–1937 for the *Survey of Libraries*: their response to the state of Russian library development was generally enthusiastic, admiring government achievements in expanding library provisions along with greatly increased education). A Communist, essentially Stalinist view of librarianship dominated, with widespread use of the Soviet classification based on Marxist-Leninist principles. Public libraries were organized into categories, the most widespread being the *massovaia biblioteka* or "library for the masses," which provided a full range of services (including a strong emphasis on chil-dren's literature) but with careful scrutiny of what readers could access. Regional librar-ies and large libraries at the head of each republic's system had a controlling interest. Censorship happened more at the point of publication than in individual libraries, with the whole Soviet publishing industry—the only source for library material—centrally controlled. All libraries came under government direction, just as all librarians were subject to Communist Party decrees. Nonetheless, communism encouraged the devel-opment of documentation and the theory and science of information (within its own parameters), in some ways exceeding Western practice.

Central control began to thaw after Stalin's death in 1953, but progress was slow and only in the 1980s and 1990s did Russian librarians begin to participate more fully in international librarianship. The breakup of the Soviet Union after 1991 led to social and economic turmoil, and the comprehensive provision of libraries across the coun-try became problematic. The Russian Library Association, founded in 1994, had some success in raising awareness, and in 1995 it launched a project to coordinate formats for electronic bibliographic records. In 2010–2011 it worked with IFLA to update its strategic plan and code of ethics, explicitly acknowledging the advantages of working in international partnerships.

Poland

Poland, whose tumultuous history included its disappearance as a state for more than a century after 1795, had nonetheless a number of early public library initiatives. The Załuski brothers founded a rich public library in Warsaw in 1747, but the Russians removed its collections to St. Petersburg in 1795; the collections returned to Poland in 1920, only to suffer heavy losses in World War II. A public library founded in Prze-myśl in 1754 had strong technical collections. The Ossolineum, founded in 1817 in Lemberg (later Lwów, now Lviv in Ukraine), was largely moved to Wrocław in 1947 to strengthen Polish presence in the former German city of Breslau; a branch opened in Lviv in 2006 to support collections left there in 1947. The Raczyński Library in Poznań (known as Posen under German rule) opened for public use in the 1820s and is housed in one of Poland's earliest library buildings. All these libraries were open to the public but were not intended for mass consumption. Nonetheless, libraries remained symbols of Poland's culture and independent spirit under alien rule.

The Warsaw Philanthropic Society, founded in 1825, opened free reading rooms in 1861; by 1897 twenty-three were operating in the city, mostly run by volunteers. After visiting English public libraries in the 1890s, Stanisław Michalski, the secretary of the society, introduced an embryonic reference and advisory service, but other society members feared too much liberalism and with the support of Russian authorities tried to restrict the range of activity. In 1890, too, Jan Władysław Dawid and his wife Jadwiga (who had written an essay on the need for a public library in Warsaw) opened a Research Reading Room intended for a more sophisticated readership. These initiatives came together as the Warsaw Public Library in 1906, which finally opened in 1914 as a public research library, although still operated by an association. In 1928 (after Poland regained independence) the association handed the library to the city authorities as a full public library. Libraries elsewhere in Poland—many of them private foundations without municipal support—were not strong, although a professional association was established in 1917 that encouraged standardization of cataloging rules for Polish libraries in the 1920s. The arrival of the National Library in 1928 stimulated professional work, and educational societies operated a wide network of libraries across the country.

During World War II the Germans aimed to extirpate Polish culture and devastated library services, instead establishing library networks intended for Germans, not Poles. After the war, domination by the Soviet Union quickly followed, with libraries forced to adapt Marxist-Leninist policies and restrict services to what the Communist Party approved. Traditional professional activity was seen as subversive: librarians were to advance communism and censor what was read. Not until the 1970s did Poland experience movement toward a freer society and more effective libraries. After administrative reforms in 1999, public libraries were founded by provincial, county, or city authorities, this allowed local control but caused funding problems only partly helped by support from national sources. Bozena Bednarek-Michalska's report illustrates the situation in 2001.

Bulgaria and Romania

The Black Sea republics of Bulgaria and Romania had a long history of being part of the Ottoman Empire, and in Bulgaria *chitalishta* or reading rooms in towns and villages played a large role in Bulgaria's struggle for independence. Although Turkish rule ended in 1878, without the political impetus the *chitalishta* did not flourish, and progress came only with a law of 1927 requiring all communities to form reading societies. These were also encouraged under Soviet rule after 1945, and by 1990 more than 3,000 of these small libraries existed. Although they had a long tradition of educational purpose, they were increasingly controlled by Communist party functionaries until the country's emergence in the 1980s. Twenty-first-century initiatives—partly with European Union and Gates Foundation support—expanded the *chitalishta* network and helped automate most libraries in the country.

Romania's borders have been fluid for centuries, with the native culture and language constantly under threat from its neighbors. In the twentieth century Romania had well-established links with western Europe and founded and supported public libraries through the early part of the century. Hungarians, South Slavs, Germans, and Roma and Romanians occupied the area known as Transylvania, and with separate foundations to serve the different communities, libraries played their part in the cultural struggles, as James Niessen records. After the Soviet takeover in 1945 the government censored the collections and made libraries vehicles of propaganda. Politically motivated practices dominated library work, a situation that changed little after the withdrawal of Soviet troops in 1958 when the Communist leader Nicolae Ceaușescu brought in three decades of tyranny. After Ceaușescu's dramatic fall in 1989, financial pressures caused more difficulties and in 1997 the government abandoned centralized control of public libraries, turning them over to impoverished municipalities, with predictably unsatisfactory results. (A *Library Trends* double issue on "Libraries in a Post-Communist World" provides a full review of the Communist legacy.) Although library education classes resumed in 1990 (they had been outlawed in the 1970s), programs aimed more at book historians and seemed unlikely to increase the prestige of libraries and librarians. Twenty-first-century automation projects promised some change in librarians' professional status.

Germany and Austria

The history of public libraries in Germany itself is positive, and many developments there have been influential elsewhere, but in other areas, including much of the former Austro-Hungarian empire, the story is varied but contains common features—particularly Catholic Church influence in some countries and the role of Jewish culture throughout Central Europe.

In the early nineteenth century historic town libraries dating back centuries were scholarly and not intended for wide public use. Many towns also hosted reading circles and commercial circulating libraries. The first move toward a modern public library came in Grossenhain in Saxony in 1828, when Karl Benjamin Preusker established a Sunday school with an attached library open to the public and accepted by the local council in 1833 as a town library, though without lasting success. Preusker wrote about the role of libraries in education and drew explicitly from the ideas of Benjamin Franklin and Henry Brougham. On a larger scale, the historian Friedrich von Raumer established four public libraries in Berlin in 1850 after visiting libraries in Britain and the United States, where he had been struck by what he had seen there, even before the British Public Libraries Act. His libraries did not become the democratic beacons he hoped for because of the degree of control exercised by the Prussian state. The oppressive political climate following the revolutions of 1848 did not favor public provision of reading material, and it was several years before things began to change, though progress was evident with the growth of workers' societies and initiatives of various Protestant churches. The Borromäus-Verein, a Catholic association founded in 1845, sponsored libraries that for many years offered strong competition to secular public libraries in much of Germany. Smaller, more liberal German states moved forward more easily. For example, the tiny Duchy of Saxe-Gotha (homeland of Queen Victoria's consort Prince Albert) voted to support public libraries in 1851. All these bore fruit later in the century, when pressure from the new Reich (established in 1871) encouraged states to support public libraries.

Constantin Nörrenberg gave German librarianship a new start. He visited the 1893 library congress in Chicago, and on his return became a vocal advocate for public libraries on the American model, rejecting the old charity-based "literary soup kitchens" as the primitive popular libraries had been dubbed. He wanted libraries free to all, by right, with extended opening hours, liberal collection-building policies, and adequate finance. "The public library is the necessary replenishment of the public school," he wrote in 1895.[6] His proposals soon blossomed into the so-called *Bücherhallenbewegung* or "book-hall movement," in some cases bringing the old town libraries into the modern age in a combination known as the *Einheitsbibliothek* or "united library," in others leading to the foundation of new public libraries. The success of the new movement, strengthened by a growth in popular education, persuaded governments to improve libraries' financial footing as they moved into the twentieth century, and new library systems appeared in many German cities. The influential Austrian scholar Eduard Reyer who, like Nörrenberg, visited Britain and the United States and became aware of the public library movements there, also supported the *Bücherhallenbewegung*. In 1895 he founded a public library in Graz, and in Vienna two years later he began the association known as the Verein Zentralbibliothek. His association quickly led to the growth of a major central library in Vienna, with one of the strongest networks of branch libraries on the continent. Reyer was one of the greatest proponents of the public library movement in Europe, though his actual achievements were always threatened by problems of financing, whether from private benefactors or municipal authorities.

Concepts from the United States and Britain that informed the *Bücherhallen* philosophy included open access, which received strong support as the movement spread across Germany and Austria. By 1910 some city libraries created networks for their rural hinterland, like Dortmund for Westphalia or Düsseldorf for the Rhineland, and in the culturally mixed province of Posen (now Poznań in Poland). Major players included Erwin Ackerknecht, city librarian in Stettin (now Szczecin in Poland), a proponent of links between libraries and adult education, who started a mobile library service in Pomerania in 1923 and remained an active polemicist as late as the 1950s. Paul Ladewig, director of "the best public library in Germany" in Essen, published *Politik der Bücherei* ("Politics of libraries") in 1912, a detailed study of the public library, encouraging close links with old town libraries to offer more open services.

A movement opposed to Ackerknecht and Ladewig sprang up under Walter Hofmann, first in Dresden, then from 1913 in Leipzig's new *Bücherhalle*. Hofmann criticized not only the principle of mass provision and open access but also the idea of expanding the scholarly town libraries into public service, which he considered antithetical to the best interests of popular education through libraries. He promoted a controlled approach to public librarianship and stressed the value of "books of true value" (particularly good fiction) in developing civic virtues, transforming *Volksbildung* or "popular education" into *Volkbildung* or "creating a people." This, he asserted, could best be promoted through serving select groups of the "public" intensively, recommending reading, recording readers' progress, and generally controlling use of the library through an advisory desk, with no public access to the shelves. His view attracted much support and linked to the "new direction" for public libraries and popular education, which developed after World War I. The debate between these two fundamental views from approximately 1910 to 1933 between Erwin Ackerknecht and Walter Hofmann split the German public library community, brought much controversy in the professional literature, and became known as the *Richtungsstreit* or "battle over direction." It also affected professional education, as Hofmann and his followers rejected the idea that library training should cover all types of libraries. They saw public libraries as distinct, sharing no common professional ground with research libraries.

This crucial debate within the profession coincided with the economic collapse of the 1920s, which left libraries with little support but huge demands from readers. Smaller libraries in rural areas in Germany and especially in Austria received meager state funding and relied largely on the church or ad hoc societies. In Austria the local mayor was often responsible. The *Survey of Libraries* of 1936–1937 noted that Germany showed contrasts between smaller and larger states (with Prussia and Bavaria dominating) and between north and south, with open access being more widespread in the north because of trading links with Britain. The British visitors thought library provision in both Germany and Austria inferior to their own, with fees for library use, stock provision aimed at the recreational reading of poorer and less educated classes, and no equivalent of county libraries. Although this was no doubt an exaggeration, comparative loans statistics (from Scandinavia and the Netherlands as well as Britain) give it credence.

The Nazi takeover in 1933 transformed public libraries in Germany (and in Austria after the *Anschluss* incorporated it into Germany in 1938). The Nazi government set up a national advisory center and gave public libraries preferential treatment over research libraries, since the former were better placed to promulgate the new politics and policies. Nazi thinking strongly supported (and distorted) Hofmann's ideas on "worthy" literature—which had not been political in origin—and compelled librarians to withdraw from their shelves any books deemed "undesirable." The state and the Nazi party (increasingly the same thing) controlled library stocks closely and pressed for the dismissal of Jewish staff, despite significant Jewish input into German professional thinking. The financial demands of a war economy after 1939 made further development difficult, and military action led to huge losses of stock and the disappearance of many library services.

After the Nazi capitulation in 1945 Germany and Austria came under four-power occupation, and redevelopment of library services showed considerable differences in the different zones. In Germany the British and U.S. zones brought in library policies— at least for public libraries—that reflected the "Anglo-Saxon" library model widely welcomed since financial support increased. The smaller French zone in the southwest initially followed French practice, but after the Federal Republic was established in 1949 libraries in all three western zones followed British and North American patterns and evolved the modern system of public libraries under the *Länder*, or federal states, rather than the central government. Johannes Langfeldt's three-volume *Handbuch des Büchereiwesens* (1965–1976), noteworthy for the space devoted to the profession as well as to library practice, was influential in setting the Federal Republic on this road. The *Bibliotheksplan '73*, a national library plan for the Federal Republic covering both research and public libraries, encouraged cooperation and modernization. The "advisory desk" pattern advocated by Walter Hofmann gave way to open access, and broader subject coverage also encouraged multimedia collections and expanded library services for children and young people. Nonetheless, elements of Hofmann's model remained in some cities such as Düsseldorf, where Joseph Peters, the library director, continued into the 1960s to attack the "populist" views of Ackerknecht and his allies—the last flaring of the *Richtungsstreit* of forty years earlier. Austrian popular libraries also continued to champion the fight against "inferior literature" into the twenty-first century, as Leitner's article in Pfoser and Vodosek's 1995 collection shows. This left Austria, a country with a strong Catholic presence and extensive rural populations, with a conservative approach to modern public librarianship, reflecting Hofmann's philosophy of an educational rather than recreational role for public libraries.

In the Soviet zone of Germany, things were different. The Soviets established the German Democratic Republic (GDR) in 1949. The Communist regime used libraries to develop a "socialist personality" and to strengthen state power. Public libraries came under the central direction of the Ministry of Culture. Local government restructuring in 1950 replaced the *Länder* with *Bezirke* and *Kreise* ("districts" and smaller "areas") that had their own public library structure alongside state-encouraged trade union library networks; these two groups became better coordinated after 1961. The early days of Soviet control saw a fight against "poisonous" books of light entertainment, and for much of its existence the GDR banned public libraries from acquiring "foreign" literature—including books from the Federal Republic. The GDR also created a new type of library—the *Wissenschaftliche Allgemeinbibliothek* or "generally available research library"—similar to Nörrenberg's *Einheitsbibliothek* half a century earlier, and often based on the larger of the *Landesbibliotheken* derived from old ducal libraries or, as in Erfurt, on a historic town library. This did not mean a complete incorporation of all library types into the public library sector but went some way toward a nationally coordinated system of research and popular libraries, quite different from the situation in the Federal Republic. These large libraries supported the smaller libraries in their districts, but their acquisitions were restricted to publications of the GDR and its sister "socialist" states, especially the Soviet Union. This public library network did its job with restricted collections (and virtually no use of electronic systems), with good results in children's work and in promoting literacy—as had been seen in the Soviet Union some decades earlier. After the unification in 1990 the restructuring of library services along "Western" lines was felt to be a mixed blessing. Although it brought huge investment in technology and access to worldwide resources, it also reduced services to readers and offered fewer employment opportunities for librarians. A rather more positive picture of changes since 1989 is given in Ulla Wimmer and Michael Seadle's article, "A Friendly Conquest" in *Library Trends* (2014).

In Switzerland (multilingual, though with a German-speaking majority) public library developments were mixed, in part because cantons and individual communities had almost total responsibility for services, as Senser's 1991 book shows. In emphasizing the preservation of sequestrated collections, cantonal libraries set up after the French Revolution had a similar role to the French *bibliothèques municipales*, and they remained more like research libraries than general public libraries. Some came to double as university libraries. Early reading societies, especially in larger towns, grew through the nineteenth and early twentieth centuries. Larger towns founded libraries without federal support, and these have often offered support to nearby rural libraries without the benefit of a national or regional structure. One wider initiative began in 1920: the association best known as *Bibliothèques pour tous* ("libraries for all") provided for small popular libraries, with a little federal support. Librarians in Switzerland tended to think internationally and follow professional activity in Germany, France, or Italy depending on the language of their canton. Because Switzerland is not part of the European Union, however, libraries have not benefited from the kinds of EU support its neighbors receive.

Central Europe

In Central Europe, largely under the Austro-Hungarian empire, the development of public libraries has similarities with Germany and Austria. (An important source for this area, covering a period long after the Austro-Hungarian empire had vanished, is a double issue of *Library Trends* [2014–2015], "Libraries in a Post-Communist World," recording developments since about 1990 in the different countries formerly under Communist rule.)

Reading societies and small local libraries grew throughout the region in the 1830s and 1840s, some developing municipal libraries the imperial authorities viewed with suspicion. In 1863 the Matica Slovenská was founded in Martin (it became the Slovak National Library in 1954, forty years before Slovakia separated from Czechoslovakia), acting specifically as a focus for Slovak culture and encouraging library growth in the Slovak lands. The creation of Czechoslovakia in 1918, following the dissolution of the Austro-Hungarian Empire, led to great enthusiasm for national education, and popular libraries benefited. Under a law of 1919 each municipality had to establish a public library; these were locally organized with central regulation but received little financial support. Nazi occupation badly affected public libraries and stocks were heavily censored. Although the 1919 act was reintroduced in 1945 and funds provided for reconstruction, Communist domination soon brought change. An act of 1959 strengthened central control that destroyed much "undesirable" stock or withdrew it into inaccessible special collections in research libraries. After 1989 a new democratic form of librarianship began in both the Czech Republic and Slovakia, with open access and accelerating automation, and although both countries experienced problems harnessing political enthusiasm to practical ends, new laws pushed libraries in both countries toward a future within EU programs.

Hungary had similar experiences, though as a major partner in the Austro-Hungarian Empire it invested more in its libraries in the nineteenth and early twentieth centuries. In Budapest and other large cities, public libraries began in the early twentieth century, though with little government support. After 1918, public libraries in provincial towns and villages developed along German lines, with untrained staff and little open access—and a modest subscription from borrowers. After Hungary became part of the Soviet "empire" in 1945 (strongly reinforced after the abortive rising of 1956), Communist methods dominated public library practices. Strong city libraries acted as centers for rural service points, open access became common, and professional education was introduced from the 1950s. Since 1989 developments have followed European practices, with considerable investment from abroad (including the European Union) and the creation of a national network of public libraries.

Farther south, the Balkan states that formed the federal republic of Yugoslavia after 1918 had a mixed history; some areas had been under Ottoman control for centuries—as had Greece, which founded libraries from 1821 as part of its struggle for independence. As Serbia, Bosnia, and Montenegro gained independence from the Ottomans, the pattern of reading societies slowly grew, matching the areas formerly under Austrian control (as in Voivodina). The present Slovenia and much of Croatia also had historically strong Italian connections, as Aleksandar Stipčević's 1989 article records. As elsewhere, these reading societies encouraged national literature and played a part in focusing nationalist movements. Many developed into public libraries, but generally they had less effect on the development of librarianship than on political and cultural matters. Some of the public libraries founded in Serbia and Croatia in the mid-nineteenth century were more research-oriented (and the largest even became virtual national libraries). The new state of Yugoslavia formed after World War I and continuing under Communist (but not Soviet) rule after 1945, developed new public library networks. These reflected the nationalist, religious, and linguistic differences between the federal states—diversity that had been particularly fierce under German occupation in World War II, and that erupted again in 1990 with little direct influence on libraries (except their destruction as in Sarajevo). The Communist government had greatly encouraged education and after the federation broke up in 1990–1991 libraries in all the new republics inherited these strong traditions. This helped libraries develop once reconstruction became possible in war-ravaged areas. A *Library Trends* double issue (2014–2015) provides details for each republic.

Belgium, the Netherlands, and Luxembourg

Belgium, the Netherlands, and Luxembourg form a group of states with much in common, but distinctive patterns of public library history. Belgium became independent in 1831; it hosts language communities speaking Flemish/Dutch and French, and also a small German-speaking community. Since 1970 the Flemish and French communities have been autonomous in cultural matters and have little common ground on libraries, looking rather to the Netherlands and France than each other for library cooperation. This hinders national professional awareness. Old Belgian cities hosted rich libraries dating back centuries, like those in Antwerp (1608) or Liège (1724), and these survive as major heritage collections. The first modern public library in the country opened in Ghent in 1856, when the Willemsfond, a society for promoting Flemish culture, established an institution there. A rival Catholic society, the Davidsfonds, began in 1875, and both established a number of small libraries across Flanders, which were taken over by local government in 1901. Other early developments included the bourgeois Ligue de l'enseignement or "League for Education," founded in Brussels in 1864, which established small libraries within primary schools, particularly in the French part of the country. These had stocks aimed at instructing the working classes and tended to see the library as "a temple of knowledge" with learned librarians as interpreters, though popular novels were heavily read.

Despite early-twentieth-century efforts by Paul Otlet and Henri La Fontaine to persuade the government to set up a public libraries commission (in 1908 they presented a manifesto on the subject at the International Conference on Bibliography held in Brussels), Belgium made little progress. Otlet and La Fontaine were joined by Joseph Nyns-Lagye, who tried to shift emphasis from "popular" to "public" libraries serving all classes of society. A 1910 international conference also pressed for public libraries to become a chain of libraries of all types, but with little effect. An organized system of public libraries had to wait until 1921, when an act of parliament aimed at reconstructing national life and culture after World War I (largely fought on Belgian soil). It gave local authorities power to incorporate small libraries and set standards for stock and regulations. All bodies that ran libraries (churches of different denominations, trade unions, etc.) could claim equal public subsidy, so that in some villages as many as four libraries competed for state support. Major cities developed their own networks of central libraries and branches, the strongest being Antwerp, Ghent, and Liège. Not until 1978 did Belgium begin monitoring this system (albeit with separate Flemish and French centers, and no national coverage), though it was more of a conglomeration than a planned network, even within the separate language areas. Flemish librarians claimed their sector as more effective, with an impressive network of public libraries, an automated central catalog, and interlibrary loan throughout Flanders (but not extending to French-speaking Wallonia). In Brussels separate "Flemish" and "French" libraries continued to compete into the twenty-first century (the former attracted more readers despite the majority of the population being French-speaking).

In the Netherlands, an independent kingdom from 1814 after nearly twenty years of French rule, a similar pattern evolved, but without the language split that handicapped Belgium's library developments. Paul Schneiders's 1999 history covers libraries of all types but is strong on public library developments. The concept of separate "pillars" representing the Netherlands' various religious divisions, which began in the later nineteenth century and lasted until 1970, brought wasteful duplication of effort, with parallel Catholic and Protestant libraries, sometimes with a third "neutral" library, even occasionally sharing the same building. Nonetheless, public libraries made strong progress, although several city libraries founded in the sixteenth and seventeenth centuries became fossilized and only recovered their place as part of the nation's heritage in the twentieth century. *Leeskabinetten* or circulating libraries often had their own reading rooms, which provided their mostly middle-class patrons with a sense of "public space." A further development came in the nineteenth century when hundreds of *nutsbibliotheken* ("people's libraries") run on a volunteer basis opened, and although intended to elevate the common man, they became very popular among the lower classes since their lending stocks came to consist mostly of recreational reading, despite the original aim.

In the later nineteenth century the growth of adult education accompanied a more serious approach to reading. It was on this basis that the first "modern" public libraries appeared, at Utrecht in 1892 and Dordrecht in 1898: local initiatives claimed support from local and state government. In 1908 the Netherlands established a Central Association for Public Reading Rooms and Libraries under the forty-year directorship of Henrik Ekkard Greve. He advocated a move away from the populist approach of the "people's libraries," which he thought had contaminated the word "library." Instead he proposed the term "public reading museum," a sacred building dedicated to providing information through largely nonfiction collections (he advised libraries to stock few "dangerous" or offensive books). This elitist movement was influential within government, and because public libraries were required to become members of the association, they dutifully made use of its training programs and selection guidelines. Libraries were largely closed-access, with all books bound uniformly. Perhaps as a result, popular use of the public libraries remained low: less than 5 percent of the Dutch population were registered users, preferring the "people's libraries" and the circulating libraries.

During the 1930s, a national financial crisis led to cutbacks. Even the small government grants were suspended, and no new libraries were founded. During the German occupation after 1940 the military government purged public libraries of some 10 percent of their stock (including all books by British and North American authors who had died after 1904) and banned Jewish staff and readers after 1941. The demoralized profession tended to submit to such direction but argued that compliance at least allowed libraries to remain open to serve the greatly increased demand during the war years. Revival after the war led to increased provision of children's services and rural libraries—though wasteful duplication of "pillarization" continued. (The "pillar" system refers to parallel provision for religious denominations that affected university libraries for part of the nineteenth and the twentieth centuries.)

In the 1960s liberalization of Dutch society and increasing prosperity brought change to public libraries. "Pillarized" libraries began to merge, to create stronger unified libraries, and as in Britain the competition from improved public libraries led to the disappearance of the "people's" and circulating libraries. The Nederlands Bibliotheek en Lectuur Centrum (NBLC; "Netherlands Centre for Libraries and Reading"), founded in 1972, provided a focus in a governmental advisory body that offered services of all kinds to public libraries. A Public Libraries Act of 1975 gave free library membership to young people, which led to increased use and improved funding. Sadly, cuts in the 1980s led to the repeal of this generous provision, and public libraries had mostly to rely on municipal funding and subscription services even while adopting advanced technology and electronic information.

France

France established "municipal libraries" in 1791 during the revolution, primarily to house and conserve the vast collections sequestrated from church and monastic libraries, and from private owners. These libraries, while open to national inspection, became the responsibility of the towns and cities where they were located but were never thought of as popular libraries or public libraries in the modern sense. Not until the middle of the nineteenth century were schemes devised to establish libraries in all communes, but these failed. The state proposed school libraries for new institutions set up after 1860, which in turn led Catholics to call for popular libraries reflecting a religious standpoint. By the end of the nineteenth century France had hundreds of small libraries, often run by volunteers, with a variety of funding models. In Paris, for example, a network set up in 1879 linked eleven groups of libraries through a single office. These popular libraries continued through the twentieth century, and in 1934 the Catholic enterprise Culture et bibliothèques assumed control of more than a thousand of these "Bibliothèques pour tous," or "libraries for all."

Most were perceived as socially and culturally inferior to the scholarly though little-used municipal libraries. This situation intrigued the Bibliothèque nationale's Eugène Morel, who initiated the French modern public library movement. He had visited England and been struck by the "democratic" nature of public libraries there; he also became aware of the American model and took inspiration from the library associations in both countries. In 1908–1909 he published his two-volume book *Bibliothèque*, studying public libraries on both sides of the Atlantic ("in the two worlds," as he put it), which in its polemic tone aroused opposition. He set up training courses for librarians in 1910–1913 and demonstrated his own professional stance in the "popular" municipal library at Levallois, where he introduced open access and pioneered use of the Dewey Decimal Classification. Morel was not a lone voice, but he was among the most articulate of those proposing change. He observed a fundamental distinction between the conservation role of libraries and the provision of "public reading" (a particularly French concept, going beyond libraries).

Advocating "public reading" was less easy because the principal professional training for librarianship took place in the École nationale des chartes, which intended to produce scholar-librarians rather than promote a "public" mentality; the American Library School, linked to the American Library in Paris, offered a wider curriculum, but it only lasted from 1924 to 1929, and other training was patchy. Despite this, Morel and others such as Gabriel Henriot and Henri Lemaître worked with the professional Association des Bibliothécaires Français to promote cooperation with U.S. libraries, and they were able not only to modernize libraries in Paris and elsewhere but also to develop the concept of "public reading." Children's libraries, many with the title *L'Heure joyeuse* or "Happy Time," opened after 1924, and mobile libraries became more common in urban and rural areas.

Because of much damage to historic libraries during World War I and subsequent financial problems, it took until 1931 for the government to attempt to standardize provision by creating different categories of public library—from the *bibliothèques classées* (or listed libraries with rich older collections) to those coming under a national inspectorate. This was not, however, accompanied by any significant improvement in funding, and French public libraries in the interwar years offered fewer services than some other countries. Closed-access libraries were common and children's services uneven, despite the encouraging efforts of the first generation of strong women librarians.

The 1938 *Survey of Libraries* does not give an encouraging view of French public libraries (even the old *bibliothèques municipales*): they were reported as often suffering from poor administration, lack of staff and book funds, and a general lack of interest from the government—though better times were hoped for. Instead, World War II brought German occupation and the imposition of a conservative policy. All libraries became subordinate to direction through the Bibliothèque nationale—and were also liable to censorship and destruction of "undesirable" stock. This sensitive period was little analyzed before Martine Poulain's powerful study in 2008, but the combination of political oppression and personal ambition left libraries in a sad state by the time of liberation in 1944.

After 1944 redevelopment began with the establishment of "central lending libraries" at the level of the Départements, the major administrative divisions, with responsibilities for ensuring better circulation of books between libraries of all kinds. Such a role was especially important for public libraries in a country with a great number of potential library authorities (more than 30,000 communes, only 800 with more than 10,000 inhabitants). In 1991 some larger municipalities were given responsibility for library services at a regional level—while still under national ministerial supervision. Libraries continued strong links with the world of reading and with adult education. Interestingly, this did not stop a widespread renaming of public libraries as *médiathèques* or "collections of media," a term not much adopted in other countries.

One milestone library—a good example of the continuing "Anglo-Saxon" model that did not become a *médiathèque*—is the Bibliothèque publique d'information or BPI, founded in Paris in 1977 and housed in the remarkable Centre Pompidou at Beaubourg in Paris. With free public access and ready availability of material in a variety of media, demand quickly overwhelmed its reading rooms and services (a major refit in the 1990s left it better able to cope). It pioneered the concept of public reference service, using electronic media to connect readers with other libraries in France and other countries, like a project linked to the central library in Berlin. The library published a twenty-five-year history, *Les 25 ans de la Bpi*, in 2003, giving a number of viewpoints on the library itself and on the role of democracy in French public library thinking.

Italy

Italy became a kingdom in 1861. Before unification, a mixture of governments and independent duchies covered the country, many with a degree of control over press freedom that did not encourage popular libraries. In the nineteenth century Italian library traditions emphasized scholarly use and conservation over the democratic diffusion of knowledge, a situation that continued for many years. Numerous commercial circulating libraries served mainly middle-class needs, like the influential Gabinetto Vieusseux in Florence, founded in 1820 and still a major Italian cultural center into the twenty-first century, as Laura Desideri's 2004 book relates. Older scholarly libraries existed throughout the country; many of them had rich collections and were often designated "public"—but they were essentially private. Such libraries were uncoordinated and public funding for them was almost unknown.

Following unification in the 1860s, popular libraries began to appear, many with links to the popular education movement. Antonio Bruni, who also produced an annual survey of libraries up to 1886, opened the first popular library in the city of Prato in 1861. Such libraries were small, with their loan collections easily available to subscribers. Shortly thereafter municipal libraries (Milan in 1867; Turin in 1869) began to emerge from old private collections, with a stock suitable for the information needs of the working classes. A 1917 law required every school in the kingdom to set up a library for its alumni and other adults attending courses, following ideas about rural schools and libraries advocated by the Florence librarian and politician Desiderio Chilovi. After 1922 Mussolini's Fascist party brought new government interest in libraries as part of the reorganization of state responsibilities. While the government supported older historic libraries because of their links to Italy's heritage, public libraries came under the Ministry of National Education in 1926, but without receiving adequate funding for their support. This situation did not improve with the 1932 establishment of the Ente nazionale per le biblioteche popolari e scolastiche (ENBPS, or "National Institute for Popular and School Libraries"), which effectively nationalized the popular libraries. (The 1917 law remained in force until 1941, and the ENBPS survived until 1978.) As in Nazi Germany, libraries had to publicize the party line and could not circulate "undesirable" literature.

Italian libraries of all kinds suffered damage in World War II, especially under the German occupation and the 1943 Allied invasion. After the war, the new constitution of 1948 gave greater power to the regions, and in 1975 a new culture ministry (the Ministero per i beni culturale e ambientale) took over responsibility for public libraries from the Ministry of Education. To some extent, however, this change indicates the Italian priority for "heritage" over "service," and many older, pre-unification libraries remained under central state control. Most responsibility passed to the regions, which each published local laws on libraries after 1976 (the last, Umbria, in 1990); but these libraries were actually run at a local rather than a regional level, without the guidance of any national policy defining their mission. Although increased investment in technology and a degree of coordination occurred in the late twentieth century, much of it concentrated on the older "heritage" libraries and neglected local provision. With virtually no national legislation or central administrative structure (the first collection of statistics on public libraries at a national level occurred only in the 1990s), and the relative weakness of Italian professional associations, usage and appreciation of library facilities remained low.

Spain and Portugal

Spain and Portugal had similar patterns of public library development. For many years, as in Italy, library priorities emphasized conservation and the "heritage" collections of older libraries, rather than libraries for a wider public. In Spain small "public" libraries opened in 1869, linked to popular education but with some provision for a general local readership. Under an 1870 decree Portugal set up similar popular libraries to cater especially to outlying areas and smaller towns. A Spanish law of 1915 also authorized popular libraries. Catalonia made notable progress under the regional government, which established a network of popular libraries. After World War I public libraries opened in Madrid and Barcelona; the latter became a center for Catalan culture, offering loan services and with a degree of open access unique in Spanish librarianship (and which came into conflict with more centralist policies after 1939). Lisbon acquired a Biblioteca Popular in 1918, established by the government specifically for public instruction and entertainment; a unique feature of Lisbon was the six "garden libraries" set up by the city council in the 1920s—small collections in public parks offering books to passers-by. The Lisbon central library, founded in 1931 for reference only, established a network of branches with lending services.

In Spain the declaration of the Second Republic in 1931 led the government to take the initiative on public libraries and to set up the Patronato de misiones pedagógicas ("Commission for educational missions") to support libraries and literacy programs, especially in rural areas, and a *Junta* or council to organize exchange and acquisition of books for public libraries, to update library stock, and to ensure its distribution to a wider range of libraries. A 1932 decree established a system of libraries to serve all sectors of the population. By the outbreak of the Spanish Civil War in 1936 about 200 smaller libraries benefited from this system. The war was already raging when in 1937 María Moliner appealed to her fellow librarians to trust in "the efficacy of their own mission" in an address to small rural libraries. Along with her other writings on the organization of libraries, this appeal provoked enthusiasm in the professional press, but the time was not right for government action, as the Republican government struggled in vain to survive.

Following the victory of Francisco Franco's nationalist armies in 1939, his Falangist regime governed Spain until 1975 and assumed central control of libraries. The government established a Dirección General de Archivos y Bibliotecas in 1939 under the Ministry for Education to direct the work of archives and libraries of all kinds, while a "national service for reading" set up in 1947 became the coordinating body for provincial libraries and subordinate municipal libraries. In Portugal, however, the Fascist government of the Salazar regime introduced a new constitution in 1933 that had little positive effect on libraries (some members of government even viewed widespread literacy as dangerous), which also suffered from the country's general impoverishment for four decades. The isolation of Spain and Portugal (both technically neutral in World War II, and under dictatorships for many years after 1945) meant that libraries experienced little input from abroad. Not until after the Franco and Salazar periods could modern library development resume.

Spain's new constitution of 1978 gave the seventeen regions authority over museums and libraries (but with little immediate effect), and a 1985 act clarified local responsibilities, requiring all municipalities of more than 5,000 inhabitants to provide public library services. Nonetheless, Spanish libraries remained underfunded and without adequate local support. Inequalities in services and collections differed between areas. Catalonia and the Basque country had stronger library traditions than other areas and gave greater support, but there was generally little encouragement to cooperate, poor investment in information technology, and little concept of public libraries as more than lending depots. In desperation, in the 1990s some Spanish librarians called for the closure of the smaller libraries to allow more investment in the larger, more forward-looking institutions. In 1998 the Ministry of Education and Culture (with help from industrial companies) began a reading campaign named after María Moliner: this concentrated on smaller towns and encouraged the promotion of libraries as a focus for reading and other social activities. The campaign was part of a more positive political framework, which stimulated the modernization of Spanish librarianship.

In Portugal, a government initiative in 1986 equipped each of the country's 308 municipalities with a public library, forming an expanding national network. In a remarkable example of philanthropy, the Fundação Calouste Gulkenkian built on this initiative to establish hundreds of public libraries across the country with the aim of stimulating recovery from the dark days of the war and Salazar's regime. José António Calixto describes this activity and later developments in his 2012 publication.

CONCLUSION

In concluding this survey of European librarianship, the question must be asked: Is there a common European model whose history can be traced in all or most of the continent? In view of the great diversity of viewpoints and practices, the answer must be "No." Certainly almost all library theory and practice, in Europe and elsewhere, has been built on the Renaissance/Enlightenment model of the sixteenth through eighteenth centuries, and certainly European societies and governments did develop cultural institutions common to all that one can call national libraries, academic and research libraries, and public libraries. Nonetheless, however, these "common" institutions were unique because they were continually and sometimes radically reinterpreted in the light of contemporary social and political contexts. Nowhere is this diversity in the common practices of librarianship more in evidence than in professional education and professional associations, two areas of librarianship not analyzed fully in this chapter. Since education for librarianship has generally always followed practice, it has varied from one country to another; and while it was influential in forming national patterns of librarianship, it reveals no single pattern. In many places the strongest emphasis in education, in earlier years, was on conservation and maintenance of libraries rather than reader service and the exploitation of information. In France, for example, the École nationale des chartes, with an emphasis on the historical approach and the physical document, was the principal professional school until the late twentieth century. It was common practice, especially in research libraries in most countries, to prefer academic qualifications (with library experience) to formal professional study. And in some countries where professional education had been successful, it was handicapped either by political control (as in the Soviet empire, where non-Soviet librarianship was treated as aberrant), or else by a division between different sectors of the library world (as in Germany, where separate career paths and library training and qualifications remain in place for four categories: public librarians, senior and lower-grade posts in research libraries, and documentation). This makes it difficult to present a single picture of what is meant by "librarianship," even in a single country at a particular time, let alone across many countries and over many years. Much the same can be said of professional associations, from which one might expect a clearer picture to emerge, but which vary considerably in their nature and their aims. The Library Association founded in London in 1877 showed a variety of attitudes to different kinds of librarianship, with a reputation through much of the twentieth century for preferring public librarianship as the standard practice, as Munford's history shows. At the beginning of the twenty-first century the LA's successor, the Chartered Institute of Library and Information Professionals, has on the one hand expanded its remit to cover the whole information profession, and on the other showed more concern with individual professional development than with libraries, as the new title implies. In other countries, public librarians and "research" librarians commonly formed separate associations, sometimes with common meeting grounds in a national organization but often without much dialogue between the sectors. In some cases the professional association became a major provider of library education and qualifications, either on its own or as a validating body. Once an association's qualifications were accepted as necessary for posts in libraries (sometimes as part of state legislation), the power of the association grew, though sometimes at the expense of its reputation for professional excellence. At this stage it could be under pressure to become more of a trade union body, protecting the interests of its members and becoming a force for both political action and conservative professional growth. It should be noted, incidentally, that in the Soviet Union and in the countries of Eastern Europe under Soviet control in the second half of the twentieth century, national or local professional associations were banned or discouraged, and it is only with the demise of communism since the late 1980s that such associations have once again been established. This is documented in a double issue of *Library Trends* (2014–2015) recording developments since the 1980s in the different countries formerly under Communist rule.

From the 1990s onward a new freedom of association internationally, together with the liberating spread of automation and electronic information, led to a more positive feel when librarians from the different parts of Europe came together, whether through their professional associations in EBLIDA or as individuals at IFLA conferences or smaller meetings. There may be no single standpoint for libraries or librarianship, but there is clearly a willingness to exchange opinions and to adapt principles and theories to the local situation, which was not the case before the 1980s.

The influence of Anglo-American thought and practice has been considerable in the history of modern European librarianship, not only in its northern part but also farther afield, especially in the twenty-first century as librarians have become able to act more freely and to consider what has been successful elsewhere. This raises another question: Is it in fact a European model that has formed libraries and librarianship in the rest of the world, through colonial developments and European influence on nineteenth-century North America? Subsequent essays in this collection address that question.

NOTES

1. Leif Kajberg and Marian Koren, "Europe: Introduction," in *Global Library and Information Science: A Textbook for Students and Educators*, ed. Ismail Abdullahi (The Hague: IFLA, 2009), 305–10.
2. James Duff Brown, *Manual of Library Economy* (London: Scott, Greenwood and Co., 1903), 280.
3. Desiderio Chilovi, *Le biblioteche universitarie* (Rome: "Nuova antologia," 1900).
4. Javier Lasso de la Vega, "University Libraries in Spain and Portugal," *Library Trends* 12, no. 4 (1964): 539–49.
5. Stanley Jast, "Library Classification," in *British Library Year Book 1900–1901: A Record of Library Progress and Work*, ed. Thomas Greenwood (London: Scott, Greenwood, 1900), 21–36.
6. Peter Vodosek, "Eduard Reyer, der Verein 'Zentralbibliothek' in Wien und das bürgerliche Engagement," in *Mäzenatentum für Bibliotheken = Philanthropy for Libraries*, ed. Peter Vodosek et al. (Wiesbaden: Harrassowitz, 2004), 49–66.

BIBLIOGRAPHY

Abb, Gustav. *Schleiermachers Reglement für die Königliche Bibliothek zu Berlin vom Jahre 1813 und seine Vorgeschichte*. Berlin: Breslauer, 1926.

Abdullahi, Ismail, ed. *Global Library and Information Science: A Textbook for Students and Educators*. Munchen, Herndon, VA: De Gruyter/K. G. Sauer, 2009.

Anghelescu, Hermina G. B. "Romanian Libraries Recover after the Cold War: The Communist Legacy and the Road Ahead." In *Books, Libraries, Reading and Publishing in the Cold War*, edited by Hermina Anghelescu and Martine Poulain, 232–52. Washington, DC: Library of Congress Center for the Book, 2001.

Arnold, Werner. "Bibliothekare und Bibliotheken im Nationalsozialismus." In *Wissenschaftliche Bibliothekare im Nationalsozialismus*, edited by Michael Knoche and Wolfgang Schmitz, 13–26. Wiesbaden: Harrassowitz, 2011.

Ashworth, Wilfred. *Handbook of Special Librarianship and Information Work*. London: Aslib, 1955.

Barbier, Frédéric. *Histoires des bibliothèques, d'Alexandrie aux bibliothèques virtuelles*. Paris: Armand Colin, 2013.

Barnett, Graham Keith. *The History of Public Libraries in France from the Revolution to 1939*. Library Association FLA thesis, 1974.

Bednarek-Michalska, Bozena. "Report on Polish Libraries 2001," http://eprints.rclis.org/20374/1 /Report%20on%20Polish%20Public%20Libraries2.pdf (cited July 15, 2014).

Benoît, Gaëtan. *Eugène Morel, Pioneer of Public Libraries in France*. Duluth, MN: Litwin Books, 2008.

Bermejo Larrea, J. Ignacio. "María Moliner, el espíritu de una bibliotecaria comprometida," http://cvc.cervantes.es/lengua/mmoliner/bermejo.htm (cited July 15, 2014).

Black, Alistair. *A New History of the English Public Library: Social and Intellectual Contexts, 1850–1914*. London: Leicester University Press, 1996.

Black, Alistair. *The Public Library in Britain, 1914–2000*. London: British Library, 2000.

Bottasso, Enzo. *Storia della biblioteca in Italia*. Milan: Bibliografica, 1984.

Bowyer, T. H. "The Founding of the Standing Conference of National and University Libraries (SCONUL)." In *University Library History: An International Review*, edited by James Thompson, 208–28. New York, London: K. G. Saur/Clive Bingley, 1980.

Brown, James Duff. *Manual of Library Economy*. London: Scott, Greenwood and Co., 1903.

Buluță, Gheorghe. *La culture écrite chez les roumains*. Bucharest, 1996.

Buluță, Gheorghe. *Scurt istorie a bibliotecilor din România*. Bucharest: Editura Enciclopedică, 2000.

Bushnell, G. H. *University Librarianship*. London: Grafton, 1930.

Buzás, Ladislaus. *Deutsche Bibliotheksgeschichte*, 3 vols. Wiesbaden: Ludwig Reichert Verlag, 1975–1978. Translated by William D. Boyd. *German Library History, 800–1945*. Jefferson, NC and London: McFarland, 1986.

Byberg, Lis. "Public Library Development in Norway in the Early Twentieth Century: American Influences and State Activity." *Libraries & Culture* 28, no. 1 (1993): 22–34.

Calixto, José António. *The Educational Role of Public Libraries in Portugal*. Lisbon: Goethe-Institut, 2012.

The Cambridge History of Libraries in Britain and Ireland, edited by Peter Hoare, 3 vols. Cambridge: Cambridge University Press, 2006.
   Vol. 2: 1640–1850, edited by Giles Mandelbrote and K. A. Manley.
   Vol. 3: 1850–2000, edited by Alistair Black and Peter Hoare.

Chilovi, Desiderio. *Le biblioteche universitarie*. Rome: "Nuova antologia," 1900.

Conigliello, Lucilla, and Anna Maria Milizia, eds. *Le biblioteche universitarie verso l'Europa*. Bologna: Projetto Leonardo, 1993.

Crawford, John C. "The Library Policies of James Coats in Early 20th Century Scotland." *Journal of Library History* 22, no. 2 (1987): 117–46.

D'Alòs-Moner, Adela, and Antonio Martin Oñate. "Public Libraries in Spain." *Bibliothek: Forschung und Praxis* 17, no. 1 (1993): 104–8.

Dalton, Margaret S. "The Borromäus Verein: Catholic Public Librarianship in Germany, 1845–1933." *Libraries & Culture* 31, no. 2 (1996): 409–21.

Desideri, Laura, ed. *Il Vieusseux: storia di un gabinetto di lettura, 1819–2003: cronologia, saggi, testimonianze*. Florence: Polistampa, 2004.

Dickson, William Purdie. *Statement of the Curator as to the Bearings of a Proposal to Grant 'Free Access' to Selected Students*. Glasgow: privately printed, 1899.

Dyrbye, Martin. "Anglo-Danish Connections in the Post-War Era: An Illustration of Cultural Aspects of the Transition from Warfare to Welfare Societies in the Years 1945 to 1964." *Library History* 24, no. 3 (2008): 230–39.

Dyrbye, Martin, et al., eds. *Library Spirit in the Nordic and Baltic Countries: Historical Perspectives*. Tampere: HIBOLIRE, 2009.

Dżurak, Ewa. "The Antecedents and Early History of the Warsaw Public Library." *Library & Information History* 27, no. 1 (2011): 17–31.

Ebert, Friedrich Adolf. *Die Bildung des Bibliothekars*, 2nd ed. Leipzig: Steinaker und Wagner, 1820.

Edwards, Edward. *Free Town Libraries, Their Formation, Management, and History: In Britain, France, Germany & America*. London: Trübner, 1869.

Edwards, Edward. "A Statistical View of the Principal Public Libraries in Europe and the United States." *Journal of the Statistical Society of London*, no. 11 (1848–1849): 250–81.

Eide, Elisabeth S. "Reading Societies and Lending Libraries in Nineteenth-Century Norway." *Library & Information History* 26, no. 2 (2010): 121–38.

Esdaile, Arundell. *The World's Great Libraries*, 2 vols. London: Grafton, 1934–1937.

Fabian, Bernhard. *Buch, Bibliothek und geisteswissenschaftliche Forschung: zu Problemen der Literaturversorgung und der Literaturproduktion in der Bundesrepublik Deutschland*. Göttingen: Vandenhoeck & Ruprecht, 1983.

Fabian, Bernhard, ed. *Handbuch der historischen Buchbestände in Deutschland*, 27 vols. Hildesheim: Olms-Weidmann, 1992–2000.

Fayet-Scribe, Sylvie. "Women Professionals in Documentation in France During the 1930s." *Libraries & the Cultural Record* 44, no. 2 (2009): 201–19.

Greenwood, Thomas, ed. *British Library Year Book 1900–1901: A Record of Library Progress and Work*. London: Scott, Greenwood, 1900.

Greenwood, Thomas. *Free Public Libraries: Their Organisation, Uses, and Management*. London: Simpkin, Marshall, 1886.

Grimes, Brendan. *Irish Carnegie Libraries: A Catalogue and Architectural History*. Dublin: Irish Academic Press, 1998.

Harris, P. R. *A History of the British Museum Library 1753–1973*. London: British Library, 1998.

Harrison, K. C. *Libraries in Scandinavia*, 2nd ed. London: André Deutsch, 1969.

Henderson, Robert. "Russian Political Emigrés and the British Museum Library." *Library History* 9, no. 1/2 (1991): 59–68.

Histoire des bibliothèques françaises, 4 vols. Paris: Promodis—Cercle de la Librairie, 1988–1992.
  Vol. 3: Les bibliothèques de la Révolution et du XIXe siècle, edited by Dominique Varry.
  Vol. 4: Les bibliothèques du XXe siècle, 1914–1990, edited by Martine Poulain.

"The History of Reading and Libraries in the Nordic Countries." *Libraries & Culture* 28, no. 1 (1993).

Hoare, Peter. "The Development of a European Information Society." *Library Review* 47, no. 8 (1998): 377–82.

Hoare, Peter. "Legal Deposit of Electronic Publications and Other Non-Print Material: An International Overview." *Alexandria* 9, no. 1 (1997): 59–79.

Hoare, Peter. "A Russian Librarian's View of European Libraries in 1859: Vol. I. Sobol'ščikov's Grand Tour." *IFLA Journal* 17, no. 4 (1991): 349–57.

Hopkins, Judith. "The 1791 French Catalogue Code and the Origins of the Card Catalogue." *Libraries & Culture* 24, no. 4 (1992): 378–404.

Houghton, Bernard. *Out of the Dinosaurs: The Evolution of the National Lending Library for Science and Technology*. London: Clive Bingley, 1972.

Humphreys, K. W. *A National Library in Theory and Practice*. Panizzi lectures 1987. London: British Library, 1988.

Humphreys, K. W. "University Libraries in Italy During the Past 100 Years." In *University Library History: An International Review*, edited by James Thompson, 250–68. New York, London: K. G. Saur/Clive Bingley, 1980.

"IFLA/UNESCO Public Library Manifesto 1994," http://www.ifla.org/publications/iflaunesco -public-library-manifesto-1994 (cited July 15, 2014).

Jast, Stanley. "Library Classification." In *British Library Year Book 1900–1901: A Record of Library Progress and Work*, edited by Thomas Greenwood, 21–36. London: Scott, Greenwood, 1900.

Jefcoate, Graham. "'A Difficult Modernity': The Library of the Catholic University of Nijmegen, 1923–1968." *Library & Information History* 27, no. 2 (2011): 104–22.

Johnson, Elmer D. *History of Libraries in the Western World*. New York: Scarecrow, 1965. (Michael H. Harris, 4th ed. Metuchen, NJ: Scarecrow, 1995.)

Jörgensen, Arne. *Universitetsbiblioteket i Helsingfors 1827–1848*. Helsinki: Mercator, 1930.

Kajberg, Leif, and Marian Koren. "Europe: Introduction." In *Global Library and Information Science: A Textbook for Students and Educators*, edited by Ismail Abdullahi, 305–10. The Hague: IFLA, 2009.

Kasinec, Edward. "L. B. Khavkina (1871–1949): American Library Ideas in Russia and the Development of Soviet Librarianship." *Libri* 37, no. 1 (1987): 59–71.

Kelly, Thomas. *History of Public Libraries in Great Britain 1845–1975*. 2nd ed. London: Library Association, 1977.

Klim, Irina. "The Impact of American Librarianship on Libraries of Communist and Post-Communist Russia." *Advances in Librarianship* 24 (2000): 209–24.

Koren, Marian, ed. *Working for Five Star Libraries: International Perspectives on a Century of Public Library Advocacy and Development*. The Hague: Vereniging van Openbare Bibliotheken, 2008.

Kubadinow, Irina. *Die Österreichische Nationalbibliothek*. Munich: Prestel, 2004.

Kunoff, Hugo. *The Foundations of the German Academic Library*. Chicago: American Library Association, 1982.

Ladewig, Paul. *Politik der Bücherei*. Leipzig: Ernst Wiegandt, 1912.

Langfeldt, Johannes, ed. *Handbuch des Büchereiwesens*, 3 vols. Wiesbaden: Harrassowitz, 1965–1976.

Lasso de la Vega, Javier. "University Libraries in Spain and Portugal." *Library Trends* 12, no. 4 (1964): 539–49.

Leitner, Gerald. "'Für das gute und werthafte Buch': Anfänge des österreichischen Volksbüchereiwesens nach 1945." In *Zur Geschichte der öffentlichen Bibliotheken in Österreich*, edited by Alfred Pfoser and Peter Vodosek, 176–92. Vienna: Büchereiverband Österreichs, 1995.

"Libraries and Librarianship in Italy." *Libraries & Culture* 25, no. 3 (1990): 307–478.

"Libraries in a Post-Communist World: A Quarter of a Century of Development in Central and Eastern Europe and Russia," edited by Hermina Anghelescu. *Library Trends* 63, no. 2 (2014): 107–314; no. 4 (2015).

Liesen, Bruno. *Bibliothèques populaires et bibliothèques publiques en Belgique 1860–1914.* Liège: CLPCF, 1990.

Lülfing, Daniela. "Die Entwicklung der Deutschen Staatsbibliothek und ihre Rolle im Bibliothekswesen der DDR." In *Geschichte des Bibliothekswesens in der DDR*, edited by Peter Vodosek and Konrad Marwinski; 145–158. Wiesbaden: Harrassowitz, 1999.

Maack, Mary Niles. "Women Librarians in France: the First Generation." *Journal of Library History* 18 (1983): 407–49.

MacKenna, R. O. "Subject Divisional Organization in a Major Scottish Research Library." In *Of One Accord: Essays in Honour of W. B. Paton*, edited by Frank McAdams, 99–103. Glasgow: Scottish Library Association, 1977.

MacKenna, R. O. "University Library Organization." In *University Library History: An International Review*, edited by James Thompson, 92–108. New York, London: K. G. Saur/Clive Bingley, 1980.

Mäkinen, Ilkka, ed. *Finnish Public Libraries in the Twentieth Century.* Tampere: Tampere University Press, 2001.

McColvin, Lionel R. *The Public Library System of Great Britain: A Report on Its Present Condition with Proposals for Post-War Reorganization.* London: Library Association, 1942.

McColvin, Lionel R., ed. *A Survey of Libraries: Reports on a Survey Made by the Library Association During 1936–1937.* London: Library Association, 1938.

McCrimmon, Barbara. *Power, Politics, and Print: The Publication of the British Museum Catalogue 1881–1900.* London: Clive Bingley, 1981.

Milkau, Fritz, ed. *Handbuch der Bibliothekswissenschaft*, 3 vols. Leipzig: Harrassowitz, 1931–1940. 2nd ed., 4 vols. in 5, edited by Georg Leyh. Wiesbaden: Harrassowitz, 1952–1965.

Miller, Edward. *Prince of Librarians: The Life and Times of Antonio Panizzi of the British Museum.* London: André Deutsch, 1967.

Minter, Catherine. "Academic Library Reform and the Ideal of the Librarian in England, France and Germany in the Long Nineteenth Century." *Library & Information History* 29, no. 1 (2013): 19–37.

Minter, Catherine. "'The Classification of Libraries and the Image of the Librarian in Nineteenth and Early Twentieth-Century Germany." *Library & Information History* 25, no. 1 (2009): 3–19.

Moliner, María. "A los bibliotecas rurales." Preface to *Instrucciones para el servicio de pequeñas bibliotecas*, ed. María Moliner. Valencia: Ministero de Instrucción Publica, 1937. Reprinted in *Educación y Biblioteca* 86 (1998): 18; and http://cvc.cervantes.es/lengua/mmoliner /bermejo.htm (cited July 15, 2014).

Morel, Eugène. *Bibliothèque: essai sur le développement des bibliothèques publiques et de la librairie dans les deux mondes*, 2 vols. Paris: Mercure de France, 1908–1909.

Munford, W. A. *History of the Library Association, 1877–1977.* London: Library Association, 1977.

Niessen, James P. "Museums, Nationality, and Public Research Libraries in Nineteenth Century Transylvania." *Libraries & the Cultural Record* 41, no. 3 (2006): 298–336.

Olenin, Alexei. *Essai sur un nouvel ordre bibliographique pour la Bibliothèque impériale de St. Petersbourg.* St Petersburg: Imprimerie du gouvernement, 1809.

Pafford, J. H. P. *Library Co-operation in Europe.* London: Library Association, 1935.

Pasztaleniec-Jarzyńska, Joanna, and Halina Tchórzewska-Kabata. *The National Library in Warsaw: Tradition and the Present Day*. Warsaw: National Library, 2000.

Petzholdt, Julius. *Katechismus der Bibliothekslehre: Anleitung zur Einrichtung und Verwaltung von Bibliotheken*. Leipzig: J. J. Weber, 1856.

Pfoser, Alfred, and Peter Vodosek, eds. *Zur Geschichte der öffentlichen Bibliotheken in Österreich*. Vienna: Büchereiverband Österreichs, 1995.

Poulain, Martine. *Livres pillés, lectures surveillées: les bibliothèques françaises sous l'Occupation*. Paris: Gallimard, 2008.

Ratcliffe, F. W. "The Growth of University Library Collections in the United Kingdom." In *University Library History: An International Review*, edited by James Thompson, 5–55. New York, London: K. G. Saur/Clive Bingley, 1980.

Raymond, Boris. *Krupskaia and Soviet Russian Librarianship 1917–1939*. Metuchen, NJ: Scarecrow Press, 1979.

Richter, Noë. *Bibliothèques et éducation permanente: de la lecture populaire à la lecture publique*. Le Mans: Bibliothèque de l'Université du Maine, 1981.

Richter, Noë. *Les bibliothèques populaires*. Paris: Cercle de la Librairie, 1978.

Schmidt-Glintzer, Helwig. "Wolfenbüttel Profiles: Collectors in a Library." In *A Treasure House of Books: The Library of Duke August of Brunswick-Wolfenbüttel* [catalogue of exhibition at the Grolier Club, New York], 9–16. Wolfenbüttel: HAB, 1998.

Schmitz, Wolfgang. *Deutsche Bibliotheksgeschichte*. Bern: Peter Land, 1984.

Schneiders, Paul. *Nederlandse bibliotheekgeschiedenis: van librije tot virtuelle bibliotheek*. The Hague: NBLC, 1999.

Schrettinger, Martin. *Versuch eines vollständigen Lehrbuches der Bibliothek-Wissenschaft, oder Anleitung zur vollkommenen Geschäftsführung eines Bibliothekars in wissenschaftlicher Form*, 3 vols. Munich: Lindauer, 1808–1810.

Séguin, Jean-Pierre. *Eugène Morel (1869–1934) et la lecture publique*. Paris: Bibliothèque publique d'information, 1993.

Senser, Christine. *Die Bibliotheken der Schweiz*. Wiesbaden: Ludwig Reichert, 1991.

Siegert, Reinhart, et al., eds. *Volksbildung durch Lesestoffe = Educating the People through Reading Material in the 18th and 19th Century*. Bremen edition: lumière, 2012.

Simsova, S., ed. *Lenin, Krupskaia and Libraries*. London: Clive Bingley, 1968.

Skorodenko, V. A., ed. *Vserossiiskaia gosudarstvnnaia biblioteka inostrannoi literatury imeni M. I. Rudomino 1922–1997*. Moscow: VGBIL, 1997.

Skouvig, Laura. "How to Observe the Librarian." *Library History* 24, no. 4 (2008): 299–306.

Sobol'shchikov, V. I. *Obzor bol'shikh bibliotek Evropy v nachalie 1859 goda*. St. Petersburg: Tip. I. Akademii nauk, 1860.

Sobol'shchikov, V. I. *Principes pour l'organisation et la conservation des grandes bibliothèques*, Paris: Vve. J. Renouard, 1859.

Sroka, Marek. "'Soldiers of the Cultural Revolution': The Stalinization of Libraries and Librarianship in Poland, 1945–1953." *Library History* 16, no. 2 (2000): 105–25.

Stam, David H., ed. *International Dictionary of Library Histories*, 2 vols. Chicago: Fitzroy Dearborn, 2001.

Stipčević, Aleksandar. "The Illyrian Reading Rooms in Croatia in the Mid-Nineteenth Century." *Libraries & Culture* 24, no. 1 (1:1989): 69–74.

Stoltzenburg, Joachim, and Günther Wiegand. *Die Bibliothek der Universität Konstanz 1965–1974: Erfahrungen und Probleme*. Pullach: Dokumentation, 1975.

Stuart, Mary. "'The Ennobling Illusion': The Public Library Movement in Late Imperial Russia." *Slavonic and East European Review* 76, no. 3 (1998): 401–40.

Stuart, Mary. "The Evolution of Librarianship in Russia: The Librarians of the Imperial Public Library, 1808–1868." *Library Quarterly* 64, no. 1 (1994): 1–29.

Sutter, Sem C. "The Lost Jewish Libraries of Vilna and the Frankfurt Institut zur Erforschung der Judenfrage." In *Lost Libraries: The Destruction of Great Book Collections since Antiquity*, edited by James Raven, 219–35. Basingstoke: Palgrave Macmillan, 2004.

Thauer, Wolfgang, and Peter Vodosek. *Geschichte der öffentlichen Bücherei in Deutschland*, 2nd ed. Wiesbaden: Harrassowitz, 1990.

Thompson, James, ed. *University Library History: An International Review*. New York and London: K. G. Saur/Clive Bingley, 1980.

Thompson, James, and Reg Carr. *An Introduction to University Library Administration*, 4th ed. London: Clive Bingley, 1987.

Traniello, Paolo. *La biblioteca pubblica: storia di un istituto nell'Europa contemporanea*. Bologna: Il Mulino, 1997.

Traniello, Paolo. *Storia delle biblioteche in Italia dall'Unità a oggi*. Bologna: Il Mulino, 2002.

Les 25 ans de la Bpi: encyclopédisme, actualité, libre accès. Paris: Bibliothèque Centre Pompidou, 2003.

Urquhart, Donald. *Mr. Boston Spa: Story of the National Lending Library and Its Librarian*. Leeds: Wood Garth, 1990.

Van Borm, J. "Belgian University Libraries Preparing for Europe." In *Le biblioteche universitarie verso l'Europa*, edited by Lucilla Conigliello and Anna Maria Milizia, 94–102. Bologna: Projetto Leonardo, 1993.

Vellekoop, P. "Transforming a 400 Years Old Library [Utrecht University Library] into a Modern Organization." In *Le biblioteche universitarie verso l'Europa*, edited by Lucilla Conigliello and Anna Maria Milizia, 87–93. Bologna: Projetto Leonardo, 1993.

Vodosek, Peter. "Eduard Reyer, der Verein 'Zentralbibliothek' in Wien und das bürgerliche Engagement." In *Mäzenatentum für Bibliotheken = Philanthropy for Libraries*, edited by Peter Vodosek et al., 49–66. Wiesbaden: Harrassowitz, 2004.

Vodosek, Peter. "Innovation and Ideology: Walter Hofmann's Library Work in Dresden-Plauen and Leipzig." *Library History* 23, no. 1 (2007): 63–76.

Vodosek, Peter. "Von der Volksaufklärung zur Gewerbebildung und Volksbildung: Karl Benjamin Preusker (1786–1871)." In *Volksbildung durch Lesestoffe = Educating the People through Reading Material in the 18th and 19th Century*, edited by Reinhart Siegert et al., 107–140. Bremen edition: lumière, 2012.

Vodosek, Peter, and J.-F. Leonhard, eds. *Die Entwicklung des Bibliothekswesens in Deutschland 1945–1965*. Wiesbaden: Harrassowitz, 1993.

Vodosek, Peter, and Konrad Marwinski, eds. *Geschichte des Bibliothekswesens in der DDR*. Wiesbaden: Harrassowitz, 1999.

Volodin, Boris Fedorovich. "Russian Library History in a European Context." *Library History* 14, no. 1 (1998): 23–28.

Volodin, Boris Fedorovich. *Vsemirnaia istoriia bibliotek*. St. Petersburg: Izd. Professiia, 2002.

Vrchotka, Jaroslav. *Dějiny Knihovny Národního muzea v Praze 1818–1892*. Prague: Národ Muzeum, [1967].

Walsh, Pat. *The Curious Case of the Mayo Librarian*. Cork: Mercier Press, 2009.

Wells, John. *Rude Words: A Discursive History of the London Library*. London: Macmillan, 1991.

Wiegand, Wayne A., and Donald G. Davis, eds. *Encyclopedia of Library History*. New York and London: Garland, 1994.

Wilks, John. *The Influence of R. W. Chambers on the Development of University Libraries*. London: H. K. Lewis, 1953.

Willison, Ian R. "The National Library in Historical Perspective." *Libraries & Culture* 24, no. 1 (1989): 75–79.

Wimmer, Ulla, and Michael Seadle. "A Friendly Conquest: German Libraries after the Fall of the Berlin Wall 1989." *Library Trends* 63, no. 2 (2014) (in press).

Woledge, G., and B. S. Page. *A Manual of University and College Library Practice*. London: Library Association, 1940.

Wolfe, Bertram D. "Krupskaia Purges the People's Libraries." In *Revolution and Reality: Essays on the Origin and Fate of the Soviet System*, 98–112. Chapel Hill: University of North Carolina Press, 1981.

Zaitsev, V., et al., eds. *The National Library of Russia 1795–1995*. St. Petersburg: Likhi Rossii, 1995.

2

United States and Canada

Wayne A. Wiegand

INTRODUCTION

Throughout their history, libraries north of the Rio Grande river operated as local institutions serving unique communities where multiple groups who founded, funded, managed, and used them interacted in numerous ways. On the one hand, these groups established and ran libraries as places to celebrate cultural commonalities. On the other, they used libraries as sites to negotiate differences these multiple systems occasioned. Naturally, library managers functioned as players in constructing many cultures whose heritages have been passed through library collections and services. Sometimes the librarianship these managers practiced served to facilitate cultural connections between groups; sometimes it served as an obstacle to slow connections, even prevent them from forming. Since the seventeenth century librarianship's choices about how to organize, what to collect, circulate, and preserve have influenced which cultural values were featured in collections and services. At the same time, however, choices librarianship made were heavily circumscribed by negotiations between funders, founders, managers, and users. Thus, American and Canadian librarianship shaped—and was shaped by—the cultures it served. Three themes persist:

- access to information resources the library has selected;
- use of those resources by an increasingly multicultural clientele; and
- the use of the library as a place.

The first was deliberately pursued as a professional goal, the second and third quietly negotiated through multiple groups upon whom the library institution depended. This chapter shows that the process by which librarianship improved access to information is constant in the profession. By concentrating some attention on use, however, the chapter also shows where librarianship has been an obstacle to cultural democracy. How people used materials to which library founders, funders, and managers provided access, and what effect this use had on librarianship constitute a record of cultural politics the literature has largely left unexplored. The same can be said for the use of the library as a place where communities bonded in the spaces libraries provided. No one can understand fully the role that American and Canadian librarianship has played in constructing the heritage of cultures unless one analyzes access, use, and place.

How can this lack of attention to use and place be explained? As capitalism evolved, the way people experienced daily life separated into "work" and "leisure." Business and government placed high value on the former, low value on the latter. A librarianship that served the information interests of business and government naturally mirrored these priorities. Eventually included with them, however, were "stories" the state regarded as so essential to the social order they constituted a canon of literature to be taught in schools and colleges, and thus collected and preserved in libraries serving both. Because they considered the library's major responsibility to collect, organize, and make available the kind of information "work" found most "useful," founders and funders wrote their own values into the agendas of institutions they established, and because they created these institutions, what they did automatically influenced patterns of development and imposed parameters that limited possibilities for change. Business, government, and authorities who assumed responsibility for educating North Americans considered commonplace stories—no matter their cultural form—less important and categorized them a "leisure" activity. Librarians either did not recognize or (more often) were slow to respond to collecting stories less dominant groups wanted. Through site use alone, however, the latter forced funders and managers to negotiate cultural priorities.

How? Because use of American and Canadian libraries has generally not been compulsory, librarians had to concern themselves with library circulation to justify funding. As a result, librarians had to address "leisure" information needs. Over time (especially in the twentieth century) librarians developed a willingness to serve the democracies of culture manifest in patrons' multiple cultural tastes by supplying stories in cultural forms millions wanted. Although they did this without much fanfare or gratitude from more dominant cultures, their professional services helped millions of users construct multiple canons unique to their own cultures and independent of a prescriptive set constructed by cultural authorities whose own "knowledge" was hardly disinterested. Finally, the library evolved as a civic institution within the public sphere, where members of many publics gathered to bond, assimilate, and practice and display acceptable community social behaviors. As a place, the library also functioned as mediator for artistic and aesthetic community standards. The history of American and Canadian librarianship detailed in this chapter tells the story of the library as a site where the collections it contained and the services it offered were consistently celebrated by its founders, funders, managers, and users. At the same time, however, these collections, services, and places—whether categorized as "work" or "leisure"—were used in many different ways.

COLONIAL AMERICA TO 1776

Native North American peoples possessed active cultures, but because none evolved sophisticated writing systems, they felt no need to develop libraries. Europeans who conquered, colonized, and settled the continent in the fifteenth and sixteenth centuries had evolved writing systems they used to record cultural messages they considered most important and (after the mid-fifteenth-century invention of moveable type) to fix them in print in book form. Like all emigrant populations, they wanted to replicate their cultures in their new homes. One way to accomplish this was carrying the books and libraries containing stories that celebrated their cultures' history and, more important, provided moral guidance they believed everyone needed to negotiate life. The colonists' first task was to clear the brush, construct houses and barns, plant crops, and meet occasional opposition from indigenous peoples. Not until this was accomplished could they begin to build cultural institutions, including libraries.

William Brewster brought a personal library with him from England to Plymouth Colony in 1620 that grew to 400 volumes in 1644. The Reverend Samuel Skelton had fifty-four mostly theological books in his library when he reached Massachusetts in 1629; later he purchased thirty-four catechisms to add to a library he intended to use to convert Native Americans. In 1631 John Winthrop carried his library of 1,000 mostly scientific books to Boston, then made them available to people interested in science. When James Logan arrived in Philadelphia in 1699, he brought a library of scientific and classical literature that grew to 3,000 volumes within a generation. Cotton Mather was his generation's most avid collector. When he died in 1728 his library reached over 4,000 volumes.

The colonial South hosted a few personal libraries. The most prominent belonged to William Byrd, II, of Virginia, who before 1740 owned 4,000 volumes rich in history, law, science, and classical and English literature. Elsewhere, plantation libraries were smaller, though no less used. Thomas Jefferson's first library burned in 1770, but by 1783 he rebuilt it to 2,500 volumes. George Washington's library was smaller but reflected his interests in English drama, fiction, and essays. Like many peers, all three regularly referenced the Bible, the classics, and French and English political philosophers—most well represented in their libraries. Once professionals like physicians and lawyers established practices, they began accumulating books, most imported from England. Many lawyers shared titles, especially William Blackstone's *Commentaries on the Laws of England* (1770), an essential work for legal practitioners that became the first law book reprinted in colonial America. Philadelphia's Pennsylvania Hospital organized the first medical library in the 1760s; by 1849 it still had the largest medical collection (10,000 volumes) on the continent. But larger collections like these were the exception.

By the mid-seventeenth century some colonists established libraries that at least some local community members could access. In 1656 merchant Robert Keayne left his library to Boston, provided the city house and maintain it. Boston placed Keayne's collection in its Town House, and even published a catalog in 1702. Over time local officials added public documents, all destroyed by fire in 1747. In 1656 Connecticut governor Theophilus Eaton bequeathed ninety-five titles to New Haven; for thirty years they resided in a town library, little used. In 1695 Anglican clergyman Thomas Bray of London, who also served as commissary to the colony of Maryland, led efforts through the Society for the Propagation of the Gospel in Foreign Parts to establish libraries in colonial churches. Some—called "Lending Libraries"—he intended for parishioners, but most—called "Parochial Libraries"—he intended for the local minister. Each generally contained less than one hundred volumes.

In 1698 a 220-volume Parochial Library arrived at New York City's Trinity Parish. That same year a 225-volume Lending Library arrived in Charleston, South Carolina; although placed in the rector's house, its maintenance eventually passed to the colonial legislature, thus showing that separation of church and state hardly existed in colonial America. In 1700 Bray sent Lending Libraries to each of Maryland's parishes, and to Pamlico, North Carolina's St. Thomas Parish, he sent both a 166-volume Parochial Library and a Lending Library of 870 volumes and pamphlets. In 1701 Bray supplemented Lending Libraries with collections of tracts written by English clergy. Between 1698 and 1730 (when Bray died), his twenty-nine Parochial Libraries and thirty-five Lending Libraries received 35,000 religious books and tracts. In addition, he also established Provincial Libraries in Boston, New York, Philadelphia, Annapolis, Charleston, and Bath, North Carolina. Over time, however, interest in these libraries diminished, and because Bray made no provisions for adding books and colonial legislatures took no responsibility for maintaining them beyond security, the libraries eventually died of neglect.

Social Libraries

In 1731 printer-entrepreneur Benjamin Franklin established the Library Company of Philadelphia. By getting fifty friends to pool forty shillings each (and promise annual contributions thereafter), he ordered from a London book agent forty-six books that included dictionaries, grammars, histories, an atlas, and scientific and agricultural literature, but no theology or fiction. Upon arrival, books were cataloged by size and subject. Louis Timothee, who opened the library several hours a week and took responsibility for monitoring circulation, became North America's first known librarian. In 1734 William Parsons succeeded Timothee, and when he moved the collections to his house shortly thereafter reported 239 volumes, 25 periodicals, and some pamphlets and papers. In 1740 Library Company collections moved to the Pennsylvania State House, where in 1787 it functioned as a reference library for the men who drafted the Constitution. In 1791 the company moved to its own quarters. In 1769 three subscription libraries established in Philadelphia between 1747 and 1757 merged with the Library Company. Then, in 1784, Franklin joined negotiations to unite the Loganian collection—3,000 volumes strong in science, mathematics, classics, and history—with the Library Company. The merger occurred in 1792, two years after Franklin died. To the end of his life, Franklin believed in social libraries. They "improv'd the general Conversation of the Americans," he said, "made the common Tradesmen and Farmers as intelligent as most Gentlemen from other Countries, and perhaps have contributed in some degree to the Stand as generally made through the Colonies in Defense of their Privileges."[1]

Before the American Revolution, New England colonies hosted fifty social libraries. Most followed the Library Company's organizational model; all looked to England for new titles. In 1733, eight founders subscribed twenty shillings each to establish the Book Company of Durham, Connecticut. In 1748, several South Carolina men pooled funds to open the Charleston Library Society as a way to collect British pamphlets and magazines. Within two years the society boasted 160 members and an acquisitions endowment. In 1747 the Redwood Library Company of Newport, Rhode Island, obtained a provincial assembly charter and three years later moved into what many claim is North America's first dedicated library building. Although members bonded there in regular meetings, its collections concentrated on "useful knowledge." In 1764 it issued a 700-title catalog (entries arranged by donor, then size); 33 percent were *belles lettres,* 19 percent science, 16 percent history, 13 percent theology, and 8 percent law. The remainder consisted of biography, travel, and the agricultural and military sciences.

Circulating Libraries

Although social libraries predominated, colonial America also hosted "circulating libraries" that made books available for a fee. Generally run out of printshops or bookstores, circulating library owners usually fronted the capital necessary to acquire a collection, then rented it by the book or time period (or combination of the two) to anyone willing to pay. Because profits depended on circulation, owners emphasized novels, an increasingly popular category of reading. And because most circulating libraries were run by businesses that did not serve alcohol, local conventions allowed women access to these establishments—one of the few public places they could frequent without male accompaniment. Circulating library successes benefited from increased literacy rates among urban, middle-class women. In 1762, for example, Annapolis, Maryland's William Rind opened what may have been colonial America's first circulating library. He charged customers (including females) twenty-seven shillings annually and allowed them to check out two books per circulation. Ten years later New York's Samuel Loudon published a 2,000-title catalog of his circulating library, available to anyone willing to pay the fee.

Academic Libraries

By contemporary standards, colonial college libraries were also small, grew mostly by donation, and were open a few hours usually one day per week. Even Harvard College, endowed in 1638 with 380 books, listed only 3,500 titles (two-thirds were religious) in its 1723 printed catalog. Library rules written in 1667 gave a "Library Keeper" responsibility for security and required him to construct a catalog alphabetically arranged by author, monitor circulation, and open the library from 11:00 a.m. to 1:00 p.m. twice a week. Rules written a century later indicated only juniors and seniors could withdraw books from the library, open and heated only on Wednesday.

By that time Yale's collection was 4,000 volumes, most theological. Established in 1700 by eleven ministers, each donated books from personal collections to mark its organization. In subsequent decades collections grew mostly by gift, including donations from Sir Isaac Newton, Reverend Elihu Yale, and Reverend George Berkeley who, in 1733, gave nearly 1,000 volumes (two-thirds consisting of theology, history, dictionaries, and grammars). To reorganize the library, in 1742 Yale hired a tutor who divided collections into sections by size, gave each book within each section a fixed location, then developed three catalogs for retrieval assistance: one arranged alphabetically by author, a second listing books in shelf location order, and a third arranged by twenty-five subject headings. Library collections in other colonial colleges experienced similar growth patterns and profiles. In 1693 the Reverend James Blair helped organize the College of William and Mary to provide training for Anglican ministers, then became the college's first president. By 1700 the college owned several hundred books, most consumed in a 1705 fire. Bequests increased the collection to nearly 2,000 by midcentury; none circulated to students. In 1757 New Jersey's governor gave 475 volumes to the College of New Jersey (later Princeton) established seven years earlier. In 1768 the college's president added 300, but a decade later the 2,000-volume collection was destroyed by British soldiers in the Revolution. The library of New York City's King's College (later Columbia) met a similar fate. Established in 1757, it grew mostly by donation to several thousand. Students at Rhode Island College (later Brown University) had limited access to their 250-volume library seven years after the college opened in 1765, but for a fee they could use the Providence Library Company's collections. Dartmouth opened its doors in 1770, and within ten years built a collection of 1,200 volumes.

Prior to the Revolution, colonial American colleges considered libraries treasures to be sequestered more than collections to be used. Theology (which mirrored the religious beliefs of institutional founders, administrators, and faculty) constituted the largest subject category. Sometimes a part-time instructor managed the library. Because he was responsible for security he tightly controlled access to collections. But students generally did not complain. The classical college curriculum did not require use of library collections; college libraries were not places they congregated. Most instruction followed eighteenth-century pedagogy designed to avoid perspectives contrary to churches that supported them, and to inculcate mental discipline instead of specialized training. For a few years, students endured a rigid curriculum focused largely on mathematics drills and the memorization and recitation of Greek, Latin, and Hebrew texts capped by a senior-level moral philosophy course (often taught by the college president), all designed to prepare them for influential positions in Christian society.

CANADA TO CONFEDERATION

Because colonial Canadians also looked to Europe for institutional models, much of their library history resembles that of colonial America. When the French settled Port Royal in 1606 in Nova Scotia's Annapolis Valley, several had books. Before 1763 twelve libraries were known to exist in New France, all attached to Roman Catholic institutions, all with carefully controlled public access. Many in New France possessed personal libraries, but most were small, and as in colonial America, works on religion, medicine, law, and philosophy dominated. Few included literary works. Hudson's Bay and North West Company fur traders carried small libraries with them, including titles by Shakespeare, Milton, and Addison. In 1786 John McKay, surgeon on the ship *Experiment*, consulted his personal library repeatedly when studying indigenous Nootka Sound peoples. North West Company trader Daniel William Harmon complained in 1813 that few company posts had enough books to satisfy his needs.

Social libraries appeared in Quebec City in 1779 and Montreal in 1796. Both had bilingual collections, both showed increased attention to literature. Their contents favored theology, history, biography, and agriculture, but little fiction. In the nineteenth century, Montreal hosted 164 libraries—two-thirds were social and circulating institutions, one-third school and academic libraries. Elsewhere social libraries were established in Niagara-on-the-Lake, Ontario, in 1800, and Halifax in 1806. The latter occupied free quarters in a government building and later merged with the Agricultural Library organized by reformer John Young. Quebec City's General Hospital had a small library when founded in 1725. Legislative libraries appeared in Nova Scotia in 1758, Prince Edward Island in 1773, New Brunswick in 1784, Ontario in 1791, and Quebec in 1792. A Halifax Law Library was organized in 1797. All emphasized legal texts, but by the early nineteenth century developed general and recreational collections to satisfy legislator and local community reading interests. Canadian government libraries took several forms. The National Museum of Agriculture began a library in 1842, the Geological Survey in 1844. By that time other Canadians had established scores of circulating and social libraries. Many supplied popular fiction. In 1825, for example, David Spence announced he was establishing a new circulating library at Nova Scotia's

Tobin's Wharf, and that he had already received novels, romances, voyages, and histories from a London supplier. Anyone willing to pay a fee could borrow books. That Spence obtained his stock from Europe was not unusual. Before the mid-nineteenth century Canada lacked a publishing industry.

Anglophone Canada

In mostly Anglophone Canada, mercantile libraries were founded in St. John's (1827), Montreal (1828), Toronto (1830), Halifax (1831), and Kingston (1834). Sometimes mercantile libraries were supported by capitalists who saw them as self-help institutions improving the skills of the clerical workers and middle-level managers they employed. More often they were a voluntary organization of skilled laborers who pooled resources to acquire books for useful knowledge and leisure reading. Each initially emphasized books of useful knowledge and literary merit, and except for authors like Dickens, Thackeray, and Bunyan, showed little desire for popular fiction. In 1835, Ontario gave the Toronto Mechanics Institute $800 and $400 to the Kingston Mechanics Institute to purchase books and scientific instruments. On the prairies, by 1846 the Sixth Regiment of Fort Guards added books purchased from England to the private libraries the Sulkirk Settlers brought to Manitoba to open the Red and Assiniboine community libraries. Victoria, British Columbia, opened its first YMCA Library in 1859 and its first Mechanics Institute Library in 1864, the latter for men only. When the institute met hard times several years later, it opened membership to women at half price. In Nanaimo, the Vancouver Coal Company president funded a "News and Reading Room" for the local Literary Institute, originally established to host public activities like debates and orations. In 1865 the collection moved to the Mechanics Institute, where it remained a subscription library until absorbed into the Vancouver Island Union Library regional system in 1936.

Several provinces followed Ontario's lead in establishing school/township libraries. There provincial Superintendent of Public Instruction Egerton Ryerson defined a "common school library" as a free public library housed in a school accessible to students, teachers, and community residents. The 1850 School Act Ryerson facilitated provided for a depository that acquired school equipment, texts, and library books, and then sold them at cost to schools and libraries. Ryerson held to four principles—common school libraries would include: (1) no "licentious, vicious, or immoral" works, or anything "hostile to the Christian religion"; (2) no controversial theological works highlighting disputes between denominations; (3) a broad range of viewpoints on historical subjects; and (4) a collection of books representing all major departments of human knowledge. For a while, Ryerson libraries prospered. By the end of 1854, all but three of Upper Canada's forty-two counties had them. Six years later, however, booksellers argued they were losing profits because the government was working directly with English wholesalers, priests complained the libraries contained books hostile to Catholicism, and local citizens found their contents uninspiring. By 1881 the depository closed, just as many Ontario mechanics' institute libraries transitioned into free public libraries.

Francophone Canada

In Francophone Quebec, library development took a different turn. There, to guide parishioners' reading interests, mid-nineteenth-century Roman Catholic parish libraries

looked to the Oeuvre des bons livres of Montréal, an institution founded by the conservative Roman Catholic Sulpician Fathers. About the same time secular, liberal Montreal
laymen organized the Institut canadien de Montréal. Almost immediately the two libraries battled, the former arguing the latter contributed to community immorality by circulating books the Church prohibited. The latter ultimately closed in the 1880s. A study
of the circulation records and membership lists of the Institut canadien de Montréal—
a combination mechanics' institute, voluntary association, and mercantile library—
between 1855 and 1883 shows most of its members came from the emerging professional and business middle classes. These members were not seeking useful knowledge,
however. Although only one-third of the collection was fiction, novels accounted for
two-thirds of circulation in 1865, more than four-fifths in 1885. And among women,
who accounted for less than 5 percent of total circulation, they chose novels nine times
out of ten.

Colonial Canadian academic libraries also mirrored institutions to the south. The
Seminary of Quebec City, founded by Jesuits, established a mission library in 1632,
a college library in 1635. By 1800 the latter boasted a 5,024-volume collection: 20
percent in theology, 17 percent classics, and 11 percent *belles lettres*. A substantial fraction represented what was probably Canada's first medical library, which the Jesuits
augmented regularly with acquisitions from France. King's College (Windsor, Nova
Scotia)—founded in 1789—issued its first book catalog in 1802. Dalhousie (Halifax),
McGill (Montreal), King's College in Upper Canada (later the University of Toronto),
and Queen's University (Kingston, Ontario) also established academic libraries before
midcentury.

UNITED STATES, 1776–1876

Social Libraries

Although colonial college libraries suffered significant losses during the American
Revolution, in large part because soldiers fighting for either side often occupied college
buildings housing collections, social libraries—many housed in private residences—
did not suffer as much. After the Revolution gave way to constitutional forms of government at federal and state levels, many states passed legislation to establish more.
New England states, for example, chartered over 500 social libraries between 1790 and
1815 (in 1802 the *Massachusetts Register* estimated the Bay State had 100), and by
the mid-nineteenth century that number jumped another 500. Small towns west of the
Appalachians established hundreds more.

Many did not survive, but their existence helped communities mark themselves as
friendly toward culture, and especially the culture of print that celebrated dominant
group moralities. Social libraries took many forms, most following the reading interests
of patrons paying for access. Collections ranged from several hundred to a few thousand. Many excluded fiction; others embraced it, sometimes totaling half the collections.
Among many authorities fiction became increasingly suspect, as early nineteenth-
century patriarchal culture responded to increased female literacy in two ways. On the
one hand, it excluded women and children from membership in social libraries. On the
other, publishers sought to protect what they perceived as women's delicate sensibilities
by altering classical texts and substituting new passages for offensive ones. Here they
followed Thomas Bowdler and his sister Harriet, whose *Family Shakespeare* (1807)

purchased by scores of American social libraries reflected a "bowdlerism" authorities thought necessary to protect the masses. Besides classical works by Aristotle, Shakespeare, and Gibbon, social libraries often specialized in collecting useful knowledge to cultivate character and provide male readers with scientific, agricultural, economic, and sociological literature to help them find a niche in—and make contributions to—the evolving United States capitalist democracy. Many maintained reading rooms, sometimes open to the general public for a fee, sometimes open only to members owning library stock. Most subscribed to English and American periodicals; all accepted gifts, some from congressional representatives who used franking privileges to forward documents the federal government distributed free.

In 1793 Thaddeus Mason Harris published *Selected Catalogue of Some of the Most Esteemed Publications in the English Language Proper to Form a Social Library*. The catalog recommended 277 books "for a *small* and *cheap* library, intended to suit the tastes and circumstances of common readers."[2] Harris adopted a conceptual frame Sir Francis Bacon originated to divide human knowledge into three major classes—memory (87 titles, including history, travel, and biography), reason (109 titles, including science, religion, and philosophy), and imagination (81 titles, including fiction, poetry, drama, and art). Book publishers and dealers quickly realized the value of cultivating social libraries with special discounts. By midcentury the growing number of social libraries constituted a major fraction of the domestic book market.

In 1805 the Boston Anthology Society approved a library of periodical subscriptions for society use. In 1807 Massachusetts passed an act incorporating the library as the Boston Athenaeum, whose purpose was, the charter explained, to build a collection of books in ancient and modern languages members could use to satisfy their intellectual curiosities. Three months later the Athenaeum sold 150 shares of stock at $350 each (no one was allowed to own more than three shares). In 1809 it issued a catalog. Nearly twenty years later the corporation agreed to allow nonshareholding subscribers. For a $5 annual fee they could draw three volumes at a time for one month. But this hardly rendered the institution democratic. "What literary advantages have the mass of our citizens derived from the Athenaeum?" a local newspaper asked in 1826. "Money buys a ticket for the wealthy to read the Hebrew language, while the industrious, worthy portion of the community, may intellectually starve upon a six-penny almanack."[3] Not until the 1830s were some women admitted to membership; one was later ousted for abolitionist views.

West of the Appalachians social library history reflects a pioneering spirit of cultural desire. In Cincinnati, for example, several citizens met in 1802 to draft a circular soliciting interest in a social library. Within a month twenty-five men paid $10 for each of thirty-four shares of stock, all for library books. In Ames, Ohio, several residents pooled money and animal pelts (especially raccoons) in 1803 to send to Boston a shareholder who carried with him letters of introduction to Thaddeus Mason Harris. He returned with sixty-one books. "He brought the books . . . in a sack, on a pack horse," a fellow subscriber described. "I was present at the untying . . . and pouring-out of the treasure. . . . There never was a library better read." Although formally organized as the Western Library Association, local lore dubbed it the "Coonskin Library."[4] A subscriber could withdraw as many books for a three-month period (a concession to pioneering work schedules) as equaled two-thirds the value of his shares priced at $2.50 each. By midcentury Ohio had chartered more than 150 social libraries. Antebellum Indiana also boasted a healthy population of social libraries. Vincennes began one in 1806.

Similar efforts occurred in the South. In 1795 fifty-nine Baltimore citizens formed a Library Company by selling shares at $30 and charging an annual $4 access fee. Five years later it had 345 members; all could access its 3,300 volumes. In 1798 Alexandria, Virginia, friends formed a subscription library; in 1856 a catalog listed 4,481 volumes. Perhaps the southern city with the most flourishing white Anglo-Saxon Protestant middle-class culture was Charleston, South Carolina, where a Library Society traced its history to 1748. The society had 15,000 volumes by 1850, but in Charleston it was hardly alone. Other social libraries included the Trinitarian Universalist and Library Society, the Franklin Library Society, the Apprentices' Library Society, and the Ramsey Library and Debating Society. Elsewhere in the Palmetto State thirty other social libraries enjoyed mixed success. In general, southern antebellum social libraries established in larger cities like Nashville and Knoxville, Tennessee; Mobile, Alabama; Augusta and Savannah, Georgia; and Wilmington, North Carolina—all run by white propertied males—had a better chance to survive hard times and the Civil War.

Although the nineteenth-century social library expanded book stock it made available to members and subscribers, local moral conventions influenced choices. In 1821 Massachusetts hosted the first U.S. obscenity prosecution against John Cleland's *Memoirs of a Woman of Pleasure* (1748). A generation later Congress prohibited the importation of obscene materials. But for young people and adults, forces pressed from other directions to influence what communities considered acceptable. "I think the test of obscenity is this," the presiding judge declared in an 1868 English court case involving alleged libel of an anti-Catholic tract, "whether the tendency of the matter charged as obscene is to deprave and corrupt those whose minds are open to such immoral influences, and into whose hands a publication of this sort may fall."[5] This definition of obscenity—referred to as the "Hicklin rule" after the judge who rendered it—fit a need. Because the rule promised a solution, the United States used it to give the Postmaster General authority to seize materials he considered obscene and punish the perpetrator with a $500 fine and a year in prison. In 1873 Congress passed the Comstock Act after Anthony Comstock, who led a movement for the YMCA Committee for the Suppression of Vice to ban books or other materials he thought indecent (this also included information on contraception or abortion) from the mails. Thirty years later George Bernard Shaw labeled overzealous efforts to purify culture "Comstockery," a term that like "bowdlerization" stuck in the censorship lexicon. Libraries dependent on the post office to deliver acquisitions took note.

New Types of Social Libraries

The early nineteenth century witnessed numerous offspring from the social library model. In 1820, for example, several New York and Boston young men established mercantile libraries. Although their predecessors were late eighteenth-century English mechanics' institutes, U.S. mercantile library collections took on a broader profile of reading materials. In the early nineteenth century young male social climbers were expected to be conversant in the language of cultural and financial capital. Many mercantile libraries connected themselves to adult education, activities and public lectures arranged by the American Lyceum that featured such prominent people as Ralph Waldo Emerson and Lyman Beecher. In some cases they were also served by the Lyceum's itinerating library system. Much more than eighteenth-century social libraries, mercantile libraries functioned as places self-selected members of the public gathered to foster community, be seen and heard, and discuss contemporary questions. New York's Mercantile Library emphasized popular fiction. It charged a $2 subscription fee, and within a year of opening had 220 members. By 1875, it had 175,000 volumes, the Boston and Philadelphia Mercantile Libraries 125,000 volumes. Baltimore's Mercantile Library Association formed in 1839, and by 1875 had 30,000 volumes. San Francisco organized its Mercantile in 1853. When it opened, a 1,500-volume collection served the information needs of 392 members.

At midcentury another type of social library appeared. In 1851 the Boston Young Men's Christian Association opened reading rooms with carefully selected books containing life lessons it intended for young men who, the YMCA believed, badly needed exposure to Christian morality instead of saloons that led them to eternal damnation. Membership fees were small, and the reading rooms themselves—which also contained approved periodicals and newspapers—stayed open twelve to fourteen hours a day (including Sunday). The collections' first aim was to support Christian education, but like most other social libraries, survival eventually influenced collection profiles, which a generation later included more general reading materials. In 1859 the United States had 145 YMCA libraries, twelve with collections exceeding 1,000. In 1875 New York's YMCA Library had 10,000 volumes, including fiction by authors like Charles Dickens and Walter Scott. In 1892 YMCA libraries peaked when 54 percent of the 1,400 reporting YMCAs indicated they housed libraries with at least fifty volumes.

Although they shared many YMCA library goals, individual churches and the Protestant denominations that supported them preferred more direct control of their parishioners' reading interests. A major means to exercise this control was Sunday school libraries, which at midcentury benefited from a sophisticated publishing and distribution system the American Tract Society (established in 1825) set up to disseminate its products through the American Sunday School Union (established in 1824). Often these collections functioned as texts for literacy instruction. Many times, in fact, they constituted the only book collections available to local populations. In 1860 the American Sunday School Union reported that the average Sunday school library had 335 volumes and was usually open only on Sunday. Secular critics argued that literature in Sunday school libraries (including bible study aids and some religious fiction) was sentimental and maudlin, and not suitable for young people. In 1870 the U.S. Census reported 33,580 Sunday school libraries containing 8,000,000 volumes.

Circulating Libraries

Nineteenth-century circulating libraries differed significantly from eighteenth-century predecessors. Unlike other types of social libraries—which rhetoricized a responsibility to improve local culture—circulating libraries made no secret that their highest priority was commercial. Where social libraries avoided stories depicting murders, hangings, and scandals of popular interest featured in newspapers like the *Boston Gazette* (1719) and *New England Gazette*, circulating libraries embraced them. Many were attached to bookstores; most existed in larger towns. And because literacy rates among middle-class white women increased significantly after the American Revolution, circulating libraries focused on the reading desires of this emerging market more than any other social library. Some circulating libraries accumulated large collections. In New York, for example, Hocquet Caritat's Circulation Library had more than 5,000 volumes seven years after opening in 1797; 20 percent were popular novels.

Academic Literary Society Libraries

In the absence of user-friendly college libraries, post-Revolution students in U.S. institutions of higher education eager to enter professions requiring rhetoric and debate skills (like law, politics, and theology) formed their own "literary societies" with libraries of printed materials society members accessed to prepare for speeches and debates. Acquisitions often came by alumni bequest, occasionally from purchases of faculty traveling through Europe. At Yale, for example, after organizing in 1769 the Linonian and the Brothers in Unity literary societies began accumulating books to provide information for weekly debates. By 1800 their combined holdings totaled 500 volumes. Competition sparked by these debates encouraged students to create bibliographic aids and make information retrieval more efficient. In 1848 student librarian William Frederick Poole of the Brothers in Unity developed a periodical literature index and had 500 copies of this *Index to Subjects Treated in the Reviews and Other Periodicals* printed that other literary societies purchased. He published an updated second index in 1853. Both demonstrated how important society librarians were. Each society developed a separate office of "librarian," who opened the facility to students who needed it and made sure materials checked out made it back to the correct location. Society officers often invited prominent alumni to attend meetings and deliver speeches, and many times the latter brought library donations. Sometimes literary society libraries also provided recreational reading. By 1870 Yale's literary society libraries held 13,000 volumes.

Other Types of Libraries

As new forms of transportation created new sites in which people had time to read, new kinds of libraries emerged. Railroads crisscrossing North America, for example, provided popular fiction for employees and passengers. In many cases, for a fee passengers could pick up a novel at the beginning of their journey and drop it off at the end for partial reimbursement. The Boston and Albany and the Baltimore and Ohio Railroads managed these kinds of libraries at midcentury; the Atchison, Topeka and Santa Fe sponsored one into the early twentieth century. Ships carrying passengers established similar library services. Other types of libraries languished, or flourished. Philadelphia's College of Physicians established a collection in the 1780s but did not cultivate it. By 1835 the library had fewer than 300 titles. In 1834, on the other hand, New York's Society of Surgeon Dentists established a library. And beginning with the *Boston Post*, U.S. newspapers established forty-two libraries in the nineteenth century. Before wire services, they shared copy. Each newspaper library also developed a "morgue"—initially a clipping file of prominent local people collected for future obituaries. Beginning in 1867 the *New York Times* began indexing the contents of its dailies, and in 1872 the *Boston Globe* enlarged its morgue into a comprehensive fee-based clipping subscription service.

By midcentury most prisons had libraries, usually consisting of the Bible and pious tracts. In 1844 New York City's Tombs prison had 150 titles of predominantly religious works. The librarian was often the prison chaplain, and funds for prison libraries usually came from visitors' fees. In the 1840s Eliza Farnham, matron of New York's Sing Sing Prison women's department, tried to expand the scope of prison library collections. Recognizing that prisoners really wanted newspapers, magazines, and novels, she began adding romances, penny magazines, and travel literature. For her efforts, prison officials accused her of immorality. She subsequently resigned. Law libraries continued to grow. Legal apprentices often used private collections, but because practitioners without access to private collections were at a significant disadvantage, bar and membership libraries emerged in the early nineteenth century. Boston's Social Law Library opened in 1804, New York's Library of the Association of the Bar soon thereafter. Over time, large private collections transitioned into bar libraries. Public law libraries also emerged. New York's Allegheny County Law Library opened in 1806; Massachusetts organized a system of county law libraries in 1815. Thirty years later the Bay State began using court filing fees to finance these libraries. But law library collections were more similar than unique and echoed the insulated professional discourse its practitioners practiced.

School District Libraries

In 1839 Secretary to the Massachusetts Board of Education Horace Mann surveyed the state for libraries. His survey showed Massachusetts had 299 social libraries containing 180,000 volumes, but the subscription fee or stock ownership most required denied access to poor people who needed them most. Libraries needed public funding, he concluded. One solution to this problem was the school district library. In 1835 New York passed a law that gave permission to school districts to tax local populations for school libraries that all local voting citizens could access. Three years later the state passed another law providing matching funds. By 1850 New York school district libraries contained 1,500,000 volumes. Massachusetts followed New York and in 1837 established a system that by midcentury housed 100,000 volumes in over 2,000 libraries. Lowell took advantage of the opportunity differently. In 1844 the city council approved a school library under the act's authority, then combined state and local funds with an annual fifty-cent user fee to maintain a 3,800-volume collection the general public could use. Connecticut, Rhode Island, Michigan, Indiana, and Ohio also passed enabling legislation for school district libraries. Although over the years school boards made teachers personally liable for the libraries' care (most were in secondary schools) and drew up specific instructions for their organization and collections, the latter did not fit the textbook-centered pedagogy in use. Most school libraries stagnated. Publishers quick to recognize a market issued entire collections of cheaply produced but previously published works (most were not protected by U.S. copyright and thus required no royalties), then sold them as "libraries" through local representatives working on commission. Funds for school district libraries were primarily used to purchase materials, not to staff, manage, and house them. As a result, collections consisted largely of textbooks and useful knowledge pitched to an audience more educated than local rural school district populations. And because districts generally lacked separate quarters to house books, many ended up in the basements and attics of teachers' and board members' homes, where they often disappeared. In 1851 the Maine Board of Education Secretary concluded that the nine towns with school district libraries failed because of insurmountable difficulties.

Predecessors of the Public Library

Some hope for a "free" public library surfaced at midcentury in New York. When John Jacob Astor died in 1848, he willed $400,000 to a foundation to establish a New York "public" library. After the legislature incorporated the Astor Library in 1849, trustees supported Director Joseph G. Cogswell's efforts to make it a noncirculating library "suited to the wants of scholars, investigators, and scientists, and to the pursuit of exact knowledge in all the arts." No one under sixteen could use the collections (youth, Cogswell said, preferred "reading the trashy" like "Scott, Cooper, Dickens, *Punch*, and the *Illustrated News*"). On opening day in 1854, Cogswell even kept most visitors away. "It would have crazed me to have seen a crowd ranging lawlessly among the books," he said, "and throw everything into confusion."[6]

The ebb and flow of nineteenth-century social library history in two cities demonstrate variety. In 1811 several St. Louis citizens started a subscription library, others a Library Society in 1819. When the latter failed quickly, others established a St. Louis Library Association in 1824. By that time St. Louis also hosted reading rooms in a hotel, a newspaper office, and a "Reading Room and Punch House." In 1839 the Library Society dissolved and sold its collections to the St. Louis Lyceum, which in turn passed them to the St. Louis Mercantile Library Association. In 1850, the Mercantile reported 589 members, including thirty life members, 211 proprietors, 306 clerks, and 142 beneficiaries. Its building—located within walking distance of the central business district—boasted a large reading room and two lecture halls with seating for 600 in one and 1,500 in the other—the city's largest indoor auditorium. In 1865 St. Louis opened a "Public School Library"—in reality a social library used mostly by teachers and students. Three years later the library moved into a city-owned building, inherited donated collections from several local libraries seeking consolidation, and by 1875 boasted 40,000 titles available to 6,000 members. In Louisiana, the Territorial Legislature had authorized a public library for New Orleans in 1805, but not until 1820 could the Crescent City claim credit for hosting a Library Society, a subscription library, a Law Library, and a "free library at the Presbyterian Church." Local philanthropist Alvarez Fisk acquired the subscription library in the 1830s, and in 1849 opened the noncirculating Fisk Free Library to local white citizens. By 1857 New Orleans added a State Library, a Young Men's Christian Association Library, a Merchants' Reading Room, and a Public School Lyceum and Society Library.

While social and circulating libraries of all types enjoyed moderate success in some communities and school district libraries struggled in others, several communities experimented with community-controlled, publicly funded institutions. In 1827 Castine, Maine, assumed ownership of a social library founded in 1801 and opened it up for public use. In 1833 Peterborough, New Hampshire, citizens followed the Rev. Abiel Abbott's recommendation to allocate part of a State Literary Fund to purchase books for a town library to be housed at the post office and monitored by the postmaster. Concerns about youthful reading sparked other early nineteenth-century initiatives. In 1803, for example, Caleb Bingham of Salisbury, Connecticut, donated 150 books to establish the Bingham Library for Youth. Lexington, Massachusetts, citizens voted to set up a library for youths in 1827 in the town church. In 1835 a local citizen's will provided West Cambridge, Massachusetts, with funds for a children's library. While each of these "public" libraries started auspiciously, communities generally failed to provide annual funds for new materials, adequate quarters, and competent staffing.

Boston Public Library

In an 1850 *Report on the Public Libraries of the United States* Charles Coffin Jewett identified 10,015 libraries in thirty-one states and the District of Columbia containing

3,701,828 volumes. But Jewett's definition of "public" was broad—all libraries not private property, he said. This definition may seem strange to twenty-first-century librarians, but for their mid-nineteenth-century predecessors it was one on which they generally agreed. It did not last long, however. Already in 1848, at the Boston City Council's request, Massachusetts passed legislation to establish and maintain a public library for Boston's citizens. For several years community leaders George Ticknor and Edward Everett, among others, agitated for an institution to supply wholesome reading to Boston's public, and especially to its lower classes increasingly replenished by uneducated, often illiterate Irish immigrants. In 1847 Mayor Josiah Quincy anonymously offered $5,000 for a public library if the city council authorized a tax to support it. When the council approved Quincy's request (efforts to convince Athenaeum shareholders to merge their collections with the public library failed), Boston began planning its public library.

In justifying enabling legislation, Massachusetts legislator John Burt Wight outlined four advantages public libraries would bring. First, they would become "needful and valuable" extensions of public schools. Second, they would "supply the whole people with ample sources of important practical information." Third, because they "will contain many instructive and excellent books" that "will be greatly increased . . . by continual additions in subsequent years," they will help effect a community's "intellectual and moral advancement." Finally, they would serve as depositories for federal, state, and local government documents. Wight was especially excited about the moral impact public libraries would have on patrons. "They will be favorable to all the moral reforms of the day, by leading to more domestic habits of life, by diminishing the circulation of low and immoral publications, and by producing higher and more worthy views of the capabilities of human nature."[7] Others states followed Massachusetts. In 1849 New Hampshire passed the first general law enabling any local government within the state to tax itself to support public libraries. Maine authorized a library tax in 1854, Vermont in 1865, and Wisconsin in 1868.

By that time other members of Boston's first families joined efforts to launch the institution. In 1851 Mayor John P. Bigelow gave $1,000, and Joshua Bates a $50,000 endowment to be used for public library collections. Everett donated 1,000 volumes, and shortly thereafter Ticknor offered his collection of Spanish history and literature. On July 6, 1852, a trustees subcommittee Everett chaired issued two reports. The first justified the Boston Public Library's existence and is often referred to as the charter of the American public library movement. The document argued for free admission to all, circulation of books for home use, and the provision of reading materials ranging from scholarly to popular. "For it has been rightly judged that,—under political, social, and religious institutions like ours,—it is of paramount importance that the means of general information should be so diffused that the largest possible number of persons should be induced to read and understand questions going down to the very foundations of social order . . . which we, as a people, are constantly required to decide, and do decide, either ignorantly or wisely."[8] Irish immigrants watching these activities recognized that founders pushing for a library represented old Beacon Hill money worried about the moral decline their community faced from pressures of industrialization, immigration, and urbanization. The second report outlined a governance structure that became the model communities opening public libraries across the country adopted. It empowered trustees to select a president, make rules and regulations, appropriate money, and care for and control the library. Annually trustees had to inspect and report to the council on the library's condition, and annually they had to elect a librarian who followed administrative rules trustees set up. Boston effectively redefined what a "public library" was a mere four years after Jewett's 1850 *Report*.

The Boston Public Library (BPL) opened March 20, 1854, in two rooms of a schoolhouse; it began circulating books on May 2. One room held the collections, the second served as a reading room with 138 periodicals, government documents, and scientific society transactions. The reading room opened every day from 9:00 a.m. to 9:30 p.m. (in 1859 trustees closed it Sundays), and any Boston resident above sixteen who possessed "a respectable character" could use the reading room and withdraw books from its closed stacks. To identify books they wanted, patrons used the public book catalog. By mid-October 6,590 people registered for borrowing privileges and withdrew 35,389 books, the majority of them fiction. To manage this new institution trustees hired Jewett, from 1847 to 1855 Smithsonian Institution librarian. After he arrived in 1857, Jewett monitored the library's move into its own building with a Lower Hall for popular materials, an Upper Hall for reference works. When Jewett issued separate catalogs for the Lower and Upper Halls in 1858, the collection totaled 100,000 volumes. Within twenty years the collection tripled. In 1868, after Jewett died, Trustee Justin Winsor, who was chair of an 1867 examining committee that scrutinized its management, became librarian. He immediately implemented managerial changes and quickly became the nation's leading authority on public library management. Directors and trustees of a mushrooming number of public libraries established across the continent constantly solicited his advice.

Library of Congress

About the time Winsor became BPL director, Librarian of Congress Ainsworth Rand Spofford had restructured the Library of Congress (LC) from mostly a congressional reference library into a national library—in fact, if not in name. Up to that time LC had a low profile, even among federal libraries. Congress created it in 1800 with an order to a London bookseller for 152 works in 740 volumes (including 104 volumes of *Parliamentary Debates*, Adam Smith's *The Wealth of Nations*, and Sir Francis Bacon's *Works*). In 1802 Congress established a joint library committee, identified borrowing privileges, and made the Librarian of Congress a presidential appointment subject to Senate approval. President Thomas Jefferson then nominated—and the Senate approved—John Beckley as the first librarian. Initially LC arranged books by size. A folio had to be returned within three weeks, a quarto within two, an octavo or duodecimo within one. When Congress was in session, LC opened from 9 to 3 and 5 to 7 Monday through Saturday. Borrowers had to leave notes promising to pay twice the book's value if they failed to return it. By 1812 the collection grew to 3,000 volumes in twenty-one broad subject headings.

Even in 1812, however, LC was not the only "federal" government library. The first was created at West Point in 1777. Fifteen years after Congress authorized the United States Military Academy in 1802 the institution appointed its first librarian. In 1818 the Army established its Medical Library, and the first surgeon general began accumulating a "Surgeon General's Library," in part to distribute medical information to field surgeons at army bases across the country. By 1840 it had a few hundred titles. The government also created a weather service library in 1809, a White House library in 1815, a Department of Justice library in 1831, a Coast Survey library in 1832, a Supreme Court library in 1843, a Naval Academy library in 1845; the Army also authorized several post libraries.

But LC still constituted the nation's foremost federal library. On August 24, 1814, however, the British entered Washington and used LC books as kindling to set fire to the Capitol. Replacing it became a national *cause célébre*. Former president Thomas Jefferson offered to sell his personal 6,000-volume library to replace LC's collections, and after political haggling, Congress accepted his offer and paid him nearly $24,000. In 1815 the librarian asked Jefferson about the collection's arrangement and the catalog that accompanied it. Jefferson had based his forty-four group subject arrangement on Sir Francis Bacon's table of science, which he modified to include law and politics. Later that year the librarian issued a catalog based on Jefferson's scheme. For most of the century this scheme was used to arrange LC collections.

In subsequent years various members of Congress and librarians tried to accelerate acquisitions, but generally to no avail. Part of the reason may have been the Smithsonian Institution, established by Congress in 1846, eight years after the United States received a bequest from Englishman James Smithson to create an agency dedicated to the increase in knowledge. Smithsonian regents wanted a museum and a library, which one senator hoped would become a national library better than any in the Western world. To run the Smithsonian, regents appointed as secretary Joseph Henry, who believed the Institution should primarily become a center and catalyst for research. To direct the library in 1848 Henry hired Charles Coffin Jewett, Brown University professor of modern languages and literature and since 1841 its librarian. Jewett saw his appointment as an opportunity to develop the nation's best reference library, and he quickly structured an agenda to achieve his goal.

In 1849 Jewett outlined a plan for a national bibliography, argued for centralized cataloging (he envisioned roving groups of catalogers systematically cataloging individual libraries by a uniform set of rules), and proposed the Smithsonian assume responsibility for developing a stereotype catalog (an idea he adopted from French librarian Chevalier de Lagarde de la Pailleterie) that would accomplish both tasks. But Jewett pushed too hard. Although prominent librarians supported him, Henry had the upper hand. On July 10, 1854, he dismissed Jewett, in part because Jewett had planted press reports critical of the secretary and his priorities. Any chance the Smithsonian had to become a national library went with him. In 1857 Henry persuaded Congress to remove the Smithsonian from copyright responsibilities it had assumed in 1846 (the State Department—the nation's official legal depository since 1796—exercised its responsibilities indifferently all that time). In 1856 the *United States Messenger* explained that the United States had no national library because the country was too divided. It also lacked a national university in the nation's capital capable of sustaining a national library. The newspaper never even considered LC a possibility. Nor did an 1851 main reading room fire that destroyed 35,000 volumes trigger thoughts of any bibliothecal grandiosity.

In 1862, however, Assistant Librarian Spofford submitted an annual report that argued LC should become the country's national library. Three years later President Abraham Lincoln appointed Spofford librarian, and he quickly began to act on his goal. First, he convinced Congress to expand the library within the Capitol. A year later he won approval to transfer Smithsonian collections to LC, and with these collections inherited the international agreements the Smithsonian set up to exchange scientific documents. In 1867 he convinced Congress to purchase an Americana collection of 22,500 books, 40,000 pamphlets, and 1,000 volumes of bound newspapers (many dated to the eighteenth century). In 1870 he helped pass a law that centralized U.S. copyright registration and deposit in the library. With collections flooding LC shelves, Spofford used his 1871 annual report to argue for a separate building.

U.S. AND CANADIAN LIBRARIANSHIP, 1876–1893

As the United States prepared for a centennial celebration in Philadelphia in 1876, the Department of Interior's Bureau of Education commissioned a report "to present, first, the history of public libraries in the United States; second, to show their present condition and extent; third, to discuss the various questions of library economy and management; and fourth, to present as complete statistical information of all classes of public libraries as practicable."[9] The definition for "public" was deliberately broad, and like Jewett's 1850 definition embraced any library to which any citizen had access. Under Commissioner John Eaton's direction, the bureau engaged thirty-five experts to write thirty-nine chapters and an introduction. As they readied *Public Libraries in the United States of America: Their History, Condition, and Management: Special Report* for publication in October of 1876, Eaton suggested to prominent librarians they might use the *Special Report* and the centennial to organize a national librarians' conference. They had precedent. In 1853 eighty-two delegates met for a New York City Librarians' Conference to exchange information, celebrate their work, and explore the possibility of establishing a national association. The 1853 conference accomplished everything except the latter.

Origins of the American Library Association

In 1876, however, library leaders seemed unenthusiastic about the idea. Into the vacuum stepped Melvil Dewey, most recently Amherst College librarian and at the time finishing a decimal classification scheme. He had just moved to Boston to begin work for educational reform, a large part of which (as he saw it) needed the American public library. On May 17, 1876, Dewey met *Publishers' Weekly* editors Frederick Leypoldt and Richard R. Bowker. Together they agreed to begin a library periodical and introduce it at a national library conference in Philadelphia coterminous with the *Special Report*'s publication. All summer Dewey worked to organize the conference, sometimes against the wishes of prominent librarians like Spofford and Cincinnati Public Library director William Frederick Poole. Once Dewey got Winsor to commit, however, other luminaries (including Poole) followed. The time was ripe. Although still in press, the *Special Report* noted the thirteen original colonies had twenty-nine "public" libraries in 1776 containing about 45,000 volumes. In 1876, the United States had 3,682 libraries containing 12,276,964 volumes and 1,500,000 pamphlets. All that printed culture needed a set of skilled professionals capable of managing it and making it available to citizens who, as Thomas Jefferson and many others believed, had an obligation to become informed.

On October 4, 1876, 103 delegates met at the Historical Society of Pennsylvania. Winsor, who chaired the Committee on Arrangements, called the meeting to order. Most of the conference consisted of papers. Poole talked about "Some Popular Objections to Public Libraries"; Samuel Swett Green of the Worcester, Massachusetts, public library argued that "a librarian should be as unwilling to allow an inquirer to leave the library with his question unanswered as a shopkeeper is to have a customer go out of his store without making a purchase." Still, much conference attention focused on the *Special Report* (which included as "Part II" Charles Ammi Cutter's *Rules for a Printed Dictionary Catalogue*), the *American Library Journal*'s first issue, and the first edition of Dewey's *Classification and Subject Index for Cataloging and Arranging the Books and Pamphlets of a Library*, a 42-page pamphlet detailing a scheme that married an inverted Baconian classification system to a decimal scheme forcing all "knowledge" into ten broad categories.

On October 5, a committee reported a constitution for a professional association. "For the purpose of promoting the library interests of the country, and of increasing reciprocity of intelligence and good-will among librarians and all interested in library economy and bibliographical studies," the preamble read, "the undersigned form themselves into a body to be known as the AMERICAN LIBRARY ASSOCIATION [ALA]." Dewey signed his name "No. 1," and before delegates left Philadelphia the next day they elected Winsor president; Spofford, Poole, and two others vice presidents; and Dewey as secretary and treasurer. For the first time, North American librarians had a professional organization to voice their concerns. In the *American Library Journal*'s first issue Dewey boldly stated: "The time has at last come when a librarian may, without assumption, speak of his occupation as a profession."[10]

Cutter's *Rules* represented a watershed in cataloging history because it successfully established catalog codes in which entries were alphabetically interfiled under author, title, and subject. Principles he laid down in 1876 sedimented into cataloging practices that were reinforced in three more editions (1889, 1891, and 1904), all carefully scrutinized at ALA conferences and in ALA publications. As a professional association ALA had a homogenizing impact on library practices and services. The nearly simultaneous publication of Cutter's rules and Dewey's classification occurred at a unique moment. First, both systems were imbued with a set of beliefs about classification inherited from previous generations that argued: (1) it was possible to view the universe as a single, cohesive whole; (2) elements of this universe had been revealed through intellectual discovery; (3) these elements existed in a hierarchical relationship; (4) listing these elements in their "natural" order would help define the essential characteristics of subject classes; (5) structuring this universe required that broadest subject classes reside at the top; and (6) to educate people and facilitate new knowledge classificatory relationships had to give order to the universe of knowledge. Second, both systems rested on the conviction that applying a universal classification scheme and set of cataloging rules to a library's collection would make the institution central to self-education by providing reliable ways to retrieve information, and thus enable citizens to inform themselves about their culture, economy, and government. The syndetic dictionary catalog allowed systematic classification and use of the alphabet to coexist in one information retrieval system. With the help of new systems of notations placed directly on their spines, books could now be arranged in subject categories relative to each other and found by referencing the notation rather than the location. The arrangement was simple and efficient.

At the ALA's 1877 conference Caroline Hewins of Hartford, Connecticut's Young Men's Institute, became the first woman to speak. Her effort not only marked women's participation in ALA, it also showed they were taking positions in libraries across the continent. In the 1870s Winsor welcomed them into the profession because "they soften our atmosphere, they lighten our labour, they are equal to our work, and for the money they cost . . . they are infinitely better than equivalent salaries will produce of the other sex." In the 1880s Dewey regularly complimented women on their "quick mind and deft fingers."[11] Shortly after the conference ALA leaders sailed to London to help launch the world's second library association. To serve its members, *American Library Journal* changed its name to *Library Journal.*

Establishing Librarianship's Jurisdiction

Like other embryonic American professions in the late nineteenth century, librarians had a professional organization and a periodical. But Dewey thought librarianship needed another anchor. After becoming librarian at New York City's Columbia College in 1883, he worked to establish a library education program. At the 1883 ALA conference he sought association approval, but extracted only a statement that expressed ALA "gratification" that Columbia trustees were willing to try the scheme. Dewey pressed on. In 1884 Columbia trustees approved the creation of a "School of Library Economy," as long as it cost no money. Initially, Dewey pilot-tested the school with a few students who traded practical experience for independent instruction. In late 1886 Dewey announced he would open the school in January. As preparations continued, however, trustees learned he planned to admit women to his first class, a move contrary to college conventions. When they protested, the college president suggested Dewey postpone opening the school. Dewey refused. Trustees then denied Dewey use of Columbia classrooms. Undaunted, Dewey went across the street and in an off-campus storeroom and "without giving a hint of the volcano on which we all stood, I welcomed the first class and launched the first library school."[12] Out of a class of twenty, seventeen were women.

The curriculum reflected what Dewey perceived to be librarianship's jurisdictional boundaries. Students would not be admitted without the right "character," a late nineteenth-century term usually marking individuals with social standing and knowledge of Western Civilization's canonical works. Once admitted, however, students had three different "faculties." For practical experience Dewey and his staff taught courses designed to develop skills in cataloging, classification, book selection, reference service, and managing the institution in which it all took place. For inspiration (his generation called this the "library faith"—an ideology that grew out of the Jeffersonian belief that for a democracy to survive it needed an informed citizenry) he imported library luminaries (e.g., Bowker, Spofford, and Hewins) as guest lecturers. For theoretical grounding, however, Dewey tapped a Saturday morning public lecture series Columbia faculty offered. In late 1886 he asked several scheduled for spring lectures to discuss the best literature in their areas of expertise and mandated his students to attend.

Thus, Dewey believed experts from outside communities like political science, literature, history, and languages would identify "best" reading for librarians in knowledge they produced in the university; they would also develop disciplinary canons against which to evaluate any new contributions to those literatures. Librarianship would take it from there. In library school students would learn how to acquire these new literatures (book selection), how to organize them (cataloging and classification), where to look for answers to questions their publics asked (reference), and finally, how to manage the institution in which these skills were exercised (management). Except to disparage and discourage it, they paid almost no attention to popular literature containing the nation's cultural stories, nor to analyzing how their publics used their libraries as places. With one exception librarians were trained to look to other cultural authorities to identify "best reading." That exception was library service for young people. When Hewins published *Books for the Young: A Guide for Parents and Children* in 1882, she claimed authority to identify best reading for children. As librarianship increasingly feminized in the late nineteenth century, experts in the patriarchal culture claiming authority to define the canons of "serious" literature for adults willingly relinquished authority to identify "serious" literature for children to women whose "natural instincts" equipped them for these decisions. Hewins worried about the negative potential she thought highly popular authors like Oliver Optic and Horatio Alger had on young readers' vulnerable minds. Her bibliography rejected books that "made 'smartness' a virtue, encourage children in cruelty, rudeness, or disrespect to their elders, contain much bad English, or make their little every-day heroes leap suddenly from abject poverty to boundless wealth."[13]

Dewey approved. It fit his concept of the profession's jurisdiction, interfered with no other profession, represented an efficient way to divide the professional workforce, and provided women a new opportunity to participate meaningfully in a profession that in his mind mirrored the natural order of things. It also fit the context of the times—child welfare advocates had begun supervising children's physical and moral development in settlement houses, juvenile courts, public playgrounds, public health programs, and now public libraries. The model for children's librarianship that characterized this pioneering generation of women included special collections, segregated areas, specially trained personnel, and services designed to bring children together with the materials adults selected for their moral and social improvement. Out of this model came the weekly story hour; in 1882 Caroline Hewins initiated a read-aloud program at her library. In 1887 the Pawtucket (RI) Public Library created a separate children's room. The Brookline (MA) Public Library followed in 1891, Minneapolis in 1893, Denver in 1894.

Other distinctions emerged. Women entering the profession organized a "Women's Meeting" at the 1892 ALA annual conference. Gender distinctions in American and Canadian library services had been prevalent for some time. The Victoria (BC) Public Library, for example, established two reading rooms when it opened in 1887—one for the general public, the other for women and children. Mixing the sexes as library employees, however, brought its own tensions. At the conference several speakers challenged conventions. One noted that women librarians "rarely receive the same pay for the same work as men." Another argued "a woman's tact and sympathy and large-heartedness can find no greater outlet in this kind of library work." A third said that although many thought women limited by social conventions, female librarians should not give up ambitions for administrative positions. Not everyone agreed with viewing the library world from a gendered perspective. Los Angeles Public Library director Tessa Kelso argued against forming an ALA "Women's Section." "There is but one standard of management for a live business," she said, "and sex has nothing to do with that standard."[14]

Academic Library Practices

Other elements affecting the profession's evolution emerged from changes in higher education. Academic library architecture was one. Most separate American and Canadian campus library buildings shared common architectural characteristics of churches constructed in the Classical Revival style in the eighteenth and the Gothic Revival style in the nineteenth centuries. Architects found that library foyers fit nicely into the narthex, transverse shelving could be accommodated in aisles and galleries, and reading rooms in naves illuminated during daylight hours by clerestory windows. In the American South the University of South Carolina (1840), the University of North Carolina (1851), and the College of Charleston (1856) all constructed libraries in the style of Greek temples. Higher education institutions in the North preferred the style of Gothic churches (Harvard in 1841, Yale in 1846, Wesleyan in 1868). Some were unique, however. To house the University of Virginia Library, Thomas Jefferson favored the classical rotunda evident at Oxford's Radcliffe Camera (and later mirrored in the Library of Congress's Reading Room). In 1846 Williams College erected an octagonal library with radial bookshelves extending inward under a dome. Princeton designed a similar library in 1873.

Academic libraries also pioneered technical services. At Brown Jewett introduced the practice of alphabetically interfiling subject entries with author and title entries in 1843. In 1861 Harvard introduced a public card catalog, recording items in the library's collection on 2x5-inch handwritten subject and author cards (work carried out by women hired as early as 1859). And at Amherst College in 1873 Dewey developed his decimal classification to control its library collections. On green cards 15x17.5 centimeters (Dewey advocated the adoption of the metric system) he placed subject entries, and on 10x5-centimeter cards he placed author entries. Dewey also pushed to homogenize library practices. In 1881 he organized the Library Bureau—which marketed Alfred Cotgreave's library inventions like the Improved Periodical Rack, the Table-Rack for Magazines, the Book-Reacher (a device to retrieve and replace books on high shelves), and the Automatic Step (a folding ladder). But Dewey also marketed the first single-card catalog tray (1894) and the first card catalog cabinet (1897). He persuaded one company to manufacture a special typewriter to produce catalog cards.

But none of these pioneering technical services significantly influenced higher education, which in the late nineteenth century was changing so rapidly academic libraries had a hard time keeping pace. In 1862, for example, the U.S. Congress passed the first Morrill Act, which supported higher education in areas like agriculture and engineering. Fourteen years later, The Johns Hopkins University became the first U.S. graduate institution based on a German university model that emphasized research, seminars, and graduate education. All three required large library collections, some of them scattered across campus. Hopkins president Daniel Coit Gilman, who had been a librarian, quickly recognized this. Harvard, Yale, Columbia, McGill, and the University of Toronto, among others, followed Hopkins's model, and each amassed collections to support seminar studies and faculty research, and meet the needs of revised undergraduate programs and a system of electives. For colleges and universities, libraries became places where students gathered routinely to learn, form, and reinforce community.

When Justin Winsor became Harvard's library director in 1877 he followed his predecessors' emphasis on acquisition but added a new mantra characteristic of his generation of librarians—use. He instituted a closed reserve system that improved student access to relatively few texts and implemented a policy of decentralization to relieve space pressure on Harvard's main library. In 1879 he argued that unpredictable research needs forced academic librarians to collect and preserve all they could, and that the new course elective systems on North American campuses transformed libraries into "intellectual hunting grounds" requiring subject catalogs and skilled reference service. Columbia represents another example of how campus libraries transitioned in the late nineteenth century. When Dewey became librarian, he changed it from a facility with closed stacks open a few hours a day a few days a week into one with open stacks for all patrons (alumni had the same borrowing privileges as students) open seven days a week from 8:00 a.m. to midnight. The library also had a separate coatroom, hourly mail pickup, and stamps, postcards, and stationery for sale at the loan desk. In 1883 he inherited a collection of 50,000 indifferently cataloged and classified volumes located in nine separate departments. Five years later the 100,000-volume collection was cataloged by ALA rules and classified by the decimal scheme in a central campus library open to all members of the Columbia community. In his first year circulation increased 500 percent, and in the five-and-a-half years he was librarian, he doubled the acquisitions budget, quadrupled the personnel budget, and structured a collection development policy. But he had help. Upon assuming his duties, Dewey hired six women. Columbia men could only grouse; no rule prevented Dewey from employing them.

Late nineteenth-century Canadian universities generally followed three models: (1) British institutions; (2) theologically controlled European universities; and (3) U.S. land grant colleges. McGill University had 11,000 volumes in 1876. In 1886 the University of Toronto held 27,000 volumes. Three years later Université Laval (formerly the Jesuit College in Quebec City) reported 100,000 volumes. By 1900 most Anglophile Canadian librarians shifted from British methods and ideas to model U.S. library institutions and services. Elsewhere in Canada, however, academic library development remained stagnant through the twentieth century's first half.

University libraries across the continent erected new buildings incorporating the nineteenth century's most influential structural modification for libraries—the multitier stack. Harvard's Gore Hall, built in 1877, consisted of six levels of structurally connected bookstacks covered with an exterior shell that per cubic foot allowed greater storage of the vast quantities of books made necessary by higher education's new requirements. Other university library buildings adapted this structure. Yale opened one in 1890, Pennsylvania in 1891, Toronto in 1892, McGill in 1893, Northwestern in 1894, Illinois in 1897, and Princeton in 1898. All hired experienced librarians to manage them. These professionals expanded hours of opening, initiated new reference services, improved bibliographic organization and access tools, and conducted instruction in library use. Before the turn of the century, many academic libraries increased their holdings tenfold. Some growth came from gifts, some from the assimilation of literary society libraries (with the new curriculum they seemed less necessary), most from increased budgets.

Shifts in service imperatives had roots in ideas about reference service, which academic librarians learned from the public library world. In the latter, reference services grew from on-demand, part-time guidance in catalog use and suggestions on choices of reading. Another part of this service imperative evolved into a "special collection," initially a concentration of books (not necessarily rare) on a specific subject. In subsequent decades, "rare books" became associated with canonical texts (especially in history and literature). When Harvard's Widener Library opened in 1915 it contained a "Treasure Room" for rare books. The New York Public Library established a Rare Book Division in 1914, and in subsequent years rare book rooms also opened at Princeton, the Library of Congress, Michigan, Wellesley, and Yale. Among the first special collections on campuses to cluster around a specific subject were law libraries. Harvard established a Law School in 1817, but not until Nathan Dane donated the profits from his *Abridgement of American Law* (1830) did Harvard's law library experience much growth. When Law School dean Christopher Langdell pioneered the case method of legal pedagogy later adopted by most law schools, access to large law library collections became essential.

Yet not until 1892 did Harvard hire its first professional to manage and develop the collection. By that time legal publishing made acquisitions easier, if not less expensive. In 1873 Frank Shephard began his case citator system to enable researchers to locate all subsequent opinions citing any reported case or statute. Competition to market systems to control this emerging literature was inevitable. In 1879 the West Publishing Company began the National Reporter System, a unified mechanism for reporting all federal and state court cases, and in 1887 developed a key-number digest scheme for indexing case law. While all these developments made law librarians partners in the practice and study of law, they also tended to separate them from other library professionals.

Public library construction also witnessed significant change. The first Boston Public Library (1856) had two galleries, the Cincinnati Public Library (1873) four, and the George Peabody Library (1878) five. After midcentury, architect Henry Richardson abandoned the Classical and Gothic styles in the one university and eight public libraries he designed by adapting Romanesque structures he witnessed in Europe. They included massive rounded arches and round or octagonal stair towers. Some of these features found their way into the Westmount Public Library in Montreal (1889), the Warder Library in Springfield, Ohio (1890), and the Cossitt Library in Memphis (1893). When Charles McKim modeled Boston's new building on Copley Square after the Bibliothèque Sainte-Geneviève by designing its facade as a Renaissance palazzo and placing its principal services on the second floor, several public library buildings followed the example (the New York Public in 1911; the Detroit Public in 1921).

U.S. AND CANADIAN LIBRARIANSHIP, 1893–1914

For U.S. and Canadian librarians, twentieth-century librarianship commenced the last decade of the nineteenth and was symbolized by two events evolving at the Chicago World's Fair in 1893 and the Library of Congress. By this time Canadian librarianship found synergy and cooperation easier with peers to the south than those across the Atlantic.

The Chicago World's Fair

The first event occurred in Chicago in 1893, where ALA (whose membership by that time included prominent Canadian librarians) gathered for its annual conference in July. For fourteen years the association labored under the motto "The best reading for the largest number at the least cost," which succinctly summarized not only a professional jurisdiction, but also reflected a professional goal of making the library a force for an ordered, enlightened, educated, and informed citizenry.

To identify the "best reading," librarians looked to a core of white Anglo-Saxon mostly Protestant (WASP) males who had the cultural pedigree and literary authority to determine what were the *belles lettres* of the day (many, in fact, ran the literary journals or served as regular reviewers in their pages), or who possessed the educational titles to research, publish, and teach in increasingly specialized areas of science, social science, and humanities on campuses across the continent. Most shared an ideology of learned reading. "Good" reading, this ideology dictated, led to good social behavior, "bad" reading to bad social behavior. (Bibliographies for youth Caroline Hewins and others produced were grounded on this ideology.) The late nineteenth-century information explosion made it relatively easy for experts with cultural pedigrees or educational titles to identify "good" reading to audiences they thought needed their evaluations. Sometimes they disagreed (were *Huckleberry Finn* and *Red Badge of Courage* "good" or "bad" literature?), but for the most part they found the Western world canons they inherited comfortable and familiar, and their recommendations for good reading were more alike than different. Librarians regarded bestseller lists regularly compiled and published after 1895 as barometers of changing tastes and fashion, but not as indicators of literary value. As the "good reading" identified by expert communities found its way to library shelves, librarians became convinced they provided "neutral" service by allowing all to access it. They did not perceive cultural bias impacting judgments of "quality" as obstacles to a professional "neutrality."

At the Chicago conference a significant marker of this ideology was the "Model Library," a 5,000-volume collection of books recommended for any public library by a committee of disciplinary experts and librarians who screened review journals for authoritative opinions. Compilers suggested a certain balance in subject categories. For example, 14 percent of citations were classified history, 12 percent biography, 15 percent fiction. The latter contrasted sharply with actual circulation figures, however; most American and Canadian public libraries experienced circulation rates of 65–75 percent fiction since they opened. That troubled librarians, and to help them combat this huge discrepancy the U.S. Bureau of Education published a bibliography of the Model Library as *Catalog of "A.L.A." Library* and made it available as a government document that congressmen could distribute free to libraries in constituent communities.

But ALA leaders did not spend much time discussing "best reading" during the conference. That problem, they believed, would take care of itself over time if only they persisted. In 1893 librarians were convinced that by inducing the public to read quality literature and consult reliable information about contemporary issues, the library would inevitably contribute to progress and social order. Dewey called this conviction the "library faith," an ideology driven by a library "spirit." Because that "faith" had sedimented into a professional *mentalité* by the late nineteenth century, ALA leaders felt it unnecessary to concentrate much conference attention on the "best reading." Instead, they showed more concern for "the largest number at the least cost." Already by 1893 embryonic efforts to capitalize on this ideology and publicize the value of library use began to manifest themselves on streetcar posters, local newspaper columns, and booklists distributed at post offices, neighborhood stores, and book deposit stations. This suited Dewey (in 1893, ALA's president) and his allies. For years, they pushed libraries to standardize library supplies and forms and adopt centralized systems such as a common classification scheme and uniform subject headings to increase the utility and efficiency of library management. Through the Library Bureau, Dewey and the ALA placed librarians squarely in the efficiency movement often identified with the Progressive Era. In addition, they sought to expand services to more Americans, including immigrants, children, women, businesses, and the physically challenged.

Because more libraries opened stacks to users, circulation systems constituted another form of service librarians made more efficient. Users came to expect a routine. Public card catalogs allowed them to identify items they wanted, and by jotting down notations they found on catalog cards that corresponded to notations on book spines, they went directly to the stacks to find books arranged on library shelves in the subject categories of increasingly common classification schemes like the Dewey Decimal, which from its second edition (1885) emphasized practical expedience more than theoretical sophistication. Open stacks and circulation systems themselves reinforced momentum to keep classification schemes practical.

Methods for recordkeeping also improved. By 1900 the number of patrons frequenting libraries made circulation's ledger system cumbersome. Some tried a two-card system: one card contained book information and a second borrower information. When the Newark (New Jersey) Public Library modified this system in 1896, it created the model for most circulation systems for the next three decades. Basic components included a book-pocket pasted inside each book's back cover, a book card inserted in the book-pocket, a date due slip, and a borrower's card. When patrons brought books to the desk, an attendant stamped a date on all three records and removed the book card. When patrons returned books, an attendant stamped the borrower's card again and replaced the book card in the book-pocket. Shortly thereafter, a rubber date stamp clipped to a pencil end became a necessary component of circulation desk supplies and helped to caricature female librarians who routinely stored them in their hairdos.

As evidence of a commitment to service "at the least cost," the 1893 ALA conference was carefully structured to consist of presentations on practical matters of library expertise and management that the Bureau of Education agreed to publish as a "Handbook of Library Economy," like the ALA *Catalog* government document novice librarians could obtain free through their congressmen. As evidence of its commitment to reaching "the greatest number," the ALA hosted meetings for three sections representing specialized library interests: college section for academic libraries, a publishing section to push for more bibliographical aids like the *Catalog*, and an Association of State Librarians (which quickly disbanded into two new sections, one for law librarians, the other for state librarians). In 1893 the library profession manifested signs of specialization that characterized other Progressive Era professions.

Library of Congress

When President William McKinley appointed Boston Public librarian Herbert Putnam librarian of Congress in 1899 (the first time a professional led the institution), LC had already assumed the trappings of a national library, in large part because Spofford laid the groundwork. In 1872, for example, he argued that three things made a separate building essential—fireproof materials, efficient organization, and sufficient space to accommodate 3,000,000 volumes. Within a year Congress authorized a committee to plan a building. Twenty-seven architects submitted plans; Smithmeyer & Pelz's Italian Renaissance design won the competition. In subsequent years Spofford consistently increased LC responsibilities. In 1875 he argued the library needed an expert to take care of the library's growing historical manuscripts collection. A year later he reported that for lack of space the library stacked many of its 199,000 volumes on floors and in hallways. In 1886 Congress appropriated $500,000 for a fireproof building east of the Capitol. Although Spofford had reason to rejoice, he realized Congress had not provided the $35,000 necessary to acquire land for the building. On Congress's last day, he hand-carried the bill authorizing the $35,000 to the White House and obtained the president's signature thirty-five minutes before both houses were scheduled to adjourn. Construction started October 28; on March 2, 1889, Congress approved $6,000,000 to carry out final plans. As the building neared completion, the Joint Committee held hearings on the scope of a national library and how it should be organized. Several librarians testified, including Dewey and Herbert Putnam. No one at the hearings questioned

LC's status as a national library—Spofford had obviously met his goal, but at age 71 it was time for a new administrator in tune with modern management principles to take over. When McKinley appointed diplomat John Russell Young in 1897 as librarian of Congress, Spofford became chief assistant librarian. Together, it was hoped, they would manage the move into the new building, which formally opened on November 1.

Although inexperienced as librarian, Young proved adept at management. He persuaded Congress to authorize 108 positions (up from 66) to meet new demands and address nagging problems (Spofford had concentrated on building collections and neglected cataloging and classification). He enlisted foreign service officers to acquire foreign documents, extended Main Reading Room hours (9:00 a.m. to 10:00 p.m.), and initiated a trust fund so the library could quickly acquire unique items the normal budget process might not accommodate. Under his leadership LC founded its Music Division and opened a Reading Room for the Blind. Among the major initiatives Young undertook was the *Library of Congress Classification* by James C. M. Hanson and Charles Martel. Although they considered Dewey's scheme and Cutter's Expansive Classification, they rejected both for several reasons: books often belonged to several subject categories; the schemes were difficult to revise and expand; many had difficulty accommodating new subjects brought by new knowledge. Their scheme, they hoped, would minimize these problems. In 1898 Hanson also began a subject headings list for LC's new dictionary catalog.

When Putnam succeeded Young (who died in 1899), he continued to emphasize reclassification. Initially, it organized only the library's 1,000,000-volume collection, but because it also accommodated new subjects without multiplying class numbers, other libraries with fast-growing collections began to adopt it. But Putnam also moved in other directions. He initiated a "National Union Catalog" project that throughout the twentieth century recorded books copyrighted in the United States and printed works collected and accessioned by hundreds of cooperating libraries throughout North America. Based on the bibliographic database LC generated, he made available for purchase LC printed catalog cards that conformed to ALA cataloging conventions. And since LC also provided subject analysis (*Subject Headings Used in the Dictionary Catalogues of the Library of Congress* appeared between 1909 and 1914) and a uniform set of added entries, librarianship's professional practices conformed to a centralized scheme. By 1901 his staff increased to 130, accessions from 31,000 in 1899 to 76,000 in 1901, and an annual appropriation from $340,000 in 1900 to $560,000 in 1902. From a distance, Canadian librarians (who still lacked a national library) watched.

Other Libraries and Library Agencies in the United States and Canada

Putnam was not the only one to preside over a federal institution pushing to become a U.S. national library. An 1862 law established a Department of Agriculture with responsibility to acquire and preserve agricultural publications. By 1876 the department had a collection of 7,000 uncataloged and unclassified volumes. In 1893 the library hired William Parker Cutter and with Josephine A. Clarke (who succeeded him in 1901), Cutter created a dictionary catalog of the growing collections, opened a reading room, and developed a cooperative acquisitions relationship with land-grant colleges and agricultural experiment stations across the country. At the same time, however, he and Clarke created a decentralized system that spread collections to departmental bureau libraries. By century's end the library held 70,000 books and pamphlets. In 1907 Claribel Barnett assumed control. During her tenure, she initiated photocopying services and extended interlibrary loan, and in 1934 negotiated an agreement with the American Documentation Institute to provide microfilm and photocopy services. Canada's Department of Agriculture also founded a library in 1910.

In 1858 Vancouver Island voted appropriations for a library for the House of Assembly, but not until 1893 did the legislature appoint a librarian, who found the library incomplete, disorganized, and of little practical value. A federally supported parliamentary library in Ottawa emerged as the country's largest when Canada became a democratic federation in 1867, and when it moved into Canada's first building specifically designed as a library in 1876, it carried a collection of 84,000 volumes. Manitoba's Legislative Assembly librarian was especially concerned with patron decorum. In 1884 he issued a set of rules prohibiting smoking, spitting on the floor, and bringing dogs into the reading room. Enabling legislation authorizing Canada's provincial communities to tax themselves to support public libraries first materialized in the late nineteenth century. Most were modeled on Great Britain's 1850 Public Library Act rather than U.S. legislation. Ontario adopted the country's first public library legislation in 1882. British Columbia followed in 1891, Manitoba in 1899, Saskatchewan in 1906, Alberta in 1907, New Brunswick in 1929, Nova Scotia in 1937, and Quebec (where the Oeuvre des bons livres de Montreal was still highly influential) not until 1959. In many cases this legislation enabled communities with mechanics' and school/township libraries in mostly Anglophone Canada to transition to public libraries, whose collections quickly added more popular novels. By 1900 fiction accounted for over 50 percent of most Canadian public library collections.

In the United States Massachusetts established a Free Public Library Commission in 1890 to advocate for public libraries. Other states followed. In New York, in 1893 the State Library sent out its first traveling libraries in small collections packed in sturdy oak boxes that doubled as bookshelves so collections could easily circulate to rural communities. The system was not the continent's first. In the early nineteenth century John McLaughlin monitored the North Pacific Coast's first traveling library out of Fort Vancouver. In 1898 the British Columbia Provincial Library Commission ran a traveling library system. Within three years thirty-five libraries circulated, each consisting of one hundred books transported in portable and lockable boxes for a three-month period to sites willing to pay six dollars per transaction. In 1905 ninety libraries circulated the province, many transported free by the Canadian Pacific Railway. By 1914 120 libraries containing 3,700 volumes circulated 2,722 titles (including some Norwegian and Swedish titles) to provincial schools, women's institutes, literary societies, and reading rooms. In the early 1900s Washington County (Maryland) librarian Mary L. Titcomb took a bookwagon to the far corners of her county. By 1900 thirty states had developed a traveling library service. Wisconsin, Oregon, and California were especially successful. Because many Wisconsin residents were isolated, a Wisconsin Free Library Commission official reported in 1909, the commission looked upon its traveling library service as an educational and social mechanism to Americanize immigrants, provide useful information to farmers, uplift the working classes, and occupy juveniles with morally acceptable literature. California pushed traveling library services in part to encourage the establishment of county libraries. As librarians continued to push "for the greatest number," traveling libraries became a tradition.

By that time library education also expanded. The Pratt Institute Library School opened in Brooklyn in 1890, the Drexel Institute Library Program in Philadelphia in

1892, the same year classes began at Chicago's Armour Institute Department of Library Science. Apprenticeship programs also operated out of the Los Angeles and Denver public libraries. In Canada, McGill inaugurated a summer program in 1904, the University of Toronto in 1911. (Not until 1927 did McGill turn its program into a full-year training course; not until 1928 did Toronto begin giving diplomas.) Library associations also proliferated. The New York State Library Association organized in 1890; Iowa founded one months later, and in rapid succession before the century's end so did thirteen other states. Chicago organized a Library Club in 1891, the District of Columbia in 1894. In 1898 four physicians and four medical librarians founded the Medical Library Association. Six months later representatives of ten state libraries founded the National Association of State Librarians. And at the 1900 conference ALA held in Montréal, Canadians resolved to form a Canadian Library Association. Efforts languished, however, and instead provincial associations emerged. The Ontario Library Association organized in 1901, the British Columbia Library Association in 1911.

The century's last decade also saw the establishment of privately endowed U.S. research libraries, especially in Chicago. On its north side, Walter Newberry estate trustees created the Newberry Library in 1887. About the same time, the will of John Crerar provided for another research library on its south side. Trustees from both agreed to specialize without duplication. The Newberry, which opened in 1893, concentrated on music theory, European map-making, the history of printing, Renaissance books and manuscripts, materials focusing on contact between Caucasian immigrants and Native Americans, and genealogy. The Crerar, which opened in 1897, concentrated on the social sciences, and technology and science (pure and applied).

Professional Practices and Publishing

By that time the world of librarianship was beginning to settle into patterns, all developing specialties that focused on "the best reading for the largest number at the least cost." Setting up mechanisms to identify "the best reading" turned into a growing industry. Over time, librarians came to "know" good books; but with one exception, that knowledge was the end product of a filtering system evolved by publishers on which that industry depended. For example, in 1901 the H. W. Wilson Company began publishing indexes like *Readers' Guide to Periodical Literature*, which, in its initial issue, covered twenty periodicals (including *Atlantic Monthly*, *Current Literature*, *Dial*, and *North American Review*), each edited by a literary authority wanting to publish only quality material. Libraries quickly subscribed to *Readers' Guide* then began favoring subscriptions to periodicals the *Guide* covered precisely because they were indexed. For the rest of the century, modification of the *Guide*'s scope came slowly.

Similarly, within the decade Wilson was also issuing bibliographical aids such as *Fiction Catalog* and *Children's Catalog*, both designed to help librarians identify "best reading." Like the ALA *Catalogs*, *Fiction Catalog* took its cues from outside experts whose reviews appeared in Wilson-indexed periodicals. *Booklist* magazine, a monthly ALA began in 1905 to guide untrained staff in small public libraries, mirrored this pattern. Over time, more librarians contributed reviews, but their evaluations were generally based on criteria they learned as undergraduates. In 1908 Arthur Bostwick summarized the profession's criteria for selection in his ALA presidential address titled "The Librarian as Censor." Three reasons to reject a book, he said: "badness" (anything reflecting undesirable morality); "falsity" (factual inaccuracies); and "ugliness" (material offensive to decency). If his ideas reflected the profession's position, librarians were as concerned with what to keep out of their collections as with what to include.

In 1896 the Chicago office of Dewey's Library Bureau began issuing the monthly *Public Libraries*, deliberately designed to contrast with *Library Journal* by directly addressing the practical interests of increasing numbers of small Midwest public libraries. There hundreds of communities were successfully applying for grants from Andrew Carnegie but later experienced difficulties finding trained staff to manage the buildings and their contents. Its first issue included John Cotton Dana's "Library Primer," later reprinted in booklet form. *Library Journal* continued to function as ALA's official organ until 1907, when ALA issued its own *Bulletin*. ALA publishing ventures benefited from interest on a $100,000 endowment Carnegie donated in 1902. Part was used for *Booklist*, part to offset publication costs of works like Alice B. Kroeger's *Guide to the Study and Use of Reference Books* (1902), predecessor to many twentieth-century editions of the *Guide to Reference Books* by Isadore Gilbert Mudge, Constance Winchell, and Eugene P. Sheehy.

Unlike *Booklist* and the ALA or *Fiction Catalogs*, however, *Children's Catalog* did not rely on authorities outside the profession. That mostly librarians supplied its contents reflected a demographic characteristic librarianship shared with few other professions. By 1920 88 percent of American librarians were women. Anne Carroll Moore, whose maxim "the right book into the hands of the right child at the right time" became an oft-quoted children's librarianship motto, began story hours at the Pratt Institute in 1896 (two years later Pratt taught the first course in children's librarianship) and incorporated them into routine New York Public Library services shortly thereafter. In 1897 the Carnegie Library of Pittsburgh hired its first director of children's work. In 1900 it started a two-year Training Class for Children's Librarians that combined classroom instruction with practical experience. Between 1904 and 1905 librarians told over 600 story hours to 460 groups of Pittsburgh children.

While many librarians pushed to extend "the greatest number" by age, only a few pushed to extend it by race. In 1905 black librarians George T. Settle and Thomas Fountain Blue established the Louisville Apprentice Class at the African American branch of the Louisville (Kentucky) Public Library to train black female (mostly southern) library workers who could get training no other way. The class continued until 1924. In a 1915 ALA conference paper titled "What of the Black and Yellow Races?" Louisville (Kentucky) Public librarian William F. Yust outlined obstacles African Americans faced gaining access to the free public libraries in the Jim Crow South. Several years later ALA established a Work with Negroes Round Table that accomplished little more than talk.

Influence of Andrew Carnegie

By the time Wilson started to publish catalogs and indexes and ALA successfully pushed the library "science" inherent in the ALA motto, steel magnate and labor union foe Andrew Carnegie had begun to give away much of his fortune. Between 1890 and his death in 1919, Carnegie gave $4,282,000 for 108 academic library buildings in the United States, and $41,000,000 for 1,679 public library buildings in 1,412 U.S. communities. To communities requesting architectural advice, Carnegie sent six models. Each contained an auditorium for community activities; some contained smaller rooms to accommodate local club meetings. Almost all followed Carnegie's models (one reason

Carnegie libraries look alike), and by World War I these buildings had not only become community centers—places people gathered for exhibits and programs of all sorts at which they modeled acceptable social behaviors—but also repositories for useful information and the kinds of printed stories readers wanted. Popular fiction—not the "best reading" librarianship pushed most in its professional practice—continued to account for two-thirds to three-quarters of total circulation. The equation was simple—public libraries either provided it or they lost readers. Most buildings went up in areas previously without public libraries (50 percent of Wisconsin's public libraries originated with Carnegie grants); most grew out of local women's club efforts to improve community culture. As a group these women's clubs campaigned for library legislation; in many cases, their members also served as local librarians. By 1923 Carnegie libraries served 32 percent of U.S. citizens.

In Canada, Carnegie spent $2,500,000 on 125 library buildings between 1901 and 1924, the vast majority (111) in Ontario, all but one (St. John, New Brunswick) west of the Ottawa River. Similar to those in the United States and other Dominion countries, most emphasized simplicity, functionalism, and prudent use of materials and space in a classically designed building. The Toronto Public Library was a prototype. Made possible by the Ontario Free Libraries Act of 1882, it grew out of the former Toronto Mechanics Institute Library. In 1884 it included 434 books as a lending library for "working classes." To expand its collections, the librarian took buying trips to Europe and on one occasion even sued the city to honor its obligation to provide operating funds, a case he ultimately won. By century's end the library had a collection largely in English, with healthy doses of French and German titles and a commitment to collect Canadiana. In pursuit of a Carnegie grant, in 1903 city officials promised to allocate at least $35,000 annually if he donated $350,000 for a new central library and three branches. Although local opposition surfaced, library advocates ignored their complaints.

Things took a different turn in Montreal, where the climate for accepting gifts was radically different. For religious, linguistic, and social reasons, in 1903 Montreal declined a Carnegie grant. In general, French-speaking Canadians looked elsewhere for their library models. In 1911, for example, Monsignor Francois-Azaric Dugas of St. Boniface, Manitoba, announced the opening of a parish library to serve French-speaking Catholics. Prairie provinces, on the other hand, welcomed Carnegie money. The Winnipeg Public Library, established in 1895, moved into its new Carnegie building in 1905, then obtained supplementary funds from Carnegie to expand it in 1908 and construct two branches. Saskatoon ultimately turned down his offer of $30,000 as inadequate to the city's needs. Calgary opened its Carnegie in 1911. In Dawson (Yukon), local officials used Carnegie money to erect a two-story wood building because of permafrost, then for insulation stuffed the facility's wall cavities with sixteen wagonloads of sawdust before opening in 1904. The new public library put out of business the Standard Library Restaurant and Hotel, which up to that time offered guests and customers services that included books, beds, bath, and bar.

Carnegie's philanthropy generated a competition between communities to establish libraries; it also encouraged other philanthropic efforts. Between 1890 and 1906 U.S. philanthropists donated $34,000,000 to fund public libraries. Baltimore's Enoch Pratt Library, Memphis's Cossitt Memorial Library, and Asheville's (North Carolina) Pack Memorial Library all started from donations by wealthy individuals. Library philanthropy took other forms. In 1896 the San Juan Bautista (California) Library Auxiliary organized to help raise funds; it served as a precursor for a "Friends of the Library" movement, which found its first American presence in the Friends of the Library of Glen Ellyn (Illinois) Free Public Library in 1922.

Although the Boston Public Library served as a prototype for public library development in the late nineteenth century, the New York Public Library (NYPL) evolved a unique profile in the early twentieth. Established in 1895 as a free public reference library, it was created out of a merger of three corporations—the Astor Library, the Lenox Library, and the Tilden Trust (which made provisions for a New York City free library). First director John Shaw Billings helped design the marble central building New York erected and maintained on Fifth Avenue and 42nd Street, and established its priorities as a bifurcated institution—one part a privately supported Reference Department dedicated to research and study, the other a publicly supported Circulation Department devoted to popular reading through local collections and services of thirty-nine branches Carnegie money erected. Use of the central facility by New York's millions of multicultural, multilingual, and recently arrived residents regularly outran the library's ability to meet demand. Branch libraries focused on neighborhood needs, and in the early twentieth century extended beyond simplistic Americanization programs that characterized many other U.S. urban public library systems. In the 1920s NYPL's Harlem branch became the site for the Schomburg Center for Research in Black Culture so central to the Harlem Renaissance.

Although the NYPL's branch system was not the first, it probably best demonstrated the value of these local facilities. Most branches were established for one or more of four reasons: (1) they took pressure off demand for popular materials at the main library; (2) because of their locations they had a better chance of reaching nonusers; (3) they enabled some people who could not afford public transportation to obtain library materials closer to home; and (4) they initiated and sustained specialized services to unique communities, especially non-English-speaking communities. A fifth reason became obvious after they opened. Branch library users turned the public space branches provided into community centers for activities that helped formed a sense of neighborhood and assimilated newcomers. In many neighborhoods branch library service built deep loyalties toward the public library system among local populations that later paid substantial dividends when politics and economics combined to threaten library budgets.

Children's Librarianship

The specializations in librarianship evident in the late nineteenth century accelerated in the early twentieth. The Cleveland Public Library's experience shows shifts in attitudes toward serving children. When it opened in 1869, children were not allowed to enter; young adults (YA) over fourteen were permitted to check out books—with parental permission. As circulation to young adults quickly rose to 15 percent of the library's total, officials decided to stop buying YA books. However, William Howard Brett, who became director in 1884, reinstituted a separate budget for children's books, opened a separate children's room in 1895, and hired Effie Lee Power to staff it. In 1896 the library eliminated all age restrictions. Within two years Power pioneered a Library League with the motto "clean hands, clean hearts, clean books" and membership in excess of 12,000 children. Other public libraries copied her model. When thousands of children tried to use the new Boston Public Library building on Copley Square in 1895, officials established a separate room for a children's collection. In 1897 the Pratt Institute said its recently opened special children's room was necessary to reduce numbers in the delivery room and to prevent children from annoying adults. An 1894 survey of 145 U.S. and Canadian public libraries also showed two-thirds allowed teachers to check out book collections for student classroom and home use, and one-third made visits to local schools.

Armed with bibliographies like Hewins's (whose first edition was updated eight years later when the ALA Publishing Section issued John F. Sargent's *Reading for the Young* through the Library Bureau), they quickly began to network. Anne Carroll Moore, who pioneered the NYPL's children's services division, exercised considerable influence over children's book publishers through newly formed children's book departments. In 1900 librarians organized a Children's Library Club within ALA. Review journals like *Booklist* and *Horn Book* (established in 1924) helped them forge professional consensus on "best," and new editions of H. W. Wilson's *Children's Catalog* (first published in 1909) reinforced these literary canons. In 1922 they began recognizing children's books they judged best (the Newbery Medal), and in 1938 the best illustrated (the Caldecott Medal). The Toronto Public Library began story hours in World War I, and by the early 1920s had turned them into "national story hours" to familiarize Toronto's children with Canadian history and heroes. In 1922 Lillian H. Smith established the successful Boys and Girls House as a branch library service to promote the "right" kind of reading for children. It represented the British Empire's first library solely for use of children's materials. In hundreds of public libraries across the continent collections like these became staple fare for the ubiquitous weekly children's story hour, often broadcast on a local radio station. They also served as a major source of voluntary reading materials for local schoolchildren.

New Libraries, Associations, and Services

Another specialization emerged in 1901 when Wisconsin's Charles McCarthy set up a Legislative Reference Library to research and draft bills for state legislators. California established a similar service in 1905, and within a decade thirty other states followed suit. Herbert Putnam hired McCarthy as a consultant when LC established its Congressional Research Service in 1915. Some urban libraries set up similar services for municipal governments, including the Enoch Pratt in 1907, Milwaukee in 1908, Kansas City in 1910, St. Louis and Toronto in 1911 (the latter located the service in City Hall), and New York in 1913. In 1860 Congress established a Government Printing Office (GPO), but the New Printing Act of 1895 also created the office of Superintendent of Documents and formalized a depository program based on congressional districts. As GPO librarian, Adelaide Hasse developed a classification scheme in the late nineteenth century that organized the 1,300 depository libraries (two-thirds in academic libraries, the remainder in public and state libraries). These depositories became intertwined with map librarianship when the GPO assumed responsibility for maps collected by the U.S. Geological Survey (established in 1895) and Defense Mapping Agency activities that grew out of the Army Map Services the federal government established in World War II.

The Association of Medical Librarians (later Medical Library Association [MLA]) organized in 1898, and shortly thereafter began the *Bulletin of the Medical Library Association*. MLA existed because of John Shaw Billings's successes as surgeon general. Under his direction the office initiated the *Index-Catalogue of the Surgeon General's Library* (a book catalog of the library's holdings) and its companion, *Index Medicus: A*

Monthly Classified Record of the Current Medical Literature of the World. By the time
he left for the New York Public Library in 1895, Billings had positioned the Surgeon
General's Library at the center of North American medical librarianship.

A 1905 American Historical Association survey revealed that just under half of the
country's seventy historical societies had libraries. Most notable were in Kansas, Massachusetts, Pennsylvania, and Wisconsin, each with collections of over 100,000 volumes.
The oldest (primarily in the East) were generally independent membership organizations receiving little public funding. Newer societies (largely in the Midwest and West)
received state support, and in some cases (like the Wisconsin Historical Society) were
chartered as official state government agencies. In 1906 several law librarians broke away
from ALA to found the American Association of Law Libraries (AALL), in part because
they identified more closely with lawyers, in part because unique bibliographic control
systems for legal materials had developed to control the literature their patrons wanted.
Within two years AALL had seventy-five members and published the *Index to Legal
Periodicals* and *Law Library Journal*. Because so many law libraries were also part of
state libraries, AALL met jointly with the National Association of State Law Libraries
until 1936, then switched to meet at American Bar Association conferences. The turn
of the century also witnessed the emergence of "special libraries." Several precedents
existed in the nineteenth century. In 1871, for example, the Confederation Life Insurance
Company established a library in Toronto. In 1898 the Sun Life Assurance Company
established one in Montreal. In 1907 four national engineering societies established the
Engineering Societies Library in New York City to serve its members and the general
public. In Newark, New Jersey, public library director John Cotton Dana developed a
"Business Branch," and based on his experiences decided to join with several corporate
librarians, including Daniel Nash Handy, to organize the Special Libraries Association
(SLA) in 1909. A year later SLA began *Special Libraries*. In 1880 Handy helped organize the Insurance Library Association of Boston (ILAB). Handy modified the DDC to
meet his own needs and started the *ILAB Bulletin* to index fire insurance and fire protec-
tion/prevention literature. As SLA president in 1913, Handy initiated projects that led to
the *Public Affairs Information Service Bulletin* and the *Industrial Arts Index*, predecessor
of the *Business Periodicals Index*, both eventually published by Wilson. Over the years
SLA established divisions, including Insurance and Employee Benefits (1922), Finance
(1925), Business (1934, which merged with Finance in 1955), and Advertising and Marketing (1942). A newspaper group organized in 1923, but with limitations. Employers
told members to discuss mutual concerns, not resource sharing.

Turn-of-the-century libraries diversified in other ways. In 1867 William Frederick
Poole set up subject-oriented reading rooms at the Cincinnati Public Library; he later
built this concept into the Newberry Library's architecture when he became its director
in 1888. In 1902 the Carnegie Library of Pittsburgh became the first U.S. public library
to have a separate department for its science and technology service. That same year
the Cincinnati Public Library opened a "useful arts" room devoted to applied science.
Brooklyn (1905), Newark (1908), St. Louis (1910), and Minneapolis (1910) followed.
And as libraries departmentalized, some employees unionized. In 1917 the first library
union formed at NYPL. Within two years similar unions formed at LC and the District
of Columbia, and the Boston Public libraries.

Professional concerns about "least cost" lost no momentum at century's turn. How
to treat serials most libraries collected constituted a major problem. The Boston Public
established a periodicals division when it opened its Boylston Street building in 1858.

LC established a separate periodicals department when it moved to its new building in 1897; so did NYPL in 1911. In 1886 Frederick Faxon started the Faxon Subscription Agency, which for a fee offered to consolidate orders into one invoice for a library's multiple subscriptions. In 1913 the Rand Company invented the Kardex, a file incorporating a system with ready-made uniform cards in slide-out trays that combined many elements of serials maintenance.

In its *Manual of Library Economy* (1907) ALA argued every large library ought to have two management sectors—"administration" and departments. The former monitored the latter, including departments for book selection, periodicals, classification, cataloging, and reading rooms. The *Manual's* 1921 edition reconfigured the four divisions, each of which could be subdepartmentalized. For example, acquisitions might contain subdepartments of periodicals, binding, gifts, exchanges, and book buying; "reading rooms" might have subdepartments for reference service and reserved books, and cataloging would include subdepartments of cataloging and classification. "Administration," however, retained "book selection" as a department directly under its control. A subsequent ALA study of staffing patterns in academic, public, school, and special libraries showed that governing boards controlled the library's major activities through its director. The hierarchy was clear; most power resided at the top. Individual staff members reported to department heads, who then reported to the library director, who in turn reported to a governing board.

BRIDGING THE WARS: 1914–1945

World War I

Because of its Dominion status, Canada became part of World War I shortly after it broke out in Europe in August, 1914. Canadian public libraries responded quickly. Many worked through the YMCA; others developed unique services. In Ontario, for example, the Windsor Public Library stocked a table with stationery and invited users to write letters to men in uniform. The library also set up a special reading room for women who worked in local war-related industries. Toronto hosted a training camp on its exhibition grounds, and the public library organized a camp library to meet trainees' reading needs. But some libraries were highly prescriptive about those reading needs. One Ottawa public library director worried about the influence of pro-German books and pacifist pamphlets in library collections. In 1917 the *Ontario Library Review* gave his concerns wider circulation in an article he wrote titled "A Contemptible Book."

Between 1914 and April 1917 the United States remained a neutral power. Once it entered the war, however, any pretense of a neutral U.S. library service disappeared. For example, public libraries willingly circulated materials printed by the government's Committee on Public Information and its Food Conservation Program, and opened their buildings to all types of war work, including Americanization programs designed to channel immigrant loyalties (especially German American). The ALA Library War Service Committee organized library services for thirty-six training camps to which thousands of libraries channeled books and periodicals collected for soldiers and sailors. "Knowledge Wins" posters designed for book collection campaigns underlined the social utility of the public library. Many librarians used the "Army Index"—a list of sometimes pro-German, sometimes pacifist materials the army did not want in training camp libraries—to purify their own collections. Some librarians even burned books the Army Index cited. At the same time, librarians watched these collections accept books one Minnesota volunteer labeled "decent but not too highbrow." By war's end, the typical camp library collection averaged 65 percent fiction. The latest edition of the ALA *Catalog* (1911), on the other hand, recommended that public library collections contain only 10.8 percent fiction.

World War I occasioned a number of other developments. Libraries in army hospitals during the war and veterans' hospitals thereafter worked to develop "bibliotherapy" as one additional approach to help heal the sick and wounded. Although as early as 1821 the Massachusetts General Hospital housed a library with books considered recreational, bibliotherapy was different. Army and veterans' hospitals built on the more recent experiences of E. Kathleen Jones, who initiated the first bibliotherapy program at the McLean Hospital (a privately endowed institution for the mentally ill) in Waverly, Massachusetts, in 1904. Working with resident physicians, she identified specific books on specific subjects for specific patients, and in her work claimed many successes that echoed the profession's ideology of learned reading. Alice S. Tyler, secretary of the Iowa Library Commission, followed Jones's lead, modeled a program of bibliotherapeutic work for patient libraries at state hospitals that other states emulated, and helped ALA form a hospital library work committee that helped organize hospital library services for World War I soldiers and sailors.

From the turn of the century, the Library Department of the National Education Association (NEA), the Library Section of the National Council of Teachers of English, and the ALA had pushed for expansion of school library services. By war's end, however, NEA pressed for separate libraries staffed and organized by school systems specifically for teachers and students, and specifically to support the school curriculum. *Certain Standards for Elementary School Libraries* appeared in 1923, and shortly thereafter some state and local governments began funding school library supervisors, issuing school library handbooks, and publishing recommended book lists. The Great Depression interrupted growth, but in postwar America school libraries began to acquire nonprint media for instruction and many quickly shifted to "instructional materials centers" or "school library and media centers."

Changing Attitudes toward Fiction

World War I also marked a shift in the profession's ideology of learned reading. Because authorities as powerful as national governments found it acceptable to circulate to soldiers and sailors the popular reading materials the vast majority of library readers wanted anyway, librarians had difficulty objecting. Besides, much was already circulating in serialized form in periodicals libraries collected and *Readers' Guide* indexed (e.g., *Saturday Evening Post* and *Ladies Home Journal*) or in local newspapers edited by men tightly connected to the local elites from which libraries drew their board members. Thus, by the 1920s librarians generally accepted that the "light" reading they had disparaged for a half-century fell somewhere between "good" and "bad," and was at most "harmless." Prewar tension surrounding their self-assumed responsibility to provide "best reading" had been modified by higher authorities, and this effect reduced the pressure librarians imposed on themselves to "elevate" popular taste.

Nonetheless, the "recreational" reading that accounted for most use in public libraries continued to occupy subordinate status in professional thinking and was largely ignored in library rhetoric. After World War I, when public libraries reported the volume of popular reading materials they circulated, they generally buried it in a larger category labeled "fiction" that lumped Edith Wharton with Mrs. E.D.E.N. Southworth, and Henry James with Oliver Optic. A preface to the 1923 *Standard Catalog for Public Libraries: Fiction Section* noted: "This is not a list of the best 2,350 novels, judged as literature, but a list of the 2,350 of the best novels for public use. This means it includes novels for highly educated and for comparatively uneducated readers, . . . and for those who want to keep in touch with present day fiction."[15] Subsequent editions also began citing previously excluded works by authors like Andre Gide, Marcel Proust, and James Joyce, mostly because cultural authorities outside the profession had reached consensus on the canonical status of these texts. Often, libraries imposed user fees on popular fiction they did not want to keep. During the war, the Victoria (British Columbia) Public Library inaugurated a duplicate pay collection for new fiction. When a citizen protested that the practice violated the principles of a Carnegie "free" library, VPL discontinued the "service." But only temporarily. In 1921 the library revived it and continued it well into the 1950s. Hundreds of other American and Canadian public libraries did likewise.

Readers' Advisors

Although the war removed some pressure to supply *only* "the best reading" and encouraged librarians to place more emphasis on reaching the "largest number at the least cost," they did not abandon a self-assumed responsibility to promote canonical literatures. Patrons could still find "best reading" in the library that was purchased through centralized systems that filtered the universe from which librarians made their choices, but beginning in the 1920s they could also tap the counsel of a new library professional—the "readers' advisor"—who was supposed to know "good books" on library shelves and through personal service meet patrons' individual needs by connecting users to appropriate library materials. Public library leaders envisioned the readers' advisor as the library's contribution to an adult education movement designed to assist independent adult learners with informal reading programs. In 1921 the Carnegie Corporation funded an ALA report, *Libraries and Adult Education*, encouraging the widespread application of advisory services. Three years later William S. Learned published another corporation report—*The American Public Library and the Diffusion of Knowledge*. It outlined the potential for the public library to function as an active agency in adult education if public libraries established a "community intelligence service" staffed by "reference experts" who would function as readers' advisors. That same year ALA established a Commission on Library and Adult Education that sought to identify weaknesses in the educational system libraries could address, laid plans for improving services to address these weaknesses, encouraged closer cooperation between schools and libraries to facilitate literacy, proposed readers' advisory services and special services to immigrants and the disabled, and advocated library extension to the unserved throughout the nation. By that time, five metropolitan public libraries (Detroit and Cleveland in 1922, Chicago and Milwaukee in 1923, and Indianapolis in 1924) had already initiated readers' advisor programs. Within a decade fifty others followed. In 1934 the Carnegie Corporation published *A Readers' Advisory Service*, a study that analyzed a decade of NYPL advisory service.

In most metropolitan public libraries, a full-time readers' advisory librarian skilled in the use of bibliographic tools and reviewing sources worked from the main library, where she conducted interviews with readers to discover their goals, interests, and capabilities. After the interview she compiled a bibliography of library titles tailor-made to the reader's needs (sometimes she also directed readers to special classes and other educational opportunities), and kept records for follow-up consultations. Sometimes readers' advisors also worked with groups by designing prepackaged reading courses. Beginning in 1925, ALA published over sixty guides in its "Reading with a Purpose" programs. During the Depression, library services often included counseling for career changes and job opportunities.

At the same time, however, patrons could use a maturing system of reference services and reference materials to research facts on which to create new knowledge or base prudent decisions to vote, to build, to invent, to purchase. It was the kind of library service Daniel Nash Handy's patrons found so valuable, the kind "serious scholars" came to expect when they did research at libraries like the Newberry and the Crerar. And because these client groups had more political, social, and economic clout than a black child or a female romance reader, the kinds of information disseminated in reference work and by "readers' advisors" became privileged. Both became part of the library's contribution to an adult education movement emerging nationwide.

In Canada, library participation in the adult education movement came later. By World War II Alberta had consolidated small school districts into larger ones, which made adult education activities easier to plan and fund. In 1943 British Columbia surveyed public libraries to determine how many adult education supervisors the province needed to support an adult education program outside public schools. Elizabeth Dafoe of the University of Manitoba took it a step further. At a meeting of the Canadian Library Council (organized in 1941) she argued that Canada needed a uniquely Canadian federal department of education (not a clone of the U.S. one) to facilitate adult education and help equalize educational opportunities across the country.

Expanding Library Services

Young adult (YA) library services also became a specialty after World War I. When Mabel Williams was named NYPL's supervisor of work with schools in 1919, she stressed that class visits (she herself made 2,500 in 1926), reading guidance, trained staff, and library sites specifically designated for youth constituted the core of YA services. Believing YA librarians were responsible for broadening youth horizons, she hired Margaret Scoggin to run the Nathan Straus Branch as a "lab" library for teenagers. There Scoggin pioneered programs and services for youth modeled elsewhere on the continent. In 1925 Jean Roos set up the Robert Louis Stevenson Room at the Cleveland Public Library. She worked with community organizations to get books and library services to youth—especially underserved and nonserved immigrants—who no longer attended school. In 1933 Margaret A. Edwards instituted "Y Work" at the Enoch Pratt. She believed that promoting the concept of world citizenship through (largely fiction) reading constituted a core value of youth services. Like Williams, she stressed class visits and book talks. By 1947 U.S. public libraries had 40 separate YA rooms, 63 separately designated alcoves, 94 special collections, and 153 full-time librarians working the library floor, writing book reviews; supervising reading, jazz, and film clubs; and providing reference services.

In the early twentieth century several wealthy philanthropists established large private research libraries of rare and unique texts they had collected. In 1919 Henry Huntington founded a library in San Marino, California, and donated to it his substantial collection of rare books. That same year, the Hoover Library of War, Revolution, and Peace opened its doors on the Stanford University campus. In 1924 J. P. Morgan Jr. turned the private collection of rare books and medieval and Renaissance manuscripts and autographed letters his father had collected into the Pierpont Morgan Library. By that time the phrase "special collections" had assumed new meaning for academic libraries. The rise of social history and the need for different kinds of documentation to support research led many academic libraries to collect manuscripts and establish archives. For example, the University of North Carolina founded the Southern Historical Collections in 1930, the University of Michigan established the Michigan Historical Collections in 1935, Smith College founded the Sophia Smith Collection in 1942, and Radcliffe established the Schlesinger Library in 1943. The latter two focused on women's history.

For centuries libraries had collected music written on paper. As early as the eighteenth century Moravian repertories at Bethlehem, Pennsylvania, and Winston-Salem, North Carolina, collected performance materials. The Harvard Musical Association organized in 1837 and published a catalog of its library thereafter. Music educator Lowell Mason bequeathed his collections to Yale, which in 1917 used them to create its School of Music Library. Joseph Drexel gave his music collection to the Lenox Library in 1888, where it became part of NYPL's Music Division in 1911 (and relocated to the Lincoln Center in 1965). But when Thomas Edison invented the sound-recording cylinder in 1877, the nature of collecting music changed. Over subsequent decades phonograph recordings became popular, and libraries began to collect them. By the mid-1920s, long-playing (LP) records had become staple public and academic library fare, and in 1927 ALA issued *The Care and Treatment of Music in a Library*. LP collections generally included classical (seldom popular or ethnic) music, foreign language instruction, and readings of plays, poetry, and speeches; collections developed for the visually impaired often included "talking books." The Music Library Association (MLA) organized in 1931, thus providing music librarians an opportunity to share ideas and celebrate the services they developed over the generations. MLA's journal, *Notes*, started in 1934 and provided music librarians with a venue to communicate research about their collections. The New Westminster Public Library became the first British Columbian library to circulate LPs in 1944; twelve years later it circulated record players. That same year the Canadian Broadcasting Corporation's library in Toronto reported a collection of 43,000 titles (including 2,500 scores), making it Canada's largest music library.

In 1934 ALA delegated George Freedley, curator of NYPL's Theatre Collection, to visit major European collections. Two years later Freedley and Rosamond Gilder published *Theatre Libraries in Collections and Museums* (1936), which sparked an effort by theater historians, librarians, and curators to organize the Theatre Library Association (TLA) in 1937, in part to facilitate preservation of "performing arts collections" (including live and recorded theatrical and dramatic performances). In subsequent years TLA published *Theatre Documentation and Performing Arts Resources* to foster the development of archives, analyses of collections, and descriptions of regional holdings. The Society of American Archivists (SAA) organized in 1936, two years after the National Archives opened in Washington, DC. The federally funded Historical Records Survey (1936–1942) greatly accelerated the development of basic archival methodologies, and together with SAA and the National Archives, helped lead the field.

During the Great Depression, American and Canadian libraries experienced increased demands on services and collections at the same time they endured decreased funding.

In response, librarians showed creativity. In the late 1930s U.S. librarians used federal work programs to build 350 new libraries, employ students and young adults (7,000 in 1938) to repair thousands of books, prepare reference materials like newspaper indexes and bibliographies, and fund rural library demonstration projects designed to encourage isolated communities to establish local library services. They also showed more sophistication in publicity efforts. In 1939 ALA organized a Public Relations Council. Four years later it created the John Cotton Dana Awards to recognize outstanding local publicity campaigns.

Sometimes local communities took care of their own reading and information needs. Independently funded reading rooms, like those Christian Scientists opened after World War I, sometimes espoused social reform. Jewish congregations helped school libraries work more closely with synagogue religious schools. A few (Temple Library in Cleveland, Wilshire Boulevard Temple Library in Los Angeles) developed collections that served the entire Jewish community.

Over time, the value of library services became closely tied to clienteles for which they were intended. Services designed to improve access to information desired by government officials, corporate executives in search of profits, or by scientists, professionals, and academics in search of facts and "truth" were more valued than services designed to improve access to information contained in reading materials desired by housewives and children. Differences in salaries earned by librarians serving each clientele reflected these values. But debates over what was "truth" continued to flavor community standards that governed the profiles of local public library collections. In Saskatoon, for example, a local branch of the Rationalist Press Association (RPA) offered the public library forty books, some of which articulated the RPA's position denying Christ's divinity. When local Christians protested that anything against Christian principles was unsuitable for a public library, trustees decided to select from the gift only those titles it thought acceptable. The RPA then withdrew its offer.

Canada

The interwar years in Canada witnessed several developments. In 1927 ALA scheduled an annual conference in Canada for the third time in its history. There, Canadian librarians resolved to form a Canadian Library Association. In part they were motivated by findings in a *Survey of Libraries in Canada* that the Dominion's Bureau of Statistics published. In part, they recognized the need for a nationally based association to increase recognition of Canadian library conditions and needs. With Carnegie Corporation help, a commission of librarians traveled the nation in 1930 to discuss library matters with federal, provincial, and education department officials, newspaper editors, normal school principals, and library professionals in all types of institutions. In 1933 the commission issued *Libraries in Canada: A Study of Library Conditions and Needs*, which noted that 80 percent of Canadians had no library service. The commission focused on public services in all types of libraries and assumed these services were a necessary part of Canada's educational system. Government libraries were woefully behind countries like France, Germany, Great Britain, and the United States, and Canada still lacked a national library that could exercise policy-making power to facilitate equitable library services to Canadians. Canada needed, the commission concluded, what the United States had in the Library of Congress. Within Canada's federal structure, each province was responsible for providing educational services, which included primary, secondary, and higher education and the libraries (including public libraries) necessary to support them. Commissioners found Canada expended about $70 per capita on students in public institutions, but libraries supporting these institutions did not receive a fair share. For public library purposes alone, it argued, Canada needed to adopt the American standard of $1.00 per capita, and for communities in Canada's vast spaces unable to expend at least $3,000 per year on a public library, the commission recommended regional library services like those in British Columbia's Fraser Valley.

The Fraser Valley Demonstration Project was an early success. It grew out of a Carnegie Corporation grant given to the British Columbia Public Library Commission to initiate a regional library service in 1930, when 10,000 books located at headquarters in Chilliwack and staffed by four professionals became available to Fraser Valley residents. Within a year the project established nine branches, six deposit stations, fifty bookmobile stations, and three elementary school libraries; it also had 13,000 registered borrowers who in one year accounted for 230,000 circulated items. When Carnegie funding ceased in 1934, the newly constituted Board of Management of the Fraser Valley Union Library assumed control. In 1944 the National Film Board of Canada made a film titled *Library on Wheels* to cameo the benefits of Fraser Valley's regional library service. No matter the commission's wishes to replicate Fraser Valley, however, the Great Depression prevented Canada from carrying out its many recommendations. Still, some libraries acted unilaterally. Public libraries of Lambton County, Ontario, pooled their resources in 1934 to create a central fund from which to effect management and service efficiencies. Where politics permitted, other counties followed their example. Alberta got even more creative. To extend the reach of its Extension Library, staff began "Book Chats" on the University of Alberta's radio station. If patrons could not have the book in hand, librarians reasoned, at least they could hear about it on the radio. Other organizations formed in the interwar years. American and Canadian librarians played influential roles in establishing the International Federation of Library Associations (IFLA) in 1929. The first Canadian chapter of the Special Libraries Association organized in Montreal in 1932, and later in Toronto to provide a forum for librarians working in some of Canada's new special libraries like the Pulp and Paper Research Institute (1927), the Ontario Research Foundation, Sheridan Park (1928), and the Canadian Industries Limited (1928). In 1931, New Brunswick appointed a Public Library Commission. In 1932, the successes of the Boys and Girls House library services the Toronto Public Library pioneered led to the creation of the Canadian Association of Children's Librarians. That same year Quebec established a bilingual Library Association. Three years later librarians from Nova Scotia, New Brunswick, and Prince Edward Island founded the Maritime Library Institute, and in 1936 the Manitoba Library Association organized. Saskatchewan founded its Library Association in 1940.

Improving Library Service

No matter their location, librarians still pushed for improved service efficiency. The Dickman Charging Machine (1927) and the Gaylord Brothers Charging Machine (1931) replaced checkout systems in many libraries. In the 1940s several libraries adopted the transaction card method, which used photography to record charges. In 1942 the Montclair (New Jersey) Public Library used IBM equipment for a circulation system. Academic librarians experimented with punch cards. The University of Texas harnessed the Hollerith card to implement a new charging system in 1936. Harvard adapted the McBee card in 1939. In the 1940s the Rapid Selector used electronics to mechanically search literature on coded microfilm. In the postwar United States Angus S. Macdonald developed the modern metal bookstack into a standard interchangeable three-foot shelf, first installed in Harvard's Widener Library in 1915, then improved into all-steel bracket shelving in Columbia University's Butler Library in 1934. By stabilizing the free-standing shelving structure from the top, the stack design made possible the modular concept so many postwar library buildings adopted. Buildings constructed in the 1930s manifested several new features; the Enoch Pratt mirrored some characteristics of department store design—vast amounts of open spaces easily modified to fit multiple tasks. Some of this reflected Macdonald's influence; "modular" construction accommodated either readers or books on any floor supported by the floors beneath. During this period the telephone also transformed reference service. In major cities like New York, public libraries set up separate telephone banks where staff answered reference questions first-come-first served, usually from a revolving bookcase of ready-reference books. But not all welcomed the shift. In 1928 the Trenton (Ontario) Public Library director complained to an Ontario Library Association audience that telephone reference services for local businesses were not intended for people too lazy to walk to the library.

In 1912 LC, NYPL, and the John Crerar all began using photostat equipment. In 1927 LC used the equipment to copy overseas materials for its collections. In 1936 Kodak produced improved cameras and projectors for micropublishing, and soon thereafter issued the 1914–1918 files of the *New York Times*. By decade's end microreproduction laboratories functioned at the University of Chicago, Columbia, Yale, Harvard, LC, NYPL, and the National Archives. Out of these laboratories came the Association of Research Libraries' Foreign Newspaper Microfilm Project (Harvard) and the University Microfilms dissertations program. Many predicted microreproduction as a solution to library growth.

Improving efficiency showed in other ways. In 1919 ALA adopted an interlibrary loan code that established a communication system linking libraries. Revised codes followed in 1940, 1952, and 1968. The 1952 code included a standard Interlibrary Loan Form that further reduced costs by creating uniformity in requests. To facilitate interlibrary loan, librarians used national union catalogs and pushed for publications like *Union List of Serials in Libraries of the United States and Canada* (H. W. Wilson published the first edition in 1927). In 1951 LC issued *Serial Titles Newly Received*, which in 1959 incorporated holdings of other libraries (including 207 Canadian libraries) and was renamed *New Serial Titles*. In 1923 Minnie Sears published *A List of Subject Headings for Small Libraries*, which with few exceptions followed the form and structure of LC subject headings. The list became staple fare in school and small public libraries throughout the United States and Canada, and in its sixth edition (1950) changed its title to *Sears List of Subject Headings*, which joined *LCSH* to plague generations of library school students forced to learn both.

And American and Canadian librarians continued to push "for the greatest number." By this time traveling libraries had become a tradition. The British Columbia Public Library Commission pioneered the Open Shelf Library in 1919, which for return postage sent any of 135 books it listed in *Agricultural Journal* to any province resident. At first the Open Shelf contained only nonfiction; it added selected fiction titles later. When British Columbia's "bush telegraph" advertised the service, use quintupled.

By 1930 the Open Shelf had 12,000 volumes. Many went to remote rural schools. A fifty-page *Manual for Small School Libraries* (1940) Vancouver school librarians put together helped the commission identify appropriate titles. In less populated Prairie provinces, traveling library service was even more important. Saskatchewan established an Open Shelf Library in 1912, then expanded to a Traveling Libraries Branch in 1915. The Saskatchewan Wheat Pool also operated a popular books mail service. Manitoba established its service in 1918 and ran it through the Manitoba Wheat Pool until the province consolidated the program with the Department of Education's Manitoba Library Service in 1949. Alberta, on the other hand, ran its library extension services through the University of Alberta's Extension Library, established in 1913. Newfoundland's Department of Education established a traveling library service for schools in 1926 but turned it over to the provincial Public Libraries Board ten years later. By 1959 the system served 420 schools.

The United States had similar experiences. Medical schools at some state universities began circulating collections to county medical societies and physicians' homes and offices. Students at Virginia's Hampton Institute took books to African Americans denied access to local public libraries, and the Brooklyn Public Library located collections in shoe and glove factories and fire departments. Elsewhere, librarians used book deposit stations, horseback libraries (California and the Appalachian Mountains), boatmobiles (Louisiana), and bookmobiles to extend services. In 1925 the Cleveland Public library formed a "hospitals and institutions" section. In 1935 the public library in Webster City, Iowa, introduced home delivery to the handicapped. A year later the Kansas City (Missouri) Public Library enlisted Girl Scouts to introduce a similar service.

Based in part on Progressive Era thinking that criminals could be rehabilitated if properly educated, librarians believed books had an important role to play in that process. In 1931 ALA published *The Education of Adult Prisoners*, which stressed the importance of reading for behavioral change. In 1932 it issued the *Prison Library Handbook*, which grew from the concept of bibliotherapy E. Kathleen Jones articulated a generation previously. Fiction became a useful tool. In 1941 the British Columbia Public Library Commission placed traveling libraries in provincial prisons, starting first with the women's ward at Oakalla Prison, later extending it to the men's section and hiring a trained librarian to staff it. By 1946 the women's collection contained 620 titles, the men's 1,500, and circulation of these "carefully selected books of fiction and nonfiction" reached nearly 36,000. "Inmates," the commission proudly announced, often complimented the library's "ameliorative influence."

Library Research

In the 1930s library education also shifted. With a substantial Carnegie Corporation grant, the University of Chicago opened a Graduate Library School (GLS) in 1928. Unlike other library schools that trained students for library practice, GLS concentrated on research and admitted only PhD students. At the time, the university was a national leader in using quantitative methods to make the social sciences more "scientific." For much of the 1930s, GLS faculty (mostly recruited from other university departments) extrapolated from political science, sociology, and education to concentrate their research on the scientific investigation of reading. The prevailing format for library research became social science empiricism with hypothesis testing sanctified by mathematical formulas. GLS faculty believed the results of such research would construct a philosophy of librarianship based on verifiable data. The germinal library research text, Pierce Butler's *An Introduction to Library Science* (1933), served two generations of library researchers and throughout the twentieth century was frequently cited. The premier research journal, *Library Quarterly*, began its first issue in 1933 with C. C. Williamson's "The Place of Research in Library Service."

But GLS's research scope also betrayed cultural biases. Led by Douglas Waples, a social scientist from Education, GLS faculty generally disregarded fiction in their research, thus ignoring reading most library users obtained at public libraries across the continent. Instead, faculty focused on nonfiction information, especially the kinds of information reference services provided. And under Dean Louis Round Wilson, GLS shifted its research focus even further from reading research to studying library management and expertise. Surveys like Wilson's *Geography of Reading: A Study of the Distribution and Status of Libraries in the United States* (1938) marked the trend. So did his *Report of a Survey of the University of Georgia Library* (1939) and Carleton B. Joeckel and Leon Carnovsky's *A Metropolitan Library in Action* (1940), which became models for other surveys. Beginning in the mid-1930s, GLS used an annual Library Institute to bring librarians together with management leaders. The principles of public administration emanating from the institute (and GLS publications studied thereafter by library school students) not only told librarians to divide their staffs into graded positions within a hierarchy of departments but it also provided them with a blueprint for career ladder-climbing.

These publications helped ground Clara Herbert's *Personnel Administration in Public Libraries* (1939), which discussed public personnel trends (such as job analysis and classification) that the federal government addressed in the previous decade. All incorporated the findings of industrial psychologist Elton Mayo, who found at the Western Electric Company's Hawthorne Plant in Chicago (1927–1932) that workers were less motivated by economic considerations than social rewards and sanctions. About the same time ALA surveyed library organizations and discovered that although special and school libraries retained the same flat staffing hierarchy considered necessary to serve their clientele, academic and public library communities had in many cases divided into "small" and "large" categories. In the latter, the survey found staff members tended to work at set tasks in closely defined departments, each headed by a specialist. Department heads—usually grouped by function, process, or campus geography—reported to a smaller set of "assistant directors," who generally had responsibilities for major services (usually "technical" and "public") and reported to a director. The director seldom performed actual library work, but instead occupied a position in an additional but elevated hierarchy of institutional administrators. Other GLS research was equally influential. Carleton B. Joeckel's *The Government of the American Public Library* (1935) laid the conceptual footings for ALA's *Post-War Standards for Public Libraries* (1943) and its many revisions. Joeckel believed that if public libraries acted in concert rather than individually, they could create more efficient and broadly based services, and thus expand their influence. Taking his cues from political scientists who wanted to reform local government, Joeckel envisioned 641 library districts spread across the nation to effect necessary changes.

As a result of more emphasis on administration and positivistic social science research, less emphasis on reading and humanities research, GLS faculty and students turned away from an opportunity to study an activity central to librarianship. On the one hand, they failed to address concerns voiced by Helen Haines, who loudly complained about "the mechanistic non-literary attitude" she thought characterized GLS research. In her *Living with Books* (1935), which became a standard selection text in library schools for two generations, Haines defended the kind of middlebrow literary tastes public library users and the new Book-of-the-Month Club patrons wanted. She championed librarians who valued the library as a repository of intellectual energy that could teach and inform, broaden and enhance life. She thought librarianship was more art than science, the librarian more missionary than technician. However, the GLS also (and to some extent Haines herself) ignored newer research on the act of reading. In 1938 Louise Rosenblatt published *Literature as Exploration*, a pioneering study written for the Progressive Education Association's Commission on Human Relations. In it she argued that because reading was not just "a passive process of absorption" but "a form of intense activity," researchers needed "to find out what happens when specific human beings, with their interests and anxieties, participate in the emotional and intellectual life" that reading "makes possible."[16]

At the time, however, library researchers were not positioned to address Rosenblatt's conclusions and extrapolate from them to the professional world they knew. In fact, *Library Literature*, the Wilson Company index to the profession's publications, listed no reviews for Rosenblatt's book and its next four editions, and for the remainder of the century, research on reading largely disappeared from the profession's discourse. Instead of pursuing ways to understand what uses most people made of the materials they obtained from libraries of all types, librarians continued to emphasize and improve professional expertise and management, and persisted in a library faith steeped in high-culture canons that over time were slow to shift.

Library Bill of Rights

Although the ideology of learned reading behind "the best reading for the largest number at the least cost" was modified after World War I, and the model of library service the profession projected to external communities extended its focus in the 1920s to encompass privileged information delivered in reference services, events occurring a continent away in the 1930s created another opportunity for the American and Canadian library communities to expand their professional responsibility. In contrast to Arthur Bostwick in 1908, Charles Beldon used his 1925 ALA presidential address to argue that the public library had to stand for intellectual freedom. In the 1930s Jesse Shera suggested that sometimes librarians' silence on public affairs constituted not neutrality, but assent. Librarians who think themselves objective professionals may, he argued, enable forces threatening civil liberties and academic freedom.

As news about book-burning events in Nazi Germany began appearing in North American newspapers and periodicals, as Chinese librarians appealed to other librarians for help against Japanese censorship, some librarians pondered their role in intellectual freedom. In 1939—a year after the Des Moines (Iowa) Public Library crafted a "Library's Bill of Rights" (LBR)—ALA adopted a similar document that outlined the library's responsibility to champion intellectual freedom and fight censorship and thus embraced, at least in abstract democratic rhetoric, the defense of intellectual freedom as a professional imperative. Books "should be chosen because of value and interest to the people of the community," it read; selection should not be "influenced by the race or nationality or the political or religious views of the writers." Yet the opinions of all sides of an issue "should be represented fairly and adequately," and library building meeting rooms ought to be open to all groups engaged in "socially useful and cultural activities."[17] The language ALA adopted allowed libraries not to offend funders and users, while at the same time appearing to adhere to LBR principles. A year later ALA created an Intellectual Freedom Committee (IFC), which for the next generation carried out ALA's IF policy and educational activities.

Issues of Race

Ironically, American librarians largely ignored civil liberties abuses of racial minorities in libraries at home and addressed racist practices only indirectly. When Thomas Fountain Blue of the Louisville Public Library discussed "Training Class at the Western Colored Branch" at the 1922 ALA annual conference, he became the first African American to participate in an ALA program—forty-six years after the association organized. ALA subsequently studied library services for blacks and called for increasing the number of African American librarians. With the help of the Carnegie Corporation and ALA, in 1925 the Hampton Institute opened a library school for African Americans, despite a National Association for the Advancement of Colored People protest that it would segregate black librarians. And so it did. In 1929 ALA's Board of Education for Librarianship surveyed library schools to discover their policies regarding admittance of blacks as students. Fourteen U.S. library schools responded (all in the North or West); four indicated they admitted African Americans. But the University of Michigan's William Warner Bishop answered differently. The board would be better off to send black students to Hampton, he argued, rather than encourage them to come to institutions where their presence was an "embarrassment." The board did nothing to discourage attitudes characterized by Bishop's comments. The Hampton school operated fourteen years, then moved to Atlanta University in 1940, where it graduated nearly 90 percent of African American librarians working in American libraries in the twentieth century.

ALA's complicity in racist practices surfaced elsewhere. Prior to the 1936 conference in Richmond, Virginia, ALA headquarters circulated a letter indicating that its black members could attend the conference but would be seated in segregated sections of meeting halls and rooms. In addition, they would not be permitted to attend meal functions or visit the conference exhibits, nor would they be allowed to register for rooms at conference hotels. After the conference concluded, African American Wallace Van Jackson wrote in *Library Journal* that the segregation of African Americans "is a shameful slide backward. What is worse, no single meeting or group at the Richmond conference so much as brought up the matter for discussion to say nothing of passing a resolution of protest." The *New Republic* projected the issue to national attention when it criticized ALA: "The explanation is made rather plaintively that these restrictions were not the fault of the ALA, but part of a law of Virginia. Query: Why should any civilized association, with Negro members, undertake to hold such a convention in Virginia or any other state that makes such distinctions?" In response, the ALA council eventually passed a resolution that "in all rooms and halls assigned to [ALA] hereafter for use in connection with its conference or otherwise under its control, all members shall be admitted upon terms of full equality."[18] It represented the first time ALA took a public position against racial discrimination, which was part of routine library practices in the American South.

World War II

As World War II erupted in Europe in September 1939, Canada was immediately involved. The Toronto Public Library, for example, developed special library collections for local factories (including one for women who filled jobs vacated by men) and military camps, and initiated special services for British children evacuated to Canada and housed at the University of Toronto. But the war also changed the contours of Canadian librarianship. More of the country became industrialized, the need for skilled technicians increased, a national media emerged, and transportation improvements diminished the isolation of the central provinces. In 1941 Quebec passed a Free Library Municipal Aid Act that made it much easier for municipal governments to develop local public library services. French Canadian librarians organized the Association Canadienne des bibliothèque catholique. With help from library associations in Alberta, British Columbia, Manitoba, the Maritimes, Ontario, Quebec, and Saskatchewan, the Canadian Library Council capitalized on nationalistic sentiment to plan a postwar campaign for increased funding and new library services. The council also agitated for a national library, initiated a publishing program, and sponsored the microfilming of early Canadian newspaper files. To the south, after the United States joined the war in December 1941, librarians mobilized to provide services to the nation's fighting forces. Librarians established over 1,000 Army Library Service post and hospital libraries and helped set up thousands of libraries on navy ships.

CONSOLIDATING GAINS: 1945–1970

The Public Library Inquiry

Postwar activities showed several priorities. In 1948 the Carnegie Corporation funded a Public Library Inquiry (PLI) to analyze the public library's purpose and especially the "library faith" that grounded it. Led by University of Chicago political science professor Robert D. Leigh, the project eventually led to seven books and five reports. Among the former were landmark studies like Oliver Garceau's *The Public Library in the Political Process* (1949), Bernard Berelson's *The Library's Public* (1949), and Alice Bryan's *The Public Librarian* (1952). In these publications authors argued that instead of supplying popular reading desired by large populations, public libraries should create a "civic" institution in which the information needs of a smaller but more influential combination of "serious" readers, community leaders, and adult education students became prime beneficiaries. Although like GLS researchers in the 1930s PLI investigators disdained popular reading and sought to reduce its monopoly on regular library services, the effect of its findings on public library practice was minimal. Some librarians ignored recommendations, some criticized it for overlooking the reading needs of less powerful groups like children, and some found fault with methodological inconsistencies in the research.

In part PLI was reacting to increasingly popular genre fiction like mystery/detective, romance, westerns, science fiction, fantasy, and horror, all part of a 1930s paperback revolution appealing to millions of readers. Public libraries responded in several ways. Some ignored this "trash." Others segregated it onto labeled shelves or spine-labeled it with a letter or other graphic device. Still others established paperback "rental shelves," where they either bought the material themselves and then rented access to pay for the book, or they contracted with commercial rental services, which allowed library patrons access to popular titles without encumbering the library with ownership and preservation. In addition, the Library Bill of Rights now gave librarians "authority" to deflect criticism about circulating popular fiction. Because intellectual freedom advocacy was so much more compelling in the world of professions than defending popular fiction, librarians had little reason to debate cultural authorities or read newer research that dealt with people's actual reading practices and behaviors, or the multiple ways in which library patrons appropriated reading materials.

Censorship Challenges

Other challenges were more compelling. Because they embraced the LBR as a fundamental professional responsibility, U.S. librarians sometimes found themselves on the nation's center stage when Wisconsin senator Joseph McCarthy accused several cultural institutions of spreading communism. In particular he picked on U.S. Information Agency libraries the State Department supported at embassies abroad for having 30,000 Communist books. Inevitably, the campaign had a ripple effect through the U.S. library world. Either to protect their jobs or because they agreed with McCarthy's goals, some librarians voluntarily withdrew controversial materials; others never acquired them. In one study for the California Library Association's Intellectual Freedom Committee, Marjorie Fiske discovered that although librarians "expressed unequivocal freedom-to-read convictions," almost two-thirds of librarians she talked to admitted they considered the controversiality of a book or author when deciding whether to buy. Even worse, nearly 20 percent "habitually avoided buying any material which is known to be controversial or which they believe might be controversial."[19] Evidence suggests many librarians in other states acted no differently, despite the profession's commitment to the LBR.

Some of this hesitation undoubtedly grew out of repeated efforts to censor. Although a federal court revised the Hicklin rule in 1933 by declaring James Joyce's *Ulysses* (1922) not obscene when considered as a whole by an average, normal adult, lower courts exercised their own discretion. Thus, when a Massachusetts court found Lillian Smith's *Strange Fruit* (1941) obscene, Bay State librarians pulled it from their shelves. When *The Nation* published several negative articles on the Catholic church in 1948, New York banned it from public school libraries for more than a decade. Similarly, when a New York court found Edmund Wilson's *Memoirs of Hecate County* (1946) obscene, the New York Public Library told its patrons reserve requests to circulate it could not be honored. In 1952 one congressman introduced a bill requiring the librarian for the LC to label subversive titles coming in for copyright. It died in committee. In 1957 Ralph Ellison led a New York City chapter of the National Association for the Advancement of Colored People to protest racial stereotypes in *Huckleberry Finn*. As a result the title was removed from the reading list of approved texts. Some librarians, however, fought McCarthy and his supporters on LBR principles. When the *Boston Herald* attacked the Boston Public Library for stocking books the newspaper said promoted communism, numerous Boston citizens, a local Catholic newspaper, and a former FBI agent joined librarians in a successful protest. In response to pressure from a Senate committee to suppress "immoral books," the ALA's Intellectual Freedom Committee joined the America Book Publisher's Council for a conference in 1953, out of which came *The Freedom to Read* statement. In June,

President Dwight D. Eisenhower implored a Dartmouth College graduating class not to be afraid to go to the library and read every book. Later that month the ALA president read a letter from Eisenhower at the annual conference encouraging librarians to resist book burners. And in a 1953 *Wilson Library Bulletin* article, "Not Censorship but Selection," University of Chicago GLS professor Lester Asheim argued that librarians should approach selection positively, always looking for value, strength, and virtue; censors, he argued, approached selection negatively, always looking for anything morally or politically offensive.

Canadian Librarianship

Many of Canada's postwar experiences ran in different directions. As the federal government established new departments in the twentieth century, many created special libraries, including the Department of Transportation (1936), the Central Housing and Mortgage Corporation (1946), the Geographical Branch of the Department of Mines and Resources (1948), and the Fisheries Research Board of Canada (1957). The Canadian Library Association (CLA) organized in 1946 and took over the work of the Canadian Library Council. In 1951 the Royal Commission on National Development in the Arts, Letters, and Sciences issued a report that pushed for a national library. Over the decades Canadian librarians kept up the pressure. When National Archives director W. Kay Lamb created the National Bibliographic Centre in 1949 and the parliamentary library experienced a fire in 1952, politicians finally succumbed. In 1953 they authorized the National Library of Canada/la Bibliothèque nationale du Canada (which in 2004 merged with the National Archives of Canada/Archives nationales du Canada to become the Library and Archives Canada/Bibliothèque et archives Canada). For a while Lamb served as director of the archives and the library (which inherited the parliamentary library's 300,000-book collection), and under his direction the library assumed responsibility for Canadian legal deposit and facilitated interlibrary cooperation and bibliographic control by maintaining a Canadian Union Catalog. It also assumed responsibility for *Canadiana*, Canada's official national bibliography that emerged from the *Canadian Catalogue of Books* (the Toronto Public Library's accessions list for its Canadiana collection). In 1963 the catalog recorded 5,000,000 catalog cards from 203 Canadian libraries. That same year the University of Toronto undertook Canada's first large-scale automated cataloging initiative for the Ontario New Universities Library Project. In 1957 the government chartered the Canadian Library Research Foundation and established the Canada Council and the Canadian National Council for UNESCO. And in 1958 CLA joined with other organizations to initiate a Canadian Library Week with financial support from the Canadian Council and the Book Publishers Association of Canada. In 1955 Canada developed standards for public libraries.

When Lamb retired in 1968 the archives and library received separate administrators, and under Guy Sylvestre, the new national librarian, the library experienced significant growth, in part because a 1969 National Library Act revision allowed Sylvestre to coordinate federal department activities, expand *Canadiana,* extend reference services, and establish new programs, including a Library Documentation Centre, a Canadian Book Exchange, a Multicultural Program, a Rare Book Department, a Children's Literature Service, and services for the disabled. The Surplus Exchange Centre it established in 1973 initially dealt only with government publications, but thereafter expanded to include trade publications and periodicals. Between 1973 and 1988 the Centre distributed 6,500,000 items. In 1962 Canada also produced a French translation of *LCSH—Repertoire de vedettes-matière*, originally prepared by the Bibliothèque de l'université Laval in Quebec. In 1967 Quebec established the Bibliothèque nationale du Québec to collect Quebec materials and produce Quebec bibliographies. In 1978 the National Library of Canada issued *Canadian Subject Headings* (revised in 1985) to include specific terms referring to unique Canadian events, concepts, history, and literature. In 1967, however, the Quebec National Assembly authorized the Bibliothèque nationale du Québec (now the Bibliothèque et Archives nationale du Québec after merging with the Archives nationales du Québec in 2006) to collect books published in Quebec, about Quebec, or by Quebec authors, and to publish the monthly *Bibliographie du Québec*. Within larger Canada, Quebec was determined to construct the heritage of its own culture.

U.S. Academic Libraries

Postwar events also changed U.S. academic libraries, and many initiatives launched in the United States depended on Canadian academic libraries for cooperation. For over a decade, returning veterans flooded the nation's campuses, placing new burdens on academic libraries. When Lawrence Powell became UCLA Library system director in 1944, for example, he inherited a collection of 462,327 volumes, a book budget of $50,000, fifty full-time staff members, and no branch libraries. That year the system circulated 300,000 items and lent a few more titles on interlibrary loan than it borrowed. When Powell retired in 1961, the UCLA Library system held 1,568,565 volumes (105,995 acquired the previous year), a book budget of $381,650, and 220 full-time staff, many of them working in the system's sixteen branches. In 1960–1961 the library circulated 1,593,204 items and on interlibrary loan borrowed 2,619 items wehile lending 9,185.

Across the continent, scholars (especially in the sciences) fought for a share of research and development money being allocated to the public sector by government and industry and in many cases formed partnerships with corporate and industrial United States and Canada to conduct that research. To cope with increased demands, academic libraries worked out cooperative acquisitions programs for rare, unique, and expensive materials. Among the most successful was the privately funded Farmington Plan, which sixty academic and research libraries (including the University of Toronto) organized in 1948 through the Association of Research Libraries (ARL). The plan sought to guarantee that at least one of fifty university libraries would obtain one copy of every new research-oriented foreign book, and that LC would list each work (and its location) in a new *National Union Catalog* edition. Each participating library accepted responsibility for collecting in specific subject areas. In its first twenty-five years the plan accounted for 11,000,000 items to member libraries, many made available by interlibrary loan practices ALA honed and revised since 1917. ARL also helped establish the Universal Serials and Book Exchange in 1948. In 1958 the exchange included nine Canadian members.

In 1949 ten U.S. midwestern universities organized the Midwest Inter-Library Center (MILC), a membership-based research library cooperative acquisitions program to collect U.S. newspapers (general circulation and ethnic), foreign newspapers, infrequently held humanities, social science, and scientific and technical journals, major microform and reprint sets, and dissertations outside the United States and Canada. In 1963 the University of Toronto joined, and in 1965 MILC changed its name to the

Center for Research Libraries. By 1990 collections totaled 3,500,000 volumes and 1,100,000 microforms, and its voting membership had grown to ninety-nine (four were Canadian) and forty associate and user members. Two other plans also helped university library acquisitions, both government-supported. In 1962 Congress passed a law allowing libraries to acquire research materials from countries with unconvertible foreign currencies the United States owned. Originally covering three countries, by 1965 the program expanded to six nations and brought in 1,500,000 items when LC established teams in the six countries to issue accessions lists.

In the late 1960s LC developed a standard format for machine-readable bibliographic records called MARC (machine-readable cataloging), first for books, later for serials and other formats. The library was under some pressure to improve efficiency. Title IIC of the 1965 Higher Education Act authorized LC to acquire as far as possible all materials of scholarly value anywhere in the world and share cataloging data with participating research libraries shortly after they were received. Named the National Program for Acquisitions and Cataloging (NPAC), the initiative called for establishing acquisition offices around the globe. The first NPAC office opened in London in 1966. Within five years thirteen more were established. By 1970 the program involved over eighty libraries and procured materials from thirty countries.

Almost all academic libraries experienced significant growth in the 1950s and 1960s, encouraging many to reclassify collections into the more accommodating LC scheme and enabling all to expand. At Harvard, Director Keyes Metcalf built the first separate rare book library in a university (Houghton), a storage library (New England Deposit Library), and the first separate undergraduate library in a university (Lamont). By that time academic library construction made necessary by spiraling enrollments adapted Macdonald's modular design into building interiors. Hardin-Simmons was the first (1947), but Princeton followed a year later, North Dakota State in 1950, and the University of Iowa in 1951. Initially, exteriors showed little inspiration, sometimes resembling warehouses, but in subsequent years architects incorporated more variety and visual interest into their designs.

In the 1960s some academic librarians promoted a "library-college idea." In part it emanated from historical context. In 1922 the NEA recommended that all teacher training schools have a course in the use of books and libraries, and in subsequent years this recommendation evolved into a proposal recognizing library skills as essential to precollege learning. In part it grew out of Harvie Branscomb's *Teaching with Books* (1940), which advocated partnerships between teaching faculty and academic librarians on assignments involving library use. Its foremost advocate was Louis Shores who, as early as the 1930s, envisioned a "librarian/teacher" actively participating in undergraduate classroom instruction by "teaching" the tools students needed to form arguments. By the 1970s, however, the idea largely slipped into the pages of library history. Except for infusing new energy into the bibliographic instruction academic librarians had provided for a century, the library-college idea did little to dent the concept that regular faculty taught information content, while librarians primarily taught information processing. James Wyer articulated this concept in *Reference Work* (1930), a text that served two generations of library school students before William Katz corroborated his scheme into a text that served another two.

Growing differences between graduate and undergraduate education led many universities to develop separate collections for the latter, and in some cases to follow Harvard's lead and construct whole buildings. In many university libraries, a double standard of reference service emerged: minimum service for large numbers of under-graduates using undergraduate libraries, and specialized services for graduate students and faculty using research collections. In the latter, staff committed to accessibility, bibliographic instruction, and reference service evolved a specialization that partially mirrored the library-college idea and influenced another emerging higher education sector—junior colleges. Because university higher education generally failed to pre-pare workers for occupations requiring technical skills, many communities developed two-year institutions in which this training took place. By midcentury junior col-leges offered vocational preparation, community service, and adult education. Librar-ies serving them placed more emphasis on service and access than collections and preservation.

Canadian Academic Libraries

The golden age of Canadian university libraries took place in the 1960s. Before then many maintained in-house classification schemes, some with the outdated Cutter system (Alberta and McGill). The University of Toronto Library labored in a crowded 1892 building. Western Ontario eliminated washrooms as an economy measure during the Great Depression. But the Soviet Union's "Sputnik" launch in 1957 affected Canadian university libraries in ways similar to the United States. Increased emphasis on research and graduate education translated into increased demand for research collections. Brit-ish Columbia responded by buying Reginald Colbeck's 50,000-volume collection of nineteenth- and twentieth-century British literature in 1966, then hiring Colbeck as its curator. McMaster purchased Bertrand Russell's library in 1972.

Canada had 246 colleges in 1959, 82 conducting classes in English, 164 in French, most with student bodies of less than 500. Half had collections less than 12,000 vol-umes, two-thirds employed no professional librarians. At the other end of the spec-trum were thirty-two major university libraries, including McGill (750,00 volumes) and the University of Toronto (1,150,000 volumes). Four reports on library sources—one for the humanities and social sciences (1962), another for medicine (1964), a third for science and technology (1966), and a fourth for general research resources (1967)—sparked increased funding, with which many developed specialized Canadiana research collections. In 1968 the National Library of Canada established an Office of Library Resources. Five years later the office became the Collection Development Branch. In the 1970s the University of British Columbia opened a new undergraduate library con-structed under the campus mall.

Information Science and Librarianship

Although Lawrence Powell was a high-profile American academic library leader, at heart he was also a humanist (he had a PhD in American literature) who argued that "books are basic" to librarianship and that to be effective professionals, librari-ans primarily had to be readers. Many in the nation's library community agreed with him. For this "fundamentalist" view, however, Powell was heavily criticized by many, most notably Jesse Shera. In the early 1950s Shera wanted librarianship to form links with an evolving scientific community with roots in World War II's Office of Scientific Research and Development. In that office Director Vannevar Bush supervised 6,000 scientists, many concerned about the rapidly expanding body of scientific and technical information. Bush anticipated that postwar America would shift the scientific energy generated by wartime efforts to peacetime uses. He also recognized that newer technologies promised improved bibliographical control of this increasingly large literature. His foresight proved accurate. In 1950 Congress authorized a clearinghouse for scientific and technical information, and, after the Soviet Union launched a satellite in 1957 (an event that catalyzed the government to supplement acquisitions funds for most types of libraries), the president's Science Advisory Committee published a report on the availability of U.S. scientific and technical information that left little doubt about why the nation was losing the space race.

By that time what Bush called "science information" was well placed to receive federal funds, and because scientists generally agreed that traditional libraries were not meeting their needs, they established science information centers and initiated their own indexing and abstracting services to more rapidly retrieve the information they needed. Out of these efforts a postwar "information science" was born, which quickly fused with other "science information" activities in medicine and allied with the gathering of military and political intelligence. Because of a well-supported, relatively powerful group of professionals who sought to serve the immediate information needs of other well-supported groups who wanted to retain or increase their influence, they understandably privileged scientific over other forms of information, especially other cultural forms of information. Nonetheless, the information science they crafted grew out of library reference services that privileged learned reading. Information scientists transformed that service, first by harnessing unique languages in particular professional discourses, and second by designing systems tailor-made to privileged literatures serving the specific information needs of particular clienteles who enjoyed political and economic power.

1956 U.S. Library Services Act

By the late 1950s the infusion of federal funds into certain sectors of the U.S. library community was having a significant impact. In 1956 President Eisenhower signed the Library Services Act (LSA), the first federal legislation intended to fund some library services. The act made it to his desk mostly because state librarians from the South convinced their congressmen and senators (many of whom held crucial committee chairs) that the act would not curtail states' rights because state library agencies would have power to determine the distribution of the funds. Services to African Americans in the South was a constant subtext in their efforts.

LSA funds gave state library agencies new power. After World War I many states consolidated library commissions and state libraries, and by World War II the consolidated agencies offered a variety of services, including legislative reference services and traveling library services to remote parts of states. Some built on a tradition of research library service. Others functioned as coordinating agencies for the state's public library system and provided interlibrary loans and traveling exhibits to city and county public libraries. Still others provided archival services focusing on state history. LSA funds, however, enabled many to buy bookmobiles to reach remote parts of their states with no library service. In the South, some states had separate bookmobiles for whites and blacks. Bookmobiles—often managed directly by a state library agency, sometimes by a newly structured county or regional library system—were stocked with titles cited in staple guides like *Fiction Catalog*, *Public Library Catalog*, and *Children's Catalog*. The bookmobile constituted yet another example of the library community's commitment to provide "the best reading for the largest number at the least cost." The 1963 *Standards for Library Functions at the State Level* developed by the ALA's Association of State Libraries listed five areas of responsibility, including research and planning, shared funding with local governments for financing public library systems, special library services specifically aimed at state government, statewide library development through use of consultants and promotion of services, and planning and coordinating statewide library resources for both the public and state government.

Libraries for Youth in the United States

In the United States at midcentury, young adults merited increased attention. In 1948 ALA published *Public Library Plans for the Teen Age*, which outlined conventional youth services that postwar public librarians inherited from previous generations. Beginning in 1960, however, when ALA published *YA Services in the Public Library*, the profession began to shift youth services from a humanistic emphasis on books to a more technical emphasis on programming. Despite the fact that youth still accounted for much of public library use (figures ranged from 25 to 60 percent), services to youth nonetheless declined in the 1970s and 1980s. This occurred in part because high school libraries increased in number, library directors did not hire YA librarians to replace those retiring, and in many cases closed rooms set up two generations earlier. In addition, articles and letters to the editors in the library press frequently complained about problems youth created when they clustered in libraries after school.

The *Standards for School Library Programs* published by the ALA in 1960 acknowledged the value audiovisual materials held for school libraries. Some schools had offered nonprint services for decades. Chicago schools established a film library in 1917; by the late 1930s over 300 school districts had film libraries. At the time most were government films, corporate-sponsored films, or reworked theatrical films (the Museum of Modern Art Film Library in New York City circulated these films to school districts in 1935). In 1938 the Association of School Film Libraries organized, then established districts as cooperatives for sharing film resources. Lyndon Johnson's 1960s Great Society legislation, including the Library Services and Construction Acts (1964, 1965), the Higher Education Act (1965), and, of particular importance to school libraries, the Elementary and Secondary Education Act (1965) significantly impacted library development in the United States. Influenced by funding from all three, the number of public school libraries increased from 50 percent of schools in 1958 (40,000) to 93 percent in 1985 (74,000). At the same time, public school library book collections increased from an average of 2,972 in 1958 to 8,466 in 1985. In 1969 ALA published *Standards for School Media Programs*, a joint project of the American Association of School Librarians and the National Education Association's Division of Audio-Visual Instructions.

Canadian Librarianship

In the late 1940s the Calgary Public Library managed 160 traveling libraries it sent to local public school classrooms for six-month periods. Calgary's situation was not unique in Alberta. The province organized a School Library Branch in 1914 to supply books funded by a School Grants Ordinance. Over time the branch exercised closer control of selections, no matter the unique needs of local children. Most schools seemed satisfied with these classroom libraries, all supplied from a distant site. In 1957, however, Alberta's Department of Education examined the province's school libraries and found a lack of trained personnel, shortages of funding, and inadequate quarters. In the late 1950s a survey of library needs for Canada's Yukon Territory led to the establishment of the Yukon Regional Library in 1960. A similar survey for the North West Territory several years later resulted in a North West Regional Library Service.

Postwar industrial development, military demobilization, immigration, and a baby boom significantly changed the Canadian economy and substantially impacted Canada's school systems. To meet anticipated demands, rural areas consolidated school systems into larger units. By 1959 the 1,000 public school systems in Canadian cities and towns contained 2,700,000 volumes that school librarians made available to 650,000 students, about one-sixth of the Canadian school population. That same year officials from several government agencies and professional associations (including CLA) met in Edmonton to prepare an outline of school library service requirements for all of Canada. The following year an Alberta commission on rural education issued minimum standards for Alberta school libraries. In 1967 Canada established standards for school libraries. Although other Canadian provincial governments provided some funds to Catholic school systems, Quebec school librarians were unique because the province supported separate educational systems—one Roman Catholic (largely French-speaking), the other Protestant (largely English-speaking). A late 1930s survey showed that in the former most had books but no central libraries. In the 1930s the Montreal Catholic School Commission appointed a school libraries director to organize a central department for all technical work. Still, by 1959 only 53 of Montreal's 300 Catholic schools had libraries. Protestant schools also lacked libraries but addressed the issue differently. In 1937 they arranged with McGill University to circulate traveling library collections of forty volumes each to Quebec's 104 rural Protestant schools for $4 per school. The first central elementary school library opened in 1927, and by 1945 75 percent had central libraries. In 1967 the Protestant School Board of Greater Montreal established a central processing office for its elementary and secondary schools. By that time most had their own central libraries staffed by a full-time professional.

Special Library Services

Special library services continued to diversify. In 1942 the secretary of agriculture asked President Roosevelt to consolidate all departmental library activities under a U.S. Department of Agriculture Library. With Executive Order 9069, he approved the request. Library director Ralph Shaw not only centralized but he also experimented with scientific management methods and initiated new programs, including the monthly *Bibliography of Agriculture* that consolidated independently issued lists, bibliographies, and related publications. In 1954 the library's collection exceeded 1,000,000 volumes. Then, by authorizing the National Agricultural Library in 1962, Congress created the third national U.S. library. In 1969 it moved into a new fifteen-story tower in Beltsville, Maryland.

The Canadian Health Library Association organized in the mid-1970s and shortly thereafter began publishing *Bibliotheca Medica Canadiana*. By 1969 the United States hosted 3,155 medical libraries, four times as many as a half-century earlier. To promote a national system of regional health science libraries to enable equal access to all health care professionals, the Medical Library Assistance Act of 1965 authorized the National Library of Medicine to coordinate a Regional Medical Library System. In the 1960s and 1970s prison inmates began asserting their "rights," among which was access to informational, educational, and inspirational materials. California's Soledad Prison inmates, for example, demanded reading materials. Surveys at other prisons showed inmates wanted the same reading available to citizens on the outside, including newspapers, magazines, mysteries, adventures, westerns, and romances. In response, ALA developed new standards for prison libraries that addressed inmate needs, including legal and vocational materials.

Modern monastic libraries also found homes in the United States. Libraries at Notre Dame University and Saint Louis University, both established by monastic orders, developed special collections. Most impressive, however, was the Cloister Library the Benedictines built at St. John's Abbey in Collegeville, Minnesota, where St. John's University also hosted the Alcuin Library of 315,000 volumes and the Hill Monastic Manuscript Library of 75,000 pre-1600 manuscripts on microfilm. The Cistercians at Gethsemani Abbey in Trappist, Kentucky, permanently loaned its collection of manuscripts and early printed books to the Cistercian Institute at Western Michigan University. In 1972 an Art Libraries Society of North America joined art librarians in Canada and the United States into one organization. Together they began *Art Documentation* (1982) and *Standards for Art Librarians and Fine Arts Slide Collections* (1983). Both provided forums for librarians from institutions like the Art Gallery of Toronto, the Vancouver Art Gallery, and the National Gallery in Ottawa. The latter opened in 1880, but not until 1913 was it designated a national gallery. By 1962 it had 15,000 volumes plus a growing collection of slides, photographs, and filmstrips.

In 1967 the American Documentation Institute (1937) changed its name to the American Society for Information Science (ASIS), in part to claim jurisdiction over an evolving professional field, in part to connect scholars, researchers, documentalists, and bibliographers who shared interests in "information science." The Association of American Library Schools organized in 1915, changed its name to Association for Library and Information Science Education in 1983, and in the pages of its *Journal of Education in Library and Information Science* it gave opportunities to many members attached to sixty accredited North American programs, fifteen smaller unaccredited programs, and ten international affiliates to publish the results of their research on library and information studies education.

Professional Literature

At the same time, the library press grew significantly, mostly to address the practical needs of the profession, especially in collections acquisition and ready reference information. The Canadian Library Association began the *Canadian Library Journal* in 1946, and its newsletter, *Feliciter,* in 1956. ALA stopped publishing its *Catalog* in mid-century, but continued *Booklist*. Most public libraries subscribed. Multiple ALA divisions, sections, and roundtables within the ALA began journals; some published applied research aimed at improving library services and management, including the Reference and Adult Services Division's *RQ* (now *RUSQ*), the American Association of School Librarians' *Top of the News* (now *School Library Research*), the Association for Library Collections and Technical Services' *Library Resources & Technical Services*, and the Association of College & Research Libraries' *College & Research Libraries*. The latter also issues *Choice* magazine (begun in 1964), a monthly list of books recommended for academic libraries. The Society of American Archivists began *American Archivist* in 1937, and ASIS changed the name of its journal from *American Documentation* (1950) to the *Journal of the American Society for Information Science* (*JASIS*) in 1970. As of this writing most are also open access online journals. The H. W. Wilson Company continued to publish *Readers' Guide*, but supplemented it with an array of other indexes, including *Abridged Readers' Guide*, *Humanities Index*, *Social Sciences Index*, and *Applied Sciences and Technology Index*. The company also began *Library Literature* in 1933 (H. G. T. Cannons's *Bibliography of Library Economy* [1927] covered the previous decade, albeit poorly). In 2011 the company merged with EBSCO Publishing. Wilson also continued *Fiction Catalog* and *Children's Catalog*, but evolved *Public Library Catalog* out of another bibliographical guide it began in the 1930s. Along with *Junior High School* and *Senior High School Library Catalog* each appeared in quinquennial editions updated by annual supplements. Librarians routinely used new editions to check collections against catalog citations, then considered titles they did not have for acquisition and titles in their collections but not in the guides for weeding. Today most of these guides are part of information retrieval systems that help construct the heritage of cultures. The R. R. Bowker Company, Scarecrow Press, Libraries Unlimited, ALA, and Neal-Schuman (now ALA-owned) also published monographs, but mostly to address librarians' practical needs. Each publisher also issued hundreds of reference titles in the twentieth century to improve library services. The most useful titles found room on reference shelves of nearly all libraries, often on revolving bookstands near the reference telephones; less utilized titles went to larger institutions.

The vast majority of postwar library literature and library research continued to address issues of library expertise and institutional management. Not even general research journals such as the *Library Quarterly*, *Library Trends*, and *Library Research* (now *Library & Information Science Research*) varied significantly from this pattern. Most bibliographical guides attempting to identify "best reading" continued to rely on a sophisticated and involved system set up at the turn of the century. Peer-reviewed journals and university presses, reputable and authoritative literary periodicals, and trade publishers worked together to evaluate newer materials and eventually formed a consensus on a hierarchy classifying the rest. Librarians followed their lead and chose from a pool whose boundaries others defined. New professionals coming out of library schools in the 1960s had little reason to question their judgment. The model of library education they inherited evolved from a training program sometimes connected to a major public library, sometimes to a university as an undergraduate program, and finally after midcentury into a professional program often located in a university graduate school that required applicants to have an undergraduate degree from an accredited institution where academic experts taught them "best reading." Once enrolled in library school, students took a core curriculum consisting of cataloging and classification, reference, management, book selection, and often a generic "library in society" course. The first four addressed institution and expertise; the last socialized students to the profession and inculcated the "library faith" by celebrating the library as an institution.

New Organizations

In 1967 ALA established an Office of Intellectual Freedom (OIF) to implement the policies of the Intellectual Freedom Committee and the ALA Council. Under Judith

Krug's direction, the office began an active program of publication, education, and public relations. In 1969 the Freedom to Read Foundation incorporated as a separate entity the OIF coordinated to provide assistance to censorship challenges. And in 1973 librarians organized an Intellectual Freedom Round Table to provide an organization within ALA through which individuals expressed opinions on specific and general intellectual freedom issues. Eleven years later the Supreme Court ruled in *Board of Education, Island Trees Union Free School District No. 26 v. Pico* that once a book was cataloged into a school library collection, school board members could not remove it just because they objected to ideas it contained. Elsewhere, fundamentalist Christians pressured librarians, school officials, and textbook publishers to remove ideas they found offensive, including Darwin's theories of evolution. In Tennessee, several parents unsuccessfully sued local public schools to have their children removed from classes that assigned readers promoting what they called "secular humanistic values." In 1976 and 1981 ALA issued ethics statements that addressed principles governing intellectual freedom, professional relationships with colleagues and vendors, and service to library patrons, among others. Like the LBR, however, the statement was unenforceable. No librarian ever suffered professional censure for violating them.

Like other professions, librarians also developed continuing education systems. Melvil Dewey introduced the issue at an 1898 ALA conference; C. C. Williamson addressed it a generation later in his landmark *Training for Library Service* (1923). Not until the 1960s, however, did the profession approach it systematically. The Continuing Library Education Network and Exchange (CLENE) formed in 1975 and nine years later became an ALA roundtable. By that time continuing education activities were offered by national, regional, state, and provincial library associations, universities and colleges, library and information schools, and individual libraries, consultants, and private vendors. Many were delivered at conferences, short courses and correspondence, and seminars, often on-site, frequently via electronic audio, video, or satellite. Almost uniformly, however, continuing education activities focused on "how to" rather than "why" questions.

AFTER 1970: "THE INFORMATION AGE"

New Research

Beginning in the 1960s, government and information scientists began to view the library as a site for "knowledge" research. Library schools that followed this perspective seldom analyzed cultural biases built into conventional definitions of "knowledge." "Information scientists" joined library school faculties, and "schools of library science" changed their names to "schools of library and information science," later "schools of information." In 1972 ALA created an Office for Research (later the Office for Research & Statistics) that generated much more quantitative than qualitative data. Library and information science research expanded its social science methodologies to cybernetics and operations research, and with the arrival of computer-based bibliographic networks and utilities laid the groundwork for user studies based on library service models encompassing online studies and reference work evaluation. Out of this milieu came "bibliometrics," a subfield designed to measure use of information products. Many—including a growing number of information scientists—continued to tout the scientific method as the most appropriate way to investigate library problems. Most, however, overlooked the social, economic, and cultural implications of power's influence on information use and the definition of "knowledge." And many library schools changed more in name than substance.

Another dimension of library research was evident in historical studies. Before the 1970s library history celebrated more than analyzed. Two published doctoral dissertations, Sidney Ditzion's *Arsenals of a Democratic Culture: A Social History of the American Public Library Movement in New England and the Middle Atlantic States from 1850 to 1900* (1947) and Jesse Shera's *The Foundations of the Public Library: The Origins of the American Public Library Movement in New England, 1629–1855* (1949) marked a shift toward analysis, but both still mirrored a positive outlook on librarianship that reinforced the "library faith." Not until the early 1970s, when Michael Harris applied revisionist educational historiography to an analysis of the Boston Public Library's origins, was the celebratory model significantly shaken. Harris argued that founders, all from Boston's first families, set up the institution primarily to control the city's new immigrants, especially the Irish. His conclusions struck at the heart of the library faith, but they also fit the times. ALA had just weathered a revolt occasioned by younger members who saw in the principle of " neutrality" advocated by veteran librarians: (1) an excuse *not* to address inequities in library practice caused by racism, sexism, and homophobia; (2) a rationale *not* to confront a government bent on conducting an unjust war in southeast Asia; and (3) a mechanism to give the Library Bill of Rights a strict construction that rendered it ineffective in the fight to include alternative perspectives in library collections. With the organization of the Social Responsibilities Round Table in 1969, these rebels found a home in ALA. Harris's and other revisionist works gave them a history that justified their actions.

Issues of Diversity

Revisionist library history grounded other efforts to correct inequities in the library profession. At the 1964 ALA annual conference, Savannah State College librarian E. J. Josey protested an Honorable Mention award given to the Mississippi Library Association (MLA) for National Library Week efforts. A decade earlier, Josey pointed out, MLA withdrew from ALA because it refused to integrate, as required by ALA bylaws. No state association should enjoy the benefits of membership, he argued, and at the same time repudiate ALA bylaws. He moved to prohibit ALA officers from attending or speaking in any official capacity at state library associations not also ALA chapters. The motion passed by a wide margin. In 1970 Josey organized the Black Caucus to monitor ALA policy and practice concerning race and to give African Americans a more prominent voice in professional matters. Shortly thereafter, the Black Caucus protested federal funding for library books for southern schools practicing segregation.

In Canada, the government initiated a Multicultural Policy that sought to promote multicultural public library services and encourage Canadian public libraries to develop programs for growing ethnic populations. Although the Toronto Public Library became a leader in the movement, it experienced serious bumps. Efforts to equalize services in all areas of the city doubled its usage between 1978 and 1983, but at the same time so stressed the staff they organized a union and in 1980 went on strike, closing the system for three weeks. Problems of a different sort preoccupied St. Boniface, which in 1953 had turned its parish library (established in 1911) into a municipal library serving both French- and English-speaking citizens. In 1972, however, Winnipeg amalgamated with other municipalities—including St. Boniface—and as a result, the St. Boniface Library became a City of Winnipeg department. By the end of the decade, library administrators and city officials made St. Boniface Winnipeg's—and Manitoba's—central French-language collection and thus deemphasized its role as a community public library. Library service to Francophones suffered as a result of municipal centralization.

African Americans were not the only minority to protest their plight within U.S. librarianship. In 1970 Israel Fishman and Janet Cooper organized an ALA Task Force on Gay Liberation (TFGL), the first openly gay and lesbian group established in a professional organization. Under Barbara Gittings's leadership after 1971, TFGL compiled bibliographies of books by and about gays and lesbians, produced conference programs, protested discrimination (including the absence of gay and lesbian press titles covered in mainstream library periodical indexes), and initiated a "best book" award ALA did not officially endorse until 1986. At the 1971 annual conference in Dallas, TFGL organized a "Hug-a-Homosexual" kissing booth that drew much local press attention. The library establishment said—and did—little to confront discriminatory practices based on sexual orientation. In 1978, for example, police arrested 105 men for homosexual solicitation at the Boston Public Library. Heterosexual librarians generally regarded this a "problem patron" activity, not unlike unruly youth, the homeless, and the mentally ill. In response, the lesbian and gay community rallied along several fronts. It created archival depositories like the Lesbian Herstory Archives in New York City, the Gay and Lesbian Historical Society of Northern California in San Francisco, and the Canadian Gay Archives in Toronto. All assumed an obligation to document the existence of gays and lesbians, a responsibility largely ignored in conventional practices librarians and information scientists often labeled "neutral." In 1988 the New York Public Library acquired the International Gay Information Center collection when it folded as a community archive. That same year Cornell established a Collection on Human Sexuality that focused on gay, lesbian, and bisexual culture.

Even in the late twentieth century, women (gay and straight) in the library profession continued to suffer sexist attitudes and practices from employers and patrons. Through the 1950s, women on the Toronto Public Library staff were not allowed to marry unless they also accepted demotion to temporary staff at a beginning salary. Some tried to subvert the practice by keeping their marriages secret. One even took to wearing a smock daily to disguise her pregnancy for a while, but once discovered she was forced to resign her position. In 1970 several women founded the Feminist Task Force of ALA's Social Responsibilities Round Table. In 1973 women in the Canadian Library Association organized a Task Force on the Status of Women. Two years later it became the Status of Women Committee and spearheaded the CLA conference theme: "Women: The Four-Fifths Minority." In a 1983 publication, Kathleen Heim pointed out that although men made up 20 percent of all U.S. librarians, they accounted for 58 percent of library school faculty members, 47 percent of the LC workforce, and 38 percent of academic librarians. Once identified, sexism in librarianship was more easily attacked wherever it surfaced.

Library Practices

For most librarians, eliminating racism, sexism, and homophobia in the profession seemed less compelling than other developments in librarianship. For example, library management literature made frequent reference to theorists like Peter Drucker, Chris

Argyris, and Douglas McGregor. In 1969 the Association of Research Libraries (ARL) created a Committee on University Library Management. In 1970 the Council on Library Resources funded ARL's Office of Management Studies, which then contracted with Booz, Allen & Hamilton to study the Columbia University Library to determine how library services might be improved. The resulting report, *Organization and Staffing of the Libraries of Columbia University* (1973), helped guide other university library managers striving to meet the demands higher education and research placed on their facilities. At the same time, however, the distribution of power in library organizations did not shift. In 1986 ARL analyzed its 109 members' organizational charts, and although it found departments for planning, budgeting, collection development, and staff relations that differed from surveys in the 1920s and 1930s, it still showed an administrative hierarchy controlling library work. Few chose to shake a system that provided a model for career advancement.

By that time support for libraries had eroded (which may explain the timing for organizing Friends of Libraries USA in 1974), and because inflation decreased purchasing power at the same time the number of publications increased and computerization of bibliographic records demanded heavy investment, "managing change" became the library administrator's primary responsibility. ARL's Office of Management Studies took several initiatives, most based on human relations and nonquantitative approaches to management science. The office established the Management Review and Analysis Project to help individual libraries review planning, control, organization development, and personnel practices; an Academic Library Development Program to improve collection development; public services and preservation at the small academic library; and the Consultant Training Program to create a corps of trained professionals to develop further studies. At many libraries administrators adapted to the management systems initiated by parent institutions (e.g., management by objectives, zero-based budgeting, and planning, programming, and budgeting systems), but they tended to avoid tools of decision theorists like operations research, economic analysis, and modeling.

As support staff assumed more responsibilities in the late twentieth century, library organizations offered much advice. In 1978 ALA issued guidelines for school libraries titled *Paraprofessional Support Staff for School Library Media Programs—A Competency Statement*. In 1985 the Council of Library/Media Technical Assistants published a collection of documents titled *Job Descriptions for Library Support Personnel*. The Canadian Library Association monitored library technician programs at community colleges. About the same time library associations, state library agencies, and universities accepted the "continuing education unit" (CEU) to reward noncredit, nontraditional learning experiences tied to job performance.

When historian Daniel Boorstin became librarian of Congress in 1974, he immediately faced two challenges—finding more space and reviewing the library's organization and functions. To address the former he oversaw construction of the James Madison Building, which, after it opened in 1980, became the third LC structure on Capitol Hill (the original structure was renamed the Jefferson Building; a second structure erected in 1939 was renamed the Adams Building). To address the latter he appointed the Task Force on Goals, Organization and Planning, and implemented many of its recommendations. Boorstin also created a Center for the Book, which opened in 1979 under the direction of LC historian John Y. Cole and quickly became a national advocate for libraries and reading, including the annual National Book Festival. When historian James H. Billington succeeded Boorstin in 1987, he became director of the world's largest library, which, at this writing, includes 32,000,000 books and 120,000,000 cataloged items, a staff of 5,000, and a budget of $700,000,000 to serve the research needs of Congress, function as the world's major producer of bibliographic data, address the needs of 700,000 blind and physically handicapped readers nationwide, and run the country's copyright agency. In 2012 LC averaged 1,700,000 visitors annually.

For most of the twentieth century U.S. and Canadian librarians worked together on cataloging and classification. Because the *Anglo-American Cataloging Rules* had not been revised since ALA and the Library Association of the United Kingdom (LAUK) compiled them in 1908 (the Depression and World War II hindered transborder cooperative work), LC appointed Seymour Lubetzky to develop *Rules for Descriptive Cataloging* in 1947, which ALA recommended for adoption as "an updated portion" of the Anglo-American Cataloging Code. Later Lubetzky produced *Code of Cataloging Rules: Author and Title Entry, an Unfinished Draft*, which an International Federation of Library Association working group on Coordination of Cataloging Rules adopted as a *Statement of Principles* in Paris in 1961. Based on these "Paris Principles," in 1967 LC, CLA, ALA, and LAUK delegates agreed to the *Anglo-American Cataloging Rules* (later known as AACR1) to unify cataloging practices in English-speaking countries. Because delegates could not agree on a final version, however, AACR1 came out in two versions, one British, the other North American. AACR2 was published in 1978, revised in 1988. By that time the Decimal Classification, used by 95 percent of North American public and school libraries and 25 percent of academic libraries, was in its twentieth edition, used in 130 countries and translated into thirty languages.

North American library communities also evolved evaluation systems for library services. In 1968 the *Bulletin of the Medical Library Association* published Richard Orr's research at the National Library of Medicine's Institute for the Advancement of Medical Communication. Orr used simulations to evaluate services, thus avoiding the need to collect data directly from library users. Several years thereafter Ernest DeProspo developed a set of performance measures for public libraries, which the Public Library Association published in 1973 as *Output Measures for Public Libraries*. The book went through several editions. The Association of Research Libraries published a manual of performance measurements shortly thereafter. The first monograph to deal comprehensively with the subject was F. W. Lancaster's *The Measurement and Evaluation of Library Services* (1977).

Elsewhere in the U.S. and Canadian public library worlds, social changes brought other effects. As white flight drained cities in the 1960s, urban public library circulation decreased, in the largest communities by as much as 16 percent. Because those who stayed did not value the kind of printed cultural forms libraries routinely collected as much as those who left, librarians had to alter traditional practices and devise new ways to address a different set of information needs. Information and referral (I&R) became one approach, most evident in the Detroit Public Library TIP (The Information Place) Program initiated in 1971. There librarians developed card file systems listing social and county organizations and the services they provided, their hours, addresses, telephone numbers, and personnel. Many files later converted to machine-readable databases. Elsewhere, public librarians took different approaches. One administrative approach to new circumstances was the evolution of federated library systems in which individually governed libraries volunteered to participate in joint efforts to purchase materials and share I&R services. Opportunities brought by improvement in electronic data processing accelerated the process.

Another was the emergence of highly successful county library systems, most notably in Broward County, Florida; Hennepin County, Minnesota; and Montgomery County, Maryland. All these developments reflected recommendations detailed in *The Public Library Mission Statement and Its Imperative for Service* that ALA issued in 1979. Public libraries should step away from acculturation, the document argued, and instead become educational, cultural, informational, and rehabilitative agencies that celebrate and serve the multicultural heritage of their communities in nontraditional ways. The popular films disdained in 1950 by the Public Library Inquiry found their way into late twentieth-century public library collections in the form of videos, which circulated to patrons like books. Another 1970s trend was the evolution of multitype systems that embraced more than one type of library in a cooperative network.

No matter the rules, however, librarians could not rid their information retrieval systems of all historic cultural biases. For example, "homosexuality" did not become an authorized LC subject heading until 1946, "lesbianism" until 1954. And not until 1972 did LC remove "see also" cross-references from these terms to "sexual perversion." Four years later LC introduced subject headings for "lesbians" and "homosexuals, male," which for the first time recognized them as classes of people. "Libraries are simply institutions that tell a story," said Winnebago tribal member Michael McLaughlin in 2005. To McLaughlin, it was clear librarianship's practices placed American Indians at a distinct disadvantage in the "story" public libraries told about them. For example, neither the LC nor DDC "adequately addresses the histories and contemporary realities of American Indians." Neither did the category "tribal sovereignty" enjoy equal status with other systems of government. Similarly, while Picasso and Monet were classified "Art," Indian sand paintings, pottery, and basketry were classified "Crafts" or "Primitive Art," and while Protestantism and Catholicism found comfortable niches in "Religion," Indian spiritualism was found in "Mythology," "Folklore," and "Other Religion." "Every American Indian perspective, accomplishment, or cultural belief, practice, or material product, according to these classification systems," McLaughlin concluded, "is of a subordinate or inferior nature." By misidentifying or refusing to identify, librarians (often unknowingly) participated in hegemony's inclination to render whole classes of people invisible.[20]

Impact of the Computer

In 1967 the Ohio College Association founded the Ohio College Library Center. For the first four years the center developed a computer systems architecture and provided catalog card production services. In 1971 it began online operation with its cataloging subsystem. Under Frederick Kilgour's leadership, within a decade the center evolved from a local college network into a national bibliographic utility known as the OCLC (Online Computer Library Center, Inc.). It also initiated online subsystems, including Interlibrary Loan, Serials Control, Acquisitions, and EPIC (a subject access system), and because OCLC adopted the MARC records, by 1990 thousands of libraries around the world used its database for cooperative cataloging. OCLC also participated in national programs, including the ARL/NFAIS A&I Project (host system for the National Serials Data Project and Serials Cataloging for LC), and the Linked Systems Project (host system for CONSER and the U.S. Newspapers Microforms Program). The CONSER Program connected national and research libraries to the OCLC network to create a large database of bibliographic records for serials. By 1990 the database contained over

150,000 records. OCLC also functioned as a contractor for GPO *Monthly Catalog* tapes. By that time, thousands of libraries had online public access catalogs and packaged automated circulation systems, and had incorporated use of CD-ROM products into traditional library services. In cooperation with the United States, Canada's National Library initiated projects like Canadian MARC format, the CONSER serials project, *Anglo-American Cataloging Rules*, Cataloging-in-Publication, and coordination of Canadian contributions to International Standard Book Numbers and International Standard Serial Numbers. In 1985 librarians on both sides of the border organized the North American Serials Interest Group to address serial pricing, acquisition, and preservation.

Elsewhere in U.S. and Canadian librarianship, efforts to prepare different futures met mixed results. In the late 1960s, for example, the Council on Library Resources (now Council on Library and Information Resources) funded MIT's Information Transfer Experiment (INTREX) Project to reconfigure the research library of the future. Because it was designed primarily by engineers who privileged the information they considered most valuable, however, the project ultimately failed to produce a prototypical all-purpose research library. In 1986, however, the council formed a Commission on Preservation and Access, produced *Slow Fires*, a film on the deterioration of paper with high acidity, and joined with other higher education and scholarly agencies (for example, the Brittle Books Program of the National Endowment for the Humanities) to focus attention on the problem that affected the printed materials held by most libraries. In 1970 NYPL established a Conservation Laboratory and two years later elevated it to a Conservation Division. In 1990 the federal government passed legislation requiring the use of alkaline paper in all government publications.

Technology continued to affect library work in the last half of the twentieth century. In the late 1950s the introduction of diffusion-transfer reversal (Thermofax) and electrostatic (Xerox) copying machines transformed library services, as students and patrons lined up to copy material from library resources. Telefacsimile did not arrive until the late 1980s. The arrival of the computer accelerated all these changes, and more. In 1972 NYPL began a computer-produced book catalog for the Research Libraries Group. The University of South Carolina was first to use a bar code and light pen to automate its circulation system. Computer Library Systems, Inc. (CLSI) pioneered online systems in the early 1970s, and by 1985 captured a major share of the market. The evolution of online public library catalogs also influenced classification systems, which were usually evaluated against the potential their notational schemes had as access points to the collections. In the 1980s a machine-readable version of DDC proved highly promising, and shortly thereafter multifunction systems incorporating classification schemes allowed libraries and their patrons not only to read all MARC information on items held but also to identify whether any title in the library collection was checked out or on the shelf. Within a decade dial access systems enabled library patrons to check on the circulation status of individual items in library collections from remote sites, to request materials via electronic mail, and to "hold" materials already in circulation. They also enabled libraries to better study use data to improve access and availability. Reference work was profoundly affected by "the online revolution," which greatly expanded and rapidly increased the speed of the reference librarian's information searching ability—and also her professional status. In many libraries database librarians set up appointments with patrons to help them tailor queries to terms systems could most easily manipulate. As a result, reference librarians assumed responsibility for guiding patrons through the intricacies of search strategies envisioned two generations earlier in the "library-college idea."

In law libraries, the full-text computer-assisted legal research systems that emerged in the 1970s forever changed law library practice. In 1973 Mead Data Central Corporation made the LEXIS legal research system commercially available, and in 1976 West Publishing introduced WESTLAW. The former was a full-text computer-assisted retrieval system designed for lawyers doing their own research. The latter utilized software developed for the Canadian-based Quick Law system to make West's headnote indexing system electronically searchable. Later, West added the full text of decisions to the database. The effect of these technological changes showed in the workforce. Beginning in the 1970s, law firms began hiring librarians to manage and manipulate these systems. Soon, law firm librarians outnumbered law school librarians in membership in the AALL. No longer were law firm libraries marked by large collections of books. Rather, they were sites where information specialists skilled at using online sources quickly satisfied lawyers' information needs. Computers also transformed information retrieval systems used by special librarians in government and industry. For example, in 1971 the National Library of Medicine transformed *Index Medicus*, a paper-copy information retrieval system originated in the 1870s, into MEDLARS (*Med*ical *L*iterature *A*nalysis and *R*etrieval *S*ystem), a computerized bibliographic system accessible through MEDLINE (MEDLARS online). Because the quantity of medical literature was growing geometrically, in 1960 the National Library of Medicine issued *Medical Subject Headings*, a flexible structured vocabulary that fit comfortably into MEDLARS language.

By 1990 the scores of consortia and networks generating and centralizing cataloging information had evolved into four major bibliographic utilities—OCLC, RLIN, WLN (initially called the Washington Library Network, later the Western Library Network), and UTLAS (for the University of Toronto Library Automated System, which developed and later sold it to a commercial organization). All four maintained online databases of authorities and bibliographic information, functioned as a source of cataloging copy for libraries with online catalogs, and produced catalog cards for libraries without online catalogs. About the same time the U.S. Defense Department's Advanced Research Projects Agency established a computer network. When several years later the government sponsored a program to establish communication protocols to integrate multiple networks, the Internet was born. In the 1980s the National Science Foundation (NSF) funded much of the research to connect selected universities and research institutions through NSFnet to NSF-assisted supercomputers. One response from the federal government to this emerging "opportunity" was the creation of the National Research and Education Network (NREN) in 1991. In anticipation of NREN, the Association of Research Libraries, the Association for the Management of Information and Technology in Higher Education, and EDUCOM (a networking consortium of colleges and universities) created the Coalition for Networked Information in 1990 to facilitate scholarship by improving access to networked information sources. Much of the activity then became subordinate to the national infrastructure initiated by the federal government.

In the first decades of the twenty-first century, U.S. and Canadian libraries of all types operated in relative transparency and generally manifested an emphasis on user needs. Users and nonusers generally considered them a public good worthy of public and philanthropic support. In 2010, among its 121,785 libraries, the United States hosted over 17,000 public libraries, including over 7,000 branches and service points in larger public library systems. Its 3,745 academic libraries included 1,160 community college libraries and 2,585 college and university libraries. Among its 8,476 special libraries were 1,436 law libraries, 1,877 medical libraries, and 1,022 religious libraries. Government libraries accounted for another 1,098 and included a library that preserved research materials for every presidential administration since Franklin Roosevelt. Larger research libraries (including some public, academic, and special libraries) modeled practices emulated across the globe. The country also hosted 99,180 elementary and secondary school libraries (81,920 public, 17,100 private, and 160 run by the Bureau of Indian Affairs). Among its 16,332 libraries Canada hosted over 1,673 public libraries with 3,415 service points. Its 205 academic libraries supported 732 service points, while its 1,047 special libraries included 156 law libraries, 206 medical libraries, and 91 religious libraries. Canada also hosted 14,451 elementary and secondary school libraries. From their beginnings, all these libraries played a role not only in constructing the heritage of cultures they served but also in many ways influencing the heritage of cultures they overlooked and/or undervalued.

ACKNOWLEDGMENT

The author would like to thank Professors Donald G. Davis, Jr., and Peter F. McNally for reading through and commenting on previous versions of this chapter. Parts of this chapter previously appeared in "Tunnel Vision and Blind Spots: What the Past Tells Us About the Present: Reflections on the 20th Century History of American Librarianship," *Library Quarterly* 69 (January 1999): 1–37.

NOTES

1. Quoted in Jesse Shera, *Foundations of the Public Library: The Origins of the Public Library Movement in New England, 1629–1855* (Chicago: University of Chicago Press, 1949), 32.

2. Thaddeus Mason Harris, *A Selected Catalogue of Some of the Most Esteemed Publications in the English Language Proper to Form a Social Library, with an Introduction upon the Choice of Books* (Boston: I. Thomas & E. T. Andrews, 1793), iii.

3. *Boston News Letter & City Record*, February 26, 1826.

4 Quoted in S. B. Cutler, "The Coonskin Library," *Publications of Ohio State Archives and Historical Society* 26 (1917): 58–77.

5. Quoted in Leon Hurwitz, *Historical Dictionary of Censorship in the United States* (Westport, CT: Greenwood Press, 1985), 158.

6. Quoted in Christopher Gray, "Streetscapes: The Old Astor Library," *New York Times*, February 10, 2002.

7. Quoted in Shera, *Foundations*, 239.

8. See Shera, *Foundations*, 269–90.

9. Bureau of Education, Department of the Interior, *Public Libraries in the United States of America: Their History, Condition, and Management; Special Report* (Washington, DC: Government Printing Office, 1876), xiii.

10. All quotes taken from Wayne A. Wiegand, *The Politics of an Emerging Profession: The American Library Association, 1876–1917* (Westport, CT: Greenwood Press, 1986).

11. Quoted in Wiegand, *Politics*, 45.

12. Wayne A. Wiegand, *Irrepressible Reformer: A Biography of Melvil Dewey* (Chicago: American Library Association, 1996), 92–93.

13. Quoted in M. S. Root, "An American Past in Children's Work," *Library Journal* (1946): 550.
14. Quoted in Wiegand, *Politics*, 73.
15. Corinne Bacon (comp.), *Standard Catalog Series: Fiction Catalog* (New York: H. W. Wilson Company, 1931), 11–12.
16. Louise Rosenblatt, *Literature as Exploration* (New York: D. Appleton-Century Company, 1938), x.
17. See Toni Samek, *Intellectual Freedom and Social Responsibility in American Librarianship, 1967–1974* (Jefferson, NC: McFarland, 2001), 148.
18. "Reader's Open Forum," *Library Journal* 61 (1936): 563; *New Republic* 87 (1936): 30.
19. Findings in Marjorie Fiske, "Action and Reaction," chap. 5 in *Book Selection and Censorship: A Study of School and Public Libraries in California* (Berkeley, CA: University of California Press, 1959), 64–85.
20. Michael McLaughlin, "The Need for American Indian Librarians," *Native American Times* 11 (2005): 8.

BIBLIOGRAPHY

Augst, Thomas. *The Clerk's Tale: Young Men and Moral Life in Nineteenth Century America.* Chicago: University of Chicago Press, 2003.

Augst, Thomas, and Kenneth Carpenter, eds. *Institutions of Reading: The Social Life of Libraries in the United States.* Boston: University of Massachusetts Press, 2007.

Augst, Thomas, and Wayne Wiegand, eds. *Libraries as Agencies of Culture.* Madison, WI: University of Wisconsin Press, 2001.

Barr, Larry J., Haynes McMullen, and Steven G. Leach, eds. *Libraries in American Periodicals before 1876: A Bibliography with Abstracts and an Index.* Jefferson, NC: McFarland, 1983.

Bay, J. Christian. *The John Crerar Library, 1895–1944: An Historical Report.* Chicago: John Crerar Library, 1945.

Beales, Ross W., and James N. Green. "Libraries and Their Users." In *The Colonial Book in the Atlantic World. Vol. 1; History of the Book in America*, edited by Hugh Amory and David D. Hall, 399–404. New York: Cambridge University Press, 2000.

Berelson, Bernard. *The Library's Public.* New York: Columbia University Press, 1949.

Bobinski, George S. *Carnegie Libraries: Their History and Impact on American Public Library Development.* Chicago: American Library Association, 1969.

Bobinski, George S., Jesse H. Shera, and Bohdan D. Wynar, eds. *Dictionary of American Library Biography.* Littleton, CO: Libraries Unlimited, 1978.

Braverman, Miriam. *Youth, Society, and the Public Library.* Chicago: American Library Association, 1979.

Bryan, Alice. *The Public Librarian.* New York: Columbia University Press, 1952.

Bundy, Mary Lee, and Frederick J. Stielow, eds. *Activism in American Librarianship, 1962–1973.* Westport, CT: Greenwood Press, 1987.

Bureau of Education, Department of the Interior. *Public Libraries in the United States of America: Their History, Condition, and Management; Special Report.* Washington, DC: Government Printing Office, 1876.

Buxton, William J., and Charles R. Acland. *American Philanthropy and Canadian Libraries: The Politics of Knowledge and Information.* Montreal: Graduate School of Library and Information Studies, McGill University, 1998.

Carmichael, James Vincent, Jr., ed. *Daring to Find Our Names: The Search for Lesbigay Library History.* Westport, CT: Greenwood Press, 1998.

Carpenter, Kenneth E. "Libraries." In *An Extensive Republic: Print, Culture, and Society in the New Nation, 1790–1840. Vol. 2: History of the Book in America*, edited by Robert A. Gross and Mary Kelley, 273–85. Chapel Hill: University of North Carolina Press, 2010.

Carpenter, Kenneth E. "Libraries." In *The Industrial Book. Vol. 3: History of the Book in America*, edited by Scott E. Casper, Jeffrey D. Groves, Stephen W. Nissenbaum, and Michael Winship, 303–18. Chapel Hill: University of North Carolina Press, 2007.

Carrier, Esther Jane. *Fiction in Public Libraries, 1876–1900.* New York: Scarecrow Press, 1965.

Carrier, Esther Jane. *Fiction in Public Libraries, 1900–1950.* Littleton, CO: Libraries Unlimited, 1985.

Casey, Marion. *Charles McCarthy: Librarianship and Reform.* Chicago: American Library Association, 1981.

Cmiel, Kenneth. "Libraries, Books, and the Information Age." In *The Enduring Book: Print Culture in Postwar America. Vol. 5: History of the Book in America*, edited by David Paul Nord, Joan Shelley Rubin, and Michael Schudson, 325–46. Chapel Hill: University of North Carolina Press, 2009.

Cole, John Y., ed. *Ainsworth Rand Spofford: Bookman and Librarian.* Littleton, CO: Libraries Unlimited, 1975.

Cole, John Y., and Jane Aikin, eds. *Encyclopedia of the Library of Congress: For Congress, the Nation & the World.* Washington, DC: Library of Congress, 2004.

Comaromi, John Phillip. *The Eighteen Editions of the Dewey Decimal Classification.* Albany, NY: Forest Press, 1976.

Conaway, James. *America's Library: The Story of the Library of Congress, 1800–2000.* New Haven, CT: Yale University Press, 2000.

Cramer, C. H. *Open Shelves and Open Minds: A History of the Cleveland Public Library.* Cleveland: The Press of Case Western Reserve University, 1972.

Cutler, Wayne, and Michael H. Harris, eds. *Justin Winsor: Scholar-Librarian.* Littleton, CO: Libraries Unlimited, 1980.

Dain, Phyllis. "The Great Libraries." In *Print in Motion: The Expansion of Publishing and Reading in the United States. Vol. 3: History of the Book in America*, edited by Carl F. Kaestle and Janice A. Radway, 452–70. Chapel Hill: University of North Carolina Press, 2009.

Dain, Phyllis. *The New York Public Library: A History of Its Founding and Early Years.* New York: New York Public Library, 1972.

Davis, Donald G., Jr., ed. *Dictionary of American Library Biography*, 2nd ed. supplement. Westport, CT: Libraries Unlimited, 2003.

Davis, Donald G., Jr., and John Mark Tucker, comps. *American Library History: A Comprehensive Guide to the Literature.* Santa Barbara, CA: ABC-CLIO, 1989.

Dickinson, Donald C. *Henry E. Huntington's Library of Libraries.* San Marino, CA: Huntington Library, 1995.

Ditzion, Sidney. *Arsenals of a Democratic Culture: A Social History of the American Public Library Movement in New England and the Middle States from 1850 to 1900.* Chicago: American Library Association, 1947.

Drolet, Antonio. *Les bibliothèques canadiennes: 1604–1960.* Ottawa: Le cercle du livre de France, 1965.

Du Mont, Rosemary R. *Reform and Reaction: The Big City Public Library in American Life.* Westport, CT: Greenwood Press, 1977.

Fiske, Marjorie. *Book Selection and Censorship: A Study of School and Public Libraries in California.* Berkeley, CA: University of California Press, 1959.

Fleming, E. McClung. *R. R. Bowker: Militant Liberal.* Norman, OK: University of Oklahoma Press, 1952.

Fleming, Patricia Lockhart, Gilles Gallichan, and Yvan Lamonde, eds. *The History of the Book in Canada. Vol. 1: Beginnings to 1840.* Toronto: University of Toronto Press, 2004.

Garceau, Oliver. *The Public Library in the Political Process.* New York: Columbia University Press, 1949.

Garrison, Dee. *Apostles of Culture: The Public Librarian and American Society, 1876–1920.* Rev. ed. Madison, WI: University of Wisconsin Press, 2003.

Geller, Evelyn. *Forbidden Books in American Public Libraries, 1876–1939.* Westport, CT: Greenwood Press, 1984.

Gerson, Carole, and Jacques Michon, eds. *History of the Book in Canada. Volume III: 1918–1980. Part 7: Reaching Readers*, 417–52. Toronto: University of Toronto Press, 2004.

Hamlin, Arthur T. *The University Library in the United States: Its Origins and Development.* Philadelphia: University of Pennsylvania Press, 1981.

Harris, Michael H., ed. *The Age of Jewett: Charles Coffin Jewett and American Librarianship, 1841–1868.* Littleton, CO: Libraries Unlimited, 1975.

Harris, Michael H. *History of Libraries in the Western World*, 4th ed. Metuchen, NJ: Scarecrow Press, 1995.

Harris, Michael H. "The Purpose of the American Public Library: A Revisionist Interpretation of History." *Library Journal* 98 (1973): 2509–14.

Hildenbrand, Suzanne, ed. *Reclaiming the American Library Past: Writing the Women In.* Norwood, NJ: Ablex, 1996.

Holley, Edward G. *Charles Evans: American Bibliographer.* Urbana, IL: University of Illinois Press, 1963.

Holley, Edward G., ed. *Raking the Historic Coals: The A.L.A. Scrapbook of 1876.* Pittsburgh: Beta Phi Mu, 1967.

Holley, Edward G., and Robert F. Schremser, eds. *The Library Services and Construction Act: An Historical Overview from the Viewpoint of Major Participants.* Greenwich, CT: JAI Press, 1983.

Holmes, Marjorie C. *Library Service in British Columbia: A Brief History of Its Development.* Victoria: Public Library Commission of British Columbia, 1959.

Jones, Plummer Alston, Jr. *Libraries, Immigrants, and the American Experience.* Westport, CT: Greenwood Press, 1999.

Kalisch, Philip Arthur. *The Enoch Pratt Free Library: A Social History.* Metuchen, NJ: Scarecrow Press, 1969.

Kaser, David. *A Book for a Sixpence: The Circulating Library in America.* Pittsburgh: Beta Phi Mu, 1981.

Kaser, David. *Books and Libraries in Camp and Battle: The Civil War Experience.* Westport, CT: Greenwood Press, 1984.

Kaser, David. *The Evolution of the American Academic Library Building.* Lanham, MD: Scarecrow Press, 1997.

Kraske, Gary E. *Missionaries of the Book: The American Library Profession and the Origins of United States Cultural Diplomacy.* Westport, CT: Greenwood Press, 1985.

Kruzas, Anthony T. *Business and Industrial Libraries in the United States, 1820–1940*. New York: Special Libraries Association, 1965.

Lamonde, Yvan, Patricia Lockhart Fleming, and Fiona A. Black, eds. *History of the Book in Canada. Vol. 2: 1840–1918. Part 5: The Evolution of Libraries*, 243–89. Toronto: University of Toronto Press, 2004.

Laugher, Charles T. *Thomas Bray's Grand Design: Libraries of the Church of England in America, 1695–1785*. Chicago: American Library Association, 1973.

Learned, William S. *The American Public Library and the Diffusion of Knowledge*. New York: Harcourt Brace, 1924.

Lee, Robert Ellis. *Continuing Education for Adults through the American Public Library, 1833–1964*. Chicago: American Library Association, 1966.

Macleod, David I. *Carnegie Libraries in Wisconsin*. Madison, WI: State Historical Society of Wisconsin, 1968.

Marcum, Deanna B. *Good Books in a Country Home: The Public Library as a Cultural Force in Hagerstown, Maryland, 1878–1920*. Westport, CT: Greenwood Press, 1994.

Martin, Robert Sidney, ed. *Carnegie Denied: Communities Rejecting Carnegie Library Construction Grants, 1898–1925*. Westport, CT: Greenwood Press, 1993.

McKechnie, Lynne E. F. "Patricia Spereman and the Beginning of Canadian Public Library Work with Children." *Libraries & Culture* 34 (1999): 135–50.

McNally, Peter F., ed. *Readings in Canadian Library History*. Ottawa: Canadian Library Association, 1986.

McNally, Peter F., ed. *Readings in Canadian Library History 2*. Ottawa: Canadian Library Association 1996.

Miksa, Francis L., ed. *Charles Ammi Cutter: Library Systematizer*. Littleton, CO: Libraries Unlimited, 1977.

Miksa, Francis L. *The Subject in the Dictionary Catalog from Cutter to the Present*. Chicago: American Library Association, 1983.

Miles, Wyndham D. *A History of the National Library of Medicine: The Nation's Treasury of Medical Knowledge*. Bethesda, MD: National Library of Medicine, 1982.

Molz, Redmond Kathleen. *National Planning for Library Service, 1935–1975*. Chicago: American Library Association, 1984.

Molz, Redmond Kathleen, and Phyllis Dain. *Civic Space/Cyberspace: The American Public Library in the Information Age*. Cambridge, MA: MIT Press, 1999.

Monroe, Margaret E. *Library Adult Education: The Biography of an Idea*. New York: Scarecrow Press, 1963.

Mount, Ellis. *Ahead of Its Time: The Engineering Societies Library, 1913–80*. Hamden, CT: Linnet Books, 1982.

Musmann, Klaus. *Technological Innovations in Libraries, 1860–1960: An Anecdotal History*. Westport, CT: Greenwood Press, 1993.

Olson, Hope A. *The Power to Name: Locating the Limits of Subject Representation in Libraries*. Dordrecht, Netherlands: Kluwer Academic Publishers, 2002.

Passet, Joanne E. *Cultural Crusaders: Women Librarians in the American West, 1900–1917*. Albuquerque: University of New Mexico Press, 1994.

Pawley, Christine. *Reading on the Middle Border: The Culture of Print in Late-Nineteenth-Century Osage, Iowa*. Boston: University of Massachusetts Press, 2001.

Pawley, Christine. *Reading Places: Literacy, Democracy, and the Public Library in Cold War America*. Boston: University of Massachusetts Press, 2010.

Peel, Bruce, ed. *Librarianship in Canada, 1946 to 1967.* Victoria: Canadian Library Association, 1968.

Pejsa, Jane. *Gratia Countryman: Her Life, Her Loves and Her Library.* Minneapolis: Nodin Press, 1995.

Raber, Douglas. *Librarianship and Legitimacy: The Ideology of the Public Library Inquiry.* Westport, CT: Greenwood Press, 1997.

Radford, Neil A. *The Carnegie Corporation and the Development of American College Libraries, 1928–1941.* Chicago: American Library Association, 1984.

Richards, Pamela Spence. *Scholars and Gentlemen: The Library of the New York Historical Society, 1804–1982.* Hamden, CT: Archon Books, 1984.

Richardson, John V., Jr. *The Gospel of Scholarship: Pierce Butler and a Critique of American Librarianship.* Metuchen, NJ: Scarecrow Press, 1992.

Richardson, John V., Jr. *The Spirit of Inquiry: The Graduate Library School at Chicago, 1921–1951.* Chicago: American Library Association, 1982.

Ring, Daniel F., ed. *Studies in Creative Partnership: Federal Aid to Public Libraries During the New Deal.* Metuchen, NJ: Scarecrow Press, 1980.

Robbins, Louise S. *Censorship and the American Library: The American Library Association's Response to Threats to Intellectual Freedom, 1939–1969.* Westport, CT: Greenwood Press, 1996.

Robbins, Louise S. *The Dismissal of Miss Ruth Brown: Civil Rights, Censorship, and the American Library.* Norman, OK: University of Oklahoma Press, 2000.

Rosenberg, Jane Aikin. *The Nation's Great Library: Herbert Putnam and the Library of Congress, 1899–1939.* Urbana, IL: University of Illinois Press, 1993.

Ross, Catherine Sheldrick, Lynne E. F. McKechnie, and Paulette M. Rothbauer, eds. *Reading Matters: What the Research Reveals about Reading, Libraries, and Community.* Westport, CT: Libraries Unlimited, 2006.

Samek, Toni. *Intellectual Freedom and Social Responsibility in American Librarianship, 1967–1974.* Jefferson, NC: McFarland, 2001.

Shera, Jesse H. *Foundations of the Public Library: The Origins of the Public Library Movement in New England, 1629–1855.* Chicago: University of Chicago Press, 1949.

Shiflett, Orvin Lee. *Louis Shores: Defining Educational Librarianship.* Lanham, MD: Scarecrow Press, 1996.

Shiflett, Orvin Lee. *The Origins of American Academic Librarianship.* Norwood, NJ: Ablex, 1981.

Sinnette, Elinor Des Verney. *Arthur Alfonso Schomburg, Black Bibliophile & Collector: A Biography.* Detroit: Wayne State University Press, 1988.

Smith, Jessie Carney. *Black Academic Libraries and Research Collections: An Historical Survey.* Westport, CT: Greenwood Press, 1977.

Smith, K. Wayne. *OCLC, 1967–1997: Thirty Years of Furthering Access to the World's Information.* New York: Haworth Press, 1998.

Smith, Karen Patricia, ed. "Imagination and Scholarship: The Contributions of Women to American Youth Services and Literature." *Library Trends* 44 (1996): 679–895.

Stone, Elizabeth W., ed. *American Library Development, 1600–1899.* New York: H. W. Wilson Company, 1977.

Sullivan, Peggy. *Carl H. Milam and the American Library Association.* New York: H. W. Wilson Company, 1976.

Swanick, Eric L., ed. *Hardiness, Perseverance, and Faith: New Brunswick Library History.* Halifax: School of Library and Information Studies, Dalhousie University, 1991.

Tucker, John Mark, ed. *Untold Stories: Civil Rights, Libraries, and Black Librarianship.* Champaign, IL: Graduate School of Library and Information Science, University of Illinois, 1998.

U.S. National Agricultural Library Associates. *The National Agricultural Library: A Chronology of Its Leadership and Attainments, 1839–1973.* Beltsville, MD: National Agricultural Library, 1974.

Vann, Sarah K. *Training for Librarianship Before 1923: Education for Librarianship Prior to the Publication of Williamson's Report on "Training for Library Service."* Chicago: American Library Association, 1961.

Van Slyck, Abigail A. *Free to All: Carnegie Libraries & American Culture, 1890–1920.* Chicago: University of Chicago Press, 1995.

Wadsworth, Sarah, and Wayne A. Wiegand. *Right Here I See My Own Books: The Woman's Building Library at the World's Columbian Exposition.* Boston: University of Massachusetts Press, 2012.

White, Carl A. *A Historical Introduction to Library Education.* Metuchen, NJ: Scarecrow Press, 1976.

Whitehill, Walter Muir. *Boston Public Library: A Centennial History.* Cambridge, MA: Harvard University Press, 1956.

Wiegand, Wayne A. *"An Active Instrument for Propaganda": The American Public Library During World War I.* Westport, CT: Greenwood Press, 1989.

Wiegand, Wayne A. "The American Public Library: Construction of a Community Reading Institution." In *Print in Motion: The Expansion of Publishing and Reading in the United States, 1880–1940. Vol. 4: History of the Book in America*, edited by Carl F. Kaestle and Janice A. Radway, 431–51. Chapel Hill: University of North Carolina Press, 2009.

Wiegand, Wayne A. "The Historical Development of State Library Agencies." In *State Library Services and Issues: Facing Future Challenges*, edited by Charles R. McClure, 1–16. Norwood, NJ: Ablex, 1986.

Wiegand, Wayne A. *Irrepressible Reformer: A Biography of Melvil Dewey.* Chicago: American Library Association, 1996.

Wiegand, Wayne A., ed. *Leaders in American Academic Librarianship, 1925–1975.* Pittsburgh: Beta Phi Mu, 1883.

Wiegand, Wayne A. *Main Street Public Library: Community Places and Reading Spaces in the Rural Heartland, 1876–1956.* Iowa City: University of Iowa Press, 2011.

Wiegand, Wayne A. *The Politics of an Emerging Profession: The American Library Association, 1876–1917.* Westport, CT: Greenwood Press, 1986.

Wiegand, Wayne A., ed. *Supplement to the Dictionary of American Library Biography.* Englewood, CO: Libraries Unlimited, 1990.

Wiegand, Wayne A., and Donald G. Davis, Jr., eds. *Encyclopedia of Library History.* New York: Garland Publishing, 1994.

Williamson, William Landram. *William Frederick Poole and the Modern Library Movement.* New York: Columbia University Press, 1963.

Winger, Howard W., ed. "American Library History: 1876–1976." *Library Trends* 25 (1976): 1–416.

Winter, Michael F. *The Culture and Control of Expertise: Toward a Sociological Understanding of Librarianship.* Westport, CT: Greenwood Press, 1988.

Wolff, Katherine. *Culture Club: The Curious History of the Boston Athenaeum.* Boston: University of Massachusetts Press, 2009.

Woodford, Frank B. *Parnassus on Main Street: A History of the Detroit Public Library.* Detroit: Wayne State University Press, 1965.

Young, Arthur P., comp. *American Library History: A Bibliography of Dissertations and Theses.* 3rd rev. ed. Metuchen, NJ: Scarecrow Press, 1988.

Young, Arthur P. *Books for Sammies: The American Library Association and World War I.* Pittsburgh: Beta Phi Mu, 1981.

3

Africa

Anthony Olden

INTRODUCTION

Egypt was the center of a great civilization in the pre-Christian era, and the library at Alexandria was known throughout much of the ancient world. But at the start of the twentieth century Egypt was under foreign rule, as was all of Africa, apart from Ethiopia—the Christian enclave in the highlands of the Horn that had succeeded in keeping the Italians out until then—and Liberia in West Africa, home of the descendants of freed American slaves and the local population they controlled. Although the twentieth century saw great changes in every continent—with advances in science, technology, and communication on the one hand and disasters ranging from war conflicts to the 1918 influenza and the 1980s AIDS pandemics on the other—it could be argued that in Africa change was greatest; most of it traveled from the beginnings of colonial rule to the end, and from the promise and excitement of independence to a more mundane reality with disappointments and failures as well as successes. The emphasis in this chapter of *A History of Modern Librarianship* is on the twentieth and early twenty-first centuries.

Kenya's Ali Mazrui points to "Africa's triple heritage of indigenous, Islamic and Western forces—fusing and recoiling, at once competitive and complementary."[1] Islam brought literacy and formal education to parts of Sub-Saharan Africa, as did the West to other parts centuries later. When publishing and libraries were introduced in the twentieth century (earlier in South Africa) they were patterned on foreign models. The library models were Western and have not always proved appropriate, in particular the Anglo-American public library model. Sections on language, literacy, education, and publishing in this chapter are provided as background to the treatment of libraries. Africa's history and socioeconomic development are touched on to provide necessary context.

War and Peace

"The hopeless continent," *The Economist* called Africa in 2000. It referred to Sierra Leone, torn apart by bad government, illicit diamond trading, and a civil war in which child soldiers committed atrocities. Diamonds and other mineral resources proved a mixed blessing in many parts of Africa. Among the minerals exported from the Democratic Republic of Congo (formerly Zaire) is coltan (columbite–tantalite), which is used in electronic products such as mobile telephones. Congo was mired in corruption and frequently in conflict and war since its independence in 1960. South Sudan, which became Africa's newest state on achieving independence from Sudan in 2011, was involved in skirmishes with the Khartoum government over their disputed border, which passes through petroleum-rich land. Botswana, on the other hand, benefited from its diamond deposits, which together with cattle raising, up-market tourism, and responsible government brought enough prosperity to support a middle-income country. This former British protectorate, which achieved independence in 1966, became stable and democratic, with a small population occupying a large geographic area, much of it the Kalahari Desert. At the time of writing Botswana was investing its money in education. The University of Botswana was fully committed to sponsoring academics for study outside the country whenever necessary. The university's library school (which also covers archives and records management) was large, with numerous faculty members holding doctorates from universities in the United States, the United Kingdom, South Africa, and elsewhere.

Although Botswana was peaceful, Somaliland (like Sierra Leone) was recovering from a devastating war. In the late 1980s Somali president Mohamed Siad Barre sent forces to attack Hargeisa, capital of the North West. Many fled across the border to Ethiopia or elsewhere. Ultimately some refugees went to the United Kingdom, the United States, Canada, and other parts of the world. One example was Mo Farah, born in the Somali capital Mogadishu of a Somaliland background. He came to Britain at the age of eight in 1991, and in the 2012 Olympics won both the 5,000- and the 10,000-meter races, making him the finest British distance runner ever. By the early 1990s the North West declared itself the Republic of Somaliland, although its independence was not recognized by other African and non-African countries. Apart from camels, goats, and sheep, Somaliland's resources were scant, but members of the diaspora scattered all over the world sent money home to support family members and promote development. Because of the conflict literacy rates were low, especially among women, while libraries in Somaliland and Somalia were destroyed. The Africa Educational Trust—which specializes in work in war-torn areas—improved the situation by training literacy teachers and establishing resource centers in a number of rural and urban primary and secondary schools. With donor money the trust selected and appointed library staff and provided them basic training. In collaboration with Book Aid International in London it provided books. It also organized workshops to encourage local writers. The results were published as pamphlets, with multiple copies placed in libraries. Users could now read material in Somali as well as in English. All books could be read on-site but not borrowed by pupils, teachers, and others. Somaliland made progress in library development and in other fields. It even started its own book fair.

"Seek ye first the political kingdom," said Kwame Nkrumah, who led Ghana to independence in 1957. His was one of the first territories to gain independence, and it did so peacefully, as did most of British Africa in the 1950s and 1960s. French West Africa and the Belgian Congo achieved independence in 1960, although Belgian lack of preparedness for the event and American and European interest in the Congo's mineral wealth were factors in the overthrow and murder of Patrice Lumumba, the new prime minister, and the gradual rise to power of Mobutu Sésé Seko, who became one of the most corrupt rulers in the world. Because of the presence of nearly a million French settlers, it took a bloody struggle with France before Algerians achieved independence in 1962. Portugal hung on to its African empire until 1975, after the government in Lisbon fell. But between the forces of their left-wing governments and rebel movements supported by apartheid South Africa and by money from the United States, war ravaged postindependence Angola and Mozambique. South Africa hung on to South-West Africa (now Namibia), originally a League of Nations mandate, until forced to back out in 1990. Eritrea fought for thirty years to extricate itself from imperial and then Marxist Ethiopia—which received support first from the United States and then from the Soviet Union—until it finally achieved its goal of independence in 1991.

Africans developed and exchanged knowledge and skills in different parts of the continent over the millennia. Knowledge of how to work and use iron spread to the region during the last millennium BCE. The introduction of the camel to North Africa early in the Christian era stimulated trans-Saharan trade and communication. The spread of Islam was especially important. By the eighth century all of North Africa was under Muslim rule. It took longer for Islam to cross the Sahara, but ultimately the empire of Kanem-Bornu in the Lake Chad area and the Hausa city-states in what is now the north of Nigeria were in touch with centers of learning as far away as Egypt and Arabia. Further to the west, Timbuktu had many Qur'anic schools in the sixteenth century. These taught basic reading and recitation. At a higher level were the *ulama*, or scholars, whose reputation was respected throughout the Islamic world. They copied manuscripts by hand because, time-consuming and expensive though this was, it cost less than buying imported books.

Shaikh Usman dan Fodio was a scholar and leader who launched a jihad in 1804 against pagan and irreligious Muslim rulers in what is now the northwest of Nigeria. He was author of numerous writings in Arabic, as was his brother Abdullahi and his son and successor as sultan of Sokoto, Muhammad Bello. Dan Fodio waged a holy war to restore what he considered a pure form of Islam. His forces brought the Hausa states under their control. Leaders of the jihad were Muslim scholars first and political and military leaders second, which is why Arabic became the official language of lands under their control. Under Usman dan Fodio and Muhammad Bello, Sokoto became a noted center of learning. Both men emphasized the importance of education for women. In East Africa trade brought Islam and the Arabic language and writing from the Gulf all along the coast.

There were Portuguese at the court of the king of Benin in the fifteenth and sixteenth centuries. The Dutch established a settlement at the Cape of Good Hope in 1652. European slave traders took millions of Africans to the Americas over several hundred years. Arab slave traders created havoc in parts of East, Central, and Southern Africa in the nineteenth century. The period of colonial rule itself was short: when Kenya gained its independence in 1963 its leader was Jomo Kenyatta. He was alive before the colony was brought into existence and died fifteen years after it came to an end. In most instances colonial rule commenced in the late nineteenth century and ended in the early 1960s.

Language Matters

Despite its brevity, however, colonial rule brought Western institutions—including libraries—and education to Africa, and spread European languages into the interior. The terms "Anglophone," "Francophone," and "Lusophone" are used regularly to describe groupings of countries in contemporary Sub-Saharan Africa. These descriptors need qualification. Whereas British East Africa and French West Africa are factually accurate terms for the territories in East and West Africa controlled by Britain or France during colonial times, the terms "Anglophone" and "Francophone" can mislead. Except for German (because Germany's colonies were mandated to Britain, France, Belgium, and South Africa by the League of Nations after World War I) and Italian (because the Italians lost the Horn of Africa during World War II, and the Republic of Somalia opted for English in preference to Italian in the 1960s), African elites are fluent in the language of the former colonizer, which is usually the official language. But this fluency is not shared by all the population. The Kenyan writer Ngũgĩ wa Thiong'o has written eloquently about the contradictions arising from this.

Ngũgĩ was an undergraduate at Makerere University College, Uganda, in 1962. He participated in the Makerere conference of "African Writers of English Expression" on the strength of two short stories he published, one of them in a student journal. Twenty years on and by then an internationally known writer and critic, he looked back on the absurdity of this. Why should a young student with no more than two stories in print be at an African writers' conference, but not Shabaan Robert (Tanzania) or Chief Fagunwa (Nigeria)? Robert wrote extensively in Kiswahili, and in Ngũgĩ's opinion was the greatest living East African writer; Fagunwa had written in Yoruba. Ngũgĩ believed the "psychological violence" of the classroom was a legacy of the physical violence of colonization. He recalled how at the school he attended in the 1950s children were beaten if caught speaking Gĩkũyũ (Kikuyu). Although English was the language of advancement in the British Empire, Ngũgĩ abandoned the Christian name (James) under which his first stories and novels had appeared. Instead, he decided to abandon the language of imperialism and switch to Gĩkũyũ and Kiswahili in his writing, although he was willing to have his work translated.

As of this writing (2013) the Nobel Prize for Literature had yet to be awarded to a Gĩkũyũ, Kiswahili, or Yoruba writer: the languages have been French, English, and Arabic. Albert Camus, born of European background in French-ruled Algeria in 1913, was awarded the Nobel Prize in 1957. Four African authors have won it since: Nigeria's Wole Soyinka (1986), Egypt's Naguib Mahfouz (1988), and South Africa's Nadine Gordimer (1991) and J. M. Coetzee (2003). Léopold Senghor, president of Senegal from 1960 to 1980, was elected to the Académie française in 1983 in recognition of his contribution to the French language and Francophone culture. The best-known African novel—Nigerian Chinua Achebe's *Things Fall Apart* (1958)—has been translated into fifty languages and sold over ten million copies. Its author lived in the United States from 1990 until his death in 2013. Unlike Ngũgĩ, Achebe never opposed writing in English. In his memoir he recalls with appreciation his education at Government College, Umuahia, in the 1940s. Referring to Nigeria's 250 ethnic groups and the efforts of the teachers to enroll students from all over the colony, he asks: "Would I have been able to communicate . . . had we not been taught one language?"[2]

Language and relevance are crucial issues in the development of library services for the general public. Following his visit to West Africa in 1964 the president of the (British) Library Association wrote that the standard of fiction in Nigerian public libraries he visited was little higher than in an English branch. He wrote without irony. The problem was that the cultural context of that fiction was foreign to most Nigerians, while the language in which it was written was foreign to all—very familiar though it was to some. Admittedly, the small amount of material available in Nigerian languages did not help. But the lack of appropriateness of the Anglo-American public library model for Africa, the limited or negligible support given to public library development by many African funding authorities, and the tiny percentage of Africans who could or would use such public libraries as did exist resulted in a sector that came to pose more and more dilemmas as years passed. The difficulty—indeed the impossibility—of avoiding the words "Anglophone," "Francophone," and "Lusophone" in an account of libraries and librarianship in Africa is illustrative of some fundamental questions still awaiting answers.

EDUCATION AND LITERACY

Missionaries, Foreign Rule, and the Struggle for Education

In ancient Egypt the papyrus plant, grown in the Nile delta, was turned into paper for writing. Later, Egypt came under Greek and then Roman rule for a thousand years, until all of North Africa came under Arab control and became part of the new Islamic world in the seventh century. Farther to the south, Christianity brought literacy to Ethiopia as early as the fourth century. However only a very small percentage of Ethiopians ever learned to read or write Ge'ez, the language of the liturgy. Literacy, which took much longer to reach other parts of Sub-Saharan Africa, has been described as the most important single innovation of foreign rule for non-Muslim areas. The foreign missionaries who brought literacy wanted young people in particular to be able to read the word of their God. "Of all the agents of imperialism it was the missionary who made the most revolutionary demands," according to Nduka.[3] Missionaries wanted Nigerian souls, not Nigerian soil or wealth from the soil. They were an integral part of the colonial world. It was said they used to ask Africans to look up at the heavens, and when Africans looked down again their lands had gone. Although the story may be apocryphal, it is revealing.

British missionaries founded Fourah Bay College in Sierra Leone in 1827, two years before the University of Cape Town. The aim was to train Africans to serve as missionaries and teachers in the region. In 1867 Fourah Bay became a college of the University of Durham, offering degrees in classics, philosophy, Hebrew, and theology. Subjects such as law were added in the twentieth century. In 1968 it severed the link with Durham and joined with two colleges to form the University of Sierra Leone. Fourah Bay was the only tertiary-level institution in Anglophone West Africa for many years, and its graduates formed an elite. The founding principal of Nigeria's University College, Ibadan, paid tribute to the work of the missionaries who taught so well at Fourah Bay. He said the reason that higher education had been established in West Africa was that missionaries had accepted conditions that few European or African lecturers would accept in the 1950s.

Elsewhere more basic Western education helped to produce the go-betweens needed by the colonial administrators and traders to interpret and explain. Many of its products became clerks, although the German colony of Cameroon had the post of secretary-interpreter. Even exceptionally able Africans receiving early Western education found that the injustices of the colonial world blocked their advance. Nigerians rose to senior positions in the late nineteenth century, but this became more difficult later. As a way to keep them subordinate, in the late 1930s Eritreans were allowed only four years of schooling—enough to learn a moderate amount of Italian, basic arithmetic, and the principles of hygiene. As for history, schools removed the *Risorgimento* from the syllabus to prevent young Eritreans getting inappropriate ideas.

Government involvement in the provision of education increased gradually during the colonial period, although as the colonial powers developed more pressing reasons for being in Africa it was never enough. Nigeria, however, did have some of the best secondary schools in the British Empire. Chinua Achebe attended Government College, Umuahia, where other pupils gave him the nickname "Dictionary." Achebe also instances King's College and Queen's College, Lagos; Government College, Ibadan; and Dennis Memorial Grammar School, Onitsha. Ngũgĩ wa Thiong'o won a place at Alliance High School, the top school for African boys in colonial Kenya. He recalled it and its principal, Edward Carey Francis, with appreciation in a memoir written more than half a century later. Days after he started in 1955 he stood at the library door, "mesmerized by the sight of shelves upon shelves of books in a building devoted to nothing else but books: I had never seen so many in my life. I could not believe that now I could go in, borrow books, return them, and get some more as often as I wanted. I swore that I would read all the books in the library."[4]

But these top-quality schools were for the few. Some colonial administrators and in particular white settlers were ambivalent about Western-educated Africans, if not indeed actively hostile to them. A lengthy report on library services in the Rhodesias and Nyasaland in 1951 includes the following comment from a director of African education (presumably British or South African): "Africans have constantly to be reminded that there has been far too much contempt for manual labour, with a contrasting admiration for book-learning and pendriving [sic], and that man is distinguished from all other creatures as a tool-using animal, and his brain has developed largely through the use of his hands."[5]

The Tanzanian leader Julius Nyerere said that on independence in 1961 his country inherited a basically illiterate society. In the early twentieth century the French wrote about their *mission civilisatrice*, but no more than a tiny elite received the equivalent of a full French education. The spread of education was uneven, and chance or a little money could make all the difference. Kenneth Kaunda remembered no free education in Northern Rhodesia (later Zambia, of which he became president) when he was a child. When he first went to school the teacher asked him for his two shillings and sixpence. He ran home in tears to ask his mother, but she did not have the money. Luckily for him a neighbor provided a loan: "for so small a thing in those days could a child for ever forfeit the privilege of his life's education."[6]

One part of Africa that took education firmly into its own hands was Eritrea during its struggle for independence from Ethiopia. It had no choice but to be self-sufficient, as the only outside support came from Eritreans overseas. The first school of the Eritrean Peoples Liberation Front was started in 1976 in a place named Zero. The pupils were the soldiers, the children of the soldiers, and civilians in the liberated areas. The curriculum included the rationale for the struggle, revolutionary theory, and the importance of equality between men and women. Schooling took place in trenches and caves because open-air gatherings were easily attacked by Ethiopian fighter planes. After independence the leader of the armed struggle became president of the new country. As his rule became more dictatorial he closed down the University of Asmara, Eritrea's sole university.

Muslim Concerns about Western Education

Muslim areas had reservations about Western education because they feared that Christian missionaries would proselytize. Early in the twentieth century Lord Lugard, the colonial administrator who was later to become governor-general of a united Nigeria, promised the Muslim north that missionaries would not be allowed into an emirate with-out the emir's consent. This policy had major repercussions as independence neared, because the north ended up with far fewer Western-educated people to fill vacancies created by the departure of expatriates than did the south of Nigeria.

Western education was a sticking point in another Muslim area under British control, the Somali coast opposite Aden. The establishment in the 1890s of a French Roman Catholic mission for homeless Somali children in the port of Berbera upset religious leader Seyyid Mohamed Abdille Hassan. Convinced Europeans stole their country—or at least its Gulf ports—he and other Somalis believed that Europeans were trying to steal their children by bringing them up as Christians. Unsuccessful at getting the mission closed, the "Mad Mullah"—as the British disparagingly referred to him—launched a remarkable military campaign that lasted until his death in 1920. In addition to conven-tional warfare he composed poems that castigated Christian colonizers and any Somalis who collaborated with them. Although Somali as a language had a rich oral tradition, it had not been written down. The Seyyid was an educated man, but most Somalis were illiterate. Many followers committed his poems to memory and traveled throughout the countryside reciting them. They had a huge impact on people for whom poetry was an integral part of life.

In 1938 the government attempted to open an elementary school for boys in Berbera. At the time Arabic was the written language of literate Somalis. R. E. Ellison, the direc-tor of education on secondment from Northern Nigeria, proposed to introduce written Somali in addition to Arabic in the Berbera school. But some mullahs countered that written Somali was against the Islamic faith, that the school was a proselytizing agency, and that the director of education was a missionary in disguise. Later they maintained that even if Ellison was not a missionary, their religion did not permit a non-Muslim to be in control of the secular education of Muslim boys. The controversy delayed the school's opening, but the governor intervened and calmed matters by forbidding the teaching of written Somali.

It is likely that most Berbera school parents were happy their sons had the oppor-tunity to learn English, useful for business purposes and advancement in general. Far more extreme is Boko Haram (Western Education Is Forbidden), the Islamic funda-mentalist group that achieved international notoriety with its kidnapping of over 270 female students in northeast Nigeria in 2014. In addition to attacking Christians the group attacks Muslims it regards as moderates. The Nigerian army has not been partic-ularly successful in fighting back, and the government has placed the entire northeast under a state of emergency. Over a million people have fled the conflict. Elsewhere in West Africa the northern half of Mali came under the control of other Islamist insur-gents in 2012. This together with a food shortage caused half a million people to flee. The followers of Ansar Dine (Supporters of the Faith) damaged the shrines of its Sufi saints in Timbuktu (a UNESCO World Heritage site of great significance in West Afri-ca's cultural and architectural history), maintaining they deviated from true Islam. The manuscript collections of the city also suffered.

The Tuareg people served in Libya in the armed forces of Colonel Qaddafi. When his regime collapsed in 2011 they returned home well armed. The Mali insurrection appears to have started as a bid for a separate homeland. Then religious extremists took over. As people of the Sahara, most Tuareg live in Niger and Mali. They were involved with the trans-Saharan trade routes, but French colonization, the replacement of the camel by new forms of transport, and other changes in twentieth-century life altered their livelihood. Famine drove some south into the north of Nigeria in the early 1970s, and the one-time desert warriors often found themselves working as night watchmen. Nigerians disliked the Tuareg, recalling times they came south hunting for slaves. A wry anecdote is told about a Tuareg error of judgment in the colonial era. Both the British and French set up schools for the sons of chiefs. When the French arrived to take the boys, the Tuareg became suspicious. They gave them the sons of their slaves instead, passing them off as their own. Then in 1960 some of these former children assumed high positions in government and the civil service as the most highly educated Africans in their newly independent territories.

Adult Education

Adult education has usually been synonymous with adult education for literacy in Africa. For those who missed out on education, adult literacy programs could offer a second opportunity. But such programs rarely met long-term success. Julius Nyerere was a strong advocate for literacy, which he made a prerequisite for membership in his political party—Tanganyikan African National Union (TANU). Mohamed Siyad Barre, who took over Somalia in a coup d'état in 1969, adopted the Roman script for the Somali language in 1972 and started a nationwide if unorthodox literacy campaign. He sent students into rural areas under the motto "If you know, teach. If you don't, learn." Although well intended, it had limited effects because not all students had teaching ability, and young people teaching their elders often lacked sensitivity. In Africa Western-educated people tended to look down on traditional knowledge that rural people passed from generation to generation, surviving often harsh conditions. Absence of opportunity explains a lack of formal education and the inability to read and write. Obtaining an education for girls, for example, has always been harder than for boys. Many African cultures expect girls to help in the home; some believe money invested in educating girls is wasted. In Africa more women than men are illiterate. Lack of respect by teachers is unlikely to promote learning. Lack of respect by librarians does not help either. Over many decades service to nonliterates was a discussion topic at conferences and in writings, but little practical progress followed.

PUBLISHING

Kenya: Charles Richards and the East African Literature Bureau

For generations libraries have depended on publishers for materials that helped construct the heritage of cultures. African libraries are no different, but how publishers served them reflected distinct cultural biases. Kenya is an appropriate case for two reasons. Its publishing industry is one of the most developed in Africa, and detailed information on how the industry developed from the 1940s to the present can be found in the writings of two individuals: Charles Richards and Henry Chakava. Richards came to Kenya from England in 1935 to run the Church Missionary Society Bookshop in Nairobi. He expanded into publishing, and in 1946–1947 his bookshop sold 250,000 of its own publications, including the popular *Woman's Work in the Home*, available in several languages. In 1948 he was invited to establish the East African Literature Bureau, which he ran until 1963. Afterward he worked briefly for Oxford University Press in Eastern Africa, and then for ten years in religious publishing in Geneva and London.

Early printing in much of colonial Africa took the form of laws, regulations, and gazettes from the government printer. Missionaries translated the Bible, or sections of it, into local languages, which were then printed. Thus, much early printing and publishing was of a religious nature, and religious publishers were and are particularly good at distributing their work both within and beyond a country's borders. The East African Literature Bureau, set up to serve Kenya, Uganda, Tanganyika, and Zanzibar, had parallels in Northern Rhodesia and Nyasaland, Northern Nigeria, and a number of other British territories. Richards felt that teaching adults to read was important, and he published appropriate reading material for the new literates in a range of languages. He worked to develop African authorship and put the most promising authors in touch with firms that could market their work internationally rather than publish it himself. His intention was not to compete with commercial firms but to develop publishing and readership in general. In a 1951 report, for example, he mentions the channels the Literature Bureau used to distribute its publications, in particular the network of church and mission bookstores. He also points out that manuscripts by African authors were being delayed or rejected because of the bureau's limited budget.

In the 1953 annual bureau report Richards mentioned that book sales to the Kikuyu had fallen away completely, although they had been among the biggest book buyers in the colony. This he attributed to the Mau Mau uprising. Kenya was an exception to what was generally a peaceful transition to independence in most of Britain's African empire. Kikuyu pressure on land and resentment toward white settlers who had taken so much of it led to Mau Mau. The colonial administration hit back with mass internment, torture, and over 1,000 executions. Much of the Kikuyu population found itself in detention camps or in villages surrounded by barbed wire. But in the camps literate inmates taught reading and writing to the semiliterate and the illiterate using sticks for writing on the dirt floors. Richards made no mention of the brutal response of colonial authorities: the bureau came under the East Africa High Commission, and the government printer in Nairobi printed its report. Richards did, however, use the bureau's civics books in what the government called the Kikuyu Rehabilitation Scheme. In 1963 Richards took up an appointment with Oxford University Press (OUP) Eastern Africa, with the task of developing it from an office with a representative to a full branch of the press. For him the OUP imprint represented the best in printing and publishing. But he did not stay. The World Council of Churches invited him to manage its Christian literature development program. Richards was happy in Kenya and happy with OUP, but he was deeply religious. He felt obliged to accept the invitation.

Kenya: Henry Chakava and Postindependence Publishing

Like Richards, Chakava entered publishing by accident. After graduating with first-class honors in literature and philosophy from the University of Nairobi, and while waiting for a scholarship to undertake doctoral studies in the United States or the United Kingdom, he took a temporary job in the Nairobi office of Heinemann Educational Books, where he became one of Africa's best known publishers. At the University of Nairobi Chakava was a student of Ngũgĩ wa Thiong'o, who as a student himself won a Literature Bureau prize provided with Rockefeller Foundation support for a new work by an East African writer. Ultimately Chakava became his publisher. Their relationship was positive and cordial, although his firm's association with such a controversial author caused the government concern. Ngũgĩ and colleagues had organized adult literacy classes in Kamirithu Community Educational and Cultural Centre, not far from Nairobi. He then upset authorities because of his play, *I Will Marry When I Want*, which he wrote in Gĩkũyũ and staged there. The content of the play was challenging, and audiences for the performances grew larger and larger until the government effectively banned them by withdrawing the licence for gatherings. Ngũgĩ soon found himself inside Kamiti Maximum Security Prison for a year without trial. His novel *Devil on the Cross*, written in the prison on toilet paper, was smuggled out with the help of a sympathetic prison warder. After his release the University of Nairobi refused to allow him to return to teaching, and Chakava provided him with a desk in the Heinemann office so he had a place to write. Apart from his children's books in Gĩkũyũ, every Ngũgĩ book became a Kenyan bestseller.

Chakava had a postindependence perspective and was a *protégé* of Heinemann publisher Alan Hill. According to Nigeria's Chinua Achebe, Hill saw the "enormous potential for indigenous publishing of African authors where those before him had seen only a market for British textbooks, modified, if need be, to give Jack and Jill brown faces and kinky hair." Heinemann established the African Writers Series in 1962 with three novels and one nonfiction title: reprints of Achebe's *Things Fall Apart* and *No Longer at Ease*, together with Cyprian Ekwensi's *Burning Grass* and Kenneth Kaunda's *Zambia Shall Be Free*. The series inspired many young authors. While other British publishers were taking on Africans as warehousemen, clerks, and salesmen, Heinemann employed Chakava as an editor and gave him training and support. The Nairobi office of Heinemann Educational Books developed into Heinemann Kenya and finally into East African Educational Publishers.

Years later Chakava criticized Richards for joining OUP, maintaining that he should have "crowned his exemplary service to publishing in Kenya by spearheading, at independence, the establishment of a locally owned commercial firm." Instead of this Richards "unleashed . . . a multinational ogre"when he joined OUP.[7]

As in Kenya, British publishing elsewhere in Africa has a mixed record. In particular, the involvement of Macmillan in Ghana, Tanzania, Uganda, and Zambia in the 1960s turned out badly. Macmillan was the family firm of Harold Macmillan, leader of the Conservative Party and British prime minister from 1957 to 1963. Because of Macmillan's personal contacts at the highest level of politics, his firm was able to enter into agreements to produce schoolbooks for four African countries (not Kenya), where the publishing industry was more advanced. Parastatal organizations were set up to supply this lucrative school market, with Macmillan providing the publishing expertise. Other British publishers were upset that an astute politician had outmaneuvered them. However, the partnerships did not last for more than a few years. African publishers consistently complained that foreign publishers operated in Africa in good economic times but departed in bad times, only to return again when the situation changed (as it did in the 1980s when the World Bank advertised contracts to provide textbooks to schoolchildren).

Publicizing African Writers

In response, in 1989 African publishers set up the African Books Collective (ABC)—a nonprofit marketing and distribution outlet. When the Modern Library—an American publishing firm owned by Random House—invited members of its editorial board to nominate the 100 best English-language novels of the twentieth century, not one African novel made the Modern Library list. "In America there is really very little knowledge of the literature of the rest of the world," Chinua Achebe noted in 2012. Achebe suggests listening to Native American poetry as a good place to start.[8] In 1998 U.S.-based Kenyan academic Ali Mazrui took steps to remedy this. He assembled an international jury to list from over 1,500 nominations Africa's 100 best twentieth-century books, including nonfiction, fiction, poetry, and books for children. Among the top twelve were Achebe's *Things Fall Apart*, Ngũgĩ's *A Grain of Wheat*, Senghor's *Oeuvre poétique*, and Soyinka's autobiographical *Aké: The Years of Childhood*.

Censorship in Apartheid South Africa

None of Ngũgĩ's books were officially banned in Kenya, but *A Grain of Wheat* was removed from the list of prescribed school literature texts in 1988, six years after he had gone into exile. Censorship in apartheid South Africa was far more draconian. When the South African edition of the second volume of the *Oxford History of South Africa* was published in 1971 it contained fifty-two blank pages—the place where the chapter on "African Nationalism in South Africa, 1910–1964" should have been, and indeed where it was in editions destined for other parts of the world. The chapter included quotations from individuals and organizations banned under South African laws. OUP felt that a volume without a chapter was better than no volume at all, as the book would certainly have been banned had it appeared in full.

Was OUP in South Africa representative of all that was good in publishing, as Charles Richards believed, or was it the multinational ogre that Henry Chakava criticized in Kenya? An investigation that drew on the company's archives reveals that by the 1970s pressure for profit led the South African branch to publish government-approved schoolbooks for black children rather than anything critical of apartheid, or indeed anything much of an academic nature. Schoolbooks for white children tended to be published by Afrikaner firms who enjoyed the backing of the government. As a result the opportunity in the market was in what the government called Bantu education, and a profitable opportunity this turned out to be for OUP. The company wanted its overseas branches to make a profit and for these profits to be returned to the United Kingdom to subsidize its academic imprint, Clarendon Press, which operated at a loss.

Between 1960 and 1990 eighty thousand people were detained without trial in South Africa, and simply possessing banned material was sufficient reason for imprisonment. The books were produced in court as evidence. Archie Dick provides an extensive account of the titles banned, of the police searches of homes, of reading in prison, and of reading in exile. Solomon Mahlangu Freedom College (SOMAFCO) was set up in Tanzania on land given to the African National Congress by the Tanzanian government, which was sympathetic to the antiapartheid movement. At its library exiles were able to read books by Nelson Mandela and Govan Mbeki that were banned at home, as well as works such as Walter Rodney's *How Europe Underdeveloped Africa* and Issa Shivji's *Class Struggle in Tanzania*. In South Africa, meanwhile, librarians colluded with authorities by removing offensive books from the shelves and burning them in municipal incinerators. One librarian Dick interviewed recalled the destruction of Martin Luther King's "I Have a Dream" speech and of a film in which Bing Crosby and Louis Armstrong sang together and held hands. Some white librarians contravened the apartheid laws and did what they could to assist nonwhite readers. Nadine Gordimer refers to such a librarian in her novel *No Time Like the Present* (2012). Gordimer, like Achebe, was one of the authors Mandela read in prison.

SUBSCRIPTION LIBRARIES

Such was the political, economic, and cultural context in which many African libraries developed. In the nineteenth and twentieth centuries South Africa had what were called public libraries, but in fact were subscription services for whites willing to pay. According to one authority who visited South Africa, the Rhodesias, and Kenya in 1928 on behalf of the Carnegie Corporation, this served as a way of keeping the nonwhites out. In Kenya the Carnegie Corporation supported a subscription library service for whites in the 1930s. Racial discrimination was a dominant feature in those parts of British Africa that had white settlers. In East Africa British officials had more to lose by African advancement as they were there permanently (or believed they were). In West Africa, however, the colonial administrators returned to the United Kingdom upon retirement. Following a visit by the Carnegie Corporation president and secretary to East and Southern Africa in 1927, a group of Kenyan settlers and administrators asked for financial help. To them Carnegie gave $40,000, which thirty years later it listed as "Government of Kenya, Public library development, 1930–35." But the money did not go to Kenyans; instead, it funded a scheme to supply books to Europeans in the colony. The McMillan Library—erected in Nairobi by the widow in her settler husband's memory—served as its base.

Carnegie money also supported a subscription library in Lagos, Nigeria, in 1932 on the initiative of Alan Burns, the colony's acting chief secretary. There was an important difference with Kenya, however, the Lagos Library was elitist but not racist. Burns saw advantages to white administrators mixing socially with highly educated Nigerians such as the lawyers Eric Olawolu Moore (the son and grandson of Church of England clergymen) and Sir Kitoyi Ajasa, a member of the colony's legislative council. In contrast to East Africa, the West African colonies had African lawyers and other professionals who had undertaken part of their education in England as far back as the nineteenth century. However, the number of subscribers to the Lagos Library was small—by 1935 no more than 481 (only 43 were Africans). The Lagos Library owed its origins to the British Council, which started subscription library services in West Africa during World War II. It was becoming clear at the time that independence for India was inevitable and that the way that members of the British administrative class had segregated themselves socially from educated Indians had damaged relationships. The council believed a different approach in Africa was desirable. In 1943 W. M. Macmillan, a senior representative for British West Africa in Accra in the Gold Coast (later Ghana) and an unapologetic elitist, saw council services as a way of bringing together the top Europeans and Africans. Not only did the council want to bring the "right" people into its libraries, it wanted to keep the "wrong" people out. One way of doing this was through subscription charges. Kate Ferguson, the council's librarian in West Africa, agreed. She determined that the Lagos Public Library, set up with council assistance, should charge a fee, because without one it would be impossible to provide a building large enough to hold all the "riff raff" who would want to come in, or to keep out those who could not read. As of this writing, some African public libraries continue to charge subscriptions.

PUBLIC LIBRARY SERVICE

The 1950s and 1960s

Modern public library development commenced at different times in different parts of Africa. The establishment of the Gold Coast Library Board enabled Ghana (as it later became) to get off to a good start in 1950. Evelyn Evans, the founding director, was able, experienced, and energetic, and went on to form an excellent working relationship with Kwame Nkrumah, who became prime minister on independence in 1957 and later became president. The Eastern Nigeria Regional Library also made great strides in the late 1950s and early 1960s under the leadership of Kalu Okorie, who also secured political backing. Tanzania started later. The library activities of the East African Literature Bureau in Tanganyika (as it then was) had been well intentioned but not particularly successful, and it took the arrival of Max Broome as founding director of the new Tanganyika Library Service Board in 1963, and the full political support of Julius Nyerere, to get things underway. Nyerere's support continued under Broome's successor, Ezekiel Kaungamno. Both Nkrumah in Ghana and Nyerere in Tanzania believed in literacy, education, and libraries, and the combination of professional expertise and hard work and strong political support brought impressive results.

The National Library Board Structure

Librarians who initiated new services in Africa were mainly British by background, and public library services at home were organized on a local basis. But in countries such as Ghana, Kenya, Uganda, Tanzania, Zambia, and Botswana the new services were set up on a national basis. In addition the new boards had national library as well as public library responsibilities. Under legal deposit legislation they received a copy of every book published in the country and produced the national bibliography on a regular basis. Ghana opted for service to various parts of the country before putting up buildings in Accra, the capital. Tanzania took the opposite approach, putting the emphasis first on a quality, professionally run service in the main city, Dar es Salaam, and then extending to other urban areas. Services operated in temporary premises until libraries were built. In 1967 Nyerere opened the National Central Library building. Financial support for new buildings came from the United Kingdom and Denmark, and scholarships to study librarianship in the United Kingdom were also provided. However, responsibilities of the Tanganyikan Library Services Board (it kept this name for many years) did not extend to Zanzibar (the offshore islands of Unguja and Pemba). As elsewhere in the world, politics influenced library development in Africa. After Tanganyika and Zanzibar merged in 1964 the latter kept much self-rule. It had its own passport and customs controls, and its own library service.

In few parts of Africa have politics had a greater impact on how public libraries were organized and structured than Nigeria. As a federation with three regions in years leading to independence in 1960 (the North, the West, and the East), three embryo regional library services evolved, of which the East was most developed. In the 1950s northern Nigeria was less advanced in Western education than the rest of the country. A new public library service was established in Kaduna, the capital, but it managed to do little outside the city by 1967. The task of providing services from scratch to a vast geographic region was so overwhelming that the Northern Regional Library largely decided to focus efforts on administrators, teachers, other professionals, and students in the capital. These library users amounted to a tiny percentage of the region's population. In 1967, as the country was sliding toward civil war, the federal government abolished the regions and put twelve states in their place. The twelve later became nineteen. As of this writing, Nigeria has thirty-six states and the federal capital territory, Abuja. As a result, in less than a half-century it has gone from three to over thirty public library authorities.

Nigeria also has a national library, set up with financial assistance from the Ford Foundation in the 1960s. Whether a national library was actually necessary was debated at the time, given that since 1950 the University of Ibadan (previously University College, Ibadan) had been performing national library functions like building up the pre-eminent collection on the country, acquiring Nigerian publications under legal deposit, and producing a national bibliography. But the Ford Foundation and its consultants were determined to give the country a present to mark its independence, and the National Library of Nigeria was the result. Later the new national library became concerned that while it was financially supported by taxes collected from all Nigerians, it was only providing a service to a very small number in Lagos, the federal capital. It decided to expand, with the aim of eventually having a branch in all thirty-six states.

What Sort of Service? And Who Is to Receive It?

Setting up and providing a public library service in Africa in the 1950s and 1960s brought particular problems. African students and teachers had similar levels of education and information needs as European or American students and teachers. Mid-twentieth-century Africans in higher education were a tiny elite. In the United Kingdom those in higher education were also an elite, although numbers there were obviously larger. While a good African academic library was similar to a good Western academic library in the 1960s, attempts to compare public libraries in the West and Africa are more difficult—indeed, comparisons often make little sense. Because library service hardly existed outside urban areas, only a small proportion of the African population used late twentieth-century public libraries. This situation was even more pronounced in the 1950s and 1960s.

The originators of the public library service were Western-world expatriates. Most of them meant well, but their familiarity with African life and culture was often limited, at least in their first years. They knew how public libraries should be run—or at least how public libraries were run in Britain, the United States, or whichever country they came from. The public library user often seemed to exist for the sake of the library rather than the library for the sake of the user. Users wanted textbooks to help them advance their level of formal education—but public libraries were not supposed to stock textbooks. Users wanted a quiet place in which to read their own study material and do their homework—but quiet places in libraries were for consulting the reference material selected with care and expense by professional staff. Users wanted help with assignments—but librarians thought of themselves as librarians, not teachers.

Then, like a rain cloud on the horizon, there lurked all those millions of nonliterates and semiliterates that nothing in the librarians' mentality or professional background had equipped them to serve. A 1963 report on the library needs of Northern Nigeria provides a good illustration of this. F. A. Sharr was a British public librarian who went on to a distinguished career in Australia. He spent almost four months in 1962–1963 researching and writing a report under the auspices of the Special Commonwealth African Assistance Plan. In his 242-page report he acknowledged: "We have no experience, and have had insufficient time fully to study the needs, of new literates and illiterates." According to Sharr the primary concern of a public library is "with those whose formal education is over." Almost all those with whom he discussed the matter in Nigeria, he stated, agreed that public library service should be aimed at the educated. He was not, however, against providing new literates or illiterates simple information verbally, should they ask.[9]

Continuing Dilemmas

The new public libraries in the 1950s and 1960s were stocked with up-to-date publications, although these publications were of no more than partial relevance to the small minority of people who used them—well-educated professionals and those striving to be well educated. In the 1970s and early 1980s Nigerian libraries still had up-to-date book stocks, because the federal and state governments had plenty of money from the country's petroleum exports. In later years the situation changed in much of Africa because funding diminished, often because African countries were under military rule and armies are expensive. Because of lack of funding some public libraries in Africa were largely stocked with out-of-date material, with the newer books being donated by organizations such as Book Aid International. All that was paid for locally were the newspapers and the salaries of the staff. Public libraries became the poor relation of the African library world, although it could be argued that school libraries in parts of the continent fell into an even worse position.

Since the mid-twentieth century the big issue remained unresolved. How could a public library reach out to the rural areas where the majority of the population lived? Most of these people received no service. In the 1950s the East African Literature Bureau circulated books to professionals and others by post, but lack of financial backing from the colonial authorities restricted the service. The bureau also circulated book boxes, but again these had limitations. The aim of some of the national library boards was to start with professionally designed, purpose-built static libraries and use these as a base for mobile library services. However, mobile libraries did not last long in Africa. The vehicles that foreign donors provided often broke down, proved too expensive to repair, were commandeered for purposes judged more important, or their parts were removed to keep other vehicles running. Sometimes animals were used as substitutes—donkeys in Zimbabwe and camels in Kenya, for example.

THE ACADEMIC LIBRARY

The Universities

It is not surprising that Egypt, with its own ancient heritage, its thousand years of Greek and then Roman civilization, and its place in the Islamic world for even longer, has the oldest university in Africa: Al-Azhar, which is linked to Al-Azhar Mosque. Originating as a *madrasa* in the tenth century, it specialized in religious studies and Arabic until the 1960s, when the curriculum was broadened to include fields such as medicine and engineering. In Sub-Saharan Africa the establishment of Fourah Bay College in Sierra Leone in 1827 has already been mentioned. In South Africa, universities with roots in the nineteenth century include Cape Town, Stellenbosch (where the medium of instruction is Afrikaans), and Witwatersrand. The University of Fort Hare played an important role in providing higher education for black South Africans such as Nelson Mandela, and for Africans from north of the border such as Robert Mugabe from Southern Rhodesia and Kenneth Kaunda from Northern Rhodesia.

Between 1945 and independence in the late 1950s to early 1960s Britain and France made efforts to advance higher education in their colonies. Dakar was the capital of French West Africa, and a school of medicine and pharmacy started there in 1916. The French Institute for Black Africa (Institut Français d'Afrique Noire) organized in the late 1930s to study the lands and people under French control. The Dakar Institute of Higher Education also began; in 1957 it became the University of Dakar and played a regional role in higher education in Francophone West Africa, and indeed more widely. Portugal lagged behind Britain and France. In 1962 it set up "higher education institutions" in what it then termed "the overseas provinces" of Angola and Mozambique. In 1968 it renamed them universities. Both were later renamed after fighters in the struggle for independence from Portugal: Agostinho Neto University in Luanda and Eduardo Mondlane University in Maputo.

British West Africa saw the establishment of university colleges in the Gold Coast and Nigeria in 1948. They had what was described as a "special relationship" with the University of London, as did Gordon Memorial College, Khartoum, and Makerere University College, Uganda. In 1957 the University College of Rhodesia and Nyasaland entered into the special relationship, as did Royal College, Nairobi, and University College, Dar es Salaam, in 1961. Students studied locally but graduated from the University of London, whose examinations they took. The papers were graded locally and then in London. One particular advantage of the arrangement for academic staff was that they could register for PhD degrees with the University of London.

Founding principal of the University College of the Gold Coast was David Balme, a classical scholar with a distinguished war record. Balme specialized in Aristotle, and the college soon had a good classics department. The subject was also on the curriculum at University College, Ibadan, where the founding principal was an entomologist with prewar research experience in East Africa. The University of London assisted with the recruitment of academic staff, and together with the two colleges it was determined to maintain the highest standards. Many other Gold Coast and Ibadan students went on to the most senior positions after independence. Initial intakes were small, because among other things members of the teaching staff were still being recruited, a process that went on for several years and had to be repeated when individuals left to return home to the United Kingdom. The first intake of students at Ibadan in 1948 numbered 104, of whom three were female. One of these three—F. A. Ogunsheye—went on to become a librarian and eventually head of the university's library school. Ibadan started in temporary premises, and years passed before a permanent campus was built, but again the standard of the new buildings was high.

Gordon Memorial College was the first to opt out of the special relationship with the University of London to become the University of Khartoum. The Gold Coast college became the University of Ghana in 1961, while Ibadan became the University of Ibadan in 1962. Makerere, Nairobi, and Dar es Salaam became colleges of the new University of East Africa in the 1960s, and ultimately independent universities in their own right after the short-lived federal institution disbanded in 1970. Ironically, the University of Nigeria, established in 1960, was the first institution of higher education to adopt the title of university in that country. Not only was it clear that a newly independent Nigeria would require far more graduates than a single university could produce, but Nigerians such as Nnamdi Azikiwe (premier of the Eastern Region between 1954 and 1960 and a U.S. university graduate himself) felt that Ibadan was perhaps overtraditional and over-academic in its approach, and that the example of American land-grant universities had more to offer in educational programs for more practical vocations. Michigan State University assisted in setting up the new University of Nigeria, which was based in Nsukka in the Eastern Region. The first two vice chancellors were American.

The number of universities in Nigeria quickly increased, with Ahmadu Bello, Lagos, and Ife being established in 1962. Statistics from the 1950s showed that Ibadan was a university for the Western and Eastern regions, the new University of Nigeria for the East. The Northern Region felt neglected. When Ibadan opened in 1948 the north simply did not have the students qualified for entry. It had, however, many with Islamic qualifications, and in the 1950s the northern premier, Sir Ahmadu Bello, returned from a visit to North Africa with the idea of establishing an Islamic university like Al-Azhar in Cairo. In fact Ahmadu Bello University (named after the premier) was established in Zaria as a secular institution by the federal government in 1962. The Kano campus of Ahmadu Bello and the Jos campus of Ibadan became universities in their own right in the 1970s. A number of Nigeria's states also established their own universities. The growth in the number of Nigerian universities continued into the twenty-first century.

In South Africa, governments set up colleges and universities on the basis of race. Fort Hare, the North, and Zululand, founded between 1916 and 1959 for black South Africans, became independent universities in 1970. The University of the Western Cape, intended for Colored (mixed race) South Africans, opened in 1960, and the University of Durban-Westville, intended for those of Indian background, in 1961. Both became independent in 1971.

Private higher education represents a recent development for much of Africa. Religious faiths started many private institutions, like Tanzania's Muslim University of Morogoro. Tumaini (Hope) University, established by the Evangelical Lutheran Church, offered the country's first undergraduate program in library science. In East Africa, Aga Khan University, linked to the Aga Khan Development Foundation (particularly involved in the education of nurses, midwives, and doctors), developed campuses in Nairobi, Dar es Salaam, and Kampala. Because government-funded universities limited the number of students, these private institutions saw opportunities. Programs offered were mainly at undergraduate level. At the beginning of the twenty-first century the University of Ghana, Ibadan in Nigeria, Makerere in Uganda, and Dar es Salaam in Tanzania—the oldest public universities—maintained enormous prestige. In some countries distance learning—for example the Open University of Tanzania—offered an alternative to full-time or part-time class attendance. By far the longest-established and largest distance education provider in Africa has been the University of South Africa, which set up a Division of External Studies in 1946. According to its website Unisa became the first correspondence university in the world in 1959.

The Libraries

Libraries serving these institutions of higher education had mixed histories. By the 1970s the University of Ibadan had a fine collection not just on Nigeria but on Africa. To a considerable extent this was due to John Harris, Ibadan's librarian from 1948 to 1968.

He accepted a number of valuable collections, including the 18,000-volume library of the late Henry Carr, a high-ranking Nigerian administrator. F. M. Dyke, a long-term employee of the United Africa Company, presented his collection of 10,000 books, including material on the oil palm industry. After the head of the history department died his family presented his books on Africa to the library. In the 1970s the libraries of Ahmadu Bello University had a good collection of books and serials: in both the main university library (Kashim Ibrahim Library) and departmental libraries (such as the Institute of Agricultural Research). Through the early 1980s acquisitions budgets were adequate in Nigerian university libraries.

University budgets in many other African countries were far from adequate in the 1980s, and the phrase "the book famine" began to be heard. An important report published by the International African Institute illustrates the situation across the continent toward the end of the century. Of libraries studied those of the University of Botswana were the best resourced. Botswana aside, the report showed no discernible difference between Anglophone, Francophone, Lusophone, and Arabaphone Africa. Serial subscriptions were the weakest area. University libraries in Côte d'Ivoire were said to be in "catastrophic decline." Departmental libraries were often of varying quality. While the Science Library at Addis Ababa University, Ethiopia, was "impressive and well run," the Medical Library was in a "sorry state," among other reasons because it was "overstaffed with people apparently hanging around doing nothing." A departmental library at the University of Dakar, Senegal, was worse: "The stock is largely outdated and physically dilapidated, there are no current journals, shelving is old and inappropriate, there are no display racks, the air-conditioning has broken down, so has the photocopier, windows are dirty and some are broken, and there is no money for equipment, furniture or repairs. Suppliers refuse to do repairs on credit because of previous unpaid bills. The chairs are set in concrete to prevent students removing them to the overcrowded lecture halls. The library is ill-sited on the top floor, the previous librarian (retired in 1994) was an invalid and for years had been unable to get up the stairs."[10]

The libraries of Eduardo Mondlane University, Mozambique, had been dependent on donors for books, journals, buildings, and staff development since the mid-1980s, the main donors being the Swedish Agency for Research Co-operation with Developing Countries, the Ford Foundation, and the American Association for the Advancement of Science. Western donor aid to Ethiopia dried up in the mid-1970s after the armed forces overthrew Emperor Haile Selassie and Mengistu Haile Mariam established a Marxist dictatorship. Before this the United States Agency for International Development built a new main library for Haile Selassie I University (later Addis Ababa University). Named after President John F. Kennedy, it was officially opened by the emperor and the president's mother, Rose Kennedy, in 1970. Ahmadu Bello University in Nigeria also had a President Kennedy Library on one of its campuses.

The demand for textbooks on the part of students was overwhelming. Whereas students at American and British universities usually bought their own textbooks, students in Africa did not, either because they could not afford them or because a local bookstore did not exist. Universities such as Makerere in Uganda established special textbook collections or "book banks." Students could borrow a textbook at the start of the academic year and return it at the end. As long ago as 1952 the East African Literature Bureau reported that many Africans came to its library centers to read but not borrow the books "presumably because the conditions of their home life are adverse to home reading."[11]

In the 1990s space in which to sit and read was the main priority of students using the University of Dakar main library.

THE LIBRARIANS

The Colonial Era and the Early Years of Independence

From the nineteenth century onward West Africans traveled overseas to qualify in law and other disciplines. But the first Nigerian to qualify professionally as a librarian did not do so until the decade preceding independence. Kalu Okorie became a fellow of the (British) Library Association in the early 1950s. In East Africa the first Kenyan was John Ndegwa, in the 1950s a staff member of the Literature Bureau in Nairobi. Both had distinguished careers, Ndegwa as librarian of the University of Nairobi and Okorie as director of public libraries in the east of Nigeria. The first professionally qualified librarians in the British territories of West and East Africa were mainly from the United Kingdom. Evelyn J. A. Evans arrived in the Gold Coast (later Ghana) as British Council Librarian in 1945. She set up the Gold Coast Library Board in 1950 and became its first director. By the time she left in 1965 she was the best known public librarian in the newly independent countries of Africa. Evans had years of English public library experience, and her relentless energy overcame many obstacles. In Nigeria the equally energetic and experienced New Zealander, John Harris, took up an appointment as librarian of the new University College, Ibadan, in 1948. His achievements over the following twenty years won him the title "father of Nigerian librarianship."

Other expatriates were not associated as closely with particular institutions or countries because they moved from library to library in the end of empire and early independence years. Two are particularly noteworthy: Wilfred J. Plumbe and Harold Holdsworth. After work in English public libraries in the 1930s and in an agricultural library in Sudan after World War II, Plumbe built up university libraries in Nigeria, Malaysia, Malawi, Guyana, and Papua New Guinea—a career that ranged over four continents. Holdsworth worked in South Africa, Jamaica (librarian of the new University College of the West Indies at Mona), and Uganda (librarian of Makerere University) before becoming librarian of the new University College in Dar es Salaam in the 1960s and later librarian of the University of the South Pacific, Fiji.

Early expatriate librarians were fully aware of their wide responsibilities. They were pioneers, establishing a profession from almost nothing. This included recruitment and training of staff who eventually took over from them, and the establishment of library associations. Looking back in 1987, Plumbe acknowledged that some of the young people he had "nudged into librarianship" in the 1950s and 1960s had become "better librarians than I ever was."[12] Eight became university librarians in Africa, Asia, and Australia. The African staff were also pioneers, starting out in a profession unknown in their countries. Some young recruits were influenced at school by teachers who passed on their love of books, and in a number of instances built up small libraries. For many others the job in the library was pure chance. The prospect of training—in particular, overseas training—served as an incentive. Gold Coast (Ghana) Library Board staff went to the United Kingdom for their professional education in the 1950s. The new Tanganyika Library Service Board emphasized similar opportunities when recruiting library assistants in the mid-1960s.

Although Africans who completed secondary education and went on to a degree or professional training in the 1950s and 1960s had to overcome considerable obstacles, Shiraz Durrani, on the staff of the University of Nairobi libraries in the 1970s and early 1980s, was critical of some. He complained that the senior librarians who were his Nairobi colleagues were more conscious of maintaining their position than of widening access to information and eliminating the injustices of the colonial era. In his opinion, it was the junior staff who had the ideas. But librarians such as Tanzania's Ezekiel Kaungamno had both ideas and energy when he succeeded Max Broome as Tanzania Library Service director in 1970. Together with Charles Ilomo (ultimately deputy director) and other colleagues he built on achievements of the founding years and expanded the service.

Changing Times

Political, economic, and social change had a tremendous impact on the lives of librarians as well as everyone else in Africa. After the first military coup in Nigeria in January 1966 the country started its slide toward civil war. Chinua Achebe (then working for the Nigerian Broadcasting Corporation) and other Igbos had to flee home to the Eastern Region, which in 1967 declared itself the Republic of Biafra. The Igbo vice chancellor of the University of Ibadan was part of this rout and was succeeded by John Harris as acting vice chancellor. In 1967 the federal government abolished the country's four regions and the Federal Territory of Lagos, replacing them with twelve states. In 1976 the twelve were replaced by nineteen plus the new Federal Capital Territory at Abuja. Over twenty years the area under the direction of one very able public librarian—Kalu Okorie—shrank to one-sixth its size before independence: from the Eastern Region to East-Central State to Imo State.

Conflict and political upheaval in the Horn of Africa at the end of the century meant deportation for one of Addis Ababa University's most senior and long-serving librarians. War broke out again between Eritrea and its former colonizer, Ethiopia. One of its outcomes was the mass deportation of people of Eritrean background from Ethiopia. In Eritrea, meanwhile, senior positions were the preserve of the fighters, those who had been active in the thirty-year armed struggle to secede. Although a just reward in one sense, in another it was an obstacle blocking the careers of younger Eritreans, many of whom found themselves enduring what seemed like endless years of compulsory military training and other forms of national service.

Long-serving library staff experienced optimism in the 1950s, when the colonial era was drawing to a close, and with the achievements of the 1960s, when so much seemed possible. In the 1970s Nigeria was under military rule, yet it was awash with oil money, and librarians at the University of Ibadan built up one of the world's best African collections. But the 1980s and 1990s were hard. Again Nigeria was under military rule, and corruption was rife. Tanzania had little money for public sector expansion after funding Ugandan insurgents who overthrew Idi Amin in 1979. Many librarians found themselves in charge of collections of increasingly old, worn-out stock. Updates came from overseas book donations. Morale suffered. Salaries in the public sector shrank. Public sector institutions in parts of Africa had once existed to provide employment almost as much as service. Now the World Bank and the International Monetary Fund were telling governments to cut staff and privatize. Many professionals such as doctors and nurses escaped into private practice, but librarians could not, although some succeeded in moving to a better post in their home country or elsewhere. Whereas Charles

Ilomo spent thirty years on the staff of the Tanzania Library Service, rising from newly recruited assistant to deputy director, a number of his able middle-ranking colleagues moved out in the mid-1980s. It looked as if those in the top jobs would be there until retirement, and library and information work for the Tanzania Commission for Science and Technology or the Institute of Finance Management, Dar es Salaam, or teaching and research at the University of Botswana, offered greater potential.

Ghanaian librarians moved to Nigeria in the 1970s, when their country's economy was in shambles. Sudanese—with the advantage of being Arabic speakers—went to Saudi Arabia and the Gulf. West and East Africans were attracted to parts of Southern Africa by the better salaries. In the early 1990s the new Faculty of Information Sciences at Moi University, Kenya, was building up a team of Kenyan lecturers with PhDs from the United Kingdom, the United States, and the Union of Soviet Socialist Republics. Then some were lured away by government appointments or by private universities in Kenya, others by teaching appointments in Botswana and South Africa. A number of African professionals managed to resettle in the United States or Europe.

The AIDS epidemic did not spare librarians in countries such as Malawi. Those who escaped the HIV virus did not necessarily escape its impact. Being a member of an extended family meant extended responsibilities. Public health provision was poor, private medical expenses high, and the children of relatives who died needed to be cared for and educated until they were old enough to support themselves. The financial pressures on African professionals were considerable, and the prospect of retirement on a pension not indexed to the cost of living was bleak in a country with a high rate of inflation. However, job perks for librarians existed, some of which predated independence. In British territories the colonial civil servants lived in set-aside areas known as government reserves and paid a nominal rent for their houses. This tradition continued in universities and in the rest of the public sector. On reaching a certain level of seniority, academics and other university staff were titled to housing on or near the campus—or to a housing allowance if nothing was available or they already had a house of their own. Similarly, a car allowance was commonly paid simply for owning a car, not just for using it for work purposes. Parking for employees was free on campuses. In Tanzania participation in certain committee and other meetings was acknowledged by the payment of an attendance allowance. For librarians who participated in one of the International Federation of Library Associations annual conferences, a U.S. State Department's tour of American libraries, or another sponsored visit to the West, the "per diem" or daily subsistence amount paid to participants to update one's professional skills often brought hard currency home, where it could make a huge difference.

African Library Literature

Consultancy reports can be bland, but one striking exception is Milton J. Ferguson's 1928–1929 report for the Carnegie Corporation. Although Ferguson was perceptive, by twenty-first-century standards he was "politically incorrect," as one of his milder comments demonstrates: "The South African is willing—perhaps has no other way out—for the native to cook his food, care for his children, keep his household in order, serve him in a personal way, carry his books to and from the library, but he would feel that an end of his regime was at hand if this same servant were permitted to open these books and to read therein."[13] Consultancy reports can also be misguided. In *The Library Needs of Northern Nigeria* (1963), consultant F. A. Sharr argued that the primary concern of a public library is "with those whose formal education is over."[14] The statement runs contrary to most late-twentieth-century African public library experiences.

When Evelyn J. A. Evans published *A Tropical Library Service: The Story of Ghana's Libraries* in 1964, Edward Sydney, former president of the (British) Library Association, wrote in an introduction that it was "impossible to over-rate the value of this book at this time to public librarianship all over the world."[15] Although Evelyn Evans's achievements were impressive, and the tribute paid her by President Kwame Nkrumah in his foreword certainly merited, her book is little more than a compendium, and Ronald Benge, then head of the Ghana Library School, said it was put together by her secretary, whom she thanked in the acknowledgments. In the book Evans provided information like the Ghana Library Service's scales of pay and financial benefits a staff member received if leaving the service other than for retirement, on account of death, or as a result of dismissal following disciplinary action. She included a recipe for homemade insecticide, which the service made up in bulk—white shellac, alcohol or industrial methylated spirit, mercuric chloride and phenol in different proportions. In the text she reproduced the Gold Coast Library Board Ordinance (1949) in full rather than as an appendix, and included J. C. Harrison's 1960 consultancy report on setting up a library school in Ghana (a document not easily found elsewhere). Photographs provided a valuable historical record, and Appendix B ("Original List of Basic Books Supplied to All Branch Libraries") gives some indication of how good a librarian Evans was. The list ranges from *Basic Principles in Electrical Engineering* to *A Course in Book-Keeping* and *Instructions to Young Footballers*. *A Tropical Library Service* has limitations, but as Evans herself used to say, she was a "do-er," not a writer.

Ronald Benge was one of the best-known library educators and authors in Anglophone West Africa in the 1960s and 1970s. His *Libraries and Cultural Change* (1970) was very influential in the United Kingdom, where he taught at Aberystwyth between posts at the Ghana Library School (which he transferred to the University of Ghana) and Ahmadu Bello University in Nigeria. He was an essayist rather than a field-worker, thinking, reading, and writing in his study, and talking with other academics in the staff club, rather than venturing into the countryside to investigate the information-seeking behavior of a scientifically selected sample of nomadic herdsmen or some other group. His *Confessions of a Lapsed Librarian* (1984) includes a section on Africa.

For Africa, Paul Sturges (Loughborough University) points to an intellectual vacuum: "a poverty of librarianship, not just a poverty of libraries."[16] He criticizes Evans, Max Broome in Tanzania, their colleagues, and their African successors for lacking the vision to break away from their professional heritage. He says the problem with African national public library services is not just lack of money but lack of ideas. His book, *The Quiet Struggle: Information and Libraries for the People of Africa*, written with Richard Neill, is a much-cited contribution to African library literature.

This literature dates from the 1950s in most of Anglophone Africa, although obviously much farther back in South Africa. One classic paper is Kingo Mchombu's "On the Librarianship of Poverty." Socioeconomic development must concern every organization, he argues. "Information units cannot continue to isolate themselves from this social struggle aimed at giving people a better life."[17] Mchombu worked for the Tanzania Library Service before teaching and researching at the University of Botswana and then serving as dean of the Faculty of Humanities and Social Sciences at the University of Namibia. Similarly, Shiraz Durrani, Kenyan author of *Information and Liberation*

(2008), was critical of conventional library services like the University of Nairobi's agricultural library. It served staff and students, he argued, but ignored local people who grew crops and raised chickens on little plots of land (by way of contrast, the Tanzania Library Service in 2012 facilitated courses to train people in poultry keeping). Durrani teased that the best places to find out what is happening in Kenya are the food kiosks where people meet. He was a librarian at the University of Nairobi until the mid-1980s, when the Kenyan police got interested in his research on political activists, after which he left the country. He worked for twenty years in public libraries in London and then taught at London Metropolitan University.

Diana Rosenberg's "Can Libraries in Africa Ever Be Sustainable?" (1994) is another provocative work. Her survey of university libraries in Africa, conducted in collaboration with local researchers, summed up their condition at the end of the twentieth century. Her career included periods as librarian of the University of Juba, Sudan (now South Sudan), as founding dean of the Faculty of Information Sciences, Moi University, Kenya, and consultant for the International African Institute and then for the International Network for the Availability of Scientific Publications (INASP). More recently University of Pretoria professor Archie Dick's *The Hidden History of South Africa's Book and Reading Cultures* (2012) covers exciting new ground. Part is based on interviews with former political prisoners and on extensive reading of their memoirs and of other relevant works. He also interviewed librarians. *Hidden History* is a vast improvement over library history that ignores social and political context.

The regional library associations set up in Africa in the 1950s started to put out newsletters. By the 1960s the emphasis shifted to national associations, and some were keen to produce journals. Few journals produced by library associations in Africa were to prove sustainable, however. Issues appeared late, which discouraged potential contributors. It also discouraged Western serials agents and indexing and abstracting services.

Some successful English-language librarianship journals include the *South African Journal of Libraries and Information Science, Innovation: Journal of Appropriate Librarianship and Information Work in Southern Africa* (University of KwaZulu-Natal), and the *African Journal of Library, Archives and Information Science*. Only the first of the journals was published by a professional association. The other two were available through African Journals Online (AJOL), a database that hosted over 400 peer-reviewed African scholarly journals. This not-for-profit scheme is based in South Africa and set up to make African scholarship more widely available within Africa itself and outside the continent. Overseas organizations supporting it include the INASP, the Ford Foundation, and the Swedish International Development Cooperation Agency.

Professional Associations

Regional associations were set up in English-speaking West and East Africa in the 1950s. The West African Library Association was an outcome of the month-long public library development seminar arranged by UNESCO in Nigeria (Ibadan) in 1953. The East African Library Association dates from 1957. These two regional associations were replaced by national associations in the 1960s. Some national associations have been more successful than others. The contribution that certain individuals made was particularly important. The drive, imagination, and hard work—or lack of it—of an association's president or chair and of other executive board members were factors that determined an association's success or failure. In the Horn of Africa, Eritrea, which secured its independence from Ethiopia in the early 1990s, did not have a library association until 2000. Somalia, which fell apart in fighting in the 1990s, hardly had libraries, let alone librarians or library associations. In South Africa a library association organized in 1930—the South African Library Association (later the South African Institute of Library and Information Science, or SAILIS). This became a whites-only association in the early 1960s, thus isolating South African librarians classified as other races by their government. In 1997 SAILIS and the African Library Association of South Africa came together to form the Library and Information Association of South Africa (LIASA). In 2000 it received funding from the Carnegie Corporation, which was much more generous supporting library development there than elsewhere in Africa.

By the early twenty-first century few African library associations had more than several hundred members. In countries such as Eritrea, Tanzania, and Zambia most members work in the largest cities: Asmara, Dar es Salaam, and Lusaka. The Internet and the mobile telephone make communication much easier now than in the days of unreliable landlines and postal services. Few associations can afford offices or paid staff.

The Standing Conference of Eastern, Central and Southern African Library and Information Professionals (SCECSAL) dates from 1974. It meets every two years, with several hundred participants. The Standing Conference of African National and University Libraries in East, Central and Southern Africa (SCANUL-ECS) and the Standing Conference of African University Libraries in West Africa (SCAULWA) are other regional groupings. The Association for Health Information and Libraries in Africa (AHILA) was founded in 1984. In 2012 it had forty-six African members, some more active than others. It holds a biennial conference; the 2012 conference took place in the Republic of Cape Verde, the Portuguese-speaking island country 350 miles off the coast of West Africa. The 2014 conference took place in Dar es Salaam, Tanzania. Many African library associations also became members of the International Federation of Library Associations (IFLA). Most attendees from Africa are librarians in senior positions or fortunate young professionals who are sponsored to attend for the first time. Twice IFLA's annual conference took place in Africa: in Nairobi, Kenya, in 1984, and in Durban, South Africa, in 2007. The 2015 conference takes place in Cape Town.

PROFESSIONAL EDUCATION AND TRAINING

By the end of the twentieth century almost all African countries had at least one university. Nigeria had more than fifty, while recently independent and sparsely populated Namibia and Eritrea had one each. Nigeria had been offering nongraduate, undergraduate, postgraduate, and research programs in library and information management for many years; Eritrea, on the other hand, had just introduced a certificate program. But Nigerian students suffered from poor information and communication technology (ICT) facilities at their universities. The library automation courses they took tended to be theoretical rather than practical. At many universities in Africa lack of up-to-date printed material was a major hurdle. At the University of Zambia books such as Evelyn J. Evans's *A Tropical Library Service* and Anna-Britta Wallenius's *Libraries in East Africa* (1971)—classics for the 1960s, even though their twenty-first-century relevance is limited—were in university library reserve collections.

The Issues

In the 1950s and 1960s professional education and training programs required the approval and support of authorities uncertain about the need for libraries and librarians, and whether to support them even if needed. Other issues included identifying the purpose of professional education; whether it should be set up to serve a region, a country, a part of a country, or even a racial group (e.g., South Africa under apartheid); its most appropriate home (professional association, library service, college, polytechnic or university department); finding and training teaching staff; the most appropriate level of the program (undergraduate or graduate); the question of Africanizing the curriculum; the need to modernize it to keep up with ICT developments; and the plight of nongraduate diploma holders whose career progression was blocked.

Taking the Library Association, London, as its model, the South African Library Association introduced professional examinations leading to a Final Diploma in the mid-1930s, and provided correspondence and vacation courses. When the University of Cape Town established a school in 1939 the association bristled because it believed all education should be under its authority. By the time other associations came into existence in Africa, however, it was clear that the old British/South African model had lost favor. After one intake in 1944 the Gold Coast Library Advisory Committee decided that unless the country established more libraries it would be unwise to take in more students. This disappointed the tutor, Ethel Fegan, who wanted her school at Achimota—the first formal training program for library staff in British West Africa—to become an African School of Librarianship. Under the auspices of the British Council she prepared fourteen students for the Elementary Examination of the Library Association in London. The Gold Coast (Ghana) did not have a library school again until 1961, when the Ghana Library Board opened one. In the interim library staff were sent to the United Kingdom to study.

Regional or National?

In 1953 a UNESCO Seminar at Ibadan recommended: "A limited number of schools of high calibre [should] be established . . . to provide full-scale professional training at the leadership level. . . . For the foreseeable future, it would probably suffice if one such school could be established to serve each of the major regional language areas of African-English speaking territories; French language areas, and Arabic for Egypt and the Sudan."[18] In fact Egypt already had a school: a four-year program leading to a diploma set up at Cairo University's Higher Institute of Archives and Librarianship in 1951.

A successful regional school for Francophone Africa organized in Dakar, Senegal, in 1963. What became L'École de Bibliothécaires, Archivistes et Documentalistes, Université Cheikh Anta Diop de Dakar took students from Benin, Burkina Faso, Burundi, Cameroun, the Central African Republic, Chad, the Comoros Islands, Congo, Côte d'Ivoire, Djibouti, Gabon, Madagascar, Mali, Mauritania, Niger, Rwanda, and Togo as well as Senegal. In Southern Africa the University of South Africa distance education programs played a regional role to a certain extent, while the school established at the University of Botswana in 1979 started with a certificate and a diploma, then added an undergraduate program and a master's degree to attract students from other countries. It was assisted in the 1980s and 1990s by German Foundation for International Development scholarships. Lusophone Africa lagged far behind. Occasional short courses were organized, and course units within history programs, but no regional or national schools.

With the exception of Botswana, political developments curtailed schools set up with regional intent in Anglophone Africa. Under Carnegie auspices Harold Lancour, University of Illinois library school assistant dean, visited Nigeria, Ghana, Sierra Leone, and the Gambia in 1957 and concluded the most important contribution Carnegie could make would be to assist in the education and training of librarians. He recommended a Postgraduate West African Institute of Librarianship be set up at University College, Ibadan. In 1960, supported by the Carnegie Corporation, the first university-level program in library studies in English-speaking West, East, and Central Africa opened there. In the mid-1960s the institute decided to stop admitting nongraduates, but years later reintroduced an undergraduate program in addition to the master's. The demand was there from the market.

Ghana also wanted its own library school—a decision put into effect by President Nkrumah himself—and set one up in 1961. On the advice of British consultant J. C. Harrison, head of Manchester's School of Librarianship, the Ghana Library School came under the authority of the Ghana Library Board. Four years later, it transferred to the University of Ghana where, under Ronald Benge, the school introduced a bachelor of arts in Library Studies, although it was discontinued and eventually replaced by a graduate program after he left in 1967.

Ahmadu Bello University, Zaria, in the north of Nigeria was the third library school in Anglophone West Africa. In 1968 it started to admit students to a three-year undergraduate program. Many librarians opposed it. Nigeria was a fast-developing country with enormous oil resources. Why should it settle for a substandard program at a regional university? Professional education at master's level was the norm in North America. Ahmadu Bello responded that the north was less Westernized than the south, with far fewer educated professionals, and the only way to produce local librarians was by enrolling them at undergraduate level, argued Benge, head of the school from 1973 to 1976. But northern graduates had many other opportunities in the 1960s. Because U.S. and other Western nations, the federal Nigerian government, the northern regional government, and successor state governments all provided generous scholarships for overseas study, northern graduates had little incentive to enroll in a postgraduate program at home.

In 1963, the East African School of Librarianship was set up with UNESCO assistance at Makerere in Uganda. By the late 1970s, however, the unsavory rule of President Idi Amin discouraged Tanzania and Kenya from sending students there to study. In Kenya, Moi University admitted its first students to an undergraduate Information Sciences program in 1988. The Tanzania Library Service (TLS) began a nongraduate certificate program in the early 1970s. In association with the National Archives of Tanzania it set up the School of Library, Archive and Documentation Studies (SLADS) at Bagamoyo, a town on the coast north of Dar es Salaam. SLADS admitted its first nongraduate diploma students in 1989. Because it expanded student intake from sixty nongraduate certificate and diploma students in 2007–2008 to over 1,000 in 2012–2013. By that time it had its own campus. The University of Dar es Salaam spent years debating whether to start a program at undergraduate or postgraduate level, eventually opting for the latter. The first students were admitted in 1997. At the time of writing Tanzania's School of Library, Archive and Documentation Studies introduced a three-month elementary program at the National Central Library in Dar es Salaam aimed at those who had not done particularly well in their school examinations. Successful completion allowed them to progress to the certificate program.

In North Africa, undergraduate programs attracted large numbers of students. Professional education for library work commenced in 1964 in Tunisia, in 1974 in Morocco, in 1975 in Algeria, and in 1976 in Libya. In the 1980s the number of library schools in Egypt increased from one to four. Arabic and French became the languages for teaching in Morocco, Algeria, and Tunisia, and Arabic in Egypt and Libya. Most other African library and information studies programs organized at universities from the beginning, although their appropriateness as homes for nongraduate certificates and diplomas has been questioned. Offering these at colleges or polytechnics is generally seen as more economical.

The Curriculum

The first curricula were drawn from Western models. This did not pose particular problems in a course on academic libraries, for example, because in the 1960s and 1970s such African libraries were similar to those of the West, although obviously newer and not as large. But a course on public libraries presented major problems. How could an American classic such as Joseph L. Wheeler and Herbert Goldhor's *Practical Administration of Public Libraries* (1962) or a British piece of legislation such as the Public Library Act (1964) be relevant to an area such as the north of Nigeria in the 1960s? Only a small percentage of the population (almost seventeen million according to the 1952–1953 census) was literate in English (or indeed in Hausa or other Nigerian languages), and public library service points amounted to no more than a handful. Such questions required major rethinking. Africanizing the curriculum needed to go far beyond consideration of the Western limitations of the Library of Congress and Dewey Decimal classification schemes. However, not all teaching staff—whether expatriate or African—were willing or able to deal with this.

In the undergraduate information sciences program at Kenya's Moi University, all students took the core curriculum, then specialized in librarianship, publishing, information technology, or archives and records management. This exposure made Moi graduates more employable. The first Africans to teach library and information science were usually graduates of the programs themselves. Departments often recruited their best students as assistant lecturers, then sponsored them for master's degrees and doctorates by providing leaves of absence with pay. In the 1960s and 1970s they usually took scholarships at universities in Western countries such as the United States, the United Kingdom, Canada, and Australia, or alternatively in the Soviet Union. In Tanzania—stable and democratic but far from wealthy—the University of Dar es Salaam sent librarians to South Africa for their PhDs: in part because South African universities had the expertise, and the fees and the cost of living were cheaper than in the West, in part because study within Africa was more relevant than study outside the continent, more focused on practices of constructing the heritage of African cultures.

LIBRARIES AND POLITICAL CHANGE: THE CASE OF THE BIBLIOTHECA ALEXANDRINA

Political change in Africa is manifest in the independence era, the election of Nelson Mandela as president of South Africa in 1994, and the move from one-party rule to multiparty democracy in a number of countries. Libraries and political change bring to mind the move away from whites-only services in colonial Kenya and apartheid South Africa. But twenty-first-century Egypt provides an example that has little to do with race and much to do with youth and the pent-up desire for change that a corrupt and authoritarian government could no longer contain. Among other developments the Bibliotheca Alexandrina (Latin for Alexandria Library) lost its chair of trustees and was linked with a corruption scandal totaling more than $140 million. The library's 2010–2011 annual report went on to celebrate the Egyptian revolution.

The Bibliotheca Alexandrina has been an ambitious project drawing inspiration from the legendary Alexandria Library of antiquity. It opened in Alexandria in 2002, having received substantial financial support from UNESCO, Arab countries, and Egypt itself. Support continued from the United States and other countries, and from private foundations like the Carnegie Corporation. Since it opened, the Bibliotheca Alexandrina has produced lengthy, informative, and well-illustrated annual reports. The institution contains not only the library (which includes services for children), but also art galleries, museums for antiquities and the history of science, a planetarium, a conference center, various research institutes including one for Alexandria and the Mediterranean, and a manuscript center with a restoration laboratory. It has a staff of 2,000.

In the first annual report (2002–2003) trustees' chair Suzanne Mubarak notes she was a supporter of the "Reading for All" campaign, in addition to being founder and president of the Suzanne Mubarak International Women for Peace Movement and founder of Egypt's National Women's Committee (NCW) and of the Arab Women's Council. She did not mention she was also the wife of Mohamed Hosni Mubarak, at that time Egypt's president for more than twenty years. In the 2009–2010 annual report Mrs. Mubarak—still trustees' chair—wrote as follows in her foreword: "I am delighted that I have seen so much of my dream for the Bibliotheca Alexandrina (BA), the new Library of Alexandria, actually implemented. I have devoted many years of my life to bring it to this stage. Today, I can say with pride that the BA has started to take its place in the international arena, and that it is indeed taking important steps to be recognized as the heir to its famous ancient namesake, for by its many activities, the spirit of the old library is revived with the tools of the new century."[19] Mrs. Mubarak also expressed her gratitude for half a million volumes from the Bibliothèque nationale de France, which made the Bibliotheca Alexandrina the main depository of French books in the Arab world and in Africa. She also mentioned that the library was planning to reach out beyond the city of Alexandria to other parts of Egypt.

In the 2010–2011 annual report, however, Suzanne Mubarak had no foreword. Her husband was no longer Egypt's president and she was no longer listed among Bibliotheca Alexandrina's trustees. The Egyptian political world had been turned upside down with the assistance of what Mrs. Mubarak described a year earlier as the tools of the new century. According to the report, the library's legitimacy now owed as much to the support of the young revolutionaries as to the quality of its work. Young people had linked hands around the perimeter of the library to protect it from possible danger, and on it laid a huge flag, which passing demonstrators cheered. In addition, "one of the most important events that occurred during the 25 January Revolution was the exposure of the presence of a secret bank account maintained by former President Mubarak in the name of the Library of Alexandria. That Account has more than 140 million dollars in it. . . . Subsequently, former President Mubarak acknowledged that he had kept it secret from the BA and its Board of Trustees and its Director."[20] The same report mentions that the Bibliotheca Alexandrina has a Memory of Modern Egypt project that documents life in the country during the nineteenth and twentieth centuries. The library immediately began documenting the 2011 revolution by archiving satellite television programs such as those of Al Jazeera, and collecting data from Facebook, YouTube, Flickr, Picasa, and Twitter.

CONCLUSION

News was forbidden to those imprisoned on Robben Island during South Africa's apartheid regime, but in his memoirs Nelson Mandela recalls how the sandwiches that the prison warders took for their lunch were often wrapped in newspapers. Prisoners gathered these surreptitiously and later read them. South African political prisoners were also permitted to register for high school qualifications or undergraduate degrees through distance learning. Some prisoners were detained for twenty years or more, and they found intellectual stimulation by registering for one undergraduate degree after another. Strict regulations governed what could be read—obviously politics was out—but an economics student managed to subscribe to *The Economist* for a short period before the censors realized its coverage ranged beyond the financial. Library books sometimes took so long to reach Robben Island that they arrived after the date they were due for return, thus automatically incurring fines. Yet at night, Mandela later recalled, his cellblock seemed more like a study hall than a prison.

At one time Heinemann's weekly in-house circular included a list of its "Authors in Prison" (including Mandela, Ngũgĩ wa Thiong'o, and Wole Soyinka), which it updated regularly. As a publishing house Heinemann was not interested in the politics or religion of authors, only in the quality of their writing. Under South African law reading and writing was forbidden to those in solitary confinement, with the exception of the Bible, which the government supplied as part of its Christian duty. Books and paper were also forbidden to Soyinka, who spent twenty-two months in solitary confinement during the Nigerian civil war. He still managed to write poetry.

At UNESCO's Public Library Seminar at Ibadan in 1953, a young Nigerian librarian, Gbole Nwikina, noted that most newly literate and semiliterate readers were students attempting to pass examinations. A decade later a Nigerian education officer said that the great majority of those using libraries were actively preparing for examinations. University students used academic libraries to help them advance their formal education; public library users wanted the same thing, including multiple copies of textbooks together with supplementary material and a quiet space in which to read and study. Over the years commentators reiterated how public libraries resembled school libraries—full of young people in their teens and twenties. After students completed their formal studies, however, libraries lost significance and they stopped using them.

Fiction reading that sustained public libraries in the Western world had been much less important in the everyday lives of most Africans. Shakespeare and Dickens were still popular in 1970s South Africa, where in black townships student activists read favorite novels like *David Copperfield* by candlelight and moonlight if necessary. What fascinated them was the divide between rich and poor in nineteenth-century England. Dickens's works also had the great advantage of being available: they were not banned by the apartheid government. In Tanzania, Julius Nyerere translated *Julius Caesar* into Kiswahili. When the director of the Ghana Library Service spoke at an exhibition of British paperbacks, she quoted Mark Antony's "Friends, Romans, countrymen" speech. Most of the Ghanaians in the room joined in with her. According to Ngũgĩ, Shakespeare was "an integral part of my intellectual formation" at his high school in Kenya in the

1950s.[21] Chinua Achebe read Shakespeare in his secondary school in Nigeria in the 1940s, as well as *David Copperfield*, Swift's *Gulliver's Travels*, Stevenson's *Treasure Island*, and Booker T. Washington's *Up from Slavery*. As a child Achebe's father introduced him to an Igbo translation of John Bunyan's *The Pilgrim's Progress*, but apart from newspapers the quantity of material available for widely spoken languages such as Hausa and Kiswahili was limited, unlike in North Africa, where in Egypt, for example, a large publishing industry produced much material in Arabic.

What of the future? According to "On the Librarianship of Poverty," the classic paper written by Tanzania's Kingo Mchombu, one or two "imposing monuments" inspired by European or North American models might be constructed in a decade, with the result that "the lucky few may have a very good service, but most people will have no service at all."[22] Perhaps Tanzania's modern library history reflects future directions for other African libraries attempting to preserve their cultural heritages. In 2014 Tanzanian districts such as Chunya, Kigoma, Lindi, Kibaha, and Ngara have been entering into a memorandum of understanding with the national library service board. They provide the building and pay for utilities and the salaries of the library assistants. The board provides the stock and pays the salary of the staff member in charge. The buildings are not purpose-built and the libraries are perhaps not as exemplary as they would be in a wealthier country such as South Africa, or if they had Carnegie backing. But they are a response to a local need and are appreciated by their users.

The Bank of Tanzania is the country's central bank, licensing and monitoring commercial banks and exchange bureaus. Its headquarters in Dar es Salaam is modern and imposing, and its library contains the latest books and serials, including the *Daily Nation* (Nairobi), the *Financial Times* (London), and *The Economist*. The bank's staff can access the International Monetary Fund's collection, as well as Tanzania's own Economic and Social Research Foundation and REPOA (Research on Poverty Alleviation). The library has ample space, and it is used in particular by staff studying for banking examinations, undergraduate degrees in business, and for MBAs. The library has branches in Zanzibar, Arusha, Mbeya, and two in Mwanza on the shores of Lake Victoria, one of which is at the training institute for bankers. When money is not an obstacle, good up-to-date library services exist.

In the center of Dar es Salaam the National Central Library, opened with pride by President Nyerere in 1967, was badly in need of renovation by the late 1990s. Under an agreement between the library board and a private sector developer, the building was extended upward by two floors and the new space rented out to businesses. After the rent went to the developer for the years specified in the agreement, it was redirected to the library board to supplement the library budget. In the twenty-first century the National Central Library opened an Internet café with new computers donated by China. Even in challenging situations good librarians adapt in inventive ways. They strive to provide better library services. As of this writing—as in the National Central Library in Dar es Salaam—these services must include modern telecommunications, although it is certain that the printed word will be around in Africa for years to come.

NOTES

1. Ali Al'Amin Mazrui, *The Africans: A Triple Heritage* (Boston: Little, Brown, 1986), 21.
2. Chinua Achebe, *There Was a Country: A Personal History of Biafra* (London: Allen Lane, 2012), 25.

3. Otonti A. Nduka, *Western Education and the Nigerian Cultural Background* (Ibadan: Oxford University Press, 1965), 10.

4. Ngũgĩ wa Thiong'o, *In the House of the Interpreter: A Memoir* (London: Harvill Secker, 2012), 159.

5. Douglas Harold Varley, *Library Service in the Rhodesias and Nyasaland: Report on Existing Facilities and Recommendations on Future Development* (Cape Town: np, 1951), Section 4.91.

6. Lalage J. Bown, ed., *Two Centuries of African English: A Survey and Anthology of Non-Fictional English Prose by African Writers Since 1769* (London: Heinemann, 1973), 143.

7. Henry Chakava, *Publishing in Africa: One Man's Perspective* (Bellagio and Nairobi: Publishing Network and East African Educational Publishers, 1996), xiii, 7.

8. Achebe, *There Was a Country*, 61.

9. Northern Region of Nigeria, Ministry of Information, *The Library Needs of Northern Nigeria: A Report Prepared under the Special Commonwealth African Assistance Plan* (Kaduna, 1963), 101, 132–33.

10. Diana Rosenberg, ed., *University Libraries in Africa: A Review of their Current State and Future Potential.* David Clow, Diana Rosenberg, and Henri Sène, eds., *Vol. 2, Case Studies: Botswana, Ethiopia, Ghana, Ivory Coast, Kenya* (London: International African Institute, 1997), 115, 168, 251.

11. East African Literature Bureau, *Annual Report, 1952* (Nairobi: East Africa High Commission, 1953), 8.

12. Wilfred John Plumbe, *Tropical Librarianship* (Metuchen, NJ: Scarecrow Press, 1987), viii.

13. Milton James Ferguson and Septimus Albert Pitt, *Memorandum: Libraries in the Union of South Africa, Rhodesia and Kenya Colony* (New York: Carnegie Corporation of New York, 1929), 10.

14. Northern Region of Nigeria, Ministry of Information, *The Library Needs*, 101.

15. Evelyn J. A. Evans, *A Tropical Library Service: The Story of Ghana's Libraries* (London: A. Deutsch, 1964), xvii.

16. Paul Sturges, "The Poverty of Librarianship: An Historical Critique of Public Librarianship in Anglophone Africa," *Libri* 51 (2001): 44.

17. K. J. Mchombu, "On the Librarianship of Poverty," *Libri* 32 (1982): 249.

18. *Development of Public Libraries in Africa: The Ibadan Seminar* (Paris: UNESCO, 1954), 117.

19. Bibliotheca Alexandrina, "Annual Report, July 2009–June 2010," http://www.biba lex.org (2010), http://www.bibalex.org/attachments_en/Publications/Files/20110406135 04943939_overview.pdf, p. 7 (cited January 12, 2014).

20. Bibliotheca Alexandrina, "Annual Report, July 2010–June 2011," http://www .bibalex.org (2011), http://www.bibalex.org/attachments_en/Publications/Files/2012080 91245249995_annualreport20102011english982012small.pdf, 15–16 (cited January 12, 2014).

21. Ngũgĩ, *In the House*, 177.

22. Mchombu, "Librarianship of Poverty," 245.

BIBLIOGRAPHY

Abdelhay, Nawaf. "The Arab Uprising 2011: New Media in the Hands of a New Generation in North Africa." *Aslib Proceedings* 64 (2012): 529–39.

Achebe, Chinua. *There Was a Country: A Personal History of Biafra*. London: Allen Lane, 2012.

Afigbo, A. E. "The Social Repercussions of Colonial Rule: The New Social Structures." In *General History of Africa, vol. 7, Africa under Colonial Domination, 1880–1935*, edited by A. Adu Boahen, 487–507. Paris: UNESCO, 1985.

African Books Collective (ABC). http://www.africanbookscollective.com (cited January 12, 2014).

African Journals Online (AJOL). http://www.ajol.info (cited January 12, 2014).

Agbodeka, Francis. *A History of University of Ghana: Half a Century of Higher Education (1948–1998)*. Accra: Woeli Publishing Services, 1998.

Aje, J. F., and Tekena N. Tamuno, eds. *The University of Ibadan, 1948–73: A History of the First Twenty-Five Years*. Ibadan: Ibadan University Press, 1973.

Amadi, Adolphe O. *African Libraries: Western Tradition and Colonial Brainwashing*. Metuchen, NJ: Scarecrow Press, 1981.

Anderson, Florence. *Library Program, 1911–1961*. New York: Carnegie Corporation of New York, 1963.

Benge, R. C. *Confessions of a Lapsed Librarian*. Metuchen, NJ: Scarecrow Press, 1984.

Benge, Ronald, and Anthony Olden. "Planning Factors in the Development of Library Education in English-Speaking Black Africa." *Journal of Librarianship* 13 (1981): 203–22.

Bibliotheca Alexandrina, "Annual Reports." http://www.bibalex.org/Publications/BA_Annual Reports_EN.aspx?Dir=1 (cited January 12, 2014).

Bown, Lalage J., ed. *Two Centuries of African English: A Survey and Anthology of Non-Fictional English Prose by African Writers Since 1769*. London: Heinemann, 1973.

"Bringing New Life to South Africa's Libraries." *Carnegie Review* (Winter 2012). http://carnegie.org/fileadmin/Media/Publications/carnegie_review_winter_2012_libraries.pdf (cited August 22, 2012).

Chakava, Henry. *Publishing in Africa: One Man's Perspective*. Bellagio and Nairobi: Publishing Network and East African Educational Publishers, 1996.

Coombs, Douglas. *Spreading the Word: The Library Work of the British Council*. London: Mansell, 1988.

Davis, Caroline. "Histories of Publishing under Apartheid: Oxford University Press in South Africa." *Journal of Southern African Studies* 37 (2011): 79–98.

Development of Public Libraries in Africa: The Ibadan Seminar. Paris: UNESCO, 1954.

Dick, Archie. *The Hidden History of South Africa's Book and Reading Cultures*. Toronto: University of Toronto Press, 2012.

Dione, Bernard, and Dieyi Diouf. "Senegal: Libraries, Archives and Museums." In *Encyclopedia of Library and Information Sciences*, edited by Marcia J. Bates and Mary Niles Maack, 3rd ed., 4687–95. London: Taylor and Francis, 2010.

Durrani, Shiraz. *Information and Liberation: Writings on the Politics of Information and Librarianship*. Duluth, MN: Library Juice Press, 2008.

Durrani, Shiraz. "Kenyan Libraries and Information in Times of Social Protest, 1960s–1970s." *Journal of Swedish Library Research* 14 (3, special issue: 2002): 21–32.

East African Literature Bureau. *Annual Report, 1952*. Nairobi: East Africa High Commission, 1953.

Elkins, Caroline. *Britain's Gulag: The Brutal End of Empire in Kenya*. London: Pimlico, 2005.

Evans, Evelyn J. A. *A Tropical Library Service: The Story of Ghana's Libraries*. London: A. Deutsch, 1964.

Ferguson, Milton James, and Septimus Albert Pitt. *Memorandum: Libraries in the Union of South Africa, Rhodesia and Kenya Colony*. New York: Carnegie Corporation of New York, 1929.

Hill, Alan. *In Pursuit of Publishing*. London: J. Murray and Heinemann, 1988.

Hodgkin, Thomas. *Nigerian Perspectives: An Historical Anthology*. 2nd ed. London: Oxford University Press, 1975.

"The Hopeless Continent." *The Economist*, May 13, 2000. http://www.economist.com/printedition/2000-05-13 (cited January 11, 2014).

International Telecommunication Union. "Key 2000–2010 Country Data." http://www.itu.int/ITU-D/ict/statistics (cited May 30, 2012).

Issak, Aissa, comp. *Public Libraries in Africa: A Report and Annotated Bibliography*. Oxford: International Network for the Availability of Scientific Publications, 2000.

Issa-Salwe, Abdisalam M., and Anthony Olden. "Somali Web Sites, History and Politics." *Aslib Proceedings* 60 (2008): 570–82.

Kaungamno, E. E., and C. S. Ilomo. *Books Build Nations*. 2 vols. London and Dar es Salaam: Transafrica Book Distributors and Tanzania Library Services, 1979.

Kenya National Library Service. "Membership." http://www.knls.ac.ke/index.php/membership (cited August 10, 2012).

Maack, Mary Niles. "Books and Libraries as Instruments of Cultural Diplomacy in Francophone Africa during the Cold War." *Libraries & Culture* 36 (Winter 2001): 60–86.

Maack, Mary Niles. *Libraries in Senegal: Continuity and Change in an Emerging Nation*. Chicago: American Library Association, 1981.

Mandela, Nelson. *Long Walk to Freedom: The Autobiography of Nelson Mandela*. London: Abacus, 1995.

Mazrui, Ali Al'Amin. *The Africans: A Triple Heritage*. Boston: Little, Brown, 1986.

Mchombu, Kingo J. "Alternatives to the National Library in Less Developed Countries." *Libri* 35 (1985): 227–49.

Mchombu, Kingo J. "Education for Information Workers in Africa: The Case of the Department of Library and Information Studies, University of Botswana." In *Education for Librarianship and Information Science in Africa*, edited by Michael Wise, 57–70. IFLA Advancement of Librarianship Programme, project report no. 5. Uppsala: Uppsala University Library, 1999.

Mchombu, Kingo J. "On the Librarianship of Poverty." *Libri* 32 (1982): 241–50.

Mchombu, Kingo J. "Which Way African Librarianship?" *IFLA Journal* 17 (1991): 26–38.

Mellanby, Kenneth. *The Birth of Nigeria's University*. London: Methuen, 1958.

Nduka, Otonti A. *Western Education and the Nigerian Cultural Background*. Ibadan: Oxford University Press, 1965.

Ngũgĩ wa Thiong'o. *Decolonising the Mind: The Politics of Language in African Literature*. London: J. Currey, 1986.

Ngũgĩ wa Thiong'o. *In the House of the Interpreter: A Memoir*. London: Harvill Secker, 2012.

Northern Region of Nigeria. Ministry of Information. *The Library Needs of Northern Nigeria: A Report Prepared under the Special Commonwealth African Assistance Plan*. Kaduna, 1963.

Ocholla, Dennis, Lyudmila Ocholla, and Omwoyo Bosire Onyancha. "Research Visibility, Publication Patterns and Output of Academic Librarians in Sub-Saharan Africa: The Case of Eastern Africa." *Aslib Proceedings* 64 (2012): 478–93.

Olden, Anthony. "Constraints on the Development of Public Library Service in Nigeria." *Library Quarterly* 55 (1985): 398–423.

Olden, Anthony. "'For Poor Nations a Library Service Is Vital': Establishing a National Public Library Service in Tanzania in the 1960s." *Library Quarterly* 75 (2005): 421–45.

Olden, Anthony. *Libraries in Africa: Pioneers, Policies, Problems*. Lanham, MD: Scarecrow Press, 1995.

Olden, Anthony. "Library Associations in Africa: Past and Present." *Innovation* 31 (2005): 1–8.

Olden, Anthony. "Somali Opposition to Government Education: R. E. Ellison and the Berbera School Affair, 1938–1940." *History of Education* 37 (2008): 71–90.

Olden, Anthony. "Sub-Saharan Africa and the Paperless Society." *Journal of the American Society for Information Science* 38 (1987): 298–304.

Olden, Anthony, and Alli A. S. Mcharazo. "Current Issues in Professional Education for Library and Information Work in Tanzania." *Education for Information* 20 (2002): 119–31.

Oluwasanmi, Edwina, Eva McLean, and Hans Zell, eds. *Publishing in Africa in the Seventies: Proceedings of an International Conference on Publishing and Book Development Held at the University of Ife, Ile-Ife, Nigeria, 16–20 December 1973.* Ile-Ife: University of Ife Press, 1975.

Pattison, Bruce. *Special Relations: The University of London and New Universities Overseas, 1947–1970.* London: University of London, 1984.

Plumbe, Wilfred John. *Tropical Librarianship.* Metuchen, NJ: Scarecrow Press, 1987.

Richards, Charles Granston, Anthony Olden, D. McD. Wilson, and Sidney Hockey. "No Carpet on the Floor: Extracts from the Memoirs of Charles Granston Richards, Founding Director, East African Literature Bureau." *African Research and Documentation* 71 (1996): 1–32.

Rosenberg, Diana. "Can Libraries in Africa Ever Be Sustainable?" *Information Development* 4 (1994): 247–51.

Rosenberg, Diana. "Imposing Libraries: The Establishment of National Public Library Services in Africa, with Particular Reference to Kenya." *Third World Libraries* 4 (1993): 35–44.

Rosenberg, Diana. "An Overview of Education for Librarianship in Anglophone Sub-Saharan Africa." In *Education for Librarianship and Information Science in Africa,* edited by Michael Wise, 11–34. IFLA Advancement of Librarianship Programme, project report no. 5. Uppsala: Uppsala University Library, 1999.

Rosenberg, Diana, ed. *University Libraries in Africa: A Review of their Current State and Future Potential, Vol. 2, Case Studies: Botswana, Ethiopia, Ghana, Ivory Coast, Kenya,* edited by David Clow, Diana Rosenberg, and Henri Sène. London: International African Institute, 1997.

Samatar, Said S. *Oral Poetry and Somali Nationalism: The Case of Sayyid Mahammad 'Abdille Hasan.* Cambridge: Cambridge University Press, 1982.

Stringer, Roger, ed. *The Book Chain in Anglophone Africa: A Survey and Directory.* Oxford: International Network for the Availability of Scientific Publications, 2002.

Sturges, Paul. "The Poverty of Librarianship: An Historical Critique of Public Librarianship in Anglophone Africa." *Libri* 51 (2001): 38–48.

Sturges, Paul, and Richard Neill. *The Quiet Struggle: Information and Libraries for the People of Africa.* 2nd ed. London, Washington, DC: Mansell, 1998.

Tamuno, Tekena N., ed. *Ibadan Voices: Ibadan University in Transition.* Ibadan: Ibadan University Press, 1981.

Underwood, Peter G., and M. C. Nassimbeni. "'We Shall All Be Changed': Professional Development and Training in the Republic of South Africa." In *Education for Librarianship and Information Science in Africa,* edited by Michael Wise, 179–98. Project report no. 5. Uppsala: Uppsala University Library, 1999.

UNESCO. "Public Library Manifesto" [1974]. http://www.unesco.org/webworld/libraries/manifestos/libraman.html (cited July 15, 2014).

Varley, Douglas Harold. *Library Service in the Rhodesias and Nyasaland: Report on Existing Facilities and Recommendations on Future Development.* Cape Town, 1951.

Wallenius, Anna-Britta, ed. *Libraries in East Africa*. Uppsala: Scandinavian Institute of African
    Studies, 1971.

Wise, Michael, ed. *Aspects of African Librarianship*. London: Mansell, 1985.

Wrong, Michela. *I Didn't Do It for You: How the World Betrayed a Small African Nation*. London,
    New York: Fourth Estate, 2005.

4

Australasia

Ross Harvey

INTRODUCTION

On casual inspection a North American or British visitor to any type of library in Australia or New Zealand in the early twenty-first century will note little that is unfamiliar. Closer scrutiny reveals some different antipodean library operations and services, the principal reason being the dichotomy these two countries experience between a past rooted in Britain and Britishness and a present situating them firmly in an Asian and Pacific reality. This chapter investigates core tensions of modern librarianship in local and regional Australian and New Zealand traditions, with a focus on colonial and postcolonial dimensions and on modernity. The approach taken combines documentary history and a critical examination of the impact of Anglo-American culture and librarianship on Australia and New Zealand. Four themes guide the chapter:

- distinctive patterns of practice based on professional understandings and outlooks of settlers from many traditions and on the traditional knowledge of the colonized;
- a reputation in Australia and New Zealand for innovation and early adoption of new ideas and technologies, arising from challenges imposed by distance, both within a very large country (Australia) and from major centers of practice;
- a high level of cooperation and convergence, shaped initially by the drive toward federation and eventually, for Australia, by the reality of federation from 1901; and
- developing new multicultural national identities that combine, in Australia, ancient indigenous knowledge systems with those of migrants since 1788, and, in New Zealand, Maori and Pacific Islander knowledge systems with those of migrants since the 1820s.

To what extent can one talk about Australasian practice? Australia and New Zealand have much in common: both are recently settled by European immigrants and sparsely populated. (Australia's population density of three people per square kilometer, compared with sixteen in New Zealand and thirty-two in the United States, had profound effects on the formation of modern Australian society and its institutions.) Australasia is not a single unified political unit. Both Australia and New Zealand have strong central governments, in comparison with the United States, more akin to the British system of government, even though Australia is a federation of states and territories. Populations are also a factor: Australia had 22 million in 2013 and New Zealand 4.4 million. These factors influence how library services developed. Library services in both Australia and New Zealand were based on Anglo-American practice, and this chapter also points out where practices differed. Although both countries were British colonies and remain within the British Commonwealth, they are increasingly aware of their geopolitical location in Asia and the Pacific, and of their indigenous populations. The three key transitions noted in this book's introduction—the development of a practical and pragmatic professionalism aimed at enhancing access to useful knowledge, its spread throughout the world, and increasing globalization of librarianship—are all evident in Australasia. The outcome is that librarianship in Australia and New Zealand lies firmly in an Anglo-American tradition, but with discernible modifications to accommodate local conditions and sensibilities.

British Roots and Emerging National Identities

The roots of Australian and New Zealand Britishness mirror John Ruskin's ideology of Empire. "This is what England must either do or perish," he lectured in 1870: "she must found colonies as fast and as far as she is able, formed of her most energetic and worthiest men; seizing every piece of fruitful waste ground she can set her foot on, and there teaching these her colonists that their chief virtue is to be fidelity to their country, and their first aim is to be to advance the power of England by land and sea."[1] By 1897 Australia's six colonies were home to four million people of British origin. They were self-governing, each with different tariffs, services, structures, and railway gauges, demonstrating a lack of unity that affected twentieth-century library services. Nineteenth-century Australians and New Zealanders may have considered themselves "simply as Britons overseas," but some distinctive characteristics of Australians and New Zealanders were already becoming apparent, including a loosening of the "old seeds of social consciousness" and "ingrained deference towards the manners and customs of the English upper classes," and a radicalism and egalitarianism that promoted equality of opportunity.[2] For example, New Zealand women were able to vote from 1893 and South Australian women won the right to vote and stand for Parliament from 1895, decades before women in Britain. Although British migrants were initially colonial Britons, their offspring, particularly after World War I, constructed new national identities as Australians or New Zealanders and distanced themselves from Britain.

World War I was a catalyst for new national identities. "White colonials had gone to war trustingly, innocently almost," Jan Morris says, "But they had gone home with different feelings. . . . They had seen the structure of British society forlornly exposed once more, and the myth of omniscience, to which they had been educated, proved a fraud." Individual national identities were discernible by the 1930s. New Zealanders were the most British of colonials but also the most exotic, living in remote islands in which the government of New Zealand was conducting socialist experiments. Their close neighbors in Australia were more strident, coming from Australian colonial beginnings in forced migration of convicts and military settlement that led to "a national character more pungent and more aggressive than that of many older States" by the 1920s.[3] But ties with

"Home" remained strong for economic reasons, as Britain and her colonies were the major markets for the products of both countries. World War II further encouraged the reinvention of national identities, as the threat of Japanese invasion and America's intervention in the Pacific expanded Australians' and New Zealanders' worldview. John Curtin, prime minister of Australia for most of the war years, declared: "Australia looks to America free of any pangs as to our traditional link or kinship with the United Kingdom."[4]

In the 1960s and 1970s the cord of economic dependence of Australia and New Zealand on Britain and Europe was severed. Greater engagement of Australia and New Zealand with Asia started from the 1970s, although New Zealand's long-standing special relationship with China predated Australia's engagement. Engagement with the United States expanded also, as exemplified by military alliances in the 1970s and 1980s. New Zealand did not participate as fully as Australia, declaring its territorial waters a nuclear-free zone from 1984 and effectively barring all U.S. Navy vessels, with the result that the United States suspended treaty obligations. New Zealand's ban on nuclear-powered ships is considered a landmark in the development of New Zealand's cultural identity and perhaps explains its less admiring attitude toward U.S. practices than is encountered in Australia. The Australian Bicentenary in 1988, celebrating 200 years since the founding of the colony of New South Wales (and ignoring the more than 40,000 years of continuous Aboriginal settlement), was a major demonstration of Australia's coming of age as a nation. Library services, practice, and collections all developed as an expression of the emerging identities of the two nations defined by their colonial heritage, history, and demographics.

At the start of the twenty-first century, library professionals in Australia and New Zealand still follow Anglo-American traditions—for example, by adhering to international standards and engaging actively in their development—but regional and national characteristics are identifiable in their practices. Differences are evident in the adaptation of Anglo-American practice to suit local imperatives, conditions, and politics, and in the way that the knowledge systems of colonized peoples have influenced practice, especially in New Zealand. Library practice in Australia and New Zealand can be characterized as globally connected, digitally proficient, based on international standards and best practice, and sometimes leading the way. One contemporary cultural commentator noted, "Australia has cherry-picked the best and weeded out the worst" to become a culturally rich and diverse country as successive waves of immigrants have made it their home, and library practice has benefited from the cherry-picking.[5]

This chapter adopts a common periodization of Australian library history: settlement to 1850; 1850 to Federation (colonial pride); 1901 to 1933 (parallel state and Commonwealth development); 1934 to 1956 (libraries for the people); 1957 to 1987 (libraries for the nation); and 1988 to date (national cooperation on an unprecedented scale). Because this chapter (and this book) is concerned primarily with the history of librarianship in the twentieth century, the period before 1900 receives only sufficient attention to contextualize later developments. This chronology also works broadly for New Zealand library history, with a later date for European settlement in the 1820s.

1788–1900: FIRST ENCOUNTERS TO FEDERATION

The relationship of Australia and New Zealand and their place in the world can be appreciated only if their early history is understood. This section sets the stage for the history of librarianship in both countries after 1900.

Australia to 1900

Australia is one of the world's longest continuously inhabited continents, having been populated for at least 40,000 years by peoples with established sophisticated traditions of preserving and transmitting knowledge. The first encounters of these peoples with European settlers, as distinct from the Portuguese, Dutch, and British explorers of the seventeenth and eighteenth centuries, occurred in 1788. Australia was declared *terra nullius* ("land without owners") by its British colonizers, denying its indigenous population any right of ownership; this legal fiction was overturned only in 1982. No formal treaties were signed, allowing the rights of Australia's indigenous population to be ignored. (The term "Aboriginal and Torres Strait Islander peoples" is used to refer to Australia's indigenous populations, and "Maori" for the inhabitants that European settlers encountered in New Zealand.) British colonizers, including convicts, soldiers, freemen, and emancipists, some with education but with little capital to purchase books, brought with them the book-based traditions and practices of their homeland, which were constantly reinforced through nostalgic reference back to "Home." The establishment of libraries, initially subscription libraries and mechanics' institutes, was among these traditions.

Some early attempts to found libraries, such as those of the Philosophical Society of Australasia in Sydney (1821–1823) and the Van Diemen's Land Scientific Society in Hobart (1829), failed. Others thrived; the State Library of New South Wales in Sydney traces its ancestry from the Australian Subscription Library and Reading Room in 1826. Athenaeums and mechanics' institutes appeared in centers with populations large enough to support them—in Hobart (1827), Sydney (1833), Newcastle (1835), and Melbourne (1838). Booksellers ran circulating libraries as early as the 1830s, such as the Derwent Circulating Library opened by Samuel Augustus Tegg in Hobart in 1839. Historical evidence shows a high premium on private libraries and reading in contexts other than libraries. In short, colonists imported an infrastructure of libraries and scholarship wholesale from Britain to Australia.

The discovery of gold in New South Wales and Victoria in 1851 attracted fortune-seekers from many nations. As new settlements sprang up in the goldfields, more athenaeums or mechanics' institutes were established. Many still exist, although their functions changed; for example, the athenaeum in the small town of Chiltern, Victoria, where gold was mined from 1858, became a museum in which much of the collection that met the recreational and educational needs of its nineteenth- and early twentieth-century users remains intact. Major cities in each of the Australian colonies grew rapidly. Gold brought prosperity to Melbourne, which became one of the world's largest and wealthiest cities by the 1880s. In 1890 its population of almost 500,000 made it the second largest city in the British Empire after London. Supreme Court judge Sir Redmond Barry was directly responsible in the 1850s and 1860s for establishing the Melbourne Public Library, the Library of the Supreme Court of Victoria, and the University of Melbourne Library, and was heavily involved in organizing the Victorian parliamentary library. Establishing the Melbourne Public Library (later the State Library of Victoria) in 1854 was an impressive manifestation of the colonists' perception that libraries were a necessary component of a civilized society. An Education Act in Victoria (1872), followed by similar acts in the other Australian colonies, signaled the availability in Australia of secular and compulsory free elementary education and resulted in high levels of literacy and education that further supported the establishment of libraries. But progress was not uniform across the country as each colony developed its own approach to providing library services. Universities were established in Sydney in 1851, Melbourne in 1853, Adelaide in 1874, and Tasmania in 1890, but their libraries were slow to develop. By the nineteenth century's end every town of any size had its mechanics' institute or athenaeum, but the library services they offered were available only to those who could afford to pay the membership subscription. Although free public libraries were established in major cities—Melbourne (1854), Sydney (1869), Hobart (1870), Perth (1884), Adelaide (1887), Brisbane (1896)—their expansion and availability beyond these cities became the key issue in the next century.

New Zealand to 1900

The development of library services in New Zealand through the nineteenth century paralleled development in Australia. Patterns of immigration into New Zealand from 1840, initially dominated by commercial operations such as the New Zealand Company, differed from Australian colonies, most of which had starter populations of transported convicts. Settlers encountered Maori, themselves colonizers from Polynesia, with their own language, belief systems, and knowledge practices, who defended their land effectively and never formally surrendered to the British army. The Treaty of Waitangi, signed in 1840 between the British Crown and tribal chiefs but largely ignored until the 1970s, has become a powerful tool for Maori and Pakeha (non-Maori New Zealanders) to define economic relationships, land ownership, and rights. The settlers were willing colonists for whom books were an essential part of their baggage, as evidenced in the plan drawn up for the Wellington settlement by the New Zealand Company's surveyors in advance of the settlers' arrival in which areas for a "Mechanics' Institution" and for a "Public Baths and Library" were allocated. Some ships carrying immigrants to New Zealand also transported printed material intended for public library collections, and libraries were established within two years of their arrival in Wellington, Auckland, and Nelson. Gold rushes in New Zealand attracted more immigrants after 1857, mainly from the British Isles but with significant representation from other parts of Europe and from China. New Zealand's highest levels of immigration occurred between 1871 and 1885 as a result of an assisted migration program from Britain.

Early settlers in New Zealand were avid readers who actively established libraries as an essential component of their new settlements; as New Zealand Company propaganda put it in 1839, "in no colony is literature more appreciated than in New Zealand." Between 1872 and 1884 there were 116 public libraries and athenaeums in the Otago region with a population in 1881 of 135,023, giving credence to the propaganda; so too does Anthony Trollope's observation during an 1872 visit to New Zealand: "In all these towns are libraries, and the books are strongly bound and well thumbed. Carlyle, Macaulay and Dickens are certainly better known to small communities in New Zealand than they are to similar congregations of men and women at home." Like their Australian counterparts, libraries in New Zealand were sites for local meetings. The Karori Library, established in 1857, not only operated a subscription library but also hosted public lectures and penny readings, at which popular works were read aloud, during the 1860s and 1870s. Libraries in New Zealand were established early and often by immigrants, largely British middle class or Scottish, who placed a high premium on education. The result was that "New Zealand appears to have achieved, within fifty years of settlement, the highest . . . number of libraries to total population ever reached in any country or state in the world," more than double the number in New England.[6] Annual government subsidies for book purchases from 1877 to 1902 on condition that an annual borrowing fee be imposed encouraged and sustained their establishment. Consequently, the availability of free library service for the New Zealand public was delayed well beyond its availability in the United States.

Australia's self-governing colonies federated as a Commonwealth on January 1, 1901. By 1900 both Australia and New Zealand were ready for expansion and diversification of libraries and their services, following the precedent of growth and expansion in Britain after 1850, when libraries started to become more widespread and librarianship more professional.

1901–1945: FEDERATION TO WORLD WAR II

The federation of the Australian colonies was the culmination of a series of actions that began with proposals for full political unification in the 1880s. By 1901 Australia's wealth and progress brought the new nation international recognition independent of its place within the British Empire, although its commercial and cultural links with Britain remained strong.

In the first half of the twentieth century Australian libraries and librarians embraced modernity (used here in the sense of modernization, transforming technologies, economies, and institutions) by taking up opportunities for international participation. Engagement with modernity and international librarianship was exemplified in a battle played out at the Melbourne Public Library (now the State Library of Victoria) in the century's first and second decades. Interaction with countries other than Britain, particularly the United States, increased. National parochialism, in the guise of an Australian system championed by Amos Brazier, confronted the international modernity of the Dewey Decimal Classification (DDC) system endorsed by Chief Librarian Edmund La Touche Armstrong. Brazier, the chief cataloger, detailed his strong objections to the Decimal scheme, which had been used successfully to classify the library's lending collections since 1900. He favored a locally developed classification scheme based on that used in the British Museum. When Armstrong proposed reclassifying the reference collections according to DDC in 1909, Brazier again objected, strenuously and offensively. Armstrong reported Brazier, who was demoted. In this conflict, values collided as new ways of thinking and practice adopted from the developing profession in the United States competed with the entrenched attitudes of an institution established in a transplanted British colonial model.

Hand in hand with international awareness was increasing professionalization, exemplified by attempts to establish professional associations. As early as 1896, librarians and others interested in libraries from Australia and New Zealand attended a conference in Melbourne and established the Library Association of Australasia. The association convened further conferences in Sydney (1898) and Adelaide (1900), and published the short-lived *Library Record of Australasia* (six issues, 1901–1902), but no record of further activities exists after 1904. State-based associations were also established, such as the Library Association of Victoria in 1912. Groups such as these stimulated exchange of ideas and public interest in libraries. By 1934, when influential Australian librarian John Metcalfe took the first of three tours of libraries in Britain, the United States, and Mexico, the profession of librarianship was already developing. Its members were middle class, and nearly all senior positions were held by males, their seniority reinforced by public service rules of employment and preferment that barred females from senior positions and paid them less than males for equivalent work. Despite these strictures, some women, such as Ida Leeson and Jean Arnot at the Public Library of New South Wales (now the State Library of New South Wales), held influential positions, even though they were denied appointment to the most senior positions.

Links with Britain were still solid and close, owing in large part to British librarians who established the first libraries and trained their successors. A consequence in Australia and New Zealand was British publishers' near stranglehold on book imports, which they did not relinquish until the 1980s, and then not without a struggle. The Berne Convention on international copyright governed British (and, therefore, Australian) practice from 1886 and the Net Book Agreement of 1900 extended British control of the Australian and New Zealand markets, resulting in British editions being heavily privileged over editions from the United States. Although U.S. publishers began to encroach on Britain's traditional markets after World War II, British publishers continued to dominate the Australian and New Zealand markets well into the 1980s.

After the excitement of new nationhood in 1901 diminished, Australia became increasingly xenophobic, exemplified in the "White Australia Policy" enshrined in the Immigration Restriction Act of 1901 and not formally rescinded until 1973. Australia severely restricted immigration from countries outside Europe. Anglo-Celtic cultural dominance persisted, with significant consequences for the nature of Australian society and its book trade, such as very little publishing or importing of foreign-language works, no publishing in indigenous languages, and very little local publishing of any sort. The British book publishers' hold affected developing library collections and services, few of which provided for non-English-speaking groups. Which cultural heritages Australian librarians helped construct in the early twentieth century was obvious.

The Munn-Pitt Report

In 1935 Ralph Munn, director of the Carnegie Library of Pittsburgh and representing the Carnegie Corporation, teamed with Ernest R. Pitt, chief librarian of the Public Library of Victoria (then Australia's largest library), to survey libraries and present a report under the auspices of the Australian Council for Educational Research (ACER). The report was scathing. Australian librarianship, they argued, was "in some respects worse than it was fifty years ago," moving from local support to heavy dependence on inadequate central government support. The result was out-of-date libraries, low levels of interest by readers, and little local pride in libraries.[7]

The Munn-Pitt report, promoting Munn's views of libraries as educational, informational, and cultural institutions, and preferring high-culture collections over popular material, had far-reaching consequences, not just for public libraries but for the wider Australian library community, library services, library associations, and education for librarianship. Its release immediately inspired newspaper headlines such as "Wanted—1,000,000 Books," and fueled media exposure of the sorry state of Australian libraries in years to come (for example, "A Neglected Library," "Australia Has Worst Libraries"). Although World War II delayed implementation of its recommendations, the report stimulated the gradual replacement of subscription libraries with free public libraries. It inspired the Free Library Movement, a coalition of concerned citizens, trade unions, and progress associations (among others) formed in 1935 to promote and establish free (that is, tax-supported) public libraries. In Australia, unlike the United States and Britain, state sponsorship of public libraries was not considered "a duty that taxpayers owed to the general welfare of society, a public obligation with personal benefits" set in a wider view of "reading and leisure . . . as collective resources that, like water, must be widely distributed and managed in the interests of an entire community's health."[8] The Munn-Pitt report introduced U.S. public librarianship traditions to Australia, and also led to the establishment of the Australian Institute of Librarians in 1937 (from 1949 the Library Association of Australia [LAA] and from 1989 the Australian Library and Information Association [ALIA]) and to the introduction in 1944 of a nationwide certification scheme for librarians.

Evolution of Public Libraries: Australia

Although Australian public libraries share many features with public libraries in other countries, they have distinctive characteristics. Public libraries often fill many roles, including preserving collective memory and supporting nationalism and national identity through collecting local and national documentary heritage; maintaining belief systems through collection development policies and practices; and societal development through providing collections and services intended to educate, typically within the constraints of limited funding. The history of public libraries in Australia is in part the story of the tensions among these roles. Visitors to Australia might wonder why the Australian public library system still does not compare favorably in its geographical coverage and collection quantity and quality with systems in other similarly developed countries. Part of the answer lies in the past dominance of subscription libraries, the mechanics' institutes, schools of arts, and institutes established in the nineteenth century and of commercial circulating (or lending) libraries in the first half of the twentieth century, which stunted the development of strong taxpayer-supported public library service. Other parts of the answer lie in the role of the state libraries in providing public library services and in the relationship between state and local government. Also relevant is the lack of connection of Australian public libraries to the concerns of Aboriginal and Torres Strait Islander peoples, since until the 1970s most in the Australian community believed indigenous peoples should assimilate into the culture of the colonizers.

Libraries in the mechanics' institutes, with their lecture rooms, newspaper reading rooms, and sometimes museums, were products of the British working-class self-improvement movement. The need to generate income to ensure their survival quickly displaced their initial aim of educating workers, so that their history from the 1890s was trying to keep marginal businesses afloat. They operated in an environment of tension between the authorities—principally local and state governments—who provided subsidies and considered them primarily as tools for workers' self-improvement, and their readers, who turned to them increasingly for popular fiction. Mechanics' institutes usually failed to resolve this dilemma and declined in number and importance as the twentieth century progressed.

Commercial circulating libraries in Australia flourished from the 1930s to the 1960s, although the earliest, the Australian Subscription Library, appeared in Sydney in 1826. Their numbers remained small until about 1930 when their growth skyrocketed; for example, Melbourne had 89 in 1930, 408 by 1940, more than 300 in 1955, declining to 87 in 1974; these figures do not include the many subscription libraries run by newsagents, chemists, florists, and other businesses. Other large Australian towns and cities were no different. The subscription libraries operated as commercial profit-making concerns, their members paying a fee that entitled them to borrow a set number of items. By comparison with their North American equivalents, which had an average collection size of about 150, Australian circulating libraries were larger, with average collection size in the low thousands and some over 20,000; some operated as members of chains. Their influence on book distribution and on reading was considerable because they provided popularly requested books, especially romances, westerns, and thrillers, and had no formal educational role. In 1938 members of a subscription library in a Melbourne working-class suburb borrowed the following types of books: romances 25 percent, westerns 22 percent, mysteries 21 percent, adventure stories 15 percent, general literature 10 percent, "better class" novels 7 percent. For a time subscriptions had a detrimental effect on municipal libraries whose collections and ideology focused on formal education rather than recreation and which were not located conveniently near railway stations. Loans from public library lending collections dropped considerably as the popularity of subscription libraries flourished.

At the same time that the popularity of the circulating libraries peaked, concerned Australians sought assistance in their quest to improve public library services. The Australian Council for Educational Research (ACER) took a leading role from 1930 to 1947 in improving library services in Australia and promoting taxpayer-funded public library services. ACER established a relationship with the Carnegie Corporation from about 1930. The corporation showed little interest in Australia before this date; Carnegie money funded four libraries, whereas in New Zealand it funded eighteen between 1902 and 1914. ACER influenced the corporation to fund Munn's 1935 visit to Australia, establish a library group to promote library services, fund a publicity campaign about the role of free public libraries, establish the Free Library Movement, and arrange the visit of British librarian Lionel McColvin in 1946–1947 and the publication of his *Public Libraries in Australia: Present Conditions and Future Possibilities*. McColvin's report proposed a program for Australian library development, recommending "a library act, a library board, a partnership between state and local government, centralized processing, a library school, a central lending library for people in very remote areas, and bulk loans, including children's books, to some local libraries."[9] The greatest influence of McColvin's visit was the debate it stimulated rather than his report and recommendations.

Changes brought by these activities were remarkable. Before World War II Australia had as many as 2,000 subscription libraries, mechanics' institutes, and schools of arts. Although some received small subsidies from local or state governments and masqueraded as public libraries, they were used by only about 3 percent of the population. The Munn-Pitt report triggered the passing of Library Acts in every state, the first in South Australia in 1939, the last in Western Australia in 1951. The legislation gave access to a public library to over 98 percent of the Australian population. The remarkable growth of public libraries in New South Wales illustrates the effect of that state's Library Act. Within eighteen months of its passing in 1944 thirty-two municipal authorities complied and sixteen indicated that they planned to comply. Seven were already providing library services. By 1946 a quarter of the state's population of nearly three million had access to a free public library, but total coverage of the state was not achieved until 1992.

In response to the challenges of distance, distinctive patterns evolved in Australian public library service in the country's sparsely populated hinterland. The use of book boxes to lend books to rural libraries was an early response, implemented in Victoria and South Australia in the 1870s and later in New South Wales. Library services in Western Australia, with its very large area and tiny population, provide a noteworthy example. Library services in that state were notoriously weak, even when compared with the minimal services provided in the more wealthy and populous states. They did not develop until the 1950s, much later than other states. McColvin's 1947 report noted no municipal libraries in Western Australia and fewer institutes than other states. By 1950 grassroots efforts pushed for legislation to ensure better services to bring Western Australia in line with most other states, culminating in the passing of legislation in 1951. Officials appointed Britain's Ali Sharr in 1953 to develop a statewide public library network in a state with a tiny number of isolated institute libraries, one subscription library, and some free children's libraries operated by volunteers. Sharr developed a model for public library provision based on loans from a central collection in the State Library. From the condition of paucity in 1953, by 1982 public library services were available in every local authority in Western Australia.

Evolution of Public Libraries: New Zealand

Provision of library services in New Zealand from 1901 to World War II was broadly similar to Australia. One difference was that fees were charged for borrowing fiction as a result of conditions attached to government aid to public libraries from 1938. In the early twenty-first century fees were still charged for fiction in some New Zealand public libraries in politically conservative towns; a 2012 informal email survey of sixty-six New Zealand public library systems showed some still charge to borrow genre fiction and some, typically smaller local authorities, charge for all fiction, although they reported exceptions for New Zealand fiction, large-print fiction, or "erudite" fiction. In 2014 the number of libraries levying charges for borrowing fiction was small.

At the beginning of the twentieth century, New Zealand made little distinction between municipally funded public libraries and their commercial counterparts. Officials viewed libraries primarily as providing readers with entertainment and, accordingly, they charged for book loans like other forms of entertainment. The role of libraries as providers of useful knowledge was valued less highly. A 1913 survey of public libraries found that 30 percent bought fiction only; 89 percent of the purchases in all but eleven major libraries were fiction. In the 1930s public libraries were, with few exceptions, subscription libraries run by municipalities or voluntary groups combining fiction and reference services, although a few had good reference services based on adequate collections. At Dunedin Public Library, however, A. G. W. Dunningham (a University of Michigan library school graduate) took a fresh approach from the late 1930s and built a collection of "quality" fiction that could be borrowed free of charge and a rental collection of genre and popular fiction for which borrowers were charged. The latter generated income that subsidized the purchase of such fiction. The debate about charging for fiction was, of course, not restricted to New Zealand, having been a preoccupation of twentieth-century North American librarians. Its widespread adoption in New Zealand was encouraged by conditions attached to the government aid available to public libraries from 1938 in the form of bulk loans from the government-run Country Library Service.

The Carnegie Corporation's role in promoting free public library service in New Zealand was substantial, although it differed from Australia where Carnegie funding secured by ACER supported the Munn-Pitt report, which then shaped consequent actions in New Zealand. Carnegie gave grants for eighteen library buildings, but of greater influence was the corporation's funding of librarians' study visits in Europe and the United States in the 1930s and 1940s. On their return these librarians transformed library services. The corporation also sponsored experts to visit New Zealand. In 1934 Ralph Munn teamed up with John Barr, chief librarian of Auckland Public Library, to tour the country. The Munn-Barr report highlighted deficiencies in New Zealand's library system, such as widespread use of the subscription system in public libraries and the lack of a national library, and recommended that public libraries be free for ratepayers and residents, a national reference library established, professional training enhanced, and more consideration given to the three functions of libraries (cultural, vocational, and recreational). The Munn-Barr report set a course for New Zealand's modern library system. In 1959 Andrew Osborn, then university librarian at the University of Sydney and with extensive experience in the United States, surveyed library resources in New Zealand. His report led to improvement of library holdings, especially in university libraries. In 1974 Sara Fenwick from the University of Chicago surveyed library services to New Zealand's children, identifying major problems such as lack of funding, lack of trained specialist librarians, and limited cooperation between school and public libraries. Her report led to the establishment of a government school library agency and to improvements in library services to children.

1945 TO DATE: AUSTRALIA SINCE WORLD WAR II

The reconstruction of the Australian economy following World War II was the backdrop for a massive expansion of library services based on the Munn-Pitt recommendations and the Free Library Movement activities. Library services in the growing universities and colleges expanded rapidly, national schemes promoting cooperation among all types of libraries developed, and awareness and adoption of international library practice increased. As Australia's population grew from 7.4 million in 1945 to 19.3 million in 2000, Australians changed their ways of living and working. Rural towns languished and urban centers sprawled, making Australia one of the world's most heavily urbanized countries. Public libraries were increasingly the only stable agencies that remained in rural areas with declining populations, economic hardship, and the withdrawal of commercial and government services. From the 1980s rural public libraries took on additional roles as local authority business transaction centers, technology service providers, and community information and learning support providers. Joint-use libraries, in which public libraries combined with school and local libraries, increased in number.

Legislation in the 1970s dismantled the White Australia policy, and Australia pursued a more open immigration regime and a commitment to multiculturalism. A 1967 referendum recognized Aboriginal and Torres Strait Islander peoples as full citizens of the nation, making it possible to begin to address inequities in land rights and attempt reconciliation in relation to earlier racist government policies. Officials began to acknowledge the information needs of Aboriginal and Torres Strait Islander peoples in library services, although painfully slowly and at first in a token way. From the 1970s a cultural maturity and a sense of identity as a self-confident nation steadily emerged. The social and political changes of the 1970s had a dramatic effect on libraries, most notably on the development of national library collections and services, and on the flourishing of local arts, writing, and publishing through the last decades of the twentieth century. The heritage of cultures Australian libraries collected and served expanded in scope.

In 1973 Harrison Bryan, as president of the Library Association of Australia (LAA), described post–World War II Australia as "still shaking itself free from war" with its enforced austerities and massive social dislocations. He also noted the level of change promoted by "the stimulation of secondary industry and the personal experience of American technology and drive." In the 1940s the Public Library of Victoria and the Public Library of New South Wales were the nation's largest libraries, whereas the Commonwealth National Library had a low profile, little national influence, and small collections. In 1948 libraries in the nation's nine universities were little changed from 1935. Australia still had no union catalog of monographs, no union list of periodicals in the social sciences and humanities, no Australian library journal, infrequent conferences of the Australian Institute of Librarians, no library school teaching any recognized curriculum; "It was a small and rather parochial library world."

"Tremendous Strides": Transforming Australian Libraries

In 1965 LAA president Peter Crisp argued that Australia's library resources did not meet the level of basic needs and acknowledged the challenges of providing library services to a small, literate, and geographically dispersed population with librarians limited in both number and training. He advocated cooperative development to meet two urgent demands: extending public library services and coordinating collection development on a national basis. The provision of library services to indigenous Australians was not on the 1965 agenda. Eight years later Bryan reported "tremendous strides . . . towards a proper provision of libraries for the nation," noting a substantial increase in bibliographical resources and the number of libraries, improvement in quality of services, a flourishing library association, six accredited library schools, and an impressive development of interlibrary cooperation.[10] Obviously, librarians accepted the responsibility for and were actively participating in the development of Australian library services.

Another postwar library development was the transformation of higher education libraries. The number of universities grew from six in 1930 to nineteen by 1980, largely because of a 1957 Commonwealth report that argued that more universities were needed to produce more educated citizens, to conduct research, and to be guardians of the nation's intellectual integrity. By 1965 university library collections rivaled the state libraries of Victoria, New South Wales, and South Australia, all founded in the nineteenth century. By 1973 they collectively constituted Australia's biggest bibliographical resource and participated fully in Australia's developing nationwide network of library services. By 2000 the number of universities doubled. With the exception of libraries in the longest-established universities (Melbourne, Sydney, and Adelaide) with substantial and well-maintained research collections, newer university library collections and services developed largely to support curriculum requirements and student needs.

As the National Library of Australia took on major coordination and leadership roles and its national influence expanded from the 1960s, state libraries challenged it. The relationship between state libraries and the National Library was sometimes difficult. Established in Melbourne as the Commonwealth Parliamentary Library in 1901, its expanding role was recognized in 1923 in a name change to Commonwealth National Library, before it moved to Australia's new national capital, Canberra, in 1927. Several state libraries overshadowed its collections, but this changed from the 1960s. In 1973 Bryan remarked on "the recent blossoming" of the National Library, noting its energetic collection building, "the long, long struggle for a significant building [which] . . . came to magnificent fruition in 1968," and the substantial expansion of services to its users.[11] In recognition of the geopolitical realities of Australia's position, Asian collections actively developed from the 1950s, formed through the acquisition of well-established personal collections and active purchase and exchange of materials in Asian languages. The collections, together with their concomitant user services, ranked among the most significant in the world by the twenty-first century. From its inception the National Library sought to comprehensively collect Australiana in printed, manuscript, and audio forms (including oral history), defining its responsibilities "in terms of national endeavour and attainment," and working closely with other institutions in Australia with major holdings of Australiana.[12] The National Library also developed a wide range of bibliographical services for the nation, including the *Annual Catalogue of Australian Publications* (1936–1960, which became the *Australian National Bibliography* in 1961) and NUCOM (the *National Union Catalogue of Monographs*) from the early 1960s. It began to participate actively in international activities. In the twenty-first century the National Library of Australia's role shifted from building a collection for the nation to coordinating multicultural services and collections across the nation.

The role of the state libraries also changed. In 1948 their collections constituted Australia's major bibliographical research resources, but by 1970 their 2.6 million books were outstripped by university libraries' collections totaling 6.3 million. State libraries sought new roles or emphasized other aspects of their mandate, particularly supporting and collaborating in public library services. One newly emphasized role was as a center for coordination and leadership in the state, reflecting at state level the National Library's role. State libraries placed greater emphasis on developing collections of rare and heritage materials and establishing positions for specialist rare books librarians to manage and develop these collections. Legal deposit legislation making the state library home for each state's publishing output enabled them to achieve this aim. State libraries also provided support for public libraries through advisory services, state-based catalogs, grants, and other services. In Tasmania the state library managed all public libraries. State libraries provided an example of increasing collaboration between libraries in Australia and New Zealand. The Council of Australian State Libraries, established in 1973 as the State Librarians' Council, was renamed National and State Libraries Australasia in 2005 to signal the expansion of its membership to include the national libraries of New Zealand and Australia.

Special libraries also benefited in this period of massive library services development. By the 1970s the Commonwealth Scientific and Industrial Research Organisation (CSIRO) library system had become a major collection in the sciences and an energetic participant in and contributor to the Australian library community. Libraries in Commonwealth and state government departments also flourished and became key components of the national library system.

The transformation of Australian school libraries began in 1968, when the Commonwealth government injected substantial funding, chiefly in response to the recommendations of the Fenwick report, the LAA's publication of standards for school libraries in 1966, and a public submission to the prime minister in 1967. Thereafter funding for capital outlay and book stock in both government and private secondary schools followed with similar support for primary school libraries from 1973. Although Australia had no national curriculum (responsibility for school education resided with the state governments), Commonwealth funding of the Australian Schools Catalogue Information Service (ASCIS) begun in 1984 had the effect of standardizing library collections and practices. ASCIS became SCIS when New Zealand joined in 1992. Its aim was to reduce the costs of and duplication of effort in cataloging resources in schools by providing a database of consistent catalog records. ASCIS provided strong support for the development of school library collections and services, as did centralized support services offered by state government agencies. School libraries were initially staffed by teachers with no library qualifications and often little interest, and later by teacher-librarians with dual credentials as both librarians and teachers from the newly established library schools from 1972.

National Cooperation

Among reasons for the vigorous expansion of library services was a high level of interlibrary cooperation. By the 1960s national cooperative schemes implemented in Australian and New Zealand libraries flourished. Collaboration continued into the twenty-first century and expanded into the wider world as Australian and New Zealand libraries participated in international activities and librarians from other countries visited Australia and New Zealand to investigate the innovation in library services for which they achieved fame. For example, a stream of visitors came to Australia and New Zealand in the century's first decade to examine the innovative digital preservation activities in both countries.

Key to this high level of cooperation in Australia was the Australian Advisory Council on Bibliographical Services (AACOBS), established in 1956 to plan coordination of bibliographical services in all Australian libraries and cooperation with international bodies. When established, AACOBS had no match elsewhere in the world for advancing the development of a nation's library services. It was a response to a particularly Australian set of issues: the need to provide library services and resources to a small population dispersed widely over a large landmass where the few major libraries were separated by great distances, and the late development of all but a handful of libraries, with the consequence that few large, comprehensive collections existed in the nation. The solution was a national approach to providing library services based on the concept of a national collection comprising all library stock, strong bibliographical services to locate resources, and a robust interlibrary lending scheme. At first only major libraries (Commonwealth National Library, state libraries, and CSIRO) were members of AACOBS, but membership expanded by 1960 to include university libraries. Eventually it became more fully representative of the nation's libraries when the organization admitted archives, special libraries, parliamentary libraries, public libraries, college libraries, and distinguished laymen to membership. One of the council's activities was the formation of the National Book Resources Development Committee, based on a regional committee structure with an effective framework for consultation among each region's major libraries, and aimed at reducing duplication of holdings of expensive resources. The Australian Libraries and Information Council (ALIC) was established in 1982 to advise the Commonwealth government on library issues, in particular to lobby for increased Commonwealth funding for libraries. In 1986 the Australian Council of Library and Information Services (ACLIS) replaced ALIC and AACOBS. ACLIS's aims were to foster development of Australian libraries and to promote and coordinate cooperation. By the time ACLIS disbanded in 1998 national cooperation was firmly embedded as a central pillar in the architecture of Australian librarianship.

Prompted in part by the decreasing value of the Australian dollar in the 1980s, which eroded the ability to purchase North American and European publications, Australian libraries formalized the concept of a national collection with the Distributed National

Collection (DNC), introduced in 1988 at the Australian Libraries Summit (another example of cooperation) as a mechanism for all Australian libraries to cooperate in managing their collecting on a national scale. The building blocks were in place, especially the Australian Bibliographic Network and the leadership of the National Library and ACLIS. Officials abandoned the DNC concept by the mid-1990s, when digital materials from overseas commercial document-delivery services became available. Cooperation continued through consortia agreements providing shared access to digital content. One example was the National and State Libraries Australasia (NSLA) E-Resources Consortium, which aimed to provide electronic resources (full-text journals, local and international newspapers, eBooks and databases) to all Australians, regardless of where in Australia they lived. Its first phase, a core set of electronic resources for all consortium libraries, was implemented in 2012.

As in other countries, Australian librarians reacted to what they considered the inadequacies of North American bibliographic tools for representing their specific needs by developing their own bibliographic tools, such as *Australia: DC Expansion* (1971) and *A List of Australian Subject Headings* (1981), and together they developed not just one, but two national bibliographic utilities, the Australian Bibliographic Network (ABN) and the Schools Catalogue Information Service (SCIS). The national resource-sharing network Libraries Australia started in 1981 as a bibliographic utility, ABN (later renamed Kinetica). Libraries of all types contributed to ABN and used its services. Other manifestations of national collaboration, not unique to Australia but demonstrating high levels of cooperation, include National and State Libraries Australasia, established in 1973 as the State Librarians Council, and the Council of Australian University Librarians (CAUL), formed in 1965.

The National Library of Australia played a major role in coordinating cooperative activities. It was instrumental in developing the national bibliographic infrastructure, in particular ABN and Kinetica, both providing vital access to information resources in Australian library collections. It assumed responsibility for managing Libraries Australia, an online service that facilitates resource sharing among Australian libraries by supplying bibliographic records for Australian and overseas publications, resource discovery, and interlibrary loan through a simple Web interface. It also developed the federated search engines Picture Australia, which provided access to major collections of images in the nation's libraries, archives, and museums and, in conjunction with the National Film and Sound Archive, Music Australia, to online and print music resources across Australia. These, together with several other collaborative specialized search services, were made searchable from a single interface, Trove, providing online access to an unprecedented range of resources and internationally acknowledged for its innovation. These initiatives were responses to the National Library's mandate to provide information for all Australians, wherever they were. In the twenty-first century the National Library of Australia continued to innovate, for example, providing access to Australian newspapers online through Trove, in collaboration with state libraries and using crowdsourcing to correct the digitized versions.

Education for Librarianship

Divergence from Anglo-American models of practice is most apparent in education for Australian librarianship. A hybrid tradition developed—unique but not entirely effective. In 1963 an Australian library educator noted, "It sometimes seems to me that in our comparatively late library development in Australia we do not profit from what has happened elsewhere. It is almost as though we say, there are a few British and American mistakes we haven't made yet; let's make them, it would be a pity to miss any."[13] A multitiered system evolved, where professional status could be claimed by holders of a Library Association of Australia–administered certificate, and by those with a three- or four-year undergraduate degree, a one-year postgraduate diploma, a master's in library and information studies, or a library technician program. The multitiered system confused potential students and uninformed employers alike. It emerged out of the shift from a workplace-based mentoring model to the regulation of entry to the profession by examinations conducted by the professional association. Until 1944, when LAA implemented a nationwide certification scheme for librarians, Australia offered no qualifications for librarianship. Before then candidates studied for the British Library Association's registration examinations in library schools within the state libraries or through correspondence courses. From the 1960s universities began to offer graduate qualifications accredited by the professional association.

Tensions arising from a series of expedient grafts of British and U.S. practice onto an established rootstock transplanted from the British educational tradition are apparent in the history of education for Australian librarianship. The model that preceded the introduction of university-based graduate qualifications in the 1960s was a "British semi-apprentice system" characterized by professional associations acting as examination rather than accreditation bodies, and placing limited value on graduate entry to the profession. Consequently, librarianship educators in Australia did not at first value North American qualifications in librarianship as highly as those from Britain. An anonymous contributor to the first issue of the *Australian Library Journal* stated: "The appointment of British librarians to senior positions in Australia should do something to dispel the idea that we are Americanized in Australia."[14] Despite this parochial view, Carnegie Corporation influence increased from the 1930s, including funding overseas study tours, which almost always included the United States. Grafted onto the British tradition, the corporation's influence resulted in a Janus-like vision for education in Australia—looking back to the colonial heritage from Britain and ahead to a future based on North American practice but modified for Australia. Library schools established in state libraries followed North American precedent rather than British tradition. A British model, however, was promoted once the Australian Institute of Librarians developed its examination system from 1944 as the path for the students to become professional librarians. This was the British Library Association model, in which the association recognized an individual's achievement, rather than the North American model, in which the American Library Association accredited library schools.

A further tension between British and North American models was apparent in the development of paraprofessional library technician qualifications. A North American model of paraprofessional education influenced programs that offered training for Australian paraprofessionals from 1970. Nevertheless, the first library technicians' program was clearly situated in the British tradition of vocational education long established in Australia. A unique and continuing tradition of paraprofessional education for Australian librarianship evolved, where library technician qualifications were recognized by the professional association and where little distinction existed in the workplace between holders of graduate and technician qualifications, which still exists at the time of this writing.

Another distinctive feature of Australian education for librarianship is distance education, developed in response to a need to educate scattered populations in a large land-mass. For most Australian students distance education has been a way of life since the 1980s. Twenty-first-century graduates were likely to have studied by distance mode, either completing their professional qualification fully online or incorporating online courses as a significant proportion of their program.

Whatever its historical influences, the state of education for Australian librarianship has consistently been viewed as less than satisfactory. Three reports (in 1989, 1996, and 2011) noted the detrimental effects of small schools of librarianship in large colleges and universities and of alliances created for administrative rather than pedagogical reasons. All identified a need for greater collaboration among the schools and with the profession, and for more educators to come from disciplines other than librarianship.

1945 TO DATE: NEW ZEALAND SINCE WORLD WAR II

Social and political changes in New Zealand had a similarly dramatic impact on the development of libraries. The Munn-Barr report of 1934 recommended a national system of libraries that included a national library with several regional headquarters, which eventuated as the National Library Service in 1945. One of its components was the Country Library Service (operated from 1938 to 1988) modeled on a library service to rural households in the Canterbury region using book vans, which began in 1930 with Carnegie Corporation funding. Officials assumed the needs of Maori were addressed by a government assimilation policy driven in large part by Maori themselves and not changed until the 1970s. Much national library service development can be attributed to one energetic and influential man, Geoffrey Alley, founding director of the Country Library Service, first director of the National Library Service, founder of the School Library Service in 1942, and New Zealand's first national librarian. Although Alley was more an implementer than a planner, under his leadership National Library services developed and consolidated.

The influence of American practice, evident in Carnegie funding of the Canterbury book van scheme, continued, and education for librarianship stands as another example of this influence. From the 1930s, and stimulated by the 1934 Munn-Barr report, British Library Association correspondence courses supplemented local training. The New Zealand Library Association (NZLA) developed and offered its own certificate from 1942. The New Zealand Library School, a unit of the National Library Service, offered graduate diplomas from 1946. Its first director was Mary Parsons, who had come to New Zealand as U.S. Information Service librarian. In 1952 the New Zealand Library School took over running of the NZLA certificate, in which students employed in New Zealand libraries attended three six-week-block courses over two years. This certificate, described as "a system of training peculiar to New Zealand," addressed the needs of the large numbers of unqualified personnel staffing many small local authority public libraries.[15] In 1980 the certificate course was transferred to Wellington College of Education and the graduate diploma course to Victoria University of Wellington.

Even after the National Library Service was established, New Zealand had three national libraries. The General Assembly Library, established in 1858 to serve members of Parliament and continually growing as a legal deposit library, performed some national library functions, such as maintaining a collection of the nation's newspapers.

The Alexander Turnbull Library, the country's premier collection of New Zealand research materials, was based on collections bequeathed to the nation in 1918 and opened to the public in 1920. In his 1960 report Andrew Osborn noted the illogicality of three national libraries reporting to three separate government agencies and proposed a single National Library. The National Library Act in 1965 combined them into the National Library of New Zealand. The coalition did not last, the General Assembly Library (in 2014 the Parliamentary Library) separating from the National Library in 1985. Three years later the National Library ended its twenty-year administrative association with the Department of Education to become an autonomous government agency, and in 2011 responsibility for the National Library passed to the Department of Internal Affairs, of which the national archives (Archives New Zealand) was already a part. Also in 1988 the National Library of New Zealand adopted an alternative Maori name, Te Puna Matauranga o Aotearoa ("wellspring of knowledge") to acknowledge New Zealand's bicultural heritage, in keeping with other government departments and organizations and in response to significant policy, societal, and economic changes in the role of Maori. As of this writing the National Library of New Zealand offers many services to Maori, including the provision of Maori-language information sources to schools throughout the country, and has a Komiti Maori to advise on matters pertaining to Maori. Maori literacy rates were exceptionally high from the earliest days of contact with missionaries in the 1820s, reflected in major collections of manuscript and printed material in the Maori language at the Auckland Public Library and the Alexander Turnbull Library (in 2014 part of the National Library of New Zealand).

Few libraries in mid-twentieth-century New Zealand seemed self-sufficient. Librarians were preoccupied with expansion from 1935 to 1980, believing that New Zealand's library development trailed countries to which it traditionally compared itself, principally Britain, former British colonies such as Australia and Canada, and the United States. School libraries were neither common nor well resourced until the 1940s, although services specifically for children in public libraries were available from 1910. The creation in 1942 of the School Library Service, a branch of the National Library, developed school libraries by providing expertise, guidance, and loan collections of books to schools, and school libraries received a further boost in 1975 with the release of the Fenwick report and other investigations into library services for schools.

New Zealand library collections, in common with those in Australia, had been dominated by the practical needs of building a nation rather than developing intellectual capital. Andrew Osborn noted in 1960 that collections were adequate if viewed on a national level, but added: "It is not altogether a matter of bringing books and periodicals into the country, although that is New Zealand's great need; to some extent it is a case of husbanding what is already present."[16] Osborn advocated mechanisms to manage transfers of duplicates and build a collection of last-resort copies so limited resources remained available to all in the nation. The National Library became the dominant player in developing and administering these mechanisms and was crucial to the expansion and strengthening of library services in New Zealand, more so than its Australian equivalent. By the 1990s the focus on building library collections abated, and librarians in New Zealand became more preoccupied with rationalization, strategic planning, and demonstrating accountability, although still keenly interested in cooperative solutions to better serve their users.

At the turn of the twenty-first century New Zealand's libraries continued to collaborate intensively, not only within the country but also increasingly with Australia and internationally. An example of national cooperation was Electronic Purchasing in Collaboration (EPIC), a licensing scheme for electronic resources available through consortium member libraries to their users. All New Zealand schools and many public libraries became consortium members. Collaboration with Australia has been illustrated by a cooperative database-purchasing scheme, the CAUL (Council of Australian University Librarians) Electronic Information Resources Committee (CEIRAC), in which the Council of New Zealand University Librarians (CONZUL) collaborated with CAUL to provide users of New Zealand university libraries with access to databases.

ACCOMMODATING ETHNIC DIVERSITY AND INDIGENOUS PEOPLES

Immigration changed the composition of Australian and New Zealand populations considerably after 1945. Although small numbers of migrants from non-European countries were common (Melbourne's Chinatown, established in 1851, is one of the oldest continuous Chinese settlements in the Western world), immigration from Europe after World War II rose to high levels. The consequences reshaped both countries, turning them from British orientations toward a much more cosmopolitan outlook. Institutions, including public libraries, also changed as they responded to demands for library services to assist new migrants to assimilate into their new environments. An Australian report noted the numbers involved—in 1966 over two million of Australia's 11,600,000 residents were born outside Australia, half from non-English-speaking countries—and tellingly advised that migrants were not using libraries because they held little material in languages other than English. To remedy this the report recommended a massive increase in foreign-language book stock, especially information in languages other than English about services, education, Australian law, and Australian customs and attitudes; an increase in the number of bilingual librarians and library assistants; and funding from the Commonwealth government rather than from local authorities, all aimed at encouraging assimilation. For the library profession, assimilation appears to have worked. In the twenty-first century librarians' demographics increasingly reflected the ethnic makeup of Australia's population.

Broadly similar conditions prevailed in New Zealand, although initially it was an influx of migrants from nearby Pacific Island nations such as Samoa and the Cook Islands, rather than Asian and European countries, that stimulated the need for diversification in library services. One significant difference between Australia and New Zealand, however, is that New Zealand adopted a formal bicultural policy from the late 1970s, largely ignoring broader multiculturalism. Neither Australian nor New Zealand colonizers showed exemplary conduct toward the peoples who inhabited either land before their arrival. Legislation and policies in the Australian colonies, in particular, disadvantaged, degraded, and restricted Aboriginal and Torres Strait Islander peoples. A policy of assimilation into mainstream culture formally adopted in 1937 remained in place until the 1960s, exemplified in the effects of the removal of children of Aboriginal and Torres Strait Islander descent from their families (the "stolen generation") who, between about 1909 and 1970, were taken from their families by government agencies and church missions and placed in foster homes. Although libraries did not appropriately and fully engage with colonized populations and although they overlooked a responsibility to collect materials documenting the cultural heritage of Aboriginal and

Torres Strait Islander peoples, they eventually initiated steps to address this failure in the late twentieth century.

Pickering and Modra's 1973 report suggested that Aboriginal and Torres Strait Islander peoples did not use libraries because "the library is a white man's establishment . . . [with] books . . . by white men. Such information as the library provides about Aboriginals is felt to be inaccurate, uninformed and biased."[17] For them libraries were not welcoming, perceived as forbidding places of authority and hostile because of the public racism, sometimes institutionalized, that persisted among most European Australians who until the 1990s had little understanding of Aboriginal and Torres Strait Islander peoples' knowledge systems. The report concluded that solutions should come from within Aboriginal and Torres Strait Islander communities, with libraries staffed by indigenous librarians.

Since 1973 library services available to Aboriginal and Torres Strait Islander peoples showed improvement. Awareness of the need for services accommodating their needs increased, especially during the 1990s, as many expressed concerns about their alienation from the nation's libraries, the offensive nature of much material about them in libraries, demeaning subject headings, and access issues. Attempts to recruit and train Aboriginal and Torres Strait Islander staff in the 1990s, supported by ALIA, had little effect. The 1995 *Aboriginal and Torres Strait Islanders Protocols for Libraries, Archives and Information Services* provided recommendations for how libraries, archives, and information services should interact with Aboriginal and Torres Strait Islander peoples and how to handle materials with Aboriginal and Torres Strait Islander content. (For example, there are traditional gender-based restrictions on who can access some categories of knowledge.) A 2004 survey of the *Protocols* led to revisions including, among other changes, a section on the digital environment. In the early twenty-first century, they were being adopted and implemented in many libraries.

The need to improve access to records documenting the lives of Aboriginal and Torres Strait Islander peoples identified in the 1997 *Bringing Them Home* report resulted in increased funding to the National Library of Australia. A series of other events in the 1990s also brought progress, such as identifying and improving access to Indigenous materials in library collections, the establishment of the Aboriginal and Torres Strait Islander Library Information and Resource Network, and the introduction of services to Aboriginal and Torres Strait Islander peoples in libraries. In the Northern Territory, Libraries and Knowledge Centres were set up, which combined traditional library models and indigenous knowledge concepts determined by local communities. Martin Nakata and his colleagues reported "evidence of an emerging area of distinct practice and a dynamic and changing Indigenous information context," but cautioned that "if Indigenous peoples are to invest in LIS services then the LIS sector must invest in Indigenous knowledge and peoples."[18]

In New Zealand, library services to Maori have a longer history. Although the Maori language was still widely spoken, English was the dominant language by the 1920s and in some schools speaking Maori was forbidden. From the 1970s Maori was again taught in schools, triggering a renaissance in Maori-language publishing. In the early 1990s libraries were encouraged to acknowledge both Maori and Pakeha cultures, and the profession held the first of a series of discussions of how to develop services to Maori. In 1992 Te Ropu Whakahau, an organization to support Maori working in libraries and promote library services to Maori, was founded, and in the following year LIANZA (Library and Information Association of New Zealand Aotearoa) initiated the Te Ara

Tika project to promote biculturalism in library services. Set within the context of major societal changes in the legal status and roles of Maori in New Zealand society, the project's report resulted in positive library service changes, such as the provision of a community space, Maori-speaking staff, separate Maori collections, bilingual interfaces in library catalogs, and bilingual signage. Diploma in Information Management and Bachelor in Information Management programs began at Te Wananga o Raukawa, a university based on traditional Maori learning practices. Maori information practices sometimes challenged European traditions of access to all. For example, *taonga* ("treasured things") placed by their *kaitiaki* ("guardians") in library collections for safekeeping may have restrictions on who accesses them.

CONCLUSION

At the start of the twenty-first century, librarianship and library services in Australia and New Zealand were highly professional. Robust professional associations, high-quality education programs, and a culture of sharing and collaboration resulted in consistent, internationally rated standards of practice. Both countries have developed distinctive practices of librarianship. Based on British traditions, they modified practice over time by influences from the United States, then from migrant groups initially from Europe and later from Asia and the Pacific, and from indigenous communities. Distinctive patterns of practice based on many traditions and on traditional knowledge, a high level of cooperation and convergence, the development of new kinds of library services for multicultural national identities, and a reputation for innovation and early adoption of new ideas and technologies, often in response to challenges imposed by distance, were the result. Not all needs were met, however. In Australia, for example, library services to Aboriginal and Torres Strait Islander peoples were still nascent, and to recently arrived migrant groups from Asia and Africa inadequate. But distinctive patterns of practice based on the needs of client groups rather than on imposed Anglo-American cultural expectations emerged. In New Zealand, services tailored to the needs and distinctive information practices of Maori and Pacific Islanders, while adequate (particularly when compared with Australia), required improvement. In both countries, school libraries continued to suffer from perceptions that they were not necessary for education.

Australian and New Zealand practitioners were considered early adopters and their practice has been innovative in many aspects of librarianship. Digital preservation is an example. An advisory report to the Library of Congress noted: "For a country with a relatively small population, Australia has a relatively large number of leading-edge online projects across all sectors."[19] The National Library of Australia became active in digital preservation in 1994, and actively shared its experience and expertise with the international library community. The National Library's early digital preservation activities included one of the world's first library digital preservation sections in 1995, building PANDORA (a Web-accessible archive of online publications) in 1996 and the PADI (Preserving Access to Digital Information) website in 1997. In another field, the National Library of Australia's Trove service provided an innovative approach to making discoverable all of the resources of the National Library, together with those of many other collecting institutions in Australia. Both Australia and New Zealand developed open-source bibliographic and digital library software suites, such as Greenstone and Koha, widely used internationally. New

Zealand's National Digital Heritage Archive has been observed by librarians around the world. Australian library professionals became well informed about developments in Britain and North America. New Zealand librarians similarly took their experience and expertise beyond local and regional borders to participate in the international library community. Around the world the quality of and innovation in New Zealand's library services was increasingly recognized, especially for its can do attitude and its bicultural focus.

Reasons for the reputation that Australian and New Zealand library services evolved for innovation and early adoption of new ideas and technologies must remain conjectural. A possible explanation is the need to develop approaches that accommodate the challenge of distance—from the hub of the empire these nations were once part of, from major centers of practice, and, in Australia's case, between population centers in a large but sparsely populated continent. Another is freedom from inherited conservative traditions and ideologies that may stultify innovation, resulting from the nature of settlement in both countries that led to a "Jack's as good as his master" attitude and to independence of practice. In Australia and in New Zealand the conviction that collaboration and information sharing are the best options to ensure that limited information resources reach the people who need them has moved beyond rhetoric; it has been put into practice. Whatever the reasons, innovation in library practice in both countries was closely observed elsewhere.

But do these factors sufficiently explain the development of libraries and library services in Australia and New Zealand? Paul Genoni offers another explanation for Australia. He suggests that the principal reasons for the development and divergence from North American (and by extension British) practice lie in part in "the broad cultural forces which have shaped the Australian character and have in turn shaped the general size and nature of our major library collections." Australia and the United States have much in common; "both are English speaking countries of the New World and both derive their cultural institutions from England, both continents are vast, and both have a history steeped in violence and the subjugation of an indigenous people." Why, then, are practices different and library collections so modest in Australia compared with those in the United States? Genoni argues that the Australian lifestyle, actively egalitarian and placing a premium on prowess in sports and connection with the land, is "unsympathetic to many of the intellectual and cultural values which are a prerequisite to building library collections of the very highest caliber" and, by extension, library services.[20] The differences, he proposes, can be explained by three influences: the nature of the people who settled each country, a more limited vision of the roles of government in Australia, and links to the land. A similar explanation could be made for New Zealand.

NOTES

1. Jan Morris, *Heaven's Command: An Imperial Progress* (New York: Harcourt Brace Jovanovich, 1973), 380.

2. James Morris, *Pax Britannica: The Climax of an Empire* (Harmondsworth, Middlesex: Penguin, 1968), 227, 446.

3. Jan Morris, *Farewell the Trumpets: An Imperial Retreat* (New York: Harcourt Brace Jovanovich, 1978), 212, 321–22.

4. John Curtin, "The Task Ahead," *Melbourne Herald*, December 27, 1941.

5. Nick Bryant, "The Derivative Country?" blog posting, January 24, 2011, Nick Bryant's Australia, http://www.bbc.co.uk/blogs/thereporters/nickbryant/2011/01/the_derivative_country .html (cited September 29, 2013).

6. J. E. Traue, "The Public Library Explosion in Colonial New Zealand," *Libraries & the Cultural Record* 42, no. 2 (2007): 151–64, quotes on 152 and 154. For quote about Carlyle, McCauley, and Dickens, see Shef Rogers, "The History of the Book in New Zealand," in *The Oxford Companion to the Book*, ed. Michael F. Suarez and H. R. Woudhuysen, 1:403–7 (Oxford: Oxford University Press, 2010), 405.

7. Ralph Munn and Ernest Roland Pitt, *Australian Libraries: A Survey of Conditions and Suggestions for Their Improvement* (Melbourne: Australian Council for Educational Research, 1935), 11.

8. Thomas Augst, "Faith in Reading: Public Libraries, Liberalism and the Civil Religion," in *Institutions of Reading: The Social Life of Libraries in the United States*, ed. Thomas Augst and Kenneth E. Carpenter, 148–79 (Amherst, MA: University of Massachusetts Press, 2007), 164–65.

9. David J. Jones, "Great Minds: Metcalfe, McColvin and *Public Libraries in Australia*," *Australian Library Journal* 54, no. 4 (2005): 386–412. Quote on p. 395.

10. Harrison Bryan, "Presidential Address, 1973: Towards Libraries for the Nation—Twenty-Five Years of Australian History 1948–1973," in *Library Association of Australia: Outpost Australian Librarianship '73: Proceedings of the 17th Biennial Conference held in Perth, August 1973*, [6]–15. Perth: Conference Committee, 1974, pp. 7, 8, 15.

11. Bryan, "Presidential Address, 1973," 9.

12. John Thompson, "To Serve the Nation: The Heritage Responsibilities of the National Library of Australia," in *Library for the Nation*, ed. Peter Biskup and Margaret Henty, 68–73 (Canberra: Australian Academic & Research Libraries [and] National Library of Australia, 1991), 9, 70.

13. Wilma Radford, "Formal Training for Library Service," *Australian Library Journal* 12, no. 1 (1963): 11–4. Quote on p. 12.

14. "Librarians Overseas and from Overseas," *Australian Library Journal* 1, no. 1 (1951): 20–21.[1]

15. Mary Ronnie, John Evans, and Melvyn D. Rainey, *Education for Librarianship in New Zealand and the Pacific Islands* (London: Mansell, 1996), 23.

16. Andrew Delbridge Osborn, *New Zealand Library Resources: Report of a Survey Made for the New Zealand Library Association under the Auspices of the Carnegie Corporation of New York* (Wellington: New Zealand Library Association, 1960), 60.

17. Des Pickering and Helen Modra, *Library Services to the Disadvantaged: A Report to the Nation* (Melbourne: Australian Library Promotion Council, 1973), 16, 37–38.

18. Martin Nakata, Alex Byrne, Vicky Nakata, and Gabrielle Gardiner, "Libraries, Indigenous Australians and a Developing Protocols Strategy for the Library and Information Sector," in *Australian Indigenous Knowledge and Libraries*, ed. Martin Nakata and Marcia Langton, 185–99 (Canberra: Australian Library and Information Association, 2005), 196–97, 199.

19. Neil Beagrie, *National Digital Preservation Initiatives: An Overview of Developments in Australia, France, the Netherlands, and the United Kingdom and of Related International Activity* (Washington, DC: Council on Library and Information Resources and Library of Congress, 2003), 14.

20. Paul Genoni, "The 'Imagining' of Australian Librarianship," In *Libraries, the Heart of the Matter: Proceedings of the Australian Library and Information Association 2nd Biennial Conference*, 115–18; Deakin: D. W. Thorpe for ALIA, 1992, 115.

BIBLIOGRAPHY

Arnold, John. "'Choose Your Author as You Would Choose a Friend': Circulating Libraries in Melbourne, 1930–1960." *La Trobe Library Journal* 40 (1987): 77–96.

Arnold, John. "The Circulating Library Phenomenon." In *A History of the Book in Australia 1891–1945: A National Culture in a Colonised Market*, edited by Martyn Lyons and John Arnold, 190–208. St Lucia, Qld: University of Queensland Press, 2001.

Augst, Thomas. "Faith in Reading: Public Libraries, Liberalism and the Civil Religion." In *Institutions of Reading: The Social Life of Libraries in the United States*, edited by Thomas Augst and Kenneth E. Carpenter, 148–79. Amherst, MA: University of Massachusetts Press, 2007.

Beagrie, Neil. *National Digital Preservation Initiatives: An Overview of Developments in Australia, France, the Netherlands, and the United Kingdom and of Related International Activity.* Washington, DC: Council on Library and Information Resources and Library of Congress, 2003.

Biskup, Peter. *Libraries in Australia.* Wagga Wagga, NSW: Centre for Information Studies, 1994.

Bryan, Harrison. "Presidential Address, 1973: Towards Libraries for the Nation—Twenty-Five Years of Australian History 1948–1973." In *Library Association of Australia: Outpost Australian Librarianship '73: Proceedings of the 17th Biennial Conference held in Perth, August 1973*, [6]–15. Perth: Conference Committee, 1974.

Bryan, Harrison, and Gordon Greenwood, eds. *Design for Diversity: Library Services for Higher Education and Research in Australia.* St. Lucia, Qld: University of Queensland Press, 1977.

Bryant, Nick. Nick Bryant's Australia, "The Derivative Country?" blog posting, January 24, 2011, http://www.bbc.co.uk/blogs/thereporters/nickbryant/2011/01/the_derivative_country.html (cited September 29, 2013).

Bundy, Alan. "Case-Study: Public Libraries—Books, Bytes, Buildings, Brains." In *Paper Empires: A History of the Book in Australia 1946–2005*, edited by Craig Munro and Robyn Sheahan-Bright, 373–81. St. Lucia, Qld: University of Queensland Press, 2006.

Byrne, Alex, Alana Garwood, Heather Moorcroft, and Alan Barries. *Aboriginal and Torres Strait Islander Protocols for Libraries, Archives and Information Services.* Canberra: Australian Library and Information Association Press, 1995.

Carroll, Mary, and Sue Reynolds. "The Great Classification Battle of 1910: A Tale of 'Blunders and Bizzareries' at the Melbourne Public Library." In *Information Beyond Borders: International Cultural and Intellectual Exchange in the Belle Époque*, edited by W. Boyd Rayward. Aldershot: Ashgate, 2014.

Committee on Australian Universities. *Report.* Canberra: Government Printer, 1957.

Crisp, M. P. "Presidential Address." *Library Association of Australia 13th Biennial Conference, Canberra: Papers*, vol. 1, [5]–14. Sydney: Library Association of Australia, 1965.

Curtin, John. "The Task Ahead." *Melbourne Herald*, December 27, 1941.

Fenwick, Sara Innis. *Library Services for Children in New Zealand Schools and Public Libraries: A Report to the New Zealand Library Association.* Wellington: New Zealand Council for Education Research and New Zealand Library Association, 1975.

Fenwick, Sara Innis. *School and Children's Libraries in Australia.* Melbourne: Cheshire, 1966.

Genoni, Paul. "The 'Imagining' of Australian Librarianship." In *Libraries: The Heart of the Matter: Proceedings of the Australian Library and Information Association 2nd Biennial Conference*, 115–18. Deakin, ACT: ALIA, 1992.

Ifould, W. H. "Australia Requires a Better Library Service." In *Proceedings of the Australian Library Conference Held at the University of Melbourne, August 1928*, 8–14. Melbourne: Government Printer, 1928.

Johnston, Lorraine (Te Rohe). "The Role of Libraries and Archival Collections in the Preservation and Revitalisation of Indigenous Knowledge: The Case of Revitalisation of Te Reo Maori." *New Zealand Library & Information Management Journal* 50 (2007): 202–15.

Jones, David J. "Great Minds: Metcalfe, McColvin and *Public Libraries in Australia*." *Australian Library Journal* 54, no. 4 (2005): 386–412.

"Librarians Overseas and from Overseas." *Australian Library Journal* 1, no. 1 (1951): 20–21.

McColvin, Lionel R. *Public Libraries in Australia: Present Conditions and Future Possibilities*. Melbourne: Melbourne University Press for ACER, 1947.

Morris, James. *Pax Britannica: The Climax of an Empire*. Harmondsworth, Middlesex: Penguin, 1968.

Morris, Jan. *Farewell the Trumpets: An Imperial Retreat*. New York: Harcourt Brace Jovanovich, 1978.

Morris, Jan. *Heaven's Command: An Imperial Progress*. New York: Harcourt Brace Jovanovich, 1973.

Morrison, Ian. "The History of the Book in Australia." In *The Oxford Companion to the Book*, edited by Michael F. Suarez and H. R. Woudhuysen, Vol. 1, 394–402. Oxford: Oxford University Press, 2010.

Munn, Ralph, and John Barr. *New Zealand Libraries: A Survey of Conditions and Suggestions for Their Improvement*. Christchurch: Libraries Association of New Zealand, 1934.

Munn, Ralph, and Ernest Roland Pitt. *Australian Libraries: A Survey of Conditions and Suggestions for Their Improvement*. Melbourne: Australian Council for Educational Research, 1935.

Nakata, Martin, Alex Byrne, Vicky Nakata, and Gabrielle Gardiner. "Libraries, Indigenous Australians and a Developing Protocols Strategy for the Library and Information Sector." In *Australian Indigenous Knowledge and Libraries*, edited by Martin Nakata and Marcia Langton, 185–199. Canberra: Australian Library and Information Association, 2005.

National Inquiry into the Separation of Aboriginal and Torres Strait Islander Children from Their Families. "Bringing Them Home." Sydney: Human Rights and Equal Opportunity Commission, 1997.

New Zealand Company. "A Proposed Plan of the City of Wellington in the First Settlement in New Zealand, Founded 1839–40" [Copy of a manuscript map drawn ca. 1839, by Samuel Cobham, held in the Alexander Turnbull Library, Wellington, New Zealand]. http://natlib.govt.nz/records/22796123 (cited August 29, 2013).

O'Reilly, R. N. "The Impasse over New Zealand Library Education." In *Outpost: Australian Librarianship '73: Proceedings of the 17th Biennial Conference held in Perth, August 1973*, 555–75. Perth: Library Association of Australia, 1974.

Osborn, Andrew Delbridge. *New Zealand Library Resources: Report of a Survey made for the New Zealand Library Association under the Auspices of the Carnegie Corporation of New York*. Wellington: New Zealand Library Association, 1960.

Pickering, Des, and Helen Modra. *Library Services to the Disadvantaged: A Report to the Nation*. Melbourne: Australian Library Promotion Council, 1973.

Radford, Wilma. "Formal Training for Library Service." *Australian Library Journal* 12, no. 1 (1963): 11–14.

Rogers, Shef. "The History of the Book in New Zealand." In *The Oxford Companion to the Book*, edited by Michael F. Suarez and H. R. Woudhuysen, Vol. 1, 403–7. Oxford: Oxford University Press, 2010.

Ronnie, Mary, John Evans, and Melvyn D. Rainey. *Education for Librarianship in New Zealand and the Pacific Islands*. London: Mansell, 1996.

Thompson, John. "To Serve the Nation: The Heritage Responsibilities of the National Library of Australia." In *Library for the Nation*, edited by Peter Biskup and Margaret Henty, 68–73. Canberra ACT: Australian Academic and Research Libraries and National Library of Australia, 1991.

Traue, J. E. "The Public Library Explosion in Colonial New Zealand." *Libraries & the Cultural Record* 42, no. 2 (2007): 151–64.

Verran, David. "Government Promotion of Public Libraries in New Zealand, 1869–1935." In *Collections, Characters and Communities: The Shaping of Libraries in Australia and New Zealand*, edited by B. J. McMullin, 35–42. Melbourne, VIC: Australian Scholarly Publishing, 2010.

"Wanted—1,000,000 Books." *The Argus* (Melbourne), January 26, 1935: 20.

Wiegand, Wayne A. "The American Library: Construction of a Community Reading Institution." In *A History of the Book in America, Vol. 4: Print in Motion*, edited by Carl F. Kaestle and Janice A. Radway, 431–51. Chapel Hill: University of North Carolina Press, 2009.

5

Digital Convergence:
The Past in the Present

Marija Dalbello

INTRODUCTION

A historical understanding of "digital convergence"—a series of innovations that are bringing about an increasingly interconnected world of recorded knowledge, documents, data, and information—requires more than a conventional technological explanation that begins with the Internet and the World Wide Web. Rather than a division between print and postprint eras, digital convergence implies a kind of continuity—as frequent and fast change coalesces to establish new information ecologies. Thomas Haigh, a historian of information technology, identified an underlying convergence among the computing, media, and telecommunications industries as a long-term development in communication technologies that includes all analog or nonelectronic information technologies in addition to those used for computer communication. Library historian Michael Harris notes multiple "advents of the information era," refers to "information explosions" of past eras, and points to the need for a larger time-scale when considering shifts in documentary cultures and practices.[1] A history of digital convergence is nested within a larger history of scholarly and scientific communication, bibliographic systematization, provision of free and universal access to public information, the world of knowledge dominated by scientific methods, and the authority of professional experts—all hallmarks of the modern "knowledge society." A rationalization of access to resources, information, and organized collections of knowledge, when paired with efficiency while ignoring cultural and social dimensions, can bring about a "tunnel vision" in the work of professionals who build tools for gathering, analyzing, disseminating, and using knowledge, as noted by Wayne Wiegand in his influential article.

This chapter focuses on digital convergence as a phenomenon of modernity in the library context. The development of tools and knowledge systematization that characterizes modernity has its roots in the fifteenth century. Peter Burke identifies a long tradition of knowledge organization and systematizations developed in medieval and early modern libraries designed for the classification of knowledge and the intellectual work of librarianship. Early modern humanists' efforts to connect with the knowledge of antiquity—by locating medical and scientific manuscripts and organizing that knowledge—include Conrad Gessner's *Bibliotheca Universalis* (1545–1549), a pioneering bibliography of printed books. The multitude of books and the perception of "information overload" prompted the development of various aids to support the work of early modern scholars (from methods of reading to note-taking)—as shown by Ann Blair in her studies of these practices from the 1550s to 1700.

Among the programs for knowledge systematization in the eighteenth century the most notable is Diderot's *Encylopédie, ou dictionnaire raisonné des sciences, des arts et des métiers* (1751–1772), a major work of the Enlightenment. The positivist projects of the nineteenth century created typologies and taxonomies in all fields of knowledge, from comparative Indo-European linguistics establishing classifications for families of languages (Franz Bopp) to geology and natural sciences establishing the lineage of species (Charles Darwin). These typologies and taxonomies exemplify techniques for systematizing knowledge that facilitated the organization of information and documents including library classifications for retrieval in the modern and late-modern periods.

The types, size, and uses of collections and libraries, and the technologies for the creation, dissemination, and utilization of knowledge relate to the meaning and values of common types of knowledge in a particular period. These types of basic knowledge (or the "epistemes") appear in succession as general epistemological structures that supersede one another. The roots of modern librarianship belong in a post-Enlightenment episteme. Intellectual techniques that were uniquely developed and depended on the expertise of specialists such as librarians and information technologists (classification systems, organization of information and documents, data management, and information storage and retrieval) fall within the scope of this chapter and occurred over a broad period. A history of techniques and technologies—digital or otherwise—in libraries as well as personal collections and digital archives and museums constitute that broader context for understanding the current convergence of computing, knowledge media, and telecommunication and media industries resulting from the mechanisms of divergence that characterize modernity.

The convergence of information technology, bibliographic control, and networking constitute an important element in the development of the digital environment that heavily influences how many people use libraries today. Understanding the role of convergence in the history of modern librarianship requires tracking the consequences of interconnected innovations from the mid-twentieth century. The 1950s and the 1960s were formative for the beginnings of library automation and computerization. The 1970s to 1990s was the golden era of the implementation of the online public access catalog (OPAC) in all types of libraries. Bibliographic and interoperational standards underlying these developments resulted from extensive negotiations within a standards community, including librarians. Standards and structured data remain key methods enabling retrieval in electronic (and paper) systems.

Further major decadal developments are tied to information technologies such as large databases of text and graphics, the Internet, and other networks constructed in the 1970s; personal computers and videotext in the 1980s; the World Wide Web in the 1990s; and the adoption of digital forms post-1990s. The common data frameworks that can be processed by machines (the so-called Semantic Web) and the participatory culture of social media constitute the most recent phenomena of this environment at the time of writing.

Between 1998 and 2002 digital libraries emerged and were broadly adopted and implemented across all types of libraries. With forerunners in large-scale information systems as well as documentation systems that stabilized in the 1980s, digital libraries formed electronic collections that changed librarianship's practices. On the one hand, the history of digital libraries from 1990 continues and builds on earlier stages of innovation in libraries that include office computing, OPACs, and networks supporting new forms of knowledge and information. On the other hand, it can be seen through an independent genealogy that shaped the discourse of technologies starting with the documentation movement at the end of the nineteenth and in the early twentieth centuries and the classificatory impulse defining a modern scientific approach. In turn, the modern scientific paradigm produced numerous cultural texts that became part of everyday life (as noted by Eviatar Zerubavel)—embedded in the organization of department stores and supermarkets as well as museums, zoos, libraries, and all types of document collections and in "how we construct age, gender, and ethnicity." Even if individuals do not "all classify reality in a precisely identical manner, yet we certainly do cut it up into rather similar mental chunks with pretty similar outlines."[2] We classify in all spheres of life, and by classifying we introduce social and moral orders in the fabric of reality and in the tools and technologies that we build.

The periodization of digital convergence that distinguishes these interconnected developments is as follows:

- origins and prototypes, 1890 to 1960s;
- 1970s into the 1990s (OPACs, the World Wide Web);
- mid-1990s to 2005 (digital libraries); and
- from 2005 (the Semantic Web and social media).

In the remaining sections, the history of digital convergence will be discussed in the context of these developments.

ORIGINS AND PROTOTYPES: 1890 TO 1960s

The first stage in the genealogy of digital convergence consists of efforts to classify and structure all knowledge in interconnected information systems. The modern ideas of networked information have roots in the work of the European documentalists Paul Marie Ghislain Otlet and Henri La Fontaine. Otlet envisioned an interconnected system of knowledge transfer in his *Traité de documentation* (1934), with its intellectual blueprint in the Mundaneum Project. Otlet and La Fontaine's Mundaneum, from its conceptualization in 1895, its institutionalization in 1910, and its implementation in the 1930s, became influential in documentation science as an interconnected information system operating on analog information technologies, based on the collection and management of millions of index cards. The Mundaneum remains a key modernist initiative and is popularly referred to as the Belgian "paper Internet." As a representation of total knowledge—presuming the possibility of classification of all knowledge and its management through a unified system that extended beyond a documentation center—it was envisioned in a "city of knowledge" to incorporate museum exhibits and archival collections.

The Mundaneum compares to other computable knowledge systems devised by phi-losophers of language and practical philosophers of information. Predecessors include Ramon Llull, Gottfried Leibniz, Gottlob Frege, and Melvil Dewey. Successors to Otlet and La Fontaine include Bertrand Russell, Ludwig Wittgenstein, Kurt Gödel, and most famously Vannevar Bush and his Memex system (1940s). Project Xanadu (1960s), the first hypertext system founded by Ted Nelson, proposed the idea of electronic text as an interconnected network of texts with connecting nodes. More recently, knowledge nav-igator applications exemplified by Google's Knowledge Graph (2013) took their place in this stream of development. In 2012 the Mundaneum (museum) in Mons (Belgium) attracted notoriety due to its partnership with the Google Corporation. Framed as a his-toricist enterprise, "dedicated to a long-ago venture to compile and index knowledge in a giant, library-style card catalog with millions of entries—an analog-era equivalent of a search engine or Wikipedia,"[3] a massive digitization of the archive's contents was at the core of controversies around corporate dominance over public knowledge that Google came to signify in Europe.

Closer to the world of libraries, work on the Mundaneum connects to the devel-opment of the Universal Decimal Classification (UDC) system (1905). While related to Dewey Decimal Classification (DDC), another analytico-synthetic system for infor-mation retrieval in large collections, the UDC has a broader vocabulary and offers far more precise and detailed content indexing and flexible notation syntax. It is difficult to imagine library and information work in a world perspective that does not—in one form or another—originate from classifications as infrastructure that underlies the heritage of cultures. Yet classifications are ideological, as are their effects on the organization of knowledge. An example of such underlying ideology is the Library and Bibliographic Classification (BBK) adopted in the former Soviet Union that presents a Marxist posi-tion on each domain of knowledge.

The library classification system and management of scholarly and scientific infor-mation making possible information retrieval in large document and library collections and information networks, play an equally important role in the historiography of infor-mation science and librarianship. Universal access through interconnected bibliographic domains to support scientific communication was a major modernist mid-twentieth-century project in librarianship. In 1951 Margaret Egan and Jesse Shera conceptualized a program of social epistemology with the goal of developing a "unified and completely articulated bibliographic system." They conceived it as a total social process of com-munication aimed at societal development, considering all types of records and bib-liographic needs of those participating in knowledge production and its consumption. The bibliographic control concerned scientific knowledge in particular. Half a century after the Mundaneum, influenced by a cybernetic approach to conceptualizing informa-tion flows, these ideas were realized in the 1970s in bibliographic forms and large-scale information systems for structuring knowledge exemplified by bibliographic utilities and indexing systems.

The interconnected bibliographic systems organizing documents by means of their bibliographic presentations, the disciplinary data structures organized in databases, and the abstracting and indexing services for retrieval of domain knowledge are all rooted in the ideas of theorists such as Samuel Bradford (1940s), who first described the pattern of retrieval within a structured information environment (known as Bradford's law). The cybernetic perspective provided a dominant grand narrative for information science through an influential work by Claude Shannon and Warren Weaver, *The Mathematical*

Theory of Communication (1949). The work of practitioners resulted in specific bibliographic artifacts for the management and retrieval of scientific information using the condensed representation of documents (data and metadata).

Other major artifacts of bibliographic control were union catalogs like the 754-volume *National Union Catalog of Pre-1956* imprints started in the 1950s. Those green-bound volumes are still found in major research libraries. The technologies of access included shared cataloging through bibliographic utilities. The Online Computer Library System (or OCLC—now Online Computer Library Center, Inc.), founded in 1967, evolved into an interconnected system of library catalog records with global participation in the bibliographic knowledge base WorldCat. Paper-based catalogs and computer library networks converged in the library world while the knowledge structures of science were made visible through comprehensive citation indexes, yet another bibliographic technique that originated in the 1960s. The underlying theorization of citation analysis resulted in bibliometrics as a discrete field of information science.

The leaders of initiatives shaping the information landscape in the 1950s and 1960s who used computers in information processing were Fred Kilgour (founding director of OCLC) and Eugene Garfield (founder of the Institute for Scientific Information). In the 1950s, the Library of Congress (LC) developed bibliographic standards for cataloging (rules and principles). Seymour Lubetzky and librarians from around the world worked on an international code for description, and in 1961 the adoption of the Paris Principles at the International Conference on Cataloguing Principles made the scaling and internationalization of bibliographic description possible. Libraries across the globe conformed to a common core standard for bibliographic processing. At the LC, Henriette Avram developed Machine-Readable Cataloging (MARC) in the late 1960s and the early 1970s. Card catalogs, printed book catalogs, and microform catalogs were the primary tools for searching in libraries until the mid-1970s.

ONLINE CATALOGS AND THE WORLD WIDE WEB: 1970s INTO THE 1990s

While online computer-based cataloging was introduced in the 1960s, it was not until the late 1990s that online catalogs became the primary access tool for identifying and accessing library materials. Nancy Eaton notes that widespread adoption was tied to the reduction of the local cost of creating records, and the wider availability of MARC and the computer networks for sharing machine-readable records. The searching capabilities and the Z39.50 search protocol (a format specified for common bibliographic searches that can be used across databases in a distributed network environment) enabled cooperation among different systems and searching efficiency, as well as the integration of the OPAC with other library systems for circulation, acquisition, interlibrary loan, and so on. By the late 1990s, online catalogs had become a norm. Shared technical capabilities for cataloging were supported by dedicated library networks, including many regional networks (i.e., library cooperatives and vendor utilities). Other chapters in this volume focus on technological advancements of the 1980s with regard to particular systems in national, academic, public, school, and special libraries and will not be covered here.

OCLC was founded in 1967. Another library cooperative—the Research Libraries Group (RLG)—was founded by a group of major U.S. research libraries in 1974. In 2006 RLG merged with OCLC and its catalog merged with WorldCat. In 2014 WorldCat. org featured this tagline on its pages, "WorldCat is the world's largest library catalog, helping you find library materials online." By that time, this global catalog of library collections for North America and the Western world was searchable in twelve languages.

In the 1990s, the Internet and World Wide Web provided the open system architecture for library online catalogs, facilitated international cooperation, and created conditions for the development of digital libraries. The standardization and internationalization presented problems for the mapping of different character sets and the display in original alphabets and scripts for diverse languages. The automated systems to handle these mappings (known as Unicode standard), text encoding, as well as computing applications and standards in the area of internationalization are, at this writing, being developed and maintained by the Unicode Consortium, incorporated in 1991. Most of its founding members were California software companies and the character encoding "Unicode" owes its conceptualization to Xerox and Apple engineers in 1988. The Unicode consortium membership includes a select number of software companies (Adobe, Apple, Microsoft, and Oracle), as well as a varied group of governmental bodies, universities, and organizations. The Unicode standard originated outside librarianship yet became a key element in the convergence of computing, media, and information exchange in libraries. Among these multiple developments, the work of librarians in preserving the heritage of cultures and providing access to human intellectual endeavor is twofold. First, it attends to tensions between public and private knowledge. Second, librarianship advocates that all perspectives be recorded and represented, advocating epistemological pluralism.

Data and various genres of documents and records can be structured to facilitate retrieval and exchange through data representations, or "metadata." Metadata emerged simultaneously with global networks in the late 1990s. Structural data are about the containers of data; content can be presented in the form of registries and lists structured for retrieval and exchange. Metadata can be applied to gene banks, geographical data, or statistical databases as well as documents. Their development is through active professional standards communities. As forms of description that extend traditional cataloging rules, metadata are not new ideas or applications.

The need for "discovery" of information across diverse epistemic communities who create and consume data and documents has prompted an effort of data integration and building applications that combine knowledge and representations. Known as Semantic Web vocabularies and ontologies, this effort is led by the World Wide Web Consortium (W3C) in accordance with its mission "to lead the Web to its full potential."

The 1990s was a decade of technological invention with profound consequences for the practice of librarianship. The availability of full-text electronic collections and full-text searching paralleled the rise of Web search engines in the 1990s: Yahoo by 1994 and Google by 1997. These were preceded by a host of now forgotten search engines from the 1990s, some built on earlier technologies to exchange files or file transfer protocols, all of which enabled access to online materials, documents, and information. Increasingly the realm of structured knowledge resided outside library collections and the ordered world of bibliographic records; full-text documents were being shared in the network. While the innovations were largely created by technologists and computer scientists, librarians implemented library sites to provide access to collections; they also reformatted paper collections for consumption as digital documents.

Methods for "preserving the Internet" and archiving digital cultural artifacts, which Brewster Kahle, founder of the Internet Archive, announced in *Scientific American* and *D-Lib Magazine* articles in 1997 and 1998, are at the core of knowledge infrastructures in their digital and remediated analog forms. Since its inception in 1996, the Internet

Archive has been an important institution for international collaboration. Its partnerships with large national libraries across the world have produced new forms of co-curated collections extracted from the Web and archiving of born-digital heritage. Archiving websites and the awareness of digital history took a decade to develop beyond experimental and research-oriented efforts. By 2014 many national libraries had formulated policies about harvesting the national "Web-spheres."

Yet at the start of the twenty-first century many libraries outside the Western world could not provide even basic access to their resources. Because of that inequity, the forms of inscriptions of human experience and heritage that were becoming visible in the new media environments called for new solutions to provide access and preserve networked knowledge of the present for all cultures and peoples. In 2010 the IFLA/UNESCO Manifesto for Digital Libraries articulated the development of digital services as a core activity and a "new channel to the universe of knowledge and information, connecting cultures across geographical and social boundaries," thus identifying a common mission and goals of international librarianship.[4]

DIGITAL LIBRARIES: MID-1990s TO 2005

The first wave of digital library development started in the 1990s with a series of projects in national, academic, public, and special libraries that made large amounts of digitized material accessible online. This transformative period exposed library institutions to critical, self-reflexive perspectives about their collections, engagement of new audiences, and the creation of new publics.

In the late 1990s and early 2000s, widespread public online access to collections coincided with the emergence of the open access movement. The Budapest Open Access Initiative, convened by the Open Society Institute in 2004, defined "open access" on their website as "free availability on the public internet, permitting any users to read, download, copy, distribute, print, search, or link to the full texts of these articles, crawl them for indexing" (i.e., systematically browse the Web using automatic indexing software).[5] This initiative was meant to ensure that authors had control over their work and were properly acknowledged and cited. The rise in popularity of disciplinary and institutional repositories to circulate e-prints of scientific papers on the model of *arXiv.org* (started by Paul Ginsparg in the 1990s) were based on the scientists' practice of prepublication and sharing preprints via email. Open access journals, open access publishing, and self-archiving surfaced amid uncertainties of budgeting and the ideal of unrestricted online access to peer-reviewed scholarly research. Librarians were active in the open access movement since they also grappled with transitioning to the electronic resource models that included building electronic journal collections, negotiating pricing for electronic resources with the publishers, and applying digital technologies to collection building.

The bimonthly *D-Lib Magazine* recorded significant events and conversations in an emergent community of practitioners of digital librarianship and is a good source of information to track and identify key events of the digital development. In its inaugural December 1995 issue, for example, it announced that Project Muse and forty-three humanities and social sciences journals had "come on the network." A "Featured Digital Collection" editorial appeared in every issue starting in January 1999, highlighting the richness and diversity of digital libraries being created and reviewing the features of these novel "libraries" in terms of content, underlying technology, interface design, and user experience.

Christine Borgman's influential definition of digital libraries (2000) emphasized the interdependent functionality of technical and social components. She noted that digital libraries are not only electronic resources with associated technical capabilities for creating, searching, and using information—an augmentation and extension of information storage and retrieval systems for the manipulation of digital data in any medium—but that they are collected and organized by and for communities of users. The new types of uses for these online collections were noted by early digital library developers. Enthusiasts and nonlibrarians becoming curators of digital libraries was another development of peer-to-peer production. Digitization altered the way people experienced documents and exposed their digital versions to the public "eye." Initially, it was sufficient for electronic collections to be viewing spectacles. The gratification of seeing the original online recalls the early fascination with the moving image. The digital "incunables" supported such responses through visual rendition of texts, and added new elements to the experience of texts. For example, the online viewing of the Gutenberg Bible at the British Library's website provided a multimedia experience through an electronic book, which offered an entry point into a broader culture of the book.

In the first period of digitization (1995–2005) the institutions focused on particular treasures displayed as online exhibitions. Reconstructive digitization projects are exemplified by the digital version of the Gutenberg Bible (1450) or the Diamond Sutra (a sacred Buddhist text from 868 written in Chinese, and the first known book using block printing). The digital facsimiles of civilizational monuments are themselves documenting earlier technologies of printing. Such digitization projects focusing on single objects became a trend in elite institutions in the Western world with a goal of highlighting national treasures. For example, the digital version of the Book of Kells was released to the public by the Trinity Library in 2014. This trend continued at the time of writing as a niche activity restricted to elite institutions.

The second type of digitization initiative was aimed at providing access to full-text editions through systematic digitization. In a series of empirical studies appearing in *Library Quarterly* from 2005 to 2009, Marija Dalbello surveyed the earliest digital collections that emerged in North American libraries. She used the Web-registries of the Association of Research Libraries and Digital Library Federation created in the late 1990s and maintained throughout the first wave of digital library development. Based on the characteristics of 378 projects, she concluded that these first libraries were spectacles, "cabinets of curiosities" typically presented in episodic narratives and often using visual documents (photographs, maps) to focus on events like the Alaska Yukon Pacific Exposition, Alexander Graham Bell's invention of the telephone, the Klondike Gold Rush, the Triangle Shirtwaist Company fire of March 25, 1911, the Chicago White Sox vs. Cincinnati Reds 1919 World Series baseball scandal, and televangelism historical broadcasts of 1949—all incidental, reflecting local interests. She also covered narratives documenting social movements (like the *Women's Suffrage, 1848–1920* collection) or those simply presenting a type of collection (e.g., anarchist posters).

She interviewed librarians and digitization experts who participated in key initiatives in European national libraries and the Library of Congress. National libraries were playing a key role in the construction of ideas around digital heritage, and digitization was conceived as a formative national event. The *American Memory, Memory of Portugal,* and *Gallica* digital libraries had as their primary purpose the re-creation of national heritage along familiar national collecting strategies. Table 1 offers a periodization of digital library development (stages and key events) in five European national digital libraries in that period.

Table 1. A Timeline of Digital Library Development in Five National Libraries, 1988–2004

Timeline	Biblioteca nacional de Portugal	Bibliothèque nationale de France	Deutsche Bibliothek	Scottish National Library	British Library
1988				Preservation microfilming	
1989		Idea of digitization and the new library building project			
1990	National bibliographic data sharing (national library consortium)				
1991					
1992					
1993					Experimental digitization of treasures
1994					
1995	Bibliotheca Universalis project	First phase of digitization		Experimentation with digital imaging	
1996			Collective/Cooperative library experimentation		
1997	Public campaign CD-ROM distributed with national newspaper				
1998			National information infrastructure prototyping		
1999	Thematic Sites—contextualizing digital objects	Transition: from comprehensive to selective thematic-encyclopedic library		Digitization strategy initiated	
2000					Restructuring phase
2001				Systematic program of development established	
2002	Transition: from experimental to functional digital library	Second project phase		Transition: from experimental to functional publicly available digital library	
2003			Model for Virtual German Library emerges		Transition: from digitization initiatives to e-strategy
2004					

These developments were focused on digitization and on the efforts to integrate electronically-born resources with the collections. The electronic resources without a media past (such as paper or print) were new forms of documents around which librarians and archivists needed to develop new procedures for preservation. In contrast, the digitized heritage and sensationalized digital versions of "reformatted" treasures required a positioning within cultural narratives of memory and tradition, civilization, or national heritage with a focus on reinterpreting the past—also led by the librarians as gatekeepers.

Chapters in this volume focus on electronic resources, reader services, and historical conservation across the Western world. Digital development in select European national libraries (Finland and Poland) and the *Europeana* project are examined in the chapter by Peter Hoare; Ross Harvey presents digital preservation projects and shared access initiatives in Australia and New Zealand—both allowing the comparison of digital heritage developments and legislation related to electronic media across cultural horizons.

While the librarians sought practical solutions for accessing digital resources, library schools responded to the digital convergence environment by adapting their curricula. A 2006 survey of fifty-six programs accredited by the American Library Association showed that forty-seven (89 percent) included some form of education in digital librarianship. This included content integrated into other courses in twenty-three programs (e.g., metadata standards covered in organization of information courses); and fifteen programs had at least one course on digital libraries. Continuing education programs also prepared librarians for the presentation of digital content and associated services. Other chapters in this volume examine education for librarianship in the "information age" post-1970s. For example, Wayne Wiegand observes how the arrival of computer-based bibliographic networks and utilities and a new focus on information science shifted education away from library service models to emphasize information handling perspectives.

As in the world of libraries, humanities scholars explored digital phenomena. The "digital humanities" movement had a separate process of institutionalization and was only partially tied to the library world. Since 1994, the Text Encoding Initiative (TEI) Consortium influenced research groups and individuals to comply with the TEI guidelines for presentation of texts for online research, teaching, and preservation. In 2014 more than 150 projects worldwide had complied with these guidelines. Research groups located at the University of Virginia, Stanford University, and George Mason University became hubs for experimentation and research with electronic text in the United States.

From the initial focus on individual collections and objects to massive digitization efforts with systematic outcomes that produced scholarly resources on the scale of large-scale microfilming projects, the development of digital libraries and digital heritage initiatives at the national and international level was a multistage process. It started with experimentation from the late 1980s and through the 1990s, and the institutionalization by the early 2000s of large-scale digitization projects. The availability of digital resources revolutionized scholarship and it also increased public awareness about these digital media, with the "electronic incunables" becoming celebrities in their own right. Libraries encouraged the educational experiences for the public. In 2014 the British Library's *Treasures in Full* page listing digital editions branded them as "high-quality digital editions, free to your desktop."[6] The users were invited to compare two copies of the Gutenberg Bible; explore a translation in English of the Magna Carta, Caxton's Chaucer, and Renaissance festival books and engage with an interactive commentary. Many of these projects were an outcome of earlier, long-term efforts by teams of librarians and scholars to identify, consolidate, and describe the objects and their preservation through imaging (i.e., microform reformatting).

Digital imaging became a technology of cultural reproduction. The national historic archive and treasures were recirculating an old canon of elite cultures. At the same time, some of the earliest collections of *American Memory* featured historical experiences of African Americans; others focused on women's suffrage and American westward expansion. At the time of writing, indigenous and Aboriginal perspectives and transnational communities found a new space for expression in "virtual" libraries, like the Center for World Indigenous Studies that archived and disseminated tribal documents and served as a portal for the Fourth World nations (self-identified as this collection's main users). The idea of the archive was becoming transformed in mid-decade as the so-called "invented archives" became available online. An example of such an archive, possible only in a digital environment, is the *Valley of the Shadow* (Virginia Center for Digital History at the University of Virginia, 1993–2007). This digital collection unified documents from various sources together with an implicit interpretation of materials that form a compendium of documents about two Civil War communities and their two viewpoints, one Northern (Franklin County, Pennsylvania) and one Southern (Augusta County, Virginia). The effect was unique, because the collection not only provided comprehensive access to primary source materials but it also blurred the usual carefully maintained distinction between an archive and a historical argument. In this example, the archive itself integrated an interpretive dialectic. The *Valley of the Shadow* helps demonstrate how reconstructive archives may contribute to changing historical understanding and offer a point-of-view perspective. Other vernacular archives and amateur projects contributed to the diversity of viewpoints, as noted by Daniel Cohen and Roy Rosenzweig in their analysis of digital history (2006). Throughout this period experimental projects were created by individuals and collectives of scholars outside the library world. These active producers of content were bringing out multiple perspectives, and in the process the content often countered official narratives, as exemplified by Jim Zwick's anti-imperialism website (1995–1999) or blurring a line between an archive and historical argument (*Valley of the Shadow*). Others were playing with the idea of an archive-museum (such as *Skarabej, Online Museum of Old Family Photographs*), a collection of found photos assembled "to create an archive of memmories [sic] of unknown people and events and make them available to everyone," as stated on its website. Like other chapters in this book pointing to biases in the process of cultural reproduction, the digital form is no exception. The Internet was becoming a total library in which what can be documented is not necessarily all that can be collected, archived, or accessed in a structured fashion. The Internet also extended "the classical space of the archive, library, and museum by an extra dimension," leading to a reconfigurable archive and open data model, with the constant rewriting and addition of recorded knowledge, exemplified by the Wikipedia peer-production model. This model is contrary to an old encyclopedia model and the possibility of "ultimate knowledge" presupposing "closed data with well-defined rules from production site to storage site" residing in their original context.[7] Distinctions between the old and the new model of knowledge created tensions for librarians who had to apply both frameworks in library work.

THE "SEMANTIC WEB" AND SOCIAL MEDIA FROM 2005

This time period is marked by four interrelated phenomena:

- the participatory, peer-production systems supporting library collections that promoted public conversation about digital resources (the digital "commons");
- scholarly digital libraries, or "humanists' laboratories" increasingly incorporated into routine library activities under the label "digital humanities" and involving librarians as collaborators;
- large-scale projects producing a critical mass of materials available online; and
- the Semantic Web for sharing of data in an international community.

The first wave of digital library development was already characterized by grassroots public engagement and the interpretation of collections, thus introducing a new voice in constructing the heritage of cultures. The consequence of primary-source collections becoming available online to a wide audience and development efforts that engaged communities of users in interpreting collections and their design are exemplified by the *American Memory* projects (and the involvement of teachers)[8] and a collaboration between the Idaho Museum of Natural History, Smithsonian anthropologist Joanna Cohan Scherer, and tribal Native communities in the identification of historical photographs accompanying their display in a digital exhibition.[9] Not until Web 2.0 and social networking platforms, however, did a new form of interaction with the library collections appear. Distribution of digitized representations of cultural artifacts that are *in situ*—located somewhere in the library or museum collections as physical objects of cultural heritage—contributed to building the connection between institutional collections and the consuming public.

The Rise of the Commons and Peer-Production

The practice of recirculating collections of digitized material via social networks can be tracked to a Library of Congress pilot initiative with the Flickr Commons in 2008. When LC turned to the social media site Flickr (an image-focused community site that was established in early 2004) to share its photographic heritage material, the Commons model for digital heritage was born. The pilot consisted of a sample of 4,000 historical photographs from the Great Depression and the World War II home front, and news photos from the early 1900s. According to a LC report published later that year, the response was surprising. The images had 500,000 views a month, and over 10,000,000 total views. The Flickr photo sharing community responded by tagging, commenting on, and annotating photos, and LC responded by including some of the commentary in the catalog metadata. The report notes an "unanticipated explosion of interest" in the LC Flickr account that in turn brought forth questions about expanded interpretive communities for libraries' resources, and how releasing content via social media increased a sense of "public ownership and shared stewardship" for public cultural heritage resources. Inscriptions of media experience and participation in electronic culture became widespread by 2010. While public attention to specific social media platforms often shifts rapidly, a persistent broader trend of crowdsourcing (i.e., using the labor of online consumers of digital media in producing content) and peer-production systems evolved. Librarians responded by integrating social media into their routine operations, from using "crowdsourcing" for reader advisory to presentation of collections online.

Librarians thus implemented a participatory model of information culture and media convergence into library work at the same time as active producers of content outside the library world adopted it.

Scholarly Digital Libraries and Digital Humanities

During this period scholars began using new tools for analysis of electronic text, developing scholarly digital libraries or "humanists' laboratories" outside the library world. The projects focused on groups of documents and networks of texts that mapped structural properties and relations of documents. For example, the *Mapping the Republic of Letters* (*Electronic Enlightenment*) project that originated at Stanford University (2009) visualizes eighteenth-century scientific correspondence and social networks. Humanist scholars looked to such multimedia collections to transform their research. Many projects later curated by libraries began as individual scholars' projects. As digital humanities projects became more ubiquitous, they brought new awareness of the materiality and aesthetics of documents and a sophisticated consumption of digital editions. Libraries often became hubs of research activity and experimentation supporting digital projects involving special collections.

Increasingly scholars in the humanities fields were embracing digital methods and unique and personality-driven projects on an in-depth research topic soon became large-scale collaborations. By 2007, 113 scholarly digital libraries in the humanities fields were operational. These projects and digital libraries were introduced in papers presented at the annual meetings of major scholarly societies such as the Modern Language Association (MLA), American Historical Association, and College Art Association. MLA hosted an inaugural panel on the digital humanities and librarianship in 2011. In 2014 MLA featured numerous such panels ranging from the bibliographical origins of digital humanities to presenting collaborative library projects.

Other digital libraries in the humanities arose from pedagogical purposes, often created collaboratively by instructors, students, and digital librarians. For instance, Edward J. Gallagher's *History on Trial*—a digital library that documents historical controversies and scandals with access to full-text documents—was built through contributions from students in seminars offered from 2009 to 2012 at Lehigh University. John Unsworth's *20th-Century American Bestsellers*—arising from student projects starting in 1998—was hosted at Brandeis University in 2014). *Perseus Digital Library* (Tufts University) has been the research and teaching tool for an interdisciplinary community of scholars since 1985.

Large-Scale Collaborations

Consolidating resources from different national contexts to create a pan-European library became a long-term cultural policy in Europe. The Consortium of European Research Libraries (CERL) began promoting European heritage (in print and manuscript) in 1994. Its efforts to control multilingual information about names and places (authority control) resulted in the creation of the *CERL Thesaurus*. Co-funded by the European Union, the *Europeana* portal was started in 2005 and launched in 2008 as a European digital library. It consolidated several networks of cultural heritage organizations (libraries, archives, museums) within the European Union and integrated different types of digital content, making the information searchable through a common

Europeana Semantic Elements metadata standard. With 2,000 institutions participating in the initiative and a portal configurable in thirty languages with English for content description, *Europeana* sought to aggregate European cultural and scientific heritage content through an open trusted source, to support innovation and advocacy, to distribute content to users without restriction on access, and to cultivate new ways for user participation in that heritage. The landing page of *Europeana* features badges of Facebook, Twitter, Pinterest, and Google+ as an invitation to share content through social media platforms and integrators of social services. Users can recirculate the emblems of cultural heritage or reuse an image with their own interpretation (and "metadata"). The *Europeana* site is a curated and reconfigurable archive that aggregates resources contributed by member libraries around *lieu de mémoire* (a term by French historian Pierre Nora to indicate common "places of memory"). In 2014 when the World War I centenary was commemorated around Europe, the *Europeana* launched "the new and improved 1914–1918 *Europeana* . . . with pan-European collection of original First World War source material" announced on its Web pages.

The *Europeana* project followed copyright laws of the contributing European nations, observing the contemporary intellectual property system. In contrast, the *Google Books* project that started around the same time (December 2004) by the Google Corporation with five U.S.- and UK-based research library partners immediately became the center of controversies around the question of who owns digital rights and heritage. In 2009 the *Google Books* project was challenged by the European Commission—whereas others in Europe praised large-scale book scanning. In another lawsuit filed by the American Authors Guild and Association of American Publishers over copyright infringement, the 2011 ruling favored the project's critics. By 2013 the *Google Books* project encompassed more than 30,000,000 scanned documents and had twenty-one research library partners from around the world.

A growing digital record of human experience was converging with other digitization efforts to bring parts of the human record online. An early book digitization project (later incorporated into the Internet Archive) was the "Million Book Project." The *Universal Digital Library: Million Book Collection* at Carnegie Mellon University (2001–2008) had 1.5 million books from the fifty scanning centers in China and India in 2007. The pioneering *Project Gutenberg* (founded in 1971 as the first digital library) focused on works in the public domain and offered over 100,000 free eBooks at the time of writing through grassroots participation. Both digitization projects were focused on making the world heritage of books accessible online, each with its own philosophy, origin, and content. The HathiTrust Research Center was launched in 2011 with the goal of integrating locally digitized content from a number of academic and research institutions in the United States and Canada to provide access to full-text books and other online content in its digital library. Other sources, some using pirated content circulated through document-sharing services, placed large selections of books online. Libraries and commercial subscription services such as Amazon and Barnes & Noble made eBooks available through e-readers and in Web browser versions (which are also incomplete versions), following the general trend in the consumption of digital media in the first decade of the twenty-first century.

Library publishing programs and librarians' involvement with scholarly publishing emerged between 2005 and 2010. Some libraries started to collaborate with university presses. According to a U.S survey, library publishing of journals, conference proceedings, technical reports, or monographs was common by 2012. For example, the Purdue e-Pubs Journal Publishing Services was launched in 2006 to publish open access journals affiliated with the university faculty, departments, or students. Other types of library publishing services consisted of "mining" the special collections for content to supplement scholarly monographs (the University of Utah Press). The new roles of librarians as publishers are reflected in neologisms such as "liblishers" and "pubrarians" that appear in popular professional discourse (e.g., in *The Lib Pub* blog devoted to library publishing).

"Semantic Web" and Data Sharing

Discovering and accessing the phenomena of digital convergence present major challenges for online information services and bibliographic infrastructures. The Linked Data and semantic network model, which combines humanly readable Web pages (hyperlinked text) with the metadata created by machines in an interrelated and seamless "Semantic Web" to represent structured knowledge, allows scholars to share information from different sources and search across sources. As of this writing, multiple projects attempt to publish open datasets and establish links among them. Multiple communities involved in these projects look to connect domain data—like geographical features worldwide, clean energy datasets, policy reports and terminology, as well as biomedical resources—with the Web evolving into a global information space to enable direct access to raw data found in Web pages, documents, and document collections.

The optimism of digital convergence made possible through these techniques of access is congruent with the "brain organization of the modern world"—the "World Brain"—that H. G. Wells discussed in the 1930s. "The world is a Phoenix," he said at the Congrès Mondial de la Documentation Universelle in Paris in 1937, "It perishes in flames and even as it dies it is born again. This synthesis of knowledge is the necessary beginning to the new world." He believed that having a structure for the "comparison, reconciliation and synthesis of common guiding ideas for the whole world" (i.e., a "common interpretation of reality") might increase the possibility of a world community and world peace.[10]

EPILOGUE

During the 2011 Arab uprising some 200,000 texts (including thousands of rare books, journals, and writings, and manuscripts from the Bonaparte era)—all held by the Institut d'Égypte in Cairo—burned in a fire believed to be part of the Egyptian revolution. As a monument to the colonial conquest of Egypt and its Western domination, the institute was set up by Napoléon Bonaparte as a research center during France's invasion and occupation (1798–1801). One of the major losses was the source manuscript for a monumental work created by 150 French scholars and scientists during a twenty-year period that documented contemporary life and contained a comprehensive description of ancient civilization and Egypt's monuments—*Description de l'Égypte* ("Description of Egypt"). Although the luxuriously printed editions of *Description de l'Égypte* that the institute produced can be found in major libraries of the world, the source manuscript was burned beyond repair.

Meanwhile, a digitized version of the *Description de l'Égypte* can be found on the open Web, the link leading to the new Bibliotheca Alexandrina (BA) in modern-day Egypt and its digital library. The digital version is a copy of a printed second edition (1820) produced in the Imprimerie royale. Presented against a sand-colored background with a decorative vignette offering stylized, nostalgic heritage framing in the digital portal, it is in sharp contrast with the main BA website. Featuring the emblematic features of a modernist library (as on the book cover of this collection), the BA mission is equally "modern"—aiming to "recapture the spirit of the original ancient Library of Alexandria" and of becoming "the world's window on Egypt, the Egypt's window on the world, the leading institution of the digital age, a center for learning, tolerance, dialogue and understanding."

The BA is a symbolic connector to the idea of the famous library of the ancient world. Even a cursory examination of the digital collections available at the BA site in 2014 support its ambition as a universal library and a deliberate continuation of the tradition of one of the great libraries of antiquity. Among its projects are those reminding us that many centuries after the demise of the great Alexandrian library, medieval Islam served as a cultural catalyst between the world of antiquity and medieval Europe (from the eleventh to thirteenth centuries). Viewers can immerse themselves in the world of digitized books, the seamless web of information. Digital convergence embodied!

As a digital library, the BA is the "third place" (this concept is attributed to cultural theorist Homi Bhabha). Third place theory comes out of postcolonial thought and claims that identity and community can be built and mediated in places where cultures meet and overlap. According to this postmodern concept, the public sphere in a modern library is extended by the possibilities of virtual spaces, where multiple origins and convergences are in play and brought together.

Amid the external turmoil in modern-day Egypt, the BA library and its world of texts presents an idea of cultural integration bridging religious and cultural tensions. The BA's physical space is modern and futuristic, its knowledge base connecting the heritage of cultures of the East and the West. The Latin form of its name "Bibliotheca" and "Alexandrina" is a paradox of sorts, in that Latin is not the *lingua franca* of the modern world, either Eastern or Western. Can this cultural institution affirm a center of learning in the African north reminiscent of the great library of antiquity, which was a melting pot of cultures of the East and the West? Or, does the BA hide another neoliberal undertaking that avails itself in the latest technologies of cultural reproduction in digital form (largely Western)? This question echoes tensions presented in the introduction to this volume, and in particular those of colonial and postcolonial society related to the uncritical import of values through Western forms of knowledge and institutions and the belief that they can be context-free.

In the contemporary BA, the digital technologies and the modern architecture that harbor a temple of knowledge make a strong political statement in the midst of several cultural tectonic plates that ground its foundation as an active "third place" offering a social space for cultural dialogue.

ACKNOWLEDGMENT

I would like to thank Anselm Spoerri for reading and commenting on versions of this chapter.

NOTES

1. Michael H. Harris, *History of Libraries in the Western World*, 4th ed. (Lanham, MD: Scarecrow Press, 1999), 257, 287.
2. Eviatar Zerubavel, *The Fine Line: Making Distinctions in Everyday Life* (New York: Free Press, 1991), 3, 76.
3. Eric Pfanner, "Google to Announce Venture with Belgian Museum," *New York Times*, March 12, 2012, http://www.nytimes.com/2012/03/13/technology/google-to-announce -venture-with-belgian-museum.html?_r=3&ref=global& (cited June 30, 2014).
4. IFLA/UNESCO Manifesto for Digital Libraries, "Bridging the Digital Divide: Making the World's Cultural and Scientific Heritage Accessible to All," http://www.ifla.org/publica tions/iflaunesco-manifesto-for-digital-libraries (cited November 17, 2014).
5. Budapest Open Access Initiative, http://www.budapestopenaccessinitiative.org/read (cited July 8, 2014).
6. Treasures in Full (British Library), http://www.bl.uk/treasures/treasuresinfull.html (cited November 17, 2014).
7. Wolfgang Ernst, "Underway to the Dual System: Classical Archives and Digital Memory," in *Netpioneers 1.0: Contextualizing Early Net-Based Art*, ed. Dieter Daniels and Günther Reisinger (Berlin: Steinberg Press, 2010), 84, 85.
8. Marija Dalbello, "A Phenomenological Study of an Emergent National Digital Library, Part II: The Narratives of Development," *Library Quarterly* 75, no. 4 (2005): e46–47.
9. Marija Dalbello, "Institutional Shaping of Cultural Memory: Digital Library as Environ- ment for Textual Transmission," *Library Quarterly* 74, no. 3 (2004): 274–75.
10. H. G. Wells, *World Brain* (London: Methuen, 1938), eBooks@adelaide, Ch. 4, http:// ebooks.adelaide.edu.au/w/wells/hg/world_brain/chapter4.html (cited July 30, 2014).

BIBLIOGRAPHY

Ariadne Database (Österreichische National Bibliothek), http://www.onb.ac.at/ev/ariadne/ari adne-database.htm (cited June 30, 2014).

Béquet, Gaëlle. *Trois bibliothèques européennes face à Google: aux origines de la bibliothèque numérique (1990–2010)*. Paris: École des chartes, 2014.

Berners-Lee, Tim, James Hendler, and Ora Lassila. "The Semantic Web." *Scientific American* (May 1, 2001): 29–37.

Bhabha, Homi K. *The Location of Culture*. Abingdon: Routledge, 2004.

Bibliotheca Alexandrina, "Mission and Objectives," http://www.bibalex.org/aboutus/mission _en.aspx (cited July 30, 2014).

Black, Alistair. "Information History." *Annual Review of Information Science and Technology* 40, no. 1 (2006): 441–72.

Blair, Ann. *Too Much to Know: Managing Scholarly Information before the Modern Age*. New Haven, CT: Yale University Press, 2011.

Borgman, Christine L. *From Gutenberg to the Global Information Infrastructure: Access to Infor- mation in the Networked World*. Cambridge, MA: MIT Press, 2000.

Borgman, Christine, and Jonathan Furner. "Scholarly Communication and Bibliometrics." *Annual Review of Information Science and Technology* 36, no. 1 (2002): 3–71.

Boyd, Rayward W. "Visions of Xanadu: Paul Otlet (1868–1944) and Hypertext." *Journal of American Society for Information Science & Technology* 45 (1994): 235–50.

Budapest Open Access Initiative, http://www.budapestopenaccessinitiative.org/read (cited July 8, 2014).

Burke, Peter. *A Social History of Knowledge: From Gutenberg to Diderot*. Malden, MA: Polity, 2000.

Burke, Peter. *A Social History of Knowledge: From the Encyclopaedia to Wikipedia*. Malden, MA: Polity, 2012.

Center for World Indigenous Studies, http://cwis.org (cited July 8, 2014).

Cohen, Dan, and Roy Rosenzweig. *Digital History: A Guide to Gathering, Preserving, and Presenting the Past on the Web*. Philadelpia, PA: University of Pennsylvania Press, 2006.

Dalbello, Marija. "Cultural Dimensions of Digital Library Development, Part I: Theory and Methodological Framework for a Comparative Study of the Cultures of Innovation in Five European National Libraries." *Library Quarterly* 78, no. 4 (2008): 355–95.

Dalbello, Marija. "Cultural Dimensions of Digital Library Development, Part II: The Cultures of Innovation in Five European National Libraries (Narratives of Development)." *Library Quarterly* 79, no. 1 (2009): 1–72.

Dalbello, Marija. "Digital Cultural Heritage: Concepts, Projects, and Emerging Constructions of Heritage." *Proceedings of the Libraries in the Digital Age (LIDA)*. Dubrovnik, Croatia, May 25–30, 2009.

Dalbello, Marija. "Institutional Shaping of Cultural Memory: Digital Library as Environment for Textual Transmission." *Library Quarterly* 74, no. 3 (2004): 265–99.

Dalbello, Marija. "A Phenomenological Study of an Emergent National Digital Library, Part I: Theory and Methodological Framework." *Library Quarterly* 75, no. 4 (2005): 391–420.

Dalbello, Marija. "A Phenomenological Study of an Emergent National Digital Library, Part II: The Narratives of Development." *Library Quarterly* 75, no. 4 (2005): e28–e70.

DeGennaro, Richard. "Library Automation and Networking: Perspectives on Three Decades." *Library Journal* 108, no. 7 (1983): 629–35.

"Description de l'Égypte," http://descegy.bibalex.org (cited March 21, 2014).

Description de l'Égypte, ou recueil des observations et des recherches qui son ete faites en Egypte pendant l'expédition de l'armée française. 2nd ed. Paris: Imprimerie royale, 1820.

"Digital Library Controversy: Google Gives Ground at EU Hearing." *Spiegel Online International*, September 8, 2009, http://www.spiegel.de/international/europe/digital-library-controversy-google-gives-ground-at-eu-hearing-a-647700.html (cited July 24, 2014).

Digital Library Federation (2004), http://old.diglib.org/pubs/techreps.htm (website no longer maintained after 2010); archived, http://www.diglib.org (cited June 30, 2014).

Drott, M. Carl. "Open Access." *Annual Review of Information Science and Technology* 40, no. 1 (2006): 79–109.

Eaton, Nancy L. "Online Catalogs." In *International Dictionary of Library Histories*, vol. 1, edited by David H. Stam, 122–24. Chicago: Fitzroy Dearborn, 2001.

Egan, Margaret E., and Jesse H. Shera. "Foundations of a Theory of Bibliography." *Library Quarterly* 22 (1987): 125–37.

Ernst, Wolfgang. "Underway to the Dual System: Classical Archives and Digital Memory." In *Netpioneers 1.0: Contextualizing Early Net-Based Art*, edited by Dieter Daniels and Günther Reisinger, 81–101. Berlin: Steinberg Press, 2010.

"Europeana.eu," http://en.wikipedia.org/wiki/Europeana (cited June 30, 2014).

Gessner, Conrad. *Bibliotheca universalis sive catalogus omnium scriptorum locupletissimus in tribus linguis Latina, Graeca et Hebraica: extantium & non extantium, veterum & recentiorum*. 1545–1549.

Haigh, Thomas. "The History of Information Technology." *Annual Review of Information Science and Technology* 45, no. 1 (2011): 431–87.

Harris, Michael H. *History of Libraries in the Western World.* 4th ed. Lanham, MD: Scarecrow Press, 1999.

Heath, Tom, and Christian Bizer. *Linked Data: Evolving the Web into a Global Data Space.* San Rafael, CA: Morgan & Claypool, 2011.

IFLA/UNESCO Manifesto for Digital Libraries, "Bridging the Digital Divide: Making the World's Cultural and Scientific Heritage Accessible to All," http://www.ifla.org/publications/iflaunesco-manifesto-for-digital-libraries (cited November 17, 2014).

Jenkins, Henry. *Convergence Culture: Where Old and New Media Collide.* New York: New York University Press, 2006.

Joint Steering Committee for Development of RDA, "A Brief History of AACR," http://www.rda-jsc.org/history.html (cited March 21, 2014).

Kaufman, Leslie. "Sharing Cultural Jewels via Instagram." *New York Times*, June 17, 2014, http://nyti.ms/1qpXK3M (cited June 30, 2014).

Moretti, Franco. *Graphs, Maps, Trees: Abstract Models for Literary History.* New York: Verso, 2005.

Mullins, James et al. *Library Publishing Services: Strategies for Success: Final Research Report.* Washington, DC: SPARC, 2012, http://docs.lib.purdue.edu/cgi/viewcontent.cgi?article=1023&context=purduepress_ebooks (cited July 30, 2014).

Nelson, Ted. "PROJECT XANADU® | Founded 1960 | The Original Hypertext Project," http://xanadu.com/#deliverable (cited June 30, 2014).

Pfanner, Eric. "Google to Announce Venture with Belgian Museum." *New York Times*, March 12, 2012, http://www.nytimes.com/2012/03/13/technology/google-to-announce-venture-with-belgian-museum.html?_r=3&ref=global& (cited June 30, 2014).

Rackley, Marilyn. "Internet Archive." In *Encyclopedia of Library and Information Sciences*, 3rd ed., edited by Marcia J. Bates and Mary Niles Maack, 2966–76. London: Taylor and Francis, 2010, https://archive.org/stream/internetarchive-encyclis/EncycLisInternetArchive#page/n0/mode/2up (cited June 30, 2014).

Saracevic, Tefko, and Marija Dalbello. "A Survey of Digital Library Education." *Proceedings of the 64th ASIST Annual Meeting, Washington, D.C., November 3–8, 2001.* Medford, NJ: Information Today, 2001.

Shannon, Claude E., and Warren Weaver. *The Mathematical Theory of Communication.* Chicago: University of Illinois Press, 1949.

"Skarabej, Online Museum of Old Family Photographs," http://www.skarabej.com/english/about_skarabej.php (cited June 30, 2014).

Springer, Michelle, et al. *For the Common Good: The Library of Congress Flickr Pilot Project. Report Summary.* Washington, D.C.: The Library of Congress, 2008, http://www.loc.gov/rr/print/flickr_report_final_summary.pdf (cited June 30, 2014).

"Thousands of Rare Books, Writings Burned at Institute d'Egypt in Cairo." *Huffington Post*, December 19, 2011, http://www.huffingtonpost.com/2011/12/19/books-burned_n_1158535.html (cited June 30, 2014).

Treasures in Full (British Library), http://www.bl.uk/treasures/treasuresinfull.html (cited November 17, 2014).

Unicode. "History of Unicode—Membership History," http://www.unicode.org/history/contributors.html (cited June 30, 2014).

"The Universal Digital Library: Million Book Collection," http://web.archive.org/web/20130704182041/http://www.ulib.org (cited July 30, 2014).

Wells, H. G. *World Brain*. London: Methuen & Co., 1938 (reprinted by eBooks@adelaide), http:// ebooks.adelaide.edu.au/w/wells/hg/world_brain/contents.html (cited July 28, 2014).

Wiegand, Wayne A. "Tunnel Vision and Blind Spots: What the Past Tells Us about the Present: Reflections on the Twentieth-Century History of American Librarianship." *Library Quarterly* 69, no. 1 (1999): 1–32.

WordStream—History of Search, http://www.wordstream.com/articles/internet-search-engines -history (cited March 22, 2014).

World Wide Web Consortium (W3C). "About W3C," http://www.w3.org/Consortium (cited June 30, 2014).

Zerubavel, Eviatar. *The Fine Line: Making Distinctions in Everyday Life*. New York: Free Press, 1991.

Zwick, Jim. *Anti-imperialism in the United States, 1898–1935*. Various domains, March 1995– February 1999 (Center for History and New Media at George Mason University), http:// chnm.gmu.edu/worldhistorysources/d/192.html (cited June 30, 2014).

Index

About the Editors and Contributors

Pamela Spence Richards (deceased) has written more than twenty journal articles, including some in Russian, French, Hungarian, and German, and authored and co-authored book chapters and three books. She is still widely known for her articles "German Libraries and Scientific and Technical Information in Nazi Germany" (1985) and "Aslib at War: The Brief but Intrepid Career of a Library Organization as a Hub of Allied Scientific Intelligence 1942–1945" (1989). Her books include *Scholars and Gentlemen: The Library of the New-York Historical Society, 1804–1982* (1984) and *Scientific Information in Wartime: The Allied-German Rivalry 1939–1945* (1994).

In addition to over one hundred scholarly articles, **Wayne A. Wiegand** is author of *History of a Hoax: Edmund Lester Pearson, John Cotton Dana and "The Old Librarian's Almanack"* (1979), *Patrician in the Progressive Era: A Biography of George von Lengerke Meyer* (1988), *Politics of an Emerging Profession: The American Library Association, 1876–1917* (1986), *"An Active Instrument for Propaganda": American Public Libraries During World War I* (1989), and *Irrepressible Reformer: A Biography of Melvil Dewey* (1996). The last three were given the G. K. Hall Award for Outstanding Contribution to Library Literature (1988, 1991, 1997). In 1994 he co-edited with Donald G. Davis Jr. the *Encyclopedia of Library History*. In 1998 he co-edited *Print Culture in a Diverse America* with James Danky, which was awarded the 1999 Carey McWilliams Award for scholarly contribution to multicultural literature, and in 2006 also co-edited with Danky *Women in Print: Essays on the Print Culture of American Women from the Nineteenth and Twentieth Centuries*. With Tom Augst, he co-edited a special issue of *American Studies* titled "The Library as an Agency of Culture" (Fall, 2001), which the University of Wisconsin Press reprinted (2002). He also edited the sixth edition of *Genreflecting: A Guide to Popular Reading Interests* (2005), in which he contributed the lead essay titled "On the Social Nature of Reading," and with Christine Pawley guest edited the Winter, 2008, issue of *Library Trends* titled "Alternative Print Culture: Social History and Libraries."

Marija Dalbello has published in the area of print culture and visual epistemology, digital library development and digital textuality, and social history of media and information. She co-edited *Print Culture in Croatia: The Canon and the Borderlands* (2006) with Tinka Katić, and *Visible Writings: Cultures, Forms, Readings* (2011) with Mary Shaw. Her articles are published in peer-reviewed journals including *The Library Quarterly, Library & Information Science Research, Analytical & Enumerative Bibliography, Journal of Documentation* (an article for which she won an award in 2012), and *Information Research.*

Peter Hoare

Peter Hoare was university librarian at the University of Nottingham for fifteen years before retiring to work on historic libraries and the history of libraries, with publications on Germany, Italy, Russia, and other European countries as well as the British Isles. In 1967 he founded the journal *Library History* (now *Library & Information History*) and is a former chair of the Library History Group. He was the general editor of the *Cambridge History of Libraries in Britain and Ireland* (3 volumes, 2006) and co-editor with Alistair Black of the third volume, covering the period 1850–2000.

Anthony Olden

Anthony Olden is academic lead for research students and associate professor at the University of West London. He worked for eight years at Ahmadu Bello University, Nigeria, initially as a librarian and then as a lecturer, and has traveled extensively in Africa, which is his main research interest. He has published in a range of research and professional journals, including *Alexandria, Aslib Proceedings, History of Education, Innovation,* the *Journal of Librarianship and Information Science,* the *Library Quarterly,* and *Libri.*

Ross Harvey

Ross Harvey is adjunct professor in the School of Business IT and Logistics, RMIT University, Melbourne, Australia, and editor of the *Australian Library Journal.* From 2007 to 2013 he was visiting professor in the Graduate School of Library and Information Science, Simmons College, Boston, and has held positions at universities in Australia, Singapore, and New Zealand. His research and teaching focus are the history of the book and the stewardship of materials in libraries and archives, particularly digital materials. He has extensive experience in research projects in Australia and the United Kingdom. He has published in the fields of library history, newspaper history, history of the book, bibliographic organization, library education, and the preservation of library and archival material, most recently the book *The Preservation Management Handbook* (AltaMira Press, 2014), co-authored with Martha R. Mahard.